YEAR OF GLORY

YEAR OF GLORY

The Life and Battles of
Jeb Stuart and His Cavalry,
June 1862–June 1863

MONTE AKERS

CASEMATE
Philadelphia & Oxford

Published in the United States of America and Great Britain in 2012 by
CASEMATE PUBLISHERS
908 Darby Road, Havertown, PA 19083
and
10 Hythe Bridge Street, Oxford, OX1 2EW

Copyright 2012 © Monte Akers

ISBN 978-1-61200-130-2
Digital Edition: ISBN 978-1-61200-142-5

Cataloging-in-publication data is available from the Library of Congress and
the British Library.

10 9 8 7 6 5 4 3 2 1

Printed and bound in the United States of America.

For a complete list of Casemate titles please contact:

CASEMATE PUBLISHERS (US)
Telephone (610) 853-9131, Fax (610) 853-9146
E-mail: casemate@casematepublishing.com

CASEMATE PUBLISHERS (UK)
Telephone (01865) 241249, Fax (01865) 794449
E-mail: casemate-uk@casematepublishing.co.uk

CONTENTS

To Harper Channing Akers, my second perfect granddaughter.

FOREWORD

When Monte Akers asked me to write the foreword for this book, I accepted the honor without hesitation. Upon brief reflection I realized the challenge such a commitment presented. How does one extol the exceptional virtues of J.E.B. Stuart without appearing to shortchange Robert E. Lee, "Stonewall" Jackson, Wade Hampton, or Jefferson Davis, let alone the ranks of Longstreets, Morgans, Forrests, Johnstons, Mosbys, and Pelhams?

It ultimately proved to be a simpler feat than I had anticipated. All I had to do was ask myself what comprised the epitome of the Southern gentleman in the antebellum South and who qualified for that title. The nearly impossible ideal required intelligence, breeding, character, health, education, courage, ambition, temperance, talent, loyalty, and spirit. The absence of any of these qualities tarnished that ideal, if only by a speck.

As I studied the list of heroes worthy of such acclaim, I found the often subtle missing components. In several, good health was absent; with some, formal education never occurred; in a few others, a handsome visage was distinctly absent; still others exhibited a tendency toward erratic or intemperate behavior, and several lacked the essential aristocratic breeding. Even the venerable Robert E. Lee, considered by many the epitome of the Southern ideal, lacked the dash, high spirits, and the robust health of many of his lieutenants.

Only James Ewell Brown Stuart epitomized all aspects of the larger-than-life ideal of Southern gentry. The rigorous standards of 1861 allowed little leeway for misbehavior, character flaws, or deviations from their rigid sense of propriety. Even accidents or youthful highjinks could be forgiven, but never forgotten.

Stuart was the scion of military heroes of the Revolution and the War of 1812, a graduate of West Point, an accomplished horseman, and possessed of a commanding physique. He was hearty and healthy, intelligent, courageous yet gentle, loyal, God-fearing, honorable, kind, well-spoken, and handsome. As a 19th century Southerner, he was beyond reproach.

His record as a junior US army officer was spotless. As a Confederate general he was exceptional. He led his command like a courtly cavalier of an earlier age with a banjo player and a troupe of accomplished officers singing popular melodies of the day. But such frivolity was balanced by its opposite extreme: the willingness to embrace any hardship no matter how grueling or dangerous.

Despite his manly demeanor, Stuart did not shy from expressing emotion, whether joy, humility, or sorrow. He was not ashamed to burst into song. Nor did he refrain from weeping at the loss of one he loved or admired. He was quick to praise another's success and slow to chide for failure. When confronted with a threat, his military prowess quickly divined how to turn defeat into victory, and he did so countless times during the war.

Stuart was stationed at remote posts in Texas and Kansas after graduation from West Point in 1854 and honed his combat skills against savage Native Americans and warring guerrilla factions in bleeding Kansas. The ceaseless hazards and fierce combats didn't result in nervous tics, thousand-yard stares from endless days on the desolate prairie, or involuntary flinching at close gunfire. He was as fearless and exuberant when racing into his last battle as he had been in his first.

Neither his successes on the frontier nor his fame in quelling John Brown's Raid at Harpers Ferry fostered an irrepressible ego. Stuart's regard for, and treatment of, his superiors and his subordinates never altered during his rise from obscurity to fame. An egotist would not have recognized and endorsed the talents of a John S. Mosby, a William Blackford, or a Richard Channing Price. Nor would he have wept openly at the death of Redmond Burke or John Pelham.

Author Akers devoted years to researching Stuart and his battles. He concentrated on Stuart's most remarkable accomplishments during twelve months of amazing feats and stunning victories from June 1862 to June 1863. He followed Stuart's footsteps across Virginia, Maryland, and Pennsylvania. He visited the battlefields, campsites, manor houses, and bivouacs where the general camped and fought. The Peninsula, Williamsburg, Manassas, South Mountain, Sharpsburg, Fredericksburg, Kelly's Ford, Chancellorsville, and Brandy Station—wherever Stuart rode, Akers followed 150 years later writing notes, taking photos, and studying the same vistas the tireless young general viewed during his campaigns.

In one year's time, Stuart earned the respect of North and South as a superlative cavalryman, a chivalrous knight, and a noble warrior cast in the mold of Arthur, Lancelot, Roland, and d'Artagnan. He captured the attention of the nation and the world with his feats of glory, *joie de vivre*, and legendary courage. Monte Akers has given us a portrait of a man the likes of whom we shall never see again—an American cavalier worthy of the world's admiration for all time.

Stephen W. Sylvia
Orange, Virginia
July 2012

PROLOGUE
The Man of the Year

*There was a land of Cavaliers and Cotton fields called the Old
South. Here in this pretty world Gallantry took its last bow. Here
was the last ever to be seen of Knights and their Ladies Fair, of
Master and of Slave. Look for it only in books, for it is no more
than a dream remembered . . . A Civilization gone with the wind.*
—Margaret Mitchell

The opening to Margaret Mitchell's classic *Gone with the Wind* invokes
significantly different reactions 150 years after the Civil War than it did
when written in 1936. Still much admired, much read, and much watched,
it is now considered almost a fairy tale. Literary proponents highlight its
value as feminist literature rather than American history. Appropriately,
critics decry its apologetic attitude toward slavery, and its depiction of the
peculiar institution as a sort of happy symbiosis. It is generally considered
to be a totally inaccurate depiction of the Old South as a land of Knights
and Ladies Fair. Let it be read or watched for its romance, its spectacle, the
celebrity of Clark Gable and Vivian Leigh, but do not take it seriously, do
not imagine there was really such a place.

Yet, in isolated places for limited periods of time, the "land of Cavaliers" did exist, and never more in any one place or for any one period of
time than in the presence of James Ewell Brown "Jeb" Stuart between June
1, 1862, and June 24, 1863.

John Thomason was a Marine Corps captain who wrote of Stuart without ever knowing him, but he captured the magnetism of the man at the

beginning of his 1930 biography of the cavalry leader:

> I sat at the feet of our old men who fought in our War of the Southern Confederacy, and asked them the questions that boys ask.
>
> 'What did Stonewall Jackson look like? What sort of man was Longstreet?—A.P. Hill? . . .'
>
> 'Well son,' after deep thought—'Old Stonewall looked—he looked like his pictures. You've seen his pictures. Longstreet, he was a thick-set sort of fellow, with a bushy beard. A.P. Hill was red-headed . . .'
>
> But when you ask about Jeb Stuart, their eyes light up and their faces quicken, and they describe details of his dress, his fighting jacket and his plume—and they hum you songs he loved and tell you how his voice sounded.
>
> Jeb Stuart filled the eye . . . .[1]

He filled more than the eye. Jeb Stuart filled a narrow niche in American legend that only a select handful of men may occupy—David Crocket, Jesse James, William F. Cody, and George Custer perhaps. Such men have become more image than reality, more hype than history, and yet, when the image and hype are stripped away, the realities are every bit as tantalizing, every bit as fascinating as the romantic tales that pass as their stories. The facts are different than the legends, but the niche they fill is one in which fantasy and fact are interchangeable.

Unlike Crockett, James, Cody and Custer, today Stuart is not a household name. Little boys no longer gallop about on stick horses wearing bath towels for capes, chicken feathers for plumes, brandishing lathes for sabers, imagining themselves to be the commander of Lee's Confederate cavalry. Precious few modern boys know who Stuart was, and just as few of their parents are anxious to describe him—one of the defenders of America's greatest shame, slavery—as someone their progeny should admire. Yet should those same parents describe the type of person who should be admired, emulated, and revered, most would describe a Jeb Stuart.

Imagine a man who proved himself, over and over, to be a winner, whose intellectual and athletic skill and tactical genius made him paparazzi-popular while being simultaneously vital to the future of his nation. Imagine a man of immense humor and popularity among his peers, who loved nothing better than raucous laughter, wrestling on the ground with young men of his staff, singing popular songs in a deep baritone voice on horseback while accompanied by a personal banjo player, or attending a joyful ball and stealing kisses from beautiful women.

Yet imagine that this same man never drank alcohol, nor used profanity, did not smoke, was never unfaithful to his wife, and was so devoutly religious that his dying words were "God's will be done." His politics were simple and had little to do with slavery. He was a Virginian. The Old Dominion was threatened, and he was willing to die to defend his home.

Add to his unlikely mix of personal attributes the ability to ride magnificently, to fight hand-to-hand in mortal combat, to intuit successful battle tactics, as well as a penchant for writing love poems. Round out the image by dressing him outrageously in black thigh-high boots with spurs of pure gold, dark blue trousers with a double gold stripe on the legs, a short, double-breasted jacket of grey wool, gold buttons, gold collar stars, and quatrefoils of rich Austrian braid on his sleeves. Place a grey cape lined in crimson on his back, a saber and pistol at his waist, and top him off with a hat pinned up on one side and sporting a long black ostrich plume.

As if that is not enough, imagine that this striking, eye-filling man, who is nearly six feet tall, who wears his hair long and who, in keeping with the latest fashion, covers his face with a huge beard, is not accustomed to being considered handsome. Imagine that in his youth he was so uncomely that his friends derisively called him "Beauty," "in inverse ratio to the compliment implied," as one of those friends explained.[2] Imagine that he overcame self-doubt about his appearance by force of personality, and that he also learned how to gild his homeliness so thoroughly that thousands proclaimed him, indeed, a striking figure.

Consider how he was perceived by his peers. General Lee said, "He was my ideal of a soldier." Stonewall Jackson said, "Stuart is my ideal of a cavalry leader, prompt, vigilant, and fearless." One of Jackson's staff officers wrote, "No more welcome guest ever came than General JEB Stuart. With clanking saber and spurs and waving black plume he came and was warmly greeted at the door. Papers and work were all hastily laid aside." Another of the same staff recalled that he "was never quiet, never depressed, always whistling, singing or laughing."

Stuart was said to be the only man who could make the stern Stonewall Jackson laugh, some said "uproariously."[3] General Lee's camp servant said, "It made no difference how quiet our headquarters was, within ten minutes of the time General Stuart rode up to visit us, everyone was laughing."[4] A

Texas soldier described him as "a dandy on dress parade, a belle at a ball, a boy in a possum hunt, and a hero in a fight."[5]

The purpose of this book is not to study the life of Stuart. His life has been chronicled many times. Nor is its purpose to defend the man, apologize for his mistakes, attempt to elevate his memory to a higher plane, or to convince parents to tell their little boys to emulate him. The purpose of this book is to focus on the single year that made the man memorable, taking it nearly day by day and event by event in order to reconstruct the times that made the legend. The work focuses on that single year, but less to chronicle events and analyze battles than to recapture and evoke, once again, the laughter, tears, and excitement of that unique time.

The year beginning in June 1862 was not Stuart's first brush with fame. He gained significant attention prior to then, having been Robert E. Lee's aide at Harpers Ferry in 1859, and having commanded cavalry at the Battle of First Manassas that were conspicuous in overrunning a regiment of Federal Zouaves. He was a brigadier general as well known as a hundred other men of that rank in the Confederate army. It was in June 1862, however, that Stuart made his first and most famous "Ride Around McClellan." It was at the beginning of that month that Robert E. Lee took command of the Army of Northern Virginia and began leading it to a series of victories in which Stuart played a vital role. It was that month that the colorful Prussian, Heros Von Borcke, joined Stuart's staff, and it was that month that Turner Ashby, theretofore the South's best known cavalier, was killed in battle. It was the month that Stuart's star made a sharp ascension and continued to climb precipitously.

Fast forward a year and a few days, to June 5, 1863. Stuart holds a grand review of his Cavalry Corps. Everyone puts on their finest uniform, polishes their leathers, shines their metals, and grooms their horses. Thousands of mounted Confederates supported by batteries of the famous Stuart Horse Artillery first walk by in military formation and then charge at a thundering gallop, with guns booming, in a large open field near Culpeper, Virginia. On the 8th of the month Stuart repeats the grand review so that Robert E. Lee and other luminaries can attend, but the noise and flurry arouses Northern curiosity. On the next day, Stuart is taken by surprise and the Battle of Brandy Station is fought. It is the largest cavalry battle in United States history and it is a victory for Stuart, but just barely. The Federal horsemen demonstrate that they are no longer inferior to their Southern counterparts. Perhaps more significantly, the newspapers of the Confederacy castigate Stuart for the battle, leaving a stinging blow to his ego that he determines to remove by another act of significant daring.

Move ahead ten days and Von Borcke is seriously wounded as he rides next to Stuart. The two will never ride together again. Move forward five more days and Stuart's massive columns of horsemen begin moving north, past the Union Army of the Potomac and ultimately to the Pennsylvania crossroads town of Gettysburg.

It is on that day, June 24, 1863, that this book, this biography of a singular year, concludes. Stuart's star has reached its zenith. Its long arc begins to descend toward its eclipse at another locale called Yellow Tavern, which it will reach in a little less than another year. After that the story of Jeb Stuart, the "Knight of the Golden Spurs," will be largely a legend and a fantasy for young boys. But it was also history, and the men who fought with and against Jeb Stuart played a major role in the American continent's greatest war. Again, quoting John Thomason, "Never, anywhere, will there be his like again."[6]

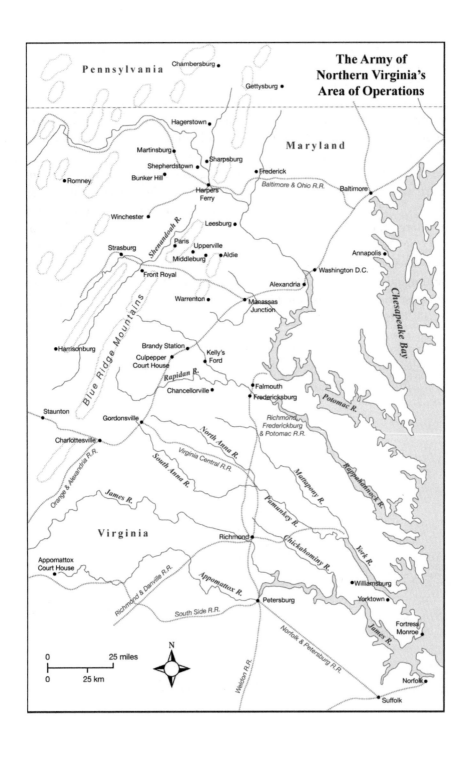

The Army of
Northern Virginia's
Area of Operations

Pennsylvania

Chambersburg

Gettysburg

Maryland

Hagerstown

Martinsburg

Sharpsburg

Shepherdstown

Frederick

Baltimore & Ohio R.R.

Baltimore

Romney

Bunker Hill

Harpers
Ferry

Winchester

Leesburg

Annapolis

Strasburg

Paris

Upperville

Shenandoah R.

Middleburg

Aldie

Washington D.C.

Front Royal

Blue Ridge Mountains

Alexandria

Harrisonburg

Warrenton

Manassas
Junction

Brandy Station

Kelly's
Ford

Culpepper
Court House

Rapidan R.

Chancellorville

Falmouth

Fredericksburg

Potomac R.

Staunton

Gordonsville

Richmond,
Fredericksburg
& Potomac R.R.

North Anna R.

Charlottesville

Virginia Central R.R.

Orange & Alexandria R.R.

South Anna R.

Mattapony R.

Rappahannock R.

James R.

Pamunkey R.

Virginia

Richmond

Chickahominy R.

York R.

Appomattox
Court House

Richmond & Danville R.R.

Appomattox R.

Williamsburg

Petersburg

Yorktown

South Side R.R.

Fortress
Monroe

Norfolk & Petersburg R.R.

James R.

0   25 miles

N

0   25 km

Weldon R.R.

Norfolk

Suffolk

Chesapeake Bay

CHAPTER ONE

STUART'S MILITARY FAMILY ASSEMBLES

Stuart was so unique that he seemed able to defy all natural laws.
—John Singleton Mosby

It was a time unique in America's history.

Even after 150 years, it does not require a great deal of imagination to conjure up the tone and tenor of June 1862. Every extension of human endeavor was at overload. Revolution was in the air. Ways of life and foundations of politics were at stake. Families, friends, and neighbors were aligning themselves according to doctrine, dogma, and desire. A person's worth was measured less by works than by perception of political philosophy. People were dying on the opposite sides of aimed rifles in the name of the same principles—freedom, loyalty, country, honor, home. Men who might immensely enjoy each other's company in society were anxious to kill each other over what each thought the other *might* believe.

Emotions were high and extremely mixed. The xenophobic zeal of politicians and the bloodlust of volunteer soldiers were offset by the deep grieving of mothers and wives and nearly everyone's dread of what might lie ahead. It was a time that will be studied, analyzed, debated, and reenacted, but for now the histories are decades in the future. The people in this place are living somewhere between believing life could not be more exhilarating and believing they can see the end of time from where they stand.

An army camp is situated behind a modest farm house. The season of the year is late spring; the place is southeastern Virginia, between Richmond and the Atlantic coast. The ground is muddy from a particularly hard, recent downpour, and by being churned by thousands of feet, hooves, and wagon wheels. The air is saturated with the smell of wood smoke, but the aromas of horse manure, cooking meat, boiling coffee, human excrement, tobacco, urine, and body odor waft about in turn as one moves through them. Away from the main camp the air grows sweeter. Wild honeysuckle and magnolia are blooming in abundance in the woods, and around the house white and red roses are blooming and climbing the walls.[1]

Tents are pitched in straight lines and grouped by companies, most of them white and billowing in the wind, some splotched with iridescent mildew that seems to pulsate in the breeze. Flags snap above a few tent flaps. Horses are tied to picket ropes in long lines. The ground slopes away gently to a sluggish creek a few feet wide located at the base of the campsite. The creek water is clear and flows over a pebbly bottom, but not far away the forest closes in and the ground becomes swampy. The noise of the camp is a steady hum of men's voices, the ring of metal on metal, horses' whickers, creaking of wagons, flapping of canvas, tramping of feet, axes chopping wood, and occasional shouts, whoops, curses, and brays of laughter.

A modern visitor gazing upon these people in this place and time sees things as they were long ago. Some of what the soldiers do, wear, say, and use seem quaint, old-fashioned, out of memory. However, the things done, worn, said, and used were not merely characteristic of the time, but were cutting edge fashionable and technologically new-hatched in 1862. Wearing facial hair, for example, was a new and exciting fad, barely two years in fashion, imported from Europe, and as exciting for men as any new gown from Paris was for a lady. In 1861, Lincoln, Lee, Jackson, Grant, and Longstreet, to name a few, grew full beards and moustaches for the first time in their lives. Long, full beards, such as became a veritable specialty of the Army of Northern Virginia—as worn by Stuart, Jackson, Longstreet, A.P. Hill, Lafayette McLaws, Fitzhugh Lee, Wade Hampton and others—were particularly daring and racy, being a step beyond the curled, oiled, whisker sculptures of Europe. Only Stuart, of those well-known Civil War leaders, has sported a beard for long—since the mid-1850s—but that was due largely to his having a chin best covered up. In December, 1861 he even included a playful poem about his beard in a letter to his wife:

And long may it wave—
For I ne'er will shave—

While my Flora approves—
Still to grow it behooves—
And "<u>nary a hair</u>"
From it will I spare.[2]

Rifled muskets and rifled cannons, six-shot revolvers, breech-loading rifles, conical projectiles, ironclad ships, telegraph wires, and hot air balloons were just a few of the numerous new-fangled gadgets either freshly invented or of such recent vintage that they were still uncommon. Technology was ablaze.

For Southerners with the new moniker of "Confederates" there were new flags, government, laws, and color for uniforms. Since Revolutionary times the American army had worn predominantly blue, but now gray was the height of military fashion. Also new, but not all that popular, was the jaunty headgear adopted from France called "kepis," forage caps, or "bummers." The symbols of rank for military officers, from lieutenant to general, were novel, and arguably better-looking than in the "old army," particularly the fancy scrolls of gold Austrian braid on the sleeves and the abandonment of shoulder boards in favor of collar insignia. Jeb Stuart even participated in the invention of improved gear by inventing a new type of sword hanger, for which he obtained a patent and was paid the princely sum of $5000, roughly equivalent to $100,000 today. Even the banjo, Jeb's favorite musical instrument, was new.

There is lot of activity near the farmhouse. Next to it is a wall tent with a canvas fly erected in front, shading a camp table and a collection of chairs, stools, and kegs. A couple of dozen yards in front of the house is a Blakely cannon, and tethered to one of its wheels is a huge raccoon that is restlessly crawling about the tube and carriage, eyeing each passerby with black eyes and hissing threateningly at anyone who comes too near. It is not a pet. It is one of several camp mascots, but is a prisoner of war rather than a volunteer. Stuart refers to the animal as "the pearl of sentinels; the paragon of coons."[3]

Men come and go from the house—the obvious headquarters of the military unit of about 1,200 men, apparently a brigade. One who settles in to watch for awhile will, sooner or later, glimpse many of the principal players in this historical adventure, or at least the players for the current season.

A huge man appears. He is six feet four inches tall and weighs 240 pounds in an age when the average man stands five feet eight and weighs 143. He laughs and speaks loudly and often but his English is so broken

and poor that only a little of what he says can be understood. Oddly, he
has filed each of his fingernails to a point, but he is handsome, with a full
head of blond hair worn long, a large, carefully cultivated and curled moustache, and chin whiskers. He is so loud and boisterous he cannot be ignored,
and he's difficult not to admire.

His name is Johann August Heinrich Heros von Borcke, and he is fresh
off a ship from Prussia. Despite his inability to speak much English, he has
consistently charmed those he has met, including Flora Stuart, the wife of
Jeb, so that he is not only accepted but welcomed with pleasure. Once
ensconced in Stuart's personal staff he will routinely and habitually carry
a carbine, a shotgun, three revolvers, and a huge saber, all at the same time,
so that Moxley Sorrell, a Georgian serving on Pete Longstreet's staff, will
describe him as "an ambulating arsenal." Although another commentator
will refer to him as a man who "complemented his [Stuart's] retinue of
'freaks.' "[4]

Von, as he is called, has been in the country for less than a month, and
has so far seen the South only from a train window. He was, as William
Blackford, a fellow staff officer, will recall, "a lieutenant in the Cuirassiers
of the Guard in Berlin, one of the household regiments officered by men
of high rank, and . . . he and his father had quarreled about money matters;
von Borcke told him if he could not support him in that regiment like a
gentleman he would resign and come to America, and this he did."[5]

Coming over from Europe on a blockade runner named *Kate*, he landed
at Charleston and made straight for Richmond. He has credentials—besides
being a lieutenant in a regiment of dragoons, he is the son of a Prussian
aristocrat who owns two large estates—one in Pomerania and the other in
what is now Poland—which Von will inherit. Unfortunately for him, his various letters of introduction were jettisoned during his ocean-crossing when
a Federal gunboat attempted to capture the *Kate*, so that he was forced to
bumble about Richmond with no papers, trying to find a sponsor. That
turned out to be the Confederate Secretary of War, George Randolph, who
out of kindness or possibly desperation, provided him with a letter of introduction to Stuart, as well as a horse, and an orderly to serve as guide.

He arrived at Stuart's headquarters only days before the 1st of June
and was immediately accepted as a volunteer aide, possibly because he was
so outlandish in appearance that Jeb could not resist. Von had managed to
hang onto a bridle and some saddle blankets he'd purchased in London,
but he did not yet have a uniform, and upon being introduced to Stuart

was decked out in a gray hunting jacket, gray leather knickers, a round white hunting hat, and tall riding boots, clothing which Von admitted was intended to call attention to himself. More likely he was accepted because, as would be proven again and again, Stuart had an eye for talent.

He arrived just in time for the Battle of Seven Pines, on May 31, and experienced an initiation into the Civil War that included not only the horrors of combat and the thrill of driving a foe, but the opportunity to accompany Stuart throughout the day and even deliver one of Jeb's first orders to either Fitz or Rooney Lee (Von may not even have known which at the time).

Von is a fierce warrior, a loyal friend, a great storyteller, a natural comedian, a graceful dancer, and a favorite of all who knew him. He will be commended repeatedly in Jeb's reports, but he tends to stretch the truth to the breaking point and beyond. His memoirs will be filled with exaggeration and colorful boasting. He will manage, just two years after the war, to irritate or insult more than one of his old comrades by taking credit for deeds they or someone else accomplished or, in some cases, simply making stuff up.

Von's tendency to exaggerate and steal other's thunder is a shame, for he really was at the epicenter of action during the upcoming year, and he deservedly gained the respect and admiration of nearly everyone who met him. Stuart would eventually urge the Richmond government to appoint him a brigadier general, either for the purpose of commanding cavalry or to act as an envoy to Europe.[6] Furthermore, of all of Stuart's staff and biographers, Von Borcke's recollections are the most detailed and contain the most personal anecdotes, chronicling the war on an almost day-by-day basis and giving readers the most intimate glimpse of Jeb and his companions. This is because he faithfully kept a journal of his adventures, writing whenever he could, sometimes while shells were falling and bullets were whizzing nearby. Douglass Southall Freeman, one of the greatest historians of the war, acknowledged that his memoirs were "useful for the correct interpretation of many incidents in the history of Stuart's cavalry."[7] Coincidentally, his arrival on the scene marked the beginning of Jeb's ascension to glory, and his departure came almost exactly at its denouement.

In contrast, a small man appears, slightly below average height and twenty pounds below average weight. He is clean-shaven and rather careless about his appearance, certainly not a man likely to become a legend. Mounted, he is a slouchy rider who exudes a disdain for military protocol. He visits the farmhouse briefly and rides away along with three companions. Even his rank seems uncertain. Had anyone watching known it was John Singleton Mosby, the future Gray Ghost of the Confederacy, they might have tried to get a better look at him.

A tall, beautiful man appears, pauses to make friends with the raccoon, and smiles when his advances are rebuffed. Handsome is a more appropriate word, but the truth is that he is beautiful, with blond hair, smooth cheeks unable to support facial hair, piercing blue eyes, and a graceful, athletic gait. The other men seem to brighten at his approach, or to gaze at him with expressions of affection. There is an odd mix about him; shy charisma if such a thing exists. He might be a teenager or might be in his mid-twenties, one can't be certain. In fact, John Pelham is twenty-four. He is a genius with artillery, and is on his way to becoming a legend.

Another giant crosses into our frame of vision. He is more hulking and hairy than Von Borcke, and seemingly less comfortable in the uniform of an officer. His name is William Henry Hagan and he is, in fact, a newly-minted lieutenant, having been promoted from the rank of corporal less than two months earlier. He is an exceptionally brave man who has already proven his mettle, as well as his cleverness, and he will prove both time and again over the next two years. He will serve Stuart faithfully for as long or longer than any other man on the staff, but will be mentioned rarely and remembered primarily, most unfairly, because another Confederate who was no fan of Stuart will single him out for study, or ridicule, in an 1875 memoir, saying:

> Almost at the beginning of the war he [Stuart] managed to surround himself with a number of persons whose principal qualification for membership of his military household was their ability to make fun. . . . He had another queer character about whom, whose chief recommendation was his grotesque fierceness of appearance. This was Corporal Hagan, a very giant in frame, with an abnormal tendency to develop hair. His face was heavily bearded almost to his eyes, and his voice was as hoarse as distant thunder, which indeed it closely resembled. Stuart, seeing him in the ranks, fell in love with his peculiarities of person at once, and had him detailed for duty at head-quarters, where he made him a corporal, and gave him charge of the stables. Hagan, whose greatness was bodily only, was much elated by the attention shown him,

and his person seemed to swell and his voice continued to grow deeper than ever under the influence of the newly acquired dignity of chevrons. All of this was amusing, of course, and Stuart's delight was unbounded. The man remained with him till the time of his death, although not always a corporal. In a mad freak of fun one day, the chief recommended his corporal for promotion, to see, he said, if the giant was capable of further swelling, and so the corporal became a lieutenant on the staff.[8]

In fact, Hagan served as an aide with the rank of corporal for only ten months, and was recommended for promotion by Stuart on April 18, 1862, because Hagan "has won a commission on the march & the battlefield if ever man did. His services are indispensable to me, while his valuable services as recognized in every report I ever made entitle him to such a mark of confidence." Rather than being in charge of the stables, he served first as commander of Stuart's escort and later as Chief of Couriers. He was always there, always faithful, but seldom mentioned, and will always be in the shadow of that one disparaging description.

Another, less ostentatious man appears. He is thin, nice-looking, with a full head of brown hair parted on the left but not worn long. He has a moustache and chin whiskers in a style known as a "handlebar and chin puff" or a "Napoleon III Imperial." He seems quiet, and perhaps a bit sickly.

John Esten Cooke is Stuart's cousin by marriage. At 32 he is a few years older than many around headquarters, and he was trained as a lawyer rather than a soldier, but he has been the latter since the mid-1850s when he joined the Richmond Howitzers. That resulted in his being sent with the company to Harpers Ferry at the time of John Brown's Raid, and he stayed with the Howitzers, rose to the rank of sergeant, and fought at the battle of First Manassas before becoming a volunteer aide and then a lieutenant on Stuart's staff.

As opposed to many of the rough and tumble men surrounding his cousin, he is retiring and intellectual, as though having the eye of a novelist and the heart of a poet. He is, in fact, both. Cooke's first published work was a poem entitled *Avalon,* published in the *Southern Literary Messenger* in 1848 when he was only 18. This was followed by a swirl of more poems, several magazine articles, a romance published serially, and finally a novel, *Leather Stocking and Silk; or, John Myers and His Times*, released in 1854. That was followed by another novel entitled *A Story of the Valley of Virginia* the next year, but the manuscript, tragically, was destroyed in a fire at the publishers before it could be printed. Nevertheless it was followed by *Henry St. John, Gentleman,* in 1859. Cooke is a bona fide literary figure, relatively well known in the bookish circles of his day.

John Esten Cooke may come closer to epitomizing the Southern gentleman than any other character of Stuart's military family. He had disdain for menial labor, a desire for proper society, a bizarre manner of dressing in the morning, and often a complete oblivion to reality. He lived for literature, and the war provided him fodder for a lifetime of more writing, for it will bring him into close contact with not only his cousin but Stonewall Jackson, Robert E. Lee and all the army's luminaries of those four years. His journal entries throughout the war will revolve around his writing plans, accomplishments, and disappointments.

He is absolutely devoted to Stuart, but the feeling is not mutual. At one point Jeb will write to Flora, "I wish I could get rid of John Esten. He is the greatest bore I ever met, and is disagreeable to everybody, but we must all suffer some."[9] In another letter to her he wrote, "Jno. Esten is a case & I am afraid I can't like him. He is like your Pa in some peculiarities."[10] On another occasion, Cooke jokingly told Flora that Jeb shaved off his beard, but Jeb saw no humor in the jibe and just barely forgave it.

A man walks rapidly from the farmhouse, scales a horse and rides away, quickly spurring his mount into a canter, seen so briefly he can scarcely be described. That is the way it will always be for Redmond Burke because so little is known of him. Another staff officer recalled him as "a rough man."[11] He is said to have "a wonderful set of yarns to tell."[12] He has "some experience constructing bridges,"[13] and he is one of Stuart's most successful and resourceful scouts. However, his appearance and exact age—probably about forty[14]—and even where he came from are uncertain. Jeb thinks he is from Texas,[15] but in all likelihood he was born in Ireland.[16] He was apparently a private in the 2nd Virginia Cavalry before coming to Stuart's staff, but the first time Stuart referred to him in writing it was as "Mr. Redmond Burke."[17] He has only a few months to live and will die nearly as mysteriously as he lived.

A knot of men come out of the house together, pulling on gauntlets, adjusting sword belts, moving with purpose toward their horses. One handsome fellow, nearly as pretty as Pelham, is much younger than everyone else. At seventeen, Chiswell Dabney is the youngest member of Stuart's staff.

Another in the group carries an air of dark determination, as though he is simultaneously highly skilled and uncertain of his skills, determined to prove himself but conscious that modesty is a virtue. The saber he wears is fancy, an officer's presentation sword perhaps, and he holds it carefully as he walks so that it neither tangles in his legs or is dinged against a solid object.[18] His name is William Downs Farley.

Farley, Burcke, Mosby, and others will serve as scouts and even spies for Stuart, sometimes accomplishing remarkable feats, often delivering vital information just when it is needed, sometimes guiding thousands of men through dangerous territory, sometimes locating the enemy and taking his measure well before anyone else. They were successful because of their knowledge of the countryside, familiarity with residents of many parts of Virginia, and, one must suspect, because they could see better than a lot of their comrades. One need only examine photos of groups of Civil War soldiers and consider the number of modern folks who wear eyeglasses to come to the conclusion that there were thousands of Civil War soldiers blissfully unaware of their own myopia. Reading glasses for middle-aged generals, such as Lee, were common, and spectacles can be dated to the Dark Ages, but the concept of having one's eyes checked or being fitted for glasses to correct nearsightedness or astigmatism was unheard of and out of financial reach for the common man of the 1860s. It is entertaining to speculate about the reputations of legendary scouts for their eagle-eyed vision, who may merely have been men who did not need to wear glasses in a sea of men who did.

The last member of the cast is heard before he is seen. He is Sam Sweeney and he is playing a five-string banjo, providing a musical score to the scene—to virtually all of Stuart's scenes—as completely and genuinely as any Hollywood composer might do for a movie.

Sam's brother, Joe, did not invent the banjo but he refined an instrument that originated among African tribes and later appeared in the Caribbean in the 17th century. In the 1830s, Joe Sweeney began playing a different version of the "banjar" on stage with his ensemble, the *Virginia Minstrels*. It had four full-length strings and a short fifth string. It was tuned differently, and had a sound box that provided a drum-like sound that became popular, particularly in the South, and spread to England, where Joe once gave a command performance for Queen Victoria. Joe died in 1860 but his younger brother and fellow band member, Sam, joined the Confederate army on January 1, 1862, as a private in Company H of the 2nd Virginia Cavalry.

That is where Jeb found him, or heard him, and just as with Von Borcke, Pelham, Mosby, and others, he recognized immediately that he was a man possessed of the type of talent with which he intended to be surrounded.

Sweeney's regimental commander was Colonel Tom Munford, and he was familiar with and proud of Sweeney's talent. Minstrel show performers were the rock stars of the day, and having Sam Sweeney in one's regiment was the modern equivalent of having Bruce Springsteen at one's football tailgate party. Munford did not appreciate it when Stuart issued an order for Sweeney to report to brigade headquarters, and then never let him return to Company H. "It was a right he [Stuart] enjoyed," Munford wrote later, "but not very pleasing to me or my regiment."

Sweeny is accompanied by other musicians—a light-complexioned African-American named Bob, or "Mulatto Bob," who is a servant of Stuart's and who plays the bones; one or more cousins of Sam's on violins, and others. They are Jeb Stuart's band, his "gleemen," his cheer leaders and his symphonic accompaniment.

Additional, important members of the cast, Henry McClellan, William Blackford, Channing Price, and others will appear later and from time to time, but those just described are sufficient for present purposes. Besides, the man stepping out of the house, placing his hat on his head and shouting in a baritone voice is the man most critical to the scene.

Jeb does "fill the eye." His outfit, already described, is striking. He is happy, even ecstatic, which is not the least bit out of character. In fact, it is part and parcel of his personality. What cannot be seen with literary eyes is best conveyed in the words of those who knew him:

Generals Joseph E. Johnston and P.G.T. Beauregard wrote jointly, when recommending him for promotion to brigadier general, that "His calm and daring courage, sagacity, zeal, and activity qualify him admirably for the command of our three regiments of cavalry, by which the outpost duty of the Army is performed. The Government would gain greatly by promoting him."[19] Writing alone, General Johnston described Stuart as "a rare man, wonderfully endowed by nature with the qualities necessary for an officer of light cavalry. Calm, firm, acute, active, and enterprising, I know no one more competent than he to estimate the occurrences before him at their true value."[20]

John Esten Cooke wrote, "A single look at him was enough to convince anybody that Stuart loved danger and adventure," and "[t]here was about

Stuart an inspiration of joy and youth. The war was evidently like play to him—and he accepted its most perilous scenes and cruelest hardships with the careless abandon of a young knight-errant seeking adventures. Nothing seemed strong enough to break down his powerful organization of mind and body; and danger only aroused and brought his full facilities into play. He greeted it with ardour and defied it with his joyous laughter—leading his column in desperate charges with a smile upon his lips. Others might despond but Stuart kept his good spirits; and while the air around him was full of hissing balls and bursting shell, he would hum his gay songs."[21]

John Mosby was succinct in his admiration for Stuart, saying he was so unique that he defied all natural laws, was the best friend Mosby ever had, and that he made him all he was in the war.[22] William Blackford, who wrote perhaps the finest, most accurate memoir of life on Stuart's staff, described him as "a little above medium height, broad shouldered and powerfully built, ruddy complexion and blue-gray eyes which could flash fire on the battlefield, or sparkle with the merry glance which ladies love."[23] Moving beyond appearance, into character, Blackford said, "He was so brave a man himself that he never seemed to attribute unworthy motives to his men,"[24] and that "[Stonewall Jackson] and Stuart were the only two men I ever knew whom I thought unconscious of the feeling of fear. There were many as brave, but these two never seemed to feel that danger existed."[25] Furthermore, "General Stuart had a warm heart, and though a member of the church and a consistent, conscientious Christian, he was fond of gay company and of ladies' society and of music and dancing. Superficial observers sometimes made the mistake of considering him frivolous, but this was not so. Stuart was closely attentive to his business and a hard worker. I have often seen him busy arranging for some of his most brilliant cavalry movements, and after all was prepared, come out of his tent, call for Sweeny and his banjo and perhaps some of the men to dance for him, and then, to our amazement, order everybody to mount and be off after the troops who were already on the march."[26]

Henry Kyd Douglass, of Jackson's staff, was not an admirer of Stuart, but that did not prevent him from recording an objective description: "The peerless chief of cavalry, never quiet, never depressed, whistling on the battlefield, singing in camp, laughing and dancing in the parlor, when he approached our Quarters was generally heard afar off. He scattered verses too, as occasion required, over the Valley or in East Virginia, or exchanged them for flowers and wreaths which the ladies sent him."[27] Douglass concluded, "Take him all in all—capacity, daring, skill, swiftness, elan—America never produced Stuart's equal as a cavalry commander. I am not forgetful of Nathan Bedford Forrest, and Phillip Sheridan and Wade Hampton, and others, but there was but one Jeb Stuart!"[28] Another member of Stonewall's staff, Jedediah Hotchkiss, wrote, "Stuart was the genuine soul, full of life and humor."[29]

Enough said, for now, about the protagonist of this tale; one can hardly add more. There is, however, another matter that must be described in order to adequately set the stage.

It is that the mood of the surrounding countryside and of people living in and near this scene is more intense, more heightened, than anywhere else on the North American continent. The Southerners in and around Richmond are terrified. However exciting and glorious the times might seem in a century-and-a-half's hindsight, and however sweet and victorious they seemed during the preceding year, the citizens of Virginia and most of the young Confederate States felt doomed at the beginning of June 1862.

The flush of victory after First Manassas is long gone. The smug delight as McClellan fiddled about and Lincoln seemed unable to mount any serious offensive has passed. Instead of holding a strong line at the very doorstep of Washington, the Confederates are clinging to a fragile defensive line at the doorstep of their own capitol. McClellan, with a huge, superbly equipped army, has now come up the Peninsula, with Joe Johnston and the Army of Northern Virginia falling back before him, and if not for some well-orchestrated, theatrical chicanery masterminded by John Magruder, plus the innate caution of McClellan, Richmond might already be in Federal hands.

To make matters worse, there have been a series of disasters—the fall of New Orleans, Fort Donelson, and Nashville, the failure of the Rebel counteroffensive at Shiloh, and the death of Albert Sidney Johnston. And Joe Johnston being knocked out of command by a serious wound on May 30, mere days earlier. He has been replaced by "Granny" Lee, nicknamed "the Queen of Spades" for his tendency to dig in and throw up earthworks rather than go on the attack. The future looks decidedly grim for the young Confederate States of America.

The South needs a new hero, a bold stroke, something to revitalize its hopes and upon which to hang its dreams anew, and it needs it immediately. Some dramatic act, some adventure must be performed . . . perhaps with an accompanying soundtrack played on five-string banjo, bones, and fiddle.

CHAPTER TWO

THE FIRST RIDE AROUND McCLELLAN

JUNE 1–15, 1862

We're the boys who rode around McClellian,
rode around McClellian, rode around McClellian.
We're the boys who rode around McClellian.
Bully boys hey; bully boys ho!
—Jine the Cavalry, *as sung by Sam Sweeney*

The first three days of June found Stuart's headquarters at a house belonging to a Mr. Fontaine on the outskirts of Richmond that Jeb described as "The sweetest place I ever saw."[1] The previous cavalry camp, also at a farmhouse[2] but located nearly a hundred miles away, between Fairfax Courthouse and Centerville, was named "Qui Vive," French for "Who Goes There?" Jeb christened the new camp as "Camp Quien Sabe," Spanish for "Who knows?"

Who knew indeed? Change was in the wind and bigger ones were coming. An old friend and mentor of Jeb's, Robert E. Lee,[3] had just been named commander of the newly named Army of Northern Virginia,[4] and Jeb wasted no time communicating his views. On June 4 he wrote a letter outlining his analysis of the situation and his recommendations for action which were, he said, "convictions derived from a close observation of the enemy movements for months past, his system of war, and his conduct in battle as well as our own."

He accurately predicted that McClellan would not simply advance and attack, but would build and perfect siege works, then bring in heavy artillery and shell the capital. "We have an army far better adapted to attack, than defend," Stuart wrote. The Confederate army should "move down with a crushing force upon our front and right flank, thwart [McClellan's] designs, and deliver our capital."[5]

Stuart did not wait for Lee to respond. On June 5th he summoned John Mosby to Camp Quien Sabe and gave him a mission, the first assignment for the future "Grey Ghost." Mosby took four men and slipped behind enemy lines. What he discovered was what Stuart suspected—the Federal right flank was open-ended, and it would be "practicable" for a force of cavalry to penetrate into the Union army's rear all the way to its supply line at the York River Railroad.

Nor did Jeb content himself with merely sending Mosby out to reconnoiter. He had other sources to draw on. On June 6 he moved from Camp Quien Sabe to a new headquarters located by a farmhouse owned by a Mr. Waddle, which Von Borcke described as "remote from the main road and surrounded on all sides by flowering bushes and thickets."[6] If the new camp received a descriptive foreign language name, it wasn't recorded. On the 8th he took Von Borcke and six couriers on a ride, ostensibly to inspect outposts in the vicinity or, if Von is to be believed, on a secret mission. Von recounted that Stuart did inspect outposts and, about evening, arrived at the last one, on the edge of enemy territory. Stuart directed all but Von Borcke to remain, then ventured further.

Von, thinking they might come upon an enemy picket post, drew a revolver to make certain it was loaded. Stuart looked at him, smiled, and said, "We do not want to use firearms except as a last resort. If we meet an enemy patrol, we must use our sabers."[7]

They continued five miles with Von Borcke "feverishly agitated that every loud rustling branch, every bird that flew past" might be the enemy. Finally they arrived at a small house where they dismounted and Stuart knocked on the door. It was answered by an Irishman who beckoned them inside. Stuart then explained to Von Borcke that he had arranged to meet "one of our spies" at the house. Why that house and who the spy was were not explained, nor, for rest of the evening, was the spy's absence. The hours crept by and the "shady character," as Von described him, did not arrive.

It is amusing to speculate about the conversations that occurred in that small, one or two-room cabin in the woods. Two colorful, charismatic characters were confined by circumstance with a family consisting of a father, his wife, their seventeen-year-old son, and a daughter or two. The enemy was within shouting distance, if Von is to be believed, but no one else knew to where Stuart had disappeared. At some or several points, Jeb tried to persuade the father or his son to go to the spy's home, which was only two miles away but much nearer—within 400 feet claimed Von—to the Federal army camp. It had begun to rain heavily. Appeals to patriotism failed, as did promises of money, as did an offer from Von to accompany one or both. Neither father nor son seemed anxious to stroll through a forest occupied by nervous, gun-toting enemy invaders in a downpour in the wee hours of the morning in the company of a giant ambulating arsenal who barely spoke English. Somewhere around midnight Stuart decided to make the trip himself.

He and Von arrived at the spy's abode "without a mishap," where they found the man so ill he could not meet them at the door. Jeb dismounted and went inside while Von, "full of the most agitated strain," stood watch for approximately fifteen minutes. Then Jeb reappeared, mounted, and the pair "hastened at full speed toward our lines" where they "were greeted with delight by anxiously awaiting comrades."[8]

What a great story! Perhaps it was true. Mosby asserted later that Von Borcke's tale of the visit to the spy was "as fictional as the adventures of Baron Munchausen in the literature of Von Borcke's native Prussia."[9]

On the morning of June 9, Stuart again summoned Mosby. They breakfasted together, and because Von wrote that at the time they were subsisting on nothing but "maize bread" and bacon, "breakfast, dinner and supper," it is safe to assume cornbread and bacon were on the menu. This time Mosby took three companions and headed south toward the Pamunkey River. He questioned residents and observed all he could, particularly that the Federal right flank and supply line were not well defended. On June 10 he returned with this news to Stuart, who was sitting in the yard of the Fontaine house beneath the trees. Mosby sat down on the ground and delivered his report. Jeb directed Mosby to write down what he'd verbalized and, with the document in his pocket, Stuart rode to General Lee's headquarters at "Highmeadows," a farm located on the Nine Mile Road owned by Mary Dabbs, widow of Josiah Dabbs.[10]

One or more writers have noted that Stuart sent a letter to General Lee on June 4 urging a particular course of immediate offense against McClellan, but that Lee never responded. Stuart's letter, in fact, is sometimes dismissed as presumptuous—the egotistic act of a young brigadier thinking he knows more than the senior commander. The fact that Jeb advocated attacking McClellan's left, whereas Lee ultimately attacked his right, is accepted as proof that Stuart's advice was not taken seriously by Lee.

The timing of events contradicts that analysis. Lee received Jeb's letter, probably on the 5th, and immediately Stuart sent Mosby to scout the enemy's right flank, then sent him a second time, after probably going out himself, then went immediately to Lee, who gave him instructions that led to completion of plans for the Seven Days Battles.

Robert E. Lee proved over and over during the war that he placed great weight on the advice of his lieutenants, particularly a small handful that included Stuart. Whether historically verifiable or not, it seems likely that Stuart's letter played a large role in what was to come, the only significant difference being that Jeb advocated "a crushing force upon our front and right flank" whereas the force that was ultimately attempted was principally on McClellan's right, or the Confederate's left flank. Why? Because Jeb Stuart provided the information needed, after June 4, to make that decision.

Stuart rode away from meeting Lee on June 10 and back to his headquarters with new, verbal, instructions. The next day, June 11, the same instructions were made formal by written orders from Lee marked "Confidential." Stuart was to "make a scout movement to the rear of the enemy posted on the Chickahominy with a view of gaining intelligence of his operations." He was directed to use reliable scouts and take only men and horses who can "stand the expedition." He should not take risks, but "accomplish all the good you can without feeling it necessary to obtain all that might be desired . . . one of the chief objects of your expedition is to gain intelligence for the guidance of future operations."[11]

Stuart issued orders to stand ready to the 1st Virginia, commanded by Colonel Fitzhugh Lee, and the 9th Virginia, commanded by Colonel Rooney Lee, and directed that each of those regiments be reinforced with half of the 4th Virginia (i.e. four companies each). He also summoned two squadrons of the Jeff Davis Legion, from Mississippi and Alabama, commanded by Lt. Colonel Will Martin; and two guns from the Horse Artillery, commanded by Lt. James Breathed. The total was about 1,200 men.[12] The "reliable scouts" selected were John Mosby, William Farley, and Redmond Burke.[13]

None of those on the expedition except Stuart knew what they were up to. He confided the details of the mission to no one, not even his senior officers. Instead the force was directed to be "quietly concentrated," as Stuart wrote, on a farm near Kilby's Station on the Richmond, Fredericksburg, and Potomac Railroad, owned by a Mrs. Mordecai.

At 2 a.m. on the morning of June 12, Jeb aroused his staff at head-quarters, five miles from the rendezvous point, with the words, "Gentlemen, in ten minutes every man must be in the saddle."[14] Stuart and his staff arrived at the Mordecai farm about 5 a.m. and the expedition set out. Each man carried three days' rations. Speculation and rumors were in everyone's thoughts, if not lips, about the purpose of their expedition.

The most popular explanation, encouraged if not planted by Jeb, was that they were off to reinforce Jackson in the Shenandoah Valley. Their march was in that direction, Jackson was heavily outnumbered and seriously engaged in the Valley, whereas all indications were that Granny Lee was expected to settle down amidst a long siege in front of Richmond. Turner Ashby, up to then the most famous cavalier in the Confederacy, had been killed on June 6, less than a week earlier. It made perfect sense that General Lee was dispatching Stuart with the flower of his cavalry to take Ashby's place and bolster the force of the Army of the Valley.

They passed through camps of Confederate infantry along the Brook Turnpike, and soldiers turned out to watch. In tried-and-true military tradition, they lobbed barbs at their rivals on horseback. "Off to see Old Stonewall? Why don't you stay where the fighting is?" were typical. When one former army comrade saw Jeb he shouted, "How long you going to be gone, Beauty?" In response, Jeb turned in his saddle and sang a refrain from *Kathleen Mavourneen:* "Oh it may be years for years, and it may be forever. . . ." Without a second's delay, Sam Sweeney and his gleemen broke into the song: "Kathleen Mavourneen, the grey dawn is breaking, the horn of the hunter, is heard on the hill. . . ."[15]

The troopers that jingled and clip-clopped down the road that morning were a striking bunch of fellows. There is an unwritten, loosely enforced rule, dating back to at least Napoleon, that the army that looks the best eventually loses, and Stuart's cavalrymen were nothing if not obedient to that rule. They were a rakish lot, very uniform and significantly not.

Overall, most were clad in gray or blue-gray shell jackets, with a touch of butternut, some with facings or cuffs of traditional yellow trim. Trousers were gray, sky-blue, butternut, or plaid. The overall impression was of uniformity by sections. The war was only a year old, and many wore some or all of the uniforms in which they'd left home. Most would not be issued uniforms by the Confederate government until 1863. Most had joined a local company with its own name and uniform that then became a designated company of a regiment. Accordingly, those companies tended to be uniform among themselves but not with the next company.

The troopers of the 9th Virginia, leading the vanguard, consisted of eight companies that enlisted between April 21 and October 24, 1861.[16] The majority of the men—53 percent—were farmers, but the ranks included physicians, lawyers, mechanics, teachers, merchants, clerks, and carpenters. The average age at the time of enlistment was 25 years. They, like everyone in the column, wore hats of their own choosing.

Confederates preferred hats with a brim over kepis or forage caps, but hardly any matched. They wore beehives, beegums, bowlers, porkpies, pillboxes, and planters' hats, with high crowns, low crowns, wide brims, and narrow brims. Some were adorned with plumes and some with turkey or hawk feathers. Some pinned up the right side of the brim and a few pinned up the front. The hats were various shades of brown, gray, black, and occasionally blue or white. Mixed in were an occasional billed mechanic's cap and even a top hat or two.

Many wore pants tucked inside cavalry boots, and many had long gauntlets tucked into belts when not worn. Belts and other leathers were black or brown. Beltplates were a wide variety of Virginia state seals, Mississippi stars, Alabama state seals, oval C.S. plates, frame buckles, forkedtongues, and a fair number of Federal "U.S." oval buckles worn upside down and standing for "Southern Nation."

Shirts were not the least bit uniform, but were not necessarily homespun or hand-sewn. The mechanical sewing machine had been around for nearly a decade and many clothes were available "off the rack." While many shirts, jackets and trousers were entirely hand-sewn, usually by mothers, wives, or sisters, and were hand-repaired by the individual soldiers, many were sewn by lockstitch machines.

The men of the Jeff Davis Legion, the only non-Virginia unit on the expedition, considered themselves to be some of the most elite troops in the cavalry, being principally from Mississippi.[17] The horses of all in the column were selected based on their ability to "stand the expedition," rather than color, but there remained a large number of black horses among the 1st and 4th Virginia, as a couple of their companies were the "Black Horse Cavalry" that had haunted the Yankees in rumor before the Battle of Manassas. Their saddles were mostly McClellans and Jennifers, with a mix of civilian styles. Some had saddlebags and most had one or more rolled blankets tied behind the seat. Their sabers were principally

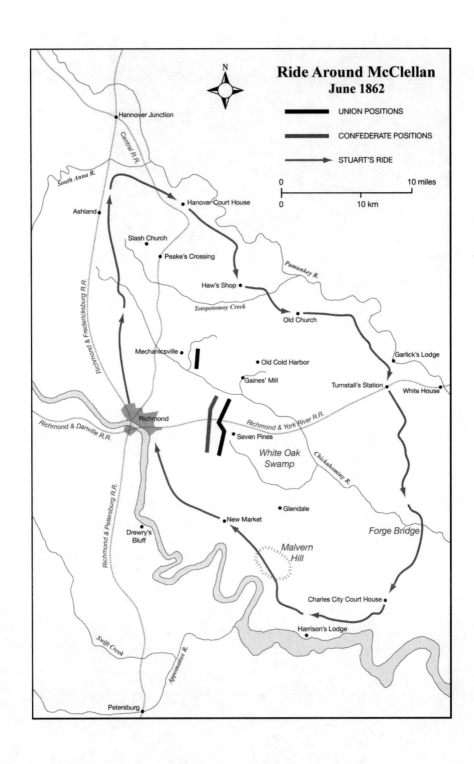

Ride Around McClellan
June 1862

UNION POSITIONS

CONFEDERATE POSITIONS

STUART'S RIDE

0 — 10 miles
0 — 10 km

N

Hannover Junction

Central R.R.

South Anna R.

Hanover Court House

Ashland

Slash Church

Peake's Crossing

Pamunkey R.

Haw's Shop

Totopotomoy Creek

Old Church

Richmond & Fredericksburg R.R.

Mechanicsville

Old Cold Harbor

Garlick's Lodge

Gaines' Mill

Turnstall's Station

White House

Richmond

Richmond & York River R.R.

Seven Pines

Richmond & Danville R.R.

White Oak Swamp

Chickahominy R.

Glendale

New Market

Forge Bridge

Richmond & Petersburg R.R.

Drewry's Bluff

Malvern Hill

Charles City Court House

Swift Creek

Appomattox R.

Harrison's Lodge

Petersburg

The 6th Pennsylvania Cavalry, known as Rush's Lancers, attempted to oppose Stuart's "ride around McClellan" in June 1862, though without success.

Below, a rare shot of a full Civil War cavalry regiment in the field, in this case the 13th New York cavalry.

After the Seven Days, a young horseman pauses on the road near the Chickahominy where Stuart's cavalry nearly became trapped by pursuing Union forces.

John Mosby, center with legs crossed, and some of his Rangers, most
of whom had also ridden with Jeb Stuart.

A Federal train wrecked by Stuart's cavalry near Manassas Junction in August 1862.

1860 Light Cavalry or 1840 "wrist breakers," with a scattering of Confederate-manufactured blades. They carried carbines, short shotguns, musketoons, and as many revolvers as each was able to lay claim.

They rode in columns of four when the width of the road allowed it, in columns of two when not, occasionally columns of squadrons, and sometimes in single file. Each company could be identified by the positioning of its officers—a captain in front, a first sergeant on the right of the first rank, other officers and non-coms alongside in designated locations. Flags were flown as they rode through the camps of the infantry, then furled and put away.

The Confederate cavalry rode all day and camped for the night on the Winston farm, near Taylorsville, having covered twenty-two miles.[18] Stuart, churning with nervous energy, did not settle down immediately. About midnight he and Rooney Lee rode five miles to "Hickory Hill," the home of Rooney's father-in-law, Henry Wickham. Lee's wife, Charlotte, was there, which was Rooney's purpose in going, and Stuart wanted to visit her brother, Col. Williams Wickham, commander of the 4th Virginia. Wickham, wounded in a skirmish on May 4, was recovering at Hickory Hill. Jeb felt it was proper, considering he had split the wounded officer's regiment into two parts and assigned them to other commanders, to at least visit the man being denied a role in the adventure. Jeb's extra energy wore off soon after he arrived, and he is reported to have spent most of his time asleep in a chair.[19]

Jeb and Rooney returned to their commands before daybreak and, as Stuart wrote later, "Our noiseless bivouac was broken early," and "without flag or bugle sound we resumed our march."[20] Flares were used to signal the resumption of the march instead of bugles.

At this point Stuart revealed the purpose of the expedition to his regimental commanders, and those in the column not told began to figure it out. Mosby, seeing they were following the same route he'd traveled four days earlier, put two and two together. They viewed their situation with new perspective and excitement. They were now in territory occupied by enemy cavalry. Because their purpose was to gain intelligence about the location and activities of McClellan's main army, or that portion north of the Chickahominy, any enemy scouts or detachments of cavalry should be taken prisoner or eliminated if possible.

The column rode east toward Hanover Court House. Mosby scouted ahead and discovered that a patrol of two squadrons of the 6th U.S. Cavalry—about 150 regulars—had just arrived at the little town from the opposite side. He sent a man back to report this to Stuart, who dispatched Fitz Lee's regiment to detour around Hanover and cut off the enemy's escape. The detour, however, took the 1st Virginia into a swamp, and while they splashed about for more solid footing the Federals spotted them and fled south.

The cat was out of the bag. The enemy could not know exactly what Stuart was up to but it could certainly guess. More important, they were likely to do something about him in response, and they had the means at hand in the form of several thousand infantry and cavalry.

Historians, analysts, and pundits who have commented on Stuart's first "Ride Around McClellan" in the years since have attributed to its commander various motivations in addition to simply carrying out Robert E. Lee's orders. Those who admire the man echoed the kind of adulation that the rest of the Confederacy would heap on him a few days hence. Those who did not wrote that his only goal was to gain personal glory, or criticized him for taking totally unnecessary and unrewarding risks in contradiction to Lee's orders. At least one writer attempted to lay blame for Lee's subsequent less-than-spectacular victories during the Seven Days Battles at Jeb's feet by writing, "With his unfortunate flair for the spectacular, Stuart exceeded his instructions and rode completely around the Federal army, thereby alerting McClellan and facilitating the latter's subsequent change of base."[21] Attributing McClellan's retreat from the gates of Richmond to Stuart's cavalry alone is overly complimentary to the cavalier, albeit amusing.

Jeb may have had another, more personal goal in mind. He knew that his father-in-law was in the area. Phillip St. George Cooke, father of Flora and uncle of John Esten Cooke, was a Virginian who refused to follow his native state, as well as most of his family, into the Confederacy. His son, John R. Cooke, was then a major and former Chief of Artillery in the Department of North Carolina who was wounded in the Battle of Seven Pines. By November 1862, John R. Cooke would be a brigadier general, the rank his father had held since November 1861. The elder Cooke was commanding the cavalry of Fitz John Porter's Corps, in whose direction Jeb and his troopers were headed. Cooke was also the author of a new book entitled *Cavalry Tactics, or Regulations for the Instruction, Formations, and Movements of the Cavalry of the Army and Volunteers of the United States*. The book was hot off the presses; Cooke's general's star was only seven months old, and he was in command of an entire division of cavalry in McClellan's army. Jeb considered him to be a traitor, and would have loved nothing more than to take him prisoner or embarrass him in a significant way.[22]

The 1,200 pressed on. They were in territory the Federals had occupied for months, and Virginians poured from their homes to welcome the perceived liberators. Von wrote that they were "greeted everywhere with enthusiasm by the inhabitants, especially by the ladies, who for a long time had seen none other than Federal troops."[23] The 9th Virginia, in the vanguard, moved quickly in order to run over Federal picket posts before they had time to flee or summon reinforcements. Von wrote that the first of these, just past Hanover Court House and near Haw's Shop, was captured to a man. However, before the prisoners could be sent to the rear the Confederate advance guard "came back at a run, hotly pursued by a large body of the enemy's dragoons." The lead squadron of the 9th Virginia flew at them and after a few moments of saber to saber clashing and crashing, the blue horsemen fled, with the Virginians on their trail and enveloped in their dust. Some were captured, but most escaped.

Interestingly, these Federals were a part of the 5th U.S. Cavalry, under the command of Captain William B. Royall. Royall was a Virginian who remained loyal to the Union, but he had served with Stuart in Kansas when both were officers of the 1st U.S. Cavalry. Furthermore, Fitz Lee had served in the 5th U.S. before the war. Small world.

The Federals rallied and took another stand further down the road. The portion of the 5th U.S. chased to that point were commanded by Lt. Edward H. Lieb, but they now reunited with the rest of the command, under Royall, and half an hour after the first clash the two forces collided again. Two squadrons of the 9th attacked, and Stuart sent Von back up the road to hasten the rest of the column to the scene. Soon the 1st Virginia arrived, but the enemy had already broken and fled. The Federals continued to flee, made one more attempt to stand, then galloped across a wooden bridge over a wide, swampy creek called the Totopotomoy, through their own camp at Old Church, and into the woods beyond, with Confederates whooping, shooting, and slashing at their rear.

It was in the attack of the 9th Virginia before the rout of the Federals that Confederate Captain William Latane ("la-ta-ney") was killed, hit by at least three bullets as he charged ahead of his squadron. While other Confederates were or would be wounded or captured, and whereas Von wrote that the Federals suffered several killed, Latane would be the only mortality Jeb's command would suffer in the expedition. Chiswell Dabney, Stuart's young aide-de-camp, reached Latane just as he died. He found his saber bent by a blow from one of the enemy's, and sticking in the ground. He gave it to one of Latane's men with directions to get it back to the family.[24]

Royall was badly wounded by a saber cut, but he escaped. The last words he was heard to shout before his wounding were, "Cut and thrust!" Latane's were "On to them, boys!"[25]

Latane was the same age as Stuart and was a physician before the war. Considered "well-born," he was widely liked in his regiment. His younger brother, James, located a farm cart, loaded the captain's body and carried it to Westwood, the nearby home of a doctor named Brockenbrough. Only Mrs. Catherine Brockenbrough was present, the rest of the menfolk being in the service of the Confederacy. No sooner had James turned over his sad bundle to her than Federal troops appeared and took him prisoner. Mrs. Brockenbrough tried to intervene, to no avail, and requested that the Yankees send one their chaplains to preside at the service for the fallen officer. Her request was refused. The next day slaves dug a grave in the garden of Westwood and a service was attended by Mrs. Brockenbrough, a few other women, and a handful of slaves. A neighbor, Mrs. Willoughby Newton, read the funeral service as the women, children, and servants looked on.

Once the raid was over, the death and burial of Latane became romanticized. John Reuben Thompson wrote a poem entitled *The Burial of Latane*, published in the July-August issue of the *Southern Literary Messenger*. It consisted of eight, six-line stanzas, including:

A little child strewed roses on his bier,
pale roses, not more stainless than his soul.
Nor yet more fragrant than his life sincere
that blossomed with good actions, brief, but whole:
The aged matron and the faithful slave
approached with reverent feet the hero's lowly grave.

and concluding with:

And when Virginia, leaning on her spear,
Victrix et vidua; the conflict done,
shall raise her mailed hand to wipe the tear
that starts as she recalls each martyred son,
no prouder memory her breast shall sway,
than thine, our early-lost, lamented Latane.

The dewy-eyed adulation did not end there. A few months after the war ended, William D. Washington produced an oil-on-canvas painting also entitled *The Burial of Latane*. It depicted five stylized women, one apparently pregnant, two little girls, one slave leaning on a shovel, and a handful of others in the shadows, around the grave. Engravings of the painting were hung in parlors throughout the South as a symbol of mourning for the Lost Cause, depicting a time when hopes were so high that the loss of a single gallant caused national mourning.

The Confederate advance from Hanover to its first encounter with Royall's men, under Lieb near Haw's Shop, to the bridge over Totopotomoy Creek and across, to Old Church, was a distance of about seventeen miles and consisted of clashes and pursuit. One Southern trooper described it as "so many blood hounds after fear-stricken deer."[26] Von wrote that after the clash in which Latane was killed, "The enemy made one more attempt to rally, but their lines were broken by our furious attack; they fled in confusion, and we chased them in wild pursuit across an open field, through their camp, and far into the woods." It is possible, even probable, that no one in the Confederate column except Stuart realized that along the way they had accomplished the principal purpose of the expedition.

The bridge over Totopotomoy Creek had not been destroyed, and the watershed along the Chickahominy and Pamunkey Rivers was not defended. Discovery of these facts made the raid a success, as the area was the probable target of Lee's offensive against the Federal right, and the bridge could serve as an important conduit for Confederate troops across the low, swampy ground. This information disproved the news mentioned in Lee's orders that the Federal right had been strengthened.

This was, as Stuart would report later, "the turning point of expedition."[27] He could turn back, job well done, or continue south, toward Tunstall's Station and McClellan's supply line to gather more intelligence and wreak havoc in the enemy's rear. Doing so was risky, and Lee had told him not to take unnecessary risks, but what else might be learned? The Southerners had already captured several of the enemy, including various officers. Might it be possible to add Phillip St. George Cooke to the bag? Even if not, what might be the result of continuing all the way around McClellan's army and back to Confederate lines? What might the depressed people in Richmond think of that?

While Jeb was seriously pondering his next step, his men were enjoying themselves. The Federal cavalry camp at Old Church was a fine prize, and the Confederates spent half an hour looting it. Von wrote that "every one tried to rescue for himself as much as possible of the articles of luxury with which the Yankees had overloaded themselves, but few succeeded . . . for . . . flames flashed up, now in one place, now in another, and in a few minutes the whole camp was enveloped in one blaze, hundreds of tents burning together presenting a wonderfully beautiful spectacle."

While this was going on, Jeb called his senior commanders, Fitz and Rooney Lee, to discuss what to do next. There were only two obvious choices: go back and claim success or go forward and risk everything, possibly for very little gain. The rail line that was McClellan's source of supply was nine miles away. The distance back to where they started was forty miles.

The two cousins were a study in both similarities and contrasts. Both were members of the same Southern aristocratic family; both were in the Federal army before the war; both now commanded regiments of Virginia Cavalry; both were close to and valued highly by Stuart; both were heavily-bearded and imposing characters; both would survive the war, would become involved in Virginia politics, and would be honored as great Southern heroes.

Fitz, however, was a graduate of West Point whereas Rooney graduated from Harvard. Fitz was a soldier's soldier. He valued military etiquette and protocol and doing things by the book. He despised guerilla warfare and unnecessary risks. Rooney was not so straight-laced. He liked what they were doing and was ready to engage in some more hit and run. Accordingly, once Jeb explained the options, Fitz adamantly opposed going forward and Rooney enthusiastically supported the idea.[28]

This may have been the response Jeb hoped for. Despite receiving the same military training as Fitz, Stuart embraced the notion of unorthodox tactics; doing what other trained West Pointers would not expect. He gave the order to advance toward McClellan's rear. John Mosby wrote later that "this was not only the turning point in the expedition, but in Stuart's life."[29]

Jeb and his companions suspected but could not know that the Federal army—under the tactical direction of none other than Phillip St. George Cooke—was hustling to bring massive forces of cavalry, infantry, and artillery to bear on the invaders. The Confederates were aided, however, in a most unusual manner. One of Captain Royall's junior officers, a Lt. Byrnes, had escaped with the rest of his regiment, and he quickly reported what had happened up the chain of command. Part of the report was that the Confederate troopers were supported by infantry.[30]

In all likelihood, Byrnes spotted some dismounted cavalrymen advancing or scouting on either side of the road, and jumped to a wild conclusion. The battle might have been his first, and he was aware of and probably in agreement with McClellan's gloomy predictions that the Federal army was woefully outnumbered and in constant peril of being overwhelmed. The treatment of Byrnes' report as it moved up the chain of command reads like a literary set of Russian nesting dolls, read from the inside out.

Byrnes reported that "when retreating, and when about one mile from Old Church, I saw the head of a column of infantry advancing on the road. . . . The pickets which were driven in saw the same body of infantry." Major Lawrence Williams, next up the line, wrote, "Lieutenant Byrnes also reported . . . he had seen infantry about a mile from me (five regiments, I think) . . . ." Brig. Gen. W.H. Emory dutifully passed on that "[Byrnes] had seen . . . five regiments of the enemy's infantry." The local infantry commander, Col. G.K. Warren, topped it off with "There was also a statement, that Lieutenant Byrnes (I believe that is the name) had seen seven regiments of Infantry at the place where the pickets were first attacked . . . ."[31]

What was happening on Old Church Road was not merely an unorthodox cavalry raid; it was a major Confederate offensive!

The reports caused the Federal commanders to over-prepare and move cautiously. The news of the advance reached Phillip St. George Cooke about 3 p.m.—several thousand Confederate cavalry are on Old Church Road in advance of several regiments of infantry. Cooke initially sent cavalry—Rush's regiment of Pennsylvania Lancers, plus a squadron of the 1st U.S. and six squadrons of the 5th and 6th U.S. Cavalry—but they'd not gotten far before someone reconsidered. They realized, or decided, they did not have enough forage for their horses for what might be an extended engagement, so they halted and sent back for more supplies in a most McClellan-esque fashion.[32]

Cooke wanted to send infantry and artillery as well, but it took awhile to gather the troops, and it wasn't until 10 p.m. that the Federals got a force of all arms in motion toward where they believed the Confederates to be. The pace was set by the infantry. The area was wooded and swampy. Roads were sometimes mere trails that looked alike, all winding and crooked. They were attempting a large military advance against a foe of unknown numbers in the dark. Nobody knew where the Confederates were, how many there might be, or when they might spring out of the brush to wreak havoc. The Federal column was eight miles long. The locals were unfriendly and unwilling to provide reliable guides or directions, which added to the Yankees's trepidation.[33]

Back at Old Church, Jeb summoned John Mosby in the afternoon and said, "I want you to ride some distance ahead." "Very well," Mosby replied, "but you must give me a guide. I don't know the road." Jeb had two locals to offer for that purpose and off they went, getting about two miles down the road before the rest of the column began to follow.[34] After traveling about four miles, Mosby found and captured a prize—a sutler and his wagon. In Civil War days sutlers were the equivalent of traveling Post Exchanges. They were licensed by the Federal government to sell supplies to the soldiers, and specialized in providing luxuries the troops could not obtain elsewhere, including cigars, sardines, oysters, personal insignia, and, oddly, gold-plated brass wedding rings.[35]

Mosby left one man to guard the treasure and proceeded onward, coming within sight of two Union supply schooners unloading at Garlick's Landing on the Pamunkey River. He sent back his other companion to alert Stuart, who dispatched one squadron each from the 9th and 1st Virginia regiments to burn the ships, plus the wagons of the 17th and 44th New York Volunteers into which the supplies were being loaded. Mosby also sent Stuart a note that urged him to quicken their progress, because "the woods are full of game."[36]

Proceeding further, now alone, Mosby came around a bend in the road near Tunstall's Station and found a Yankee quartermaster wagon loaded with Colt revolvers, boots, shoes, and blankets. The driver and lone trooper assigned to accompany the wagon quickly surrendered, but the historical record doesn't reveal whether Mosby got the prize to Jeb's men or whether he set it afire. Considering that he continued alone past Tunstall's station, the latter option was probably what occurred, but not necessarily. Mosby wrote that both the driver and the vidette went into a stupor "with bedazzled looks on their faces as though they had just seen a ghost."[37] They may have been content to sit still and wait until Stuart's men arrived.

Mosby then came upon a company of Pennsylvania cavalry and "bluffed" them into "withdrawing without firing a shot."[38] He stayed in position until the main body came up, which rushed forward and captured the Federals.

Von Borcke's report was consistently and characteristically inflated. "On either side of the road we constantly seized upon unsuspecting Federal soldiers, who had no idea of the close proximity of the dreaded Stuart until collared by his horsemen. A considerable number of waggons (sic) laden with provisions and goods fell into our hands, among them one containing the personal stores of General McClellan, with his cigars, wines, and other dainties. But we could not be burdened with booty, so the entire train was committed to the flames, the champagne popped bootlessly, and the cabanas wasted their fragrance on the air. Three transport-ships which lay in the river Pamunkey near at hand, laden with wheat, corn, and provisions from all quarters, were seized by us, together with the guard and the agents stationed there, and ere long the flames mounting towards heaven proclaimed how complete was our work of destruction."[39]

One suspects that to Von the lone sutler wagon became the personal property of the Federal commander, two wagons became a train, two ships became three, and that the fragrances and fires in the air were stronger and brighter in the old warrior's memory than in reality.

Jeb and his troopers were now fully invested, incontrovertibly committed to riding completely around McClellan's army. It was believed, or assumed, that Federals were gathering en masse on the road behind them and that they knew that the Confederates comprised only about twelve hundred men. Federal camps were all around, some plainly visible.[40]

Stuart would write in his report, defending a perilous venture subject to criticism, that the decision to continue the ride around McClellan instead of going back was "the quintessence of prudence."[41] Any critical hindsight on the part of folks not there misses a major point. Stuart may have been behaving recklessly and partially for personal gain, but his tactics were working remarkably—the enemy was simply stunned. Mosby wrote that at one point twenty demoralized Federal cavalrymen raced to overtake the raiders in order to surrender. Federal infantrymen at Tunstall's Station did not even have their weapons loaded. His "bluff" of the company of Pennsylvania cavalry consisted of stopping in the middle of the road, drawing his saber, waving it in the air and shouting, "Come on boys, Come on." Had he done the logical thing, turned and ran, the Pennsylvanians would have chased him down on their fresher horses and captured him. His theatrics convinced them, instead, to turn and vanish.[42] The Confederates were bamboozling the Yankees and having great fun doing it.

Rooney Lee's 9th Virginia still led, followed by Fitz's 1st Virginia, with Martin's Jeff Davis Legion and Breathed's two guns bringing up the rear. As such, the gray column arrived at the railroad line at Tunstall's Station—McClellan's vital source of supplies—about sunset. As Jeb's father-in-law was still waiting to gather a force sufficient to repulse the perceived Confederate offensive, Jeb directed Mosby, Burke, and Farley to cut the telegraph lines and poles, saw to it that the dismayed Federal infantrymen were rounded up, directed that the railroad lines be cut and that a nearby railroad bridge be burned, and ordered that all supplies and rolling stock be set afire.

Hardly had that work begun than the sounds of an approaching train were heard. The tracks had not yet been cut, so troopers hastily threw up a barricade of logs and ties, but not in time for it to be a significant obstacle. The train plowed through and kept going, but its loss was not mourned. The wagonloads of supplies the Southerners found at Tunstall's were like the best Christmas in their lives, so much so it is surprising the raid did not end then and there with 1,200 swollen-bellied, sickened troopers.

In addition to clothing, shoes, pistols, blankets, and tobacco, they found all sorts of exotic foodstuffs. John Esten Cooke wrote that he consumed "figs, beef tongue, pickle, candy, catsup, preserves, lemons, cakes, sausages, molasses, crackers, and canned meats.[43] Von recorded finding "pickles, oysters, preserved fruits, oranges, lemons, and cigars," and recalled that one soldier presented him with a bottle of champagne with the observation that "Captain, you did pretty hot work to-day. I got this bottle of champagne for you out of McClellan's waggon. It will do you good." Von recalled that he was so parched that his tongue was cleaving to the roof of his mouth and "Never in my life have I enjoyed a bottle of wine so much."[44]

A private in the 4th Virginia wrote, "We broke up the sutlers and got all their good eating. . . . We had a gay time." There was more than they could carry and they had no choice but to put most of it to the torch. As a member of the Jeff Davis Legion explained, "It would have been a loss of everything if we had attempted to bring off wagons and it was all we could do to get through with the prisoners, horses and mules."[45]

Darkness had fallen. The Confederates had ridden forty miles in a day filled with combat, pursuit, overeating, and lots of "pretty hot work," but they could not simply stop and go to sleep. The temptation was to proceed directly to the "White House," which was Rooney Lee's farm on the Pamunkey River that was captured by McClellan and turned into his primary supply depot. It was only four miles away, and the vast, rich stores there would make those at Tunstall's Station seem like hors d'oeuvres in comparison.

The temptation was overwhelming, but Stuart knew the depot would be guarded by gunboats as well as infantry, whom he could assume had been alerted to a possible attack. If any doubt remained, it was vanquished when a body of Federal cavalry rode out of the woods to the east, observed the scene at Tunstall's Station, and retired in the direction of the White House.[46]

From Tunstall's Station they proceeded south toward Talleysville, which consisted of only three or four houses, where they halted about 8:30 p.m. for a few hours of rest. About midnight or early in the morning of June 14, they pressed on with only moonlight to brighten the road. The period of rest was inadequate. Many soldiers fell asleep at they rode, and at one point even Jeb nodded off. John Esten Cooke wrote that "He had thrown one knee over the pommel of his saddle, folded his arms, dropped the bridle and—chin on chest, his plumed hat drooping over his forehead—was sound asleep. His sure-footed horse moved steadily, but the form of the General tottered from side to side, and for miles I held him erect by the arm," upright in his saddle.[47]

They were heading toward the Chickahominy River, which they planned to cross at a privately owned ford at "Sycamore Springs," the home of the Christian family. Lt. Jones Christian, a son, was a member of the column and he led them to the site.[48] Jeb and his staff arrived at the ford about 5 a.m., but they were dismayed to find that recent rains and upstream runoff had caused the river to crest at nearly fifteen feet.[49]

Rooney Lee and a handful of his men attempted to swim it on horseback, but whereas the Colonel made it, some of his men were nearly swept away and the horses of others became entangled in tree roots and other obstructions on the bank, so that they could only be rescued "with great difficulty." Colonel Lee swam his horse back rather than be separated from the column, as it was obvious that any hope of getting the entire body of troopers and guns across there should be abandoned.[50] When he regained the near bank, John Esten Cooke asked his opinion of the situation. "I think we are caught," responded Lee.[51]

To compound the crisis, the rear guard reported they were being pursued. It was Rush's Lancers, and they were only about four miles away. Von Borcke wrote that it was an entire division of the enemy. Stuart's men and horses were exhausted, such that it had become necessary to double the number of horses pulling the two artillery pieces. Fitz Lee must have been thinking, "I told you so."

Stuart displayed an uncharacteristic touch of anxiety earlier. As the column was leaving Tunstall's Station, its rear lighted by blazing wagons and the front in complete darkness, John Esten Cooke was startled when Jeb shouted "Who is there?" from the side of the road and then, upon ascertaining it was Cooke, demanded to know the location of Rooney Lee.

"I think he has moved on, General, "Cooke replied.

"Do you KNOW it?" Stuart responded.

"No, but I believe it," Cooke said, to which Jeb answered in a strained voice, "Will you *swear* it? I must know! He may take the wrong road and the column will get separated."

Cooke rode forward and almost immediately encountered a courier from Rooney who reported that the rest of the 9th Virginia was a mile ahead. "Good!" Stuart exclaimed from the darkness. The General's worry about taking the wrong road was a valid one, but not as critical a concern as that he faced at the river crossing. At the Chickahominy Jeb was up against an obstacle every bit as formidable as a rock, with a force of the enemy, very much a mobile hard place, approaching from behind.

"Anxiety at this time was reflected on the face of every one of those dusty and begrimed rebels," wrote one trooper.[52] "Every face showed anxious care except that of Stuart himself, who sat upon his horse stroking his long beard, as was his custom in moments of serious thought," said another.[53] "Every one looked with anxiety towards our leader, who, with the greatest possible calmness and coolness, gave his orders and made his arrangements," wrote Von.[54]

Jeb did not panic. A staff officer recalled that "Stuart was rarely excited by anything," and he could "think with entire calmness."[55] He was one of those rare individuals who might become impatient, irritated, or perturbed at minor inconveniences, but who became calm and reflective during genuine crises.

He did two things. He dispatched a courier—Corporal Turner Doswell —to Robert E. Lee to advise him of the situation and request that "a diversion might be made in his favor on the Charles River Road."[56] Second, he began casting about for a means of extracting his command from its "unpleasant position." He soon discovered the remains of a destroyed bridge about a mile downstream, where the road from Providence Forge, a local plantation, crossed the river to the Charles City Court House. Additionally, a large wooden warehouse, or barn, stood abandoned nearby that could be dismantled and used to repair the bridge. The group rode downstream to the new site.

Two regiments and the artillery were put in position to protect the workers. Redmond Burke and Corporal Henry Hagan "had some experience repairing bridges," and were assigned the task of overseeing the project. A skiff was used as a pontoon and boards were laid to form a low, rickety bridge, adequate to support a man but not a horse. The troopers then began crossing on foot, each carrying his saddle and equipment and leading his horse as it swam beside the bridge. Von claimed to have personally led 65 horses over in this manner.[57] Jeb sat nearby observing, in what Mosby noted was "the gayest humor I have ever seen him."[58]

Once across, however, they discovered they were on an island. The men searched and splashed about in desperation and finally located a swampy crossing at the island's western end. About half of the column then crossed to the south bank of the river, but this was not going to work for the artillery.

"Heavier blows resounded from the old barn," wrote Cooke. "Huge timbers approached borne on brawny shoulders, and descending into the boat anchored in the middle of the stream, the men lifted them across. They were just long enough; the ends resting on the abutments and immediately thick planks were hurried forward and laid crosswise." Stuart was in the middle of the second project, working alongside the men in the boat while singing.[59]

The second bridge took about three hours to complete. By approximately 1 p.m. everyone was across, including the artillery, which was pulled across the planks by hand, as well as all the horses, mules, prisoners, and troopers. The men cheered and gave the Rebel Yell lustily, then set their feat of engineering ablaze.

Fitz Lee was the last man to cross, and as he did, one of Rush's Lancers took a shot at him. The Federals had made appearances while the bridge repair was underway, but each time they did, Fitz advanced troopers and they retired.[60] Less than two hours away when Stuart first reached the swollen river at about 5 a.m., they had dawdled nervously and done nothing of significance for seven hours.

Colonel Rush's entire force arrived about ten minutes after the last of the rebels were across, as if they'd been in hot pursuit and living up to the commander's surname all along. A few shots were exchanged, but no damage was done and Rush did not attempt a similar feat of bridge construction. Later in the day he stopped at the home of a lady in New Kent, "looking weary, broken down and out of humour." When she asked if he had caught Stuart, he said "No, he has gone in at the back door. I only saw his rear guard as it passed the swamp."[61]

The Confederate column was now safe from pursuit, but was not yet out of the miasma. The area was full of water and holes, such that they were forced to swim their horses at several points. The prisoners, which numbered 165, were mounted on captured mules and horses, often riding double, and having less than a jolly time. The mounts frequently fell, or their riders fell off, and many blue uniforms became the color of mud. John Esten Cooke recalled that after managing to get across two swampy rivers, the column came to a third and one of the prisoners exclaimed indignantly, "How many damned Chicken—hominies are there, I wonder, in this infernal country."[62]

The Confederate column finally made it to Charles City, where it halted and got some much-needed rest. It was Sunday and some of the men had not slept since Friday. The main body stopped at Buckland, the home of J.M. Wilcox, but Stuart and his staff rode on to the home of Judge Isaac Christian. There the general and his staff lay down on a carpet spread on the lawn and went to sleep. After two hours Jeb was up again, "fresh as a lark," according to Cooke. He and the staff ate all the Christian family had to offer and then, leaving orders for the column to follow in five hours, Jeb took Private Richard Frayser, who served as a guide on the expedition, plus one courier, and pushed on to Richmond. Cooke claimed he was invited to go, but had to decline because his horse was worn out.[63]

The trio had thirty more miles to ride, which they did with only one stop, at Rowland's Mill for a cup of coffee. They arrived at Lee's headquarters about sunrise on June 15. Frayser was sent to inform Mrs. Stuart of their safe return and then to report the same to Virginia's Governor John Fletcher.[64] The first "Ride Around McClellan" was complete, but there would be a great deal of aftermath.

CHAPTER THREE

_____

THE SEVEN DAYS AND THE JAMES
JUNE 15–JULY 3, 1862

"He loved a joke, and would ring the changes on
one until a better one turned up."—W.W. Blackford

*Then McClellan followed soon, both with spade and balloon to try
the Peninsular approaches, but one and all agreed that his best rate
of speed was no faster than the slowest of slow coaches. Instead of
easy ground, at Williamsburg he found a Longstreet indeed and
nothing shorter, and it put him in the dumps, that spades wasn't
trumps, and the Hills he couldn't level "as he orter."*
—Richmond is a Hard Road to Travel, *as sung by Sam Sweeny*

The response to Jeb's "Ride Around McClellan" was immediate and
tumultuous. It was just what the doctor ordered for the ailing spirits in and
around Richmond. Having spent weeks observing a veritable Federal jug-
gernaut inexorably inching all the way to the gates of Richmond, the news
that Confederate cavaliers had ridden around the behemoth, making a
mockery of Union pursuit, was a tonic of cheer for the defenders.

Jeb's welcome home as a hero began as soon as the exhausted troops
entered the capital city. Residents lined the streets, cheering. Young ladies
spread bouquets and flower petals before Stuart and his men. A girl placed
a garland around Jeb's horse's neck. Women held out loaves of bread and
other edibles to the troopers. The *Richmond Dispatch* proclaimed that "Stuart
and his troopers are now forever in history." The *Richmond Examiner* de-

scribed the expedition as "one of the most brilliant affairs of the war, bold in its inception and most brilliant in its execution." Robert E. Lee wrote that the scout he had ordered "was executed with great address and daring by that accomplished officer." Maj. Gen. D.H. Hill, never generous with compliments, commented that "no more dashing thing [was] done in the war."[1]

On Monday, June 16, Jeb strolled to the capitol building. His purpose was to soak up all the adulation he could, for unlike Lee, Jackson, and other leaders of the Confederacy, he was not modest. He was as much in his element as the center of attention as he was in the saddle.

He attended a military drill, but everyone recognized and began cheering him. Demands for a speech were shouted, and one witness wrote, "The people, citizens and soldiers were pretty near crazy to hear the gallant General speak."[2] Jeb climbed the steps of the Governor's Mansion and said a few words. He did not overdo it, and took no personal credit for anything grand. Instead he talked about the importance of "the spirit of the people, the grand object of Southern deliverance, and the determined and heroic character of the army."[3]

Jeb later learned something as satisfying as all the cheers and admiration—he had seriously, permanently, embarrassed his father-in-law. Phillip St. George Cooke. Cooke's commander, Fitz John Porter, wrote in his report that "I have seen no energy or spirit in the pursuit by General Cooke." Cooke was ordered to make a statement explaining how and why he let the rebels escape.[4] More than a few people in important positions wondered if Cooke had intentionally let his son-in-law escape, and where the Virginian's loyalties actually lay. Cooke stewed for days and wrote his report, but his career was on a downhill slide. He remained in the army for the duration of the war but never again held a significant military command.[5]

Jeb spent the next few days at his headquarters, taking care of paperwork, resting up, and accepting the congratulations of visitors, companions, and peers. On June 17 he wrote his report to General Lee, a congratulatory order to his command, and an appendix to his report singling out nine officers for promotion. These were Fitzhugh Lee, Rooney Lee, W.T. Martin, Assistant Surgeon J.B. Fontaine, Heros Von Borcke, Redmond Burke, William Farley, John Mosby, and Lt. W.T. Robins, adjutant of the 9th Virginia.[6]

Others were praised in the report, which began "in compliance with your written instructions . . ." but blossomed into such prose as "on dashed

Robins, here skirting a field, there leaping a fence," and in which Latane did not merely die, but "sealed his devotion to his native soil with his blood."[7] Stuart's congratulatory order to his command said, "History will record in imperishable characters and a grateful country will remember with gratitude that portion of the First, Fourth, and Ninth Virginia Cavalry, the Jeff Davis Legion, and the section of the Stuart Horse Artillery engaged in the expedition. What was accomplished is known to you, to the public, and to the enemy . . ." and "Proud of his command, the general trusts that it will never lose sight of what is at stake in this struggle—the reputation now its providence to maintain."[8]

On June 23, General Lee issued Order No. 74 congratulating Stuart and his command, calling the mission a "brilliant exploit" in which "the general commanding takes great pleasure in expressing his admiration of the courage and skill so conspicuously exhibited throughout by the general and the officers and the men under his command." Lee even reached down to congratulate four soldiers not mentioned by Stuart—Private Thomas D. Clapp of the 1st Virginia, Privates Ashton, Brent, R. Herring, and F. Coleman of the 9th Virginia, plus one man with no rank Stuart did single out—John Mosby.[9]

Mosby was getting other public attention. His ruse on the Federal company of cavalry at Tunstall's Station earned him an account in the *Richmond Dispatch* in which he was called "the gallant Lieutenant." The *Abingdon Virginia,* reported, "We hold this a bright record, alike for bravery, intelligence and enterprise. Mosby is evidently of the same stuff that Morgan and Ashby and such men are made of."

Nevertheless, Mosby was restless. He was not cut out for regular military service, even when it allowed him to scout independently in advance. He also was not comfortable at Stuart's headquarters because of the frequent presence of a man he could not abide and who despised him—Fitz Lee. These two famous men were united in a common cause under the leadership of the same beloved commander, but they hated each other for reasons bordering on the ridiculous.

When Mosby joined the army he became adjutant in the 1st Virginia Cavalry, commanded by William E. "Grumble" Jones, whom Mosby admired and Stuart disliked. Jones was irascible, threadbare, and slovenly, which satisfied Mosby just fine. Mosby's later photos show a natty dresser, but that wasn't the image he cultivated at the beginning of the war. He rode a civilian saddle and wore red facings on his uniform instead of cavalry yellow. A Mosby biographer described him as the soldier in his company "most likely to drop out first," with "indifference and distaste for military courtesy [that] hung over him like a cloud."[10]

Jones was not popular with the regiment, whereas his second-in-command, Fitz Lee, was both well liked and was a by-the-book West Pointer. Lee, however, recognized Mosby as the sneaky irregular the Grey Ghost would become, and he wasted no time letting Mosby know.

The first incident occurred when Jones was absent and Adjutant Mosby formed the regiment for dress parade. Such an exercise is not an actual parade, but a formation accomplished once or twice daily in which the regiment forms in line of battle facing its commander to receive orders. It is one of the few formations in which the adjutant plays a critical role, but Mosby did not perform with the military pomp Lee expected.

Mosby ambled up to Lee and said "Colonel, the horn has blowed for dress parade," and Lee exploded.

"Sir, if I ever again hear you call that bugle a horn, I will put you under arrest!"

Mosby hadn't seen that coming.

The catalyst for the next incident was a Northern newspaper, the *Washington Star*, which Mosby had taken from a Federal prisoner. Stuart being absent, Mosby carried it to Fitz Lee saying, "Colonel, here's a copy of today's paper." Lee glared at him, refused to take the paper and said with venom, "The ruling passion strong in death."

This phrase means nothing to most of us today, but Lee was quoting from a poem by Alexander Pope titled *An Epistle to Right Honourable Richard Temple, Lord Visct. Cobham*. Both Lee and Mosby were learned men and familiar with the poem, which includes the aphorism "as the twig is bent, so's the tree inclined." The poem's theme is that each man has an inner passion that will lead to his death and which cannot be disguised by acts contrary to that passion. The message Lee delivered cryptically was "I know what you really are, that you are no honorable man, and that you will get what you deserve."[11] Mosby got the message.

On April 23, 1862, the Confederate army elected officers. This unmilitary yet democratic exercise was enacted into law as part of the Confederate Conscription Act. This first-ever Southern draft not only threatened to take men into the army by force but extended one-year enlistments to three. Allowing men to elect their own officers was a bone thrown to the soldiers for such ungentlemanly treatment. In the 1st Virginia it meant the unpopular Jones was voted out and Fitz Lee was voted in. Mosby resigned from the regiment within an hour.[12]

He became a scout, with no rank, and Stuart selected him to go behind enemy lines, then ride around McClellan. Mosby was successful but he wanted more. He told Stuart he was considering transferring to the Virginia State Line, a new brigade commanded by John B. Floyd created by the Confederate Congress in March. Its members would act as guerillas, partisans, and independent raiders, which Mosby considered ideal.

Stuart did not want to lose him and proposed another idea. On June 20th, Jeb wrote a letter to Secretary of War Randolph proposing the formation of a company of sharpshooters within his command under Mosby. Mosby delivered the letter to Randolph, but it was not approved, and Mosby continued to chafe.[13]

Stuart was in and around camp from the 17th through the 23rd of June, taking care of paperwork. On the 23rd he wrote Lt. Col. Thomas Rosser, a friend and former West Point roommate of John Pelham, to inform him he was promoted Colonel to command the newly formed 5th Virginia Cavalry, a promotion Stuart had lobbied the War Department to award. In his letter Jeb wrote, "Come to me at daylight in the morning and I will give you the particulars. You are in my brigade and must play an important role in the next battle. Come a-runnin'."[14]

Another important player in the drama, William W. Blackford, joined, or rather re-joined, Stuart about then. Blackford was an engineer who had served under Jeb at the beginning of the war in the 1st Virginia Cavalry. He was Stuart's adjutant until Jeb was promoted to Brigadier General on September 24, 1861, and Grumble Jones, the new regimental commander, appointed Mosby as adjutant. A week later Blackford was commissioned captain, but was arrested by Jones for allegedly violating an order against having fires on picket lines.[15] It took weeks for a court martial to find Blackford innocent, during which the army reorganization and election of officers occurred, so that he was not elected captain of a company and was left without a command.

His misfortune was fortune for those desiring to learn more about Jeb Stuart, because he was next commissioned captain in the Confederate Corps of Engineers and assigned to Stuart as brigade engineer. More importantly, he survived the war and penned a clear-minded, engaging account of the war, devoted principally to his service with Stuart's cavalry. He arrived on June 24, 1862, just as things started popping again.

Bucolic bliss at cavalry headquarters ended that day with the issuance of General Lee's Order No. 75, a directive for the campaign that would become the Seven Days' Battles. It was also the culmination of three weeks of planning, scouting, and the gathering of information accomplished in Jeb's ride around McClellan. Lee explained his plans to his senior commanders—Longstreet, Jackson, and the two Hills, A.P. and D. H. They were to strike McClellan's right in the vicinity of a community named Mechanicsville. Stuart would cover the army's flanks, particularly Jackson's, who was to spearhead the assault.

Jackson had commanded the Shenandoah Valley District and the Army of the Valley since October, 1861, and for the previous four months was engaged in what has been called "One of the most brilliant operations in military history."[16] On June 25, Jeb rode from Richmond north by the Brook Turnpike to meet him. With him rode the 1st, 4th and 9th Virginia Cavalry regiments, the cavalry of the Cobb, Jeff Davis, and Hampton Legions, and the Stuart Horse Artillery, about 2,000 men. He left behind the 3rd, 5th, and 10th Virginia, and three companies of the 1st North Carolina to guard the right flank of the Confederate army.[17]

Stuart and Jackson had served together the previous year, beginning May 10, 1861, at Harpers Ferry, where Stuart took command of companies that became the 1st Virginia Cavalry while Jackson organized and trained what became the Stonewall Brigade.

The two men shared some characteristics—both were about six feet tall and weighed about 175 pounds with blue eyes; and both were devout Presbyterians who neither smoked, swore, nor drank liquor—but otherwise they were polar opposites. Stuart was jovial and boisterous; Jackson was quiet and taciturn. Jeb loved music and singing while Jackson was notoriously tone-deaf. Stuart wore fine, well-adorned, braided, and decorous uniforms while Jackson was threadbare and disheveled. Stuart loved to joke, tease, and frolic while Jackson rarely laughed, told, or responded to a joke. Stuart's health seemed indestructible while Jackson suffered from dyspepsia and harbored odd theories about how his body functioned and what was needed to keep it in balance. Stuart was a youthful twenty-eight while Jackson was an almost middle-aged thirty-eight. Yet somehow, in one of the war's endearing developments, the two were not merely companions, but devoted friends.

Those who saw them together marveled. "Jackson unbent to Stuart more perhaps than anyone else in the army, and Stuart, more than any one else was free and easy with him," wrote David Boyd, a friend of Stuart's.[18] An Aide de Camp to Jackson, Lt. James Power Smith, wrote that Jackson's "fondness for General J.E.B. Stuart was very great, and the humor and frolic of the genial and splendid cavalryman was a source of unbounded delight."[19] Jeb, a bit ahead of his time, collected autographs, and carried a book for that purpose in which the signatures of the South's luminaries were written. In it he pasted a clipped signature of Jackson's in which Stonewall wrote, "To my friend, to whom I am much attached." They were so comfortable with each other that Jeb did not think anything, after a hard day of campaigning, of crawling into bed with Jackson, a habit which elicited a rare, memorable witticism from Jackson.

Stuart met Jackson near Ashland on June 24. The Army of the Valley had marched twenty miles that day, on top of 646 miles during the latter part of their campaign. They were exhausted, dusty, and ragged, but Jackson and his men brightened when they saw Jeb. "He [Jackson] was delighted to see General Stuart and rode out to one side of the road with him to have a consultation. Stuart's fame had spread, and Jackson's men cheered wildly as they passed, for they knew well enough what was brewing when these two men conferred in that way."[20]

The same day that Stuart rode to meet Jackson, McClellan surprised everyone by attacking Lee's army in the first of the Seven Days' battles. It was a small affair remembered by many names—Oak Grove, Henrico, King's School, and The Orchards—but nothing of significance occurred.

In fact, there is not a lot to be said about Stuart's role in the battles that immediately followed, being Mechanicsville on the 26th, Gaines' Mill on the 27th, Garnett's and Goldings Farms on the 27th and 28th, Savage Station and Allen's Farm (aka Peach Orchard) on the 29th, White Oak Swamp (aka Glendale, Charles City, New Market Crossroads, or Frayser's Farm) on the 30th, and Malvern Hill on July 1st. The role of the cavalry was to screen Jackson's movements, cover the army's flanks and keep tabs on McClellan to make certain nothing unexpected occurred. Various adventures were had along the way.

On June 27, as the Federal army began to withdraw, Stuart's men encountered a regiment of Pennsylvania Lancers they had read about. Northern newspapers described them as "the finest body of troops in the world," and William Blackford attested to the accuracy of that claim because they were very well dressed; they were very well mounted; when lined up in battle two or three hundred yards off with their pointed lances erect and glittering, they looked splendid; and once they saw the Confederates attacking they turned and ran so fast the Confederates couldn't catch them. Blackford was particularly proud of the speed of his horse, Comet, but testified that even she "couldn't overtake them in a mile or two race, and them only having a hundred yards head start."[21] Von Borcke opined that only twenty of the 700 lancers retained their awkward weapon, the rest being strewn for miles along their route of retreat.[22]

Stonewall Jackson, for reasons never fully understood, performed poorly during the opening battles. He was slow, lackluster, and unlike himself. Exhaustion is a likely cause, although not an excuse, but his performance allowed John Pelham an opportunity to do good work and advance a growing fame.

On June 27 Jackson was hours behind schedule, and once his nine brigades got into position, about 4:30 p.m., they immediately came under the fire of two Federal batteries.[23] Jackson's artillery had not arrived, but Stuart sent Pelham forward with a Blakely rifle and a twelve-pounder Napoleon. The Blakely was knocked out of action but Pelham continued the duel with the Napoleon.

At short range for close to an hour, Pelham fought twelve Federal cannons with a single gun. Jackson was amazed. He watched the duel from afar and sent Jeb a message asking who was the officer directing his fire so accurately against overwhelming numbers. Stuart proudly identified Pelham, and after Jackson's artillery arrived to help drive the Federals from the battlefield, Jeb brought the young captain to Stonewall for an introduction.

"This is Captain Pelham, General," Stuart announced. "He fought with one gun that whole battalion on the hill, at pointblank range, for nearly an hour." Jackson extended his hand and Pelham took it, blushed, bowed low, and withdrew shyly, overwhelmed at the attention. Jackson seemed energized by Pelham's performance, and subsequently singled him out for praise in his battle report.[24]

While preoccupied with Pelham's exploits, Jeb missed two events that would have pleased him mightily. First, Confederate infantry under John Bell Hood finally broke through the Federal line near its center. Once the formidable position had been punctured the Federal line began to crumble right and left. Second, more personal, Jeb's Unionist farther-in-law, Phillip St. George Cooke, attempted to do something about it by ordering a cavalry charge against the onrushing Confederates.

A basic rule since the invention of the rifled musket had been "don't attack infantry head-on with cavalry." A visceral, layman's analysis might hold that mounted men riding toward dismounted men have an advantage, and Hollywood has bolstered that impression, but the opposite is true. Concentrated infantry fire brings down horses, empties saddles, and tangles the remaining riders long before the cavalry can do damage. If the mounted force makes it to the infantry, unless the infantrymen decide to flee, a lot of horses get bayoneted and their riders can't get close enough to use a saber or sit steady enough to fire well-aimed shots from a plunging horse.

Cooke, in his opus *Cavalry Tactics*, devoted over 200 pages to training, marching, drilling, and every kind of maneuver, from "posts of the officers and non-commissioned officers of the field and staff of a regiment in line" on page 4, to "running at the heads and pistol practice" on page 154, to "marching in open column to form line faced to the left, to the front and to the rear" on page 188, but only five pages to the "Charge." There was nothing therein about not attacking infantry head on.

Accordingly, when Cooke decided the best way to save the Union artillery was by counterattacking the Rebels who had just breached the Federal line, the result was, as Federal corps commander Fitz John Porter put it, "confusion. The bewildered and uncontrollable horses wheeled about, and, dashing through the batteries, satisfied the gunners that they were charged by the enemy. To this alone I always attributed the failure on our part longer to hold the battlefield and to bring off all our guns . . ."[25] While the Confederate infantry simply stood and shot down the galloping Yankees, the Federal artillery either felt compelled to cease fire or else drop exploding shells into the middle of their own cavalry. When the surviving horsemen stampeded back through their own guns the chaos was made complete.

The Federals lost twenty-two guns at Gaines' Mill, most of them on the part of the field where Cooke made his charge. To be fair, Brigadier General Evander Law, who led part of the Rebel breakthrough, failed to share Porter's disdain for Cooke's action: ". . . the batteries, having no infantry supports, did not check our advance for a moment," he wrote. "The diversion by the cavalry, on the other hand, did delay their capture for the short period it took to repulse it, and gave time for the artilleriststs to save some of their guns."[26] The postwar view of an enemy commander, however, did not save Cooke from Fitz John Porter's immediate wrath.

Jeb missed the entire spectacle, which was the last opportunity he had to embarrass his father-in-law. Gaines' Mill was to be Cooke's last combat of the war. He spent the rest of the conflict on court martial and recruiting duties, plus a lackluster command in Baton Rouge. The next evening his nephew, John Esten Cooke, enjoyed dinner in his abandoned headquarters.[27]

About this time, Stuart and his staff were sitting on their horses observing the battle when an enemy battery, as Blackford said, "noticed us by a round." The shell came close, flying over the heads of the mounted men, and most of the staff officers being "not so well accustomed to artillery as we became afterwards," ducked. John Esten Cooke, in fact, ducked so low that he lost his balance and tumbled from his horse.

Thinking his cousin-in-law might be wounded, Stuart leaned down and said, "Hallo Cooke, are you hit?" John Esten stood up, embarrassed, dusted himself off and said, "No General, I only dodged a little too far."

The entire staff, most particularly Stuart, erupted in laughter, "until we could scarcely keep our seats in our saddles," Blackford recalled. Thereafter, not merely for days or weeks, but months, nearly every time Jeb saw Cooke he would repeat the scene or some variation of it. "Cooke, are you awake or did you just dodge too far?" "Cooke, I need a man who knows how to dodge; do you have anyone to recommend?"

Cooke took it in good humor, considering he had no choice, and Jeb's ribbing was not malicious. Stuart, as Blackford described, "loved a joke and would ring the changes on one until a better one turned up."[28] The term "ring the changes," is a phrase popular in the 19th Century that has fallen into disuse. It originated with the practice of bell ringing, and dates to the 17th Century. When multiple bells were rung, each pattern in the order of ringing was called a change, and to "ring the changes" meant to strike all the patterns and then come back to the beginning. An 1859 dictionary defined it as "changing bad money for good; in respectable society the phrase is sometimes employed to denote that the aggressor has been paid back in his own coin, as in practical joking, when the laugh is turned against the jester."[29] In Jeb's case the phrase definitely referred to a jester rather than a money changer.

John Esten Cooke was not the only man who was the butt of serious change ringing. General McClellan was not victorious at Mechanicsville on the 26th, was whipped at Gaines' Mill on the 27th, was generally defeated and chased on the 28th through the 30th, and managed to salvage his army by repulsing Lee's repeated assaults on Malvern Hill on the 1st, after which he continued his retreat. The news he sent north, however, was that he simply accomplished a "change of base" from the York to the James River.[30]

When the Rebels got wind of Little Mac's report, they thought it was hilarious. McClellan was clearly skedaddling and "changing one's base" became a watchword rung through the army's changes on an epic scale. As Blackford wrote, "If two dogs fought and one ran, the men cheered and shouted 'Look at him changing his base'; if a man fell in the mud, his comrades would laugh and ask him what he was changing his base for; or if the rain flooded the place where they were sleeping they would say 'Come, fellows, let's change our base'."[31]

Late on the night of June 27th, after Jeb and his staff were asleep, General Jackson came to their camp. Jeb was roused and the two generals conferred in the dark.[32] They agreed that McClellan was certain to retreat toward his remaining base of supplies, and that maybe he could be cut off from doing so."[33] Consistent with that analysis, Stuart led his command early the next morning toward the White House on the Pamunkey River. This historic, six-room plantation house was once the home of Martha Custis, and there George Washington courted her. In 1857, Rooney Lee inherited it from his grandfather, but for the previous three months it was McClellan's supply depot. Tons of Federal supplies were stacked and stored around the plantation, and Stuart went there to hinder or prevent McClellan's efforts to remove them.

Their route took them back to Tunstall's Station, where they had adventured two weeks earlier. Now they found it entrenched, as if the raid of June 13 impressed upon the Federals that doing so was a sound idea. Missing, however, were Federal soldiers to occupy the fieldworks. They had withdrawn across Black Creek—more a swamp than a creek—destroyed the bridge behind them, and were on high ground on the far side of the swamp with artillery and bad attitudes.

Stuart shelled the high ground and sent Farley and a squadron of dismounted men to drive off sharpshooters who could fire down on the bridge. Then he commanded Blackford to rebuild it, which took up the rest of the day.[34]

The Federals decided to destroy their supplies, a decision Blackford credited to Stuart sending dismounted men to march about in sight of the enemy and make them think they were infantry while Pelham fired his cannons at long range and changed the position of his guns frequently to make them think there were a great number.[35] This ruse, Blackford wrote, "succeeded and soon after nightfall great columns of smoke and a bright illumination announced that they were setting fire to the great town of canvas and board houses that had sprung up at the place since its occupation by the Northern army."[36]

Von Borcke was unable to accompany Stuart to the White House on the 28th. The previous day, while riding back from delivering Jeb's orders to a regiment of Georgians, he felt a sudden blow to his spine that sent horse and rider to on the ground. Getting to his feet, Von examined his mount, a chestnut, and found no injuries. A solid shot had passed so close to them that the "windage" had knocked both to the ground. It was a somewhat common occurrence during the war, and Von Borcke suffered no injury from the experience, but his horse did not recover. The next morning his servant reported that the chestnut could not rise, and it never did, so Von stayed behind to help sort out prisoners.[37]

Later in the day he borrowed a horse and rode out to see the Gaines' Mill battlefield, the carnage of which aroused a sense of the macabre. In some places he saw bodies piled three and four deep, and he was particularly affected by the site of two dead Confederates lying on their backs side by side. One was silver-haired and over the age of fifty, shot in the head, and the other was a boy of about sixteen, his hands crossed over his chest, shot in the heart.

He recognized the body of one of Jackson's infantryman. The man, a Mississippian, was, in Von's words "a perfect giant," larger than all around him and all the more fearsome in appearance because he wore a bearskin vest. That day, however, he lay dead with a small hole in his chest that was "sufficient to make an end at once of all his strength and vigour."[38]

Someone told him that at one spot on the battlefield a Texan and a Federal Zouave had squared off, bayonet to bayonet, that each had pierced the other "and that their dead bodies were found standing erect in the very attitude in which each had received his deathwound." Accordingly, "Curiosity carried me to the spot."[39] He found it but not the standing dead men. Instead he found the red-pantalooned Zouaves "scattered about all over the ground like the scarlet poppies in a corn-field" where "the never-erring bullet of the famous Texan marksmen had brought them down, not the bayonet." He became fully engaged in the endeavor, dismounted, and examined several corpses, but found only three or four bayonet-wounds, and those evidently received after the soldiers were shot. He concluded that the accounts of bayonet fights, which seemed to accompany every general engagement, "rarely if ever occur, and exist only in the imagination."[40]

Von Borcke was not the only sightseer. John Pelham took a stroll across the battlefield that night. Among the carnage, broken bodies, weapons, and accouterments, he spied and salvaged a souvenir—an Episcopal Book of Common Prayer. [41] John Esten Cooke wrote of the battlefield, saying, "Dead Yankees as thick as leaves. Hundreds of red legged Zouaves lying on their backs—toes up. No pity for them. . . ."[42]

Stuart and his men spent the night of the 28th and the early hours of the 29th watching the Federal supply dump burn. Blackford said the fire was so large that it lit the countryside like day for miles around, that clouds of smoke rose hundreds of feet into the air and that the sound of exploding shells and ammunition sounded like a battle.[43]

When dawn came, they saw a gunboat, the *Marblehead*, on the river. Stuart advanced seventy-five men from the 1st and 4th Virginia regiments and the Jeff Davis Legion, plus one of Pelham's howitzers, and a skirmish followed, after which the gunboat steamed away.[44] Stuart, his staff, and the 9th Virginia rode forward to claim what remained around the White House.

Once again it was Christmas come early. Although tons of supplies were reduced to ash, tons more survived. The Confederates found "quantities of barrels of sugar, lemons by the millions, cases of wine, beer, and other liquors of every description, confectionary, canned meats, . . . fruits and vegetables, and great quantities of ice, all still in excellent condition."[45] Of particular interest were barrels of fresh eggs shipped and stored in barrels of salt to minimize breakage. The fires had cooked but not destroyed them. "The salt was fused into a solid cake with the eggs, deliciously roasted, distributed throughout the mass; it was only necessary to split off a block and then pick out the eggs, like the meat of a nut."[46]

The supply depot also served as an embalming center for dead soldiers, and the fleeing Federals had not carried away the subjects of that treatment. They—Union casualties of recent battles—were stretched out on tables, in coffins, and in rows on the ground. Blackford described it as a ghastly spectacle and noted that many of the dead were officers but that there was no record of their names.

Liquor attracted the attention of troopers, and several began drinking or storing bottles away for future consumption. This led Rooney Lee to issue a report that the fleeing Federals had poisoned the liquor, left it behind on purpose, and that several Southerners had already died in agony. The trick worked, and soon bottles of whiskey, beer, and champagne were sailing through the air and exploding like small shells while the imaginations of those who'd already imbibed inflicted the type of stomach pains that *might* have been a symptom of arsenic.[47]

The lemons, ice, and sugar were transformed into buckets of lemonade, and the Confederates, who were subsisting on salt meat and crackers, shared and sampled pickled oysters, canned beef and ham, French rolls, cakes, confectionaries, coffee, and Havana cigars in addition to the roasted eggs, with their iced lemonade.[48] The consumables were not the only prizes. One soldier found a box containing two dozen pairs of white kid gloves, worn by officers on special occasions. He started to toss them into the fire but a comrade grabbed his arm and exclaimed "Don't burn them things up! Don't you know Richmond is full of weddings these days, and all the officers want gloves to wear? Save 'em and you can ask your own price in town." The soldier did and the gloves served at numerous "gallant affairs."[49]

Of greater value was a train of pontoons used for the construction of temporary bridges, which were hauled away for later use. There was also railroad stock—locomotives and new cars, but salvaging them posed a challenge. There were no tracks available to transport them into Confederate territory, and there was a distinct possibility the Federals would send gunboats or troops to retrieve them. Jeb decided to damage the locomotives enough to put them out of commission, but not so badly they could not be repaired. Blackford was given the task of making the locomotives inoperable, and he did so with a rifled cannon. Setting it up fifty yards from the engines, he put a shot through the boiler of each, rendering it useless but repairable.[50]

Von Borcke caught up about noon. He found Jeb in high spirits, drinking lemonade beneath a banana tree, and after sharing some he continued his tour, wandering about the half-burned depot, marveling at the delicacies, observing small mountains of hams and bacon and enough equipment and rifles to arm 10,000 soldiers. He also examined the corpse of a freshly embalmed officer rumored to be a "French prince of the Orleans family" who had served on McClellan's staff.[51] He also found a new horse to replace the one he'd lost but, characteristically, he lost the prize soon thereafter.

The next day, June 30, Stuart spent a few hours sorting through, securing, and distributing supplies, then left the depot under guard of Cobb's Legion and moved his cavalry to a bridge over the Chickahominy, eight miles distant.[52] There they expected to take a slap at the flank of McClellan's retreating army, but were too late, so they backtracked to Forge Bridge and discovered Federal infantry, cavalry, and two pieces of artillery on the far side among thickly wooded hills. Pelham opened up with two howitzers, aiming some personally, and there followed a spirited duel in which each of Pelham's shots was said to hit either a man or a horse or to cause someone to flee. The Federals finally withdrew and Stuart's men went into camp for the night near the bridge.[53]

Early on July 1—about 3:30 a.m.—a courier brought orders from Lee for Stuart to rejoin Jackson, and Jeb rode forty-two miles trying to do so, to no avail.[54] He arrived on the left flank of the army late in the afternoon and went into camp that night near Malvern Hill, where the final and bloodiest battle of the Seven Days had just been fought. McClellan had dug in on high ground and Lee hurled his divisions against him in repeated, fruitless assaults. Despite holding his own and gaining something to brag about, McClellan continued retreating the next day.

The morning of July 2 brought rain that lasted three hours and continued off and on thereafter.[55] Stuart, Jackson, Longstreet, Lee, and Jefferson Davis, who had ridden out from the capital on the 30th, weathered the downpour and met at Lee's headquarters. They'd started to discuss the army's condition and its options for continuing the offensive when word came that the Federals had abandoned Malvern Hill and were withdrawing farther down the James River. Jeb returned to his command and went in pursuit, capturing stragglers and chasing the main body of the enemy army to within sight of the river and the gunboats *Monitor* and *Galena*. Lt. Col. Martin, commanding the Jeff Davis Legion and temporarily the 4th Virginia, captured a sailor from the *Monitor*, plus 150 other prisoners.[56]

As darkness was falling, Jeb sent Pelham with one gun and a squadron of the 1st Virginia down the road to find the enemy and, if he was attempting to escape downriver, shell him.[57] Stuart then went into camp and, about 10 p.m., sent a courier to General Lee to say he would continue the pursuit at daybreak and that McClellan was "doubtless awaiting for his transports" so he could go back north where it was safer.[58] It was a straightforward, accurate plan and message. Jeb had no way of knowing it would lead to the first serious error of his year of glory, even though what he did seems correct in hindsight.

Before dawn on the 3rd, a courier rode in from Pelham carrying a detailed message. Pelham had driven in enemy pickets at a farm belonging to Allen Bradley. Bradley told him that all of McClellan's wagons and cattle were located on a "beautiful plain" at the Westover and Berkeley mansions

commanded by a high hill called Evelynton Heights, located two miles from
Stuart's position. Pelham said that guns placed on the heights could command everything as far as the river. He had found McClellan's army,
"tightly bunched along a three-mile front," with the river at their back and
unguarded high ground looking down on them.[59] The Confederates had
McClellan bottled up and at their mercy.

Stuart sent a message to Jackson, who forwarded the news to Lee, and
set off for Evelynton Heights. When Jeb arrived, he found Pelham's men
questioning Federal prisoners, who confirmed that the entire Federal army
lay below the heights, miserable in the rain, the mud, and their disgrace.

Jeb set up a line of skirmishers and watched as the oblivious Federal
soldiers prepared breakfast. He waited, hoping Jackson or Longstreet would
arrive, but an hour passed and no Confederate infantry appeared. Jeb
feared the enemy would discover his position and send a force to seize the
heights, which any commander worth his salt would have occupied hours
previously. When there was still no sign of support by 9 a.m., Jeb ordered
Pelham to open fire.

He did so with a single twelve-pounder howitzer, causing great conster-
nation among the Federals, but also alerting them to their situation and the
importance of holding the heights. Gunboats returned fire, lobbing eleven-
inch naval shells "as big as flour barrels,"[60] and forcing Pelham to fall back.
He did so, changed location again when the Federals got his range, and
fired and moved, fired and moved, knowing Longstreet or Jackson would
arrive any minute to deliver a severe, possibly final, blow to McClellan's
army. No Confederate infantry appeared.

Federal skirmishers came up the slope and Stuart moved sharpshooters
forward to stop them. Stuart unloosed a battery of Congreve rockets, which
were marvelously frightening but woefully inaccurate, setting tents ablaze
and scalding some mules.[61]

For five hours the two sides blazed away at each other but the Confederate infantry did not appear. Longstreet had taken the wrong road and
was still six miles away. The rockets were exhausted, the dismounted cavalrymen were running out of ammunition, and Pelham was down to only
solid shot. A battery of Union artillery, supported by infantry, was uncomfortably close. Pelham fired his last round, and a little after 2 p.m. Stuart
ordered a retreat. McClellan seized the heights. Longstreet did not arrive
until after dark.[62]

A marvelous opportunity was lost. Stuart got the blame.

"Stuart, glorious Stuart," wrote Lee's Assistant Adjutant General, Walter Taylor. "Always at the front and full of fight. . . . The temptation was too strong to be resisted; he commanded some of his guns to open fire. . . . It frightened the enemy but it enlightened him. . . . The enemy, not slow in comprehending his danger, soon advanced his infantry in force, to dislodge our cavalry and to possess the heights. . . . Had the infantry been up, General Lee would have . . . dictated to McClellan terms of surrender. . . ."[63] Another of Lee's staff, Charles Venable, described Stuart's action as "a grave error."[64] Still, it was the failure of the Confederate infantry to launch concerted attacks while McClellan's force was strung out in retreat toward the James that comprised the greatest error. General Lee, in his report of the campaign, wrote that "the Federal army should have been destroyed," and Edward Porter Alexander recorded that the commanding general was "deeply, bitterly disappointed."[65]

Still, the war was yet young. The notion, so prevalent a year earlier, that once the two sides had one good battle the war would be over, the winner of the battle the winner of the war, was still alive in some hearts, apparently even Robert E. Lee's.

The Seven Days Battles, particularly Gaines' Mill and Malvern Hill, were brutal and far exceeded the carnage that shocked both nations at First Manassas. Von Borcke's and Pelham's reviews of the dead were matched by Blackford, who toured the field at Malvern Hill in front of Jackson's position. He reported that artillery fire had cut many men in two, while others were headless and that "fragments of bodies and limbs were strewn about in every direction." He announced that it was "a fact well-known among medical students . . . that under certain circumstances the condition of the [human] system is such that when death comes suddenly from a wound the muscles become, instantly, perfectly rigid and so remain." To this and the fatigue and excitement of Jackson's men, he attributed the extreme looks and postures of some of the dead. He saw one on his back with his legs raised in the air, one hand clutching a handful of grass on the ground, the other holding a bunch of turf aloft, over his head, at which the man stared with eyes wide open. Another was sitting against a tree, arms resting on his knees, his chin on his breast in a natural attitude, but a cannonball had passed through the tree and taken off the top of his head to the roots of his hair. Several held their rifles with one or both hands, and one soldier died in the act of loading, one hand grasping the musket, the other the ramrod, the body fallen to the ground.[66]

So ended the Seven Days Battles. Jeb did not know he would be criticized for it not being a greater victory than it was. Instead he wrote to Flora on July 5 that he had been "marching and fighting for one solid week. Generally on my own hook, with the cavalry detached from the main body. I ran a gunboat from the White House and took possession. What do you think of that?" and "on the 3d I had the satisfaction of slipping around to the enemy's rear and shelling his camp at Westover. If the army were up with me we could have finished this business."[67]

Jeb was into the swing of things in his year of glory. He had eleven months to go.

CHAPTER FOUR

VERDIERSVILLE TO SECOND
MANASSAS, JULY 4–AUGUST 31, 1862

Then Lincoln said to Pope, "You can make the trip, I hope. I
will save the Universal Yankee nation. To make sure of no defeat,
I'll leave no lines of retreat, and issue a famous proclamation."
But that same dreaded Jackson, this fellow laid his whacks on and
made him, by compulsion, a seceder. So Pope took rapid flight from
Manassas' second fight; 'twas his very last appearance as a leader
—Richmond is a Hard Road to Travel *as sung by Sam Sweeny*

About the 4th of July, Stuart established his headquarters near those of
Generals Lee and Longstreet "in the extensive farmyard of a Mr. Phillips,"
on the James River. Here the cavalry rested and recuperated for a couple
of days, making certain McClellan was withdrawing.

July 5 was quiet. Stuart and his men spent the day in camp and that
evening Jackson's command arrived nearby.[1] On July 6 Stuart took the 1st
and 4th Virginia regiments and six guns, under Pelham, to demonstrate
against Federal gunboats and, if possible, to ambush transports carrying
Union soldiers. Six transports loaded with troops came along and were
peppered by the Horse Artillery. Von Borcke claimed that the smallest of
the six ships sank, but nobody else took note of this fact. As soon as they
saw Federal gunboats, with their "ponderous 100-pounder guns," the Confederates withdrew.[2]

Von provided Jeb with a new joke to start ringing the changes on that
day. Intending to ride out with Stuart to ambush the transports, he was

delayed by what he said was a duty at headquarters. Considering he'd just returned from riding to and from Richmond and the Confederate column left well before dawn, it's likely he simply did not get out of bed in time. He was now alone, it was dark, and he knew enemy patrols were in the area, so when he heard hooves on a small bridle path on the right side of the road, he halted, drew a revolver, and waited. Sure enough, a mounted soldier wearing a Federal uniform appeared.

"Halt, what is your regiment?" Von Borcke demanded. "Eighth Illinois," came the reply. Von rushed up with leveled revolver and took the man prisoner. He escorted him back up the road to the 9th Virginia's camp by Stuart's headquarters. The prisoner seemed relaxed, and "entertained" Von with stories about the Yankee army, how long he had served, and so forth. Von noted that the man was riding "an admirable horse," and having lost the one he captured at the White House, he regarded the animal "with infinite satisfaction as already my property."

When they reached the Confederate camp, however, the prisoner suddenly changed his story and claimed he was a Confederate private who had traded his tattered uniform for that of a Federal and, hearing Von Borcke's Prussian accent, mistook him for a Yankee. Von would have nothing to do with such a preposterous story.

"I lost all patience with him, and again leveling my pistol at him, I gave him to understand that I would make short work of him at any future repetition of his jests." He then carried the man straight to the commanding officer, Colonel Rooney Lee, whereupon to Von's chagrin, Lee immediately recognized the man as one of his regiment sent out on a scouting mission.

Stuart loved the story, of course, and for the next few days or weeks seldom saw Von Borcke without asking, "How many prisoners of the 9th Virginia have you taken lately?"[3] Von Borcke, probably the one who told the story on himself to Stuart, accepted the teasing good-naturedly, his greatest regret being that he had not obtained his prisoner's admirable horse.

Cooke did not accompany Stuart on the expedition of the 6th. He was in Richmond obtaining a new horse and tending to other affairs, and rode most of the night of July 5–6 to get back to Stuart's headquarters, anticipating a big battle that did not occur. When he arrived in camp he startled everyone, as though he was resurrected from the dead. Indeed, a report had reached camp that he and another officer were riding toward Long Bridge when they were fired upon by 200 of the enemy and Cooke was killed. The report was that the men there removed Cooke's boots and buried him. Von Borcke cried. Both he and Farley vowed to retrieve his remains. Cooke was flattered, and closed his diary entry for the day with, "Not this time mes amis! Here I am writing on the grass under the locusts, the Gen. sleeping yonder."[4]

Another of the staff, William Blackford, enjoyed a different type of frolic about the same time. He had two horses at headquarters, his favorite being a mare named Comet, but he concluded that the demands of serving on Stuart's staff were so great that two horses were not enough. Accordingly he sent for another horse, a cousin of Comet's named Magic. Both horses were purchased from a Mr. B.K. Buchanan, and Magic was a blooded mare standing sixteen hands high, dark Chestnut and four years old, but she had suffered an ignominious experience—Yankees had bred her to a jackass. As a result, she had a mule colt that Blackford referred to as a "disreputable baby" that had to be weaned before she could be of service in the field.

This was finally accomplished and she arrived at Stuart's camp on July 2. Blackford found her to be high strung and suffering from the equine equivalent of Attention Deficit Disorder. Anything distracted her, and in an army camp there was plenty to do that. When eating, should troops march by or cheer, she would prick up her ears, cock and toss her head, and forget to swallow whatever she had in her mouth. If artillery fired anywhere near, she would prance, paw, and kick for hours unless Blackford petted and soothed her.

After letting her become accustomed to the camp for a few days, Blackford had her bridled and saddled for a first ride. Stuart and the entire staff turned out to see the show. Gilbert, Blackford's servant, brought her out, "looking sleek and fine but with the devil in her eye." Blackford had to coax and sweet talk her before she would let him approach, and then let him put one hand on her mane and one foot in the stirrup, which was "all I needed her consent for."

He swung into the saddle and Magic exploded, first rearing and then bolting for open space. For half a mile she ran at full tilt, then allowed Blackford to rein her in to a moderate gait. However, the countryside was littered with carcasses of horses and men, and every time one came in sight, Magic would screech to a halt and begin snorting and wheeling, while Blackford "tried to reason the matter with her." He would talk sweetly and let her put her nose to the ground and snuff, then ease her a little closer to the offensive object. The first one or two took more than an hour to approach, but she gradually became less and less terrified, until finally she began accepting the unnatural things as natural.

The image of that Confederate officer and his wild-eyed horse, tearing across the countryside and then scoping out the detritus of war is unique, and not one to be seen again. Magic proved thereafter to be, in Blackford's words, "as fleet as the wind and as active and quick as a cat, and no fence or ditch could stop her with my weight on her back." However, he also wrote that her nervous, flighty ways continued, and that on long marches her prancing and fretting would go on for hours "until it required a strong exercise of patience to keep me from blowing her brains out."[5]

Some famous generals had famous horses—Lee's Traveler, Jackson's Little Sorrell, Meade's Baldy, Sheridan's Winchester—but Stuart is not remembered for a single mount. The reason is simple—he rode them so hard that no single one could stand up to the challenge.

Jeb had a number of horses, including Skylark, Star of the East, Lilly of the Valley, Maryland My Maryland, Shiloh, Lady Margrave, Highflyer, Chancellor, The Light Fantastic, Virginia, and, the one he rode at Yellow Tavern, General. He preferred large animals, hunter-types, preferably blood bays with black points. General was a gray. His brother, William Alexander, was given the task of watching out for and acquiring such animals when possible, but sometimes Jeb found his own, one of which he spent $350 of his brother's money to acquire in early August 1862.[6] Admirers gave him horses, or fellow officers captured them and turned them over to him, as Mosby did with a sorrel. Maryland was such a gift, and was, along with Lily of the Valley, one of his horses gentle enough for Flora to ride.

They suffered different fates—Chancellor was killed, appropriately, at Chancellorsville; Maryland sickened with "the glanders," a bacteria-borne disease often fatal to mules and horses; Virginia died of distemper; The Light Fantastic was left, "broken down," in Maryland; Margrave and Skylark were both captured when Stuart's servant, Bob, went to sleep on the march and fell into the enemy's hands, although both horses were apparently left with a friendly Marylander and recovered. Some that Jeb lost were noted without being named—a captured horse he had killed for unstated reasons at Funkstown in mid-1863; one that died of "the farcy" (another name for glanders) in February 1864, another he bought from Von Borcke that died in the first week of March 1864, in Augusta, and another that lost all its hooves from disease about the same time. Shiloh had the shortest duration of ownership. On May 1, 1862, Jeb wrote his brother thanking him for the horse and predicting that "his feats on the field will make you proud of him," but on May 4, 1862 he wrote to say, "I have in accordance with your wishes disposed of Shiloh & will either send you a draft or get a horse here as a present from you." The reasons for getting rid of the animal were not stated. Lily of the Valley had the happiest-ever-after in that dangerous time. She was a gift to Stuart from his relatives, the Hairstons, who paid $800 for her, but she proved too light for the General's needs and he sold her to Theodore Garnett of his staff. Garnett then traded her to William Blackford, who wanted her for his wife, but after the war he traded her to Alexander Stuart, the General's brother, for two carloads of salt valued at $500 Federal, thus bringing her back to the Stuart family for the rest of her days.[7]

Von Borcke was remembered by Blackford as being careless with his horses, guilty of "negligence in attention to them and his unmerciful treatment . . . that rendered them unfit for use." He theorized that he was accustomed, in Prussia, to having grooms who attended the horses, whereas Von's idea of attending them was to "dash about at full speed, regardless of his horse."[8] Von Borcke's memoirs bear this out, as he frequently lost horses or had none to use, although he never attributed any fault to himself. On July 8, 1862, Von received a new horse from the quartermaster in Richmond to replace the chestnut disabled by artillery "windage," a coal-black animal Von credited with saving his life several times in later campaigns by "its speed and magnificent jumping."[9]

It is interesting that the Confederate government chose to supply him with a horse, as that was not the custom for cavalrymen. Rebels, officers and men alike, were expected to supply their own mounts, but the government then took charge of the animal, crediting the trooper with a fair valuation and paid each soldier for the animal's use at a rate of forty cents per day. If the horse was killed in action, the Confederate government reimbursed the trooper, but did not provide a new horse. If the animal was captured, fell sick, or became worn out and broken down, that was the owner's loss.[10] This bureaucratic system led to a great number of Rebels becoming dismounted. As Blackford recalled, the most courageous men were the ones most likely to have their horse shot out from under them, and when that occurred the soldier was expected to either find another mount or to become a member of "Company Q."

There is no "Q," (or "J,") in the normal designation of companies in a regiment, and those in Stuart's command who lost their horses, often some of the best soldiers in any regiment, were assigned to that group, together with "the invariable fringe of riffraff, malingerers, and inefficient" who considered it safest to be dismounted.[11] Whereas men from Mississippi, Georgia, and other distant Confederate states had to secure a furlough and make a long journey home and back in order to stay in the cavalry, Von Borcke, probably because of the South's longing for European recognition, issued the large Prussian at least one horse.

On July 9 the enemy made a sudden, noisy demonstration, driving in Confederate pickets but then retired when they confronted organized resistance. On the 10th word came that McClellan was definitely loading his transports at Harrison's Landing and heading north. The same day Stuart received orders to move to Hanover Court House where, it was hoped, more horses and better provisions could be secured. Despite hauling in tons of foodstuffs at the White House, the soldiers were nearly out of supplies and forage. Captain Hardeman Stuart—a double third cousin to Jeb—and Von Borcke spent a day digging up a garden to retrieve only a few onions and a "diseased potato."[12] The entire area east of Richmond to the James River was devastated. Besides having been stripped of everything eatable and ridable, portions of the countryside caught fire during the battles, and a scattered herd of dead horses and mules still festered in the sun.

So it was with no regret that Jeb left the Peninsula and led his troops north. Leaving the column behind, he took Von Borcke for a detour into Richmond, stopping, Von claimed, at the same Irishman's house where the pair had awaited the spy who didn't come in from the rain a month earlier. After enjoying milk and blackberries provided by the lady of the house, they proceeded to the capital, where Stuart met with President Davis and Von bought a new uniform. After spending July 11th in Richmond, Stuart and Von Borcke proceeded to the new cavalry camp in Hanover County near Atlee's Station at a farm belonging to a Mr. Timberlake.[13] The Timberlake house was located in a forest of oak and hickory trees with fields stretching about, and Timberlake, having two sons serving under Stuart, went out of his way to make Jeb and his staff comfortable.[14]

On the 14th, Mrs. Stuart and the two children—James, or Jimmie, aged three, and little Flora, aged five—arrived, and for a few days Jeb was united with both of his clans—military and actual—which Von described as a single family. On the 15th, Stuart received the resignation of Major

Dabney Ball as staff commissary. Ball was the former chaplain of the 1st Virginia, and was sometimes referred to as the "fighting parson." When Stuart received his brigadier's star in September 1861, he tapped Ball to become his captain of commissary, and then had him promoted to major, effective October 4. The two men were friends, but the strain of the Peninsula campaign placed too great a strain either on Ball's skills, Stuart's patience, or both. The contents of Ball's resignation letter are essentially the only explanation for what occurred, but it is well known that getting sufficient supplies and rations from the Confederate government, then getting them in adequate quantities to the soldiers, was a Herculean task. Apparently on July 14 Ball failed to get rations to four cavalry regiments when they were expected. Stuart sent him an angry note by courier, and the next day Ball replied in a passive-aggressive manner, "I have the honour to report, in response to [Stuart's] inquiry . . . that Col. Rosser's Reg't received their rations yesterday, by his Commissary . . .[and] 'arrangements' have been made to supply the three regiments east of Richmond that your orders specified. . . . I send herewith my resignation as commissary in the C.S. Army. . . . Hoping you may speedily fill the place with someone whose manner of doing business will be less annoying to you, and who will not be so 'disconcerted and diverted' from the high and responsible duty of feeding the men, I am with Great Respect, Your obt.svt., Dabney Ball." Ball went back to being a chaplain but he and Stuart remained friends and Jeb tried unsuccessfully on more than one occasion to secure him promotions or better paying positions."[15]

On July 17 Jeb held a review of the cavalry, which was admired by "all the ladies in the country round," whom Blackford, Von and the rest of the staff were given the "agreeable duty" of entertaining.[16] After the review, Stuart galloped from carriage to carriage to invite everyone to his headquarters, about a mile away, to socialize. Von Borcke and Captain Norman Fitzhugh were sent ahead to make arrangements, and Von reported that with Mr. Timberlake's permission and assisted by "a little army of negro servants," they "plundered his house of its chairs and sofas, which were disposed in a semicircle outside beneath an immense tent-fly that was among the spoils taken from the enemy at the White House." For refreshments they had fresh milk and ginger cakes, plus mint juleps for any gentleman that cared for one. After animated talk about the war, the review, the Peninsula campaign, and what might lie ahead, the guests left, taking with them, Von opined, "the impression that camplife was not so bad after all."[17]

Stuart traveled to Richmond on July 18 and returned to find an English visitor—Lord Edward St. Maur, the son of the Duke of Somerset.[18] Blackford described him as a "gawky youth" of about twenty. The headquarters larder was nearly bare. Staff members had been fishing for perch and catfish and hunting for rabbits or squirrels, and Von Borcke was able to furnish two of the latter to prepare for St. Maur. Von's servant, William, produced a meat pie that Von said the Lord relished. He stayed only a day but would not be the last foreign dignitary to visit Stuart's headquarters.[19]

On Sunday the 20th, church services were held in camp in an open meadow in the middle of a forest. The Reverend Landstreet, chaplain of the 1st Virginia Cavalry, officiated, and hundreds of gray-clad, bearded troopers attended, sitting and lying on the grass, listening respectfully beneath the canopy of limbs.[20] Later that day Jeb wrote a letter of introduction for John Mosby to Stonewall Jackson. Mosby was still agitating for work as an irregular, and had approached Jeb with a request for twelve men and permission to go raiding in the rear of a new Yankee army that was getting organized in Washington D.C. under the command of John Pope. Stuart declined Mosby's request, saying he could not spare any men in light of the upcoming campaign. Instead, he assigned to Mosby a courier named Mortimer Weaver, who happened to have a club foot, and wrote the letter to Jackson, saying, "The bearer, John S. Mosby, . . . is en route to scout beyond the enemy's lines toward Manassas and Fairfax. He is bold, daring, and discreet. The information he may obtain and transmit to you may be relied upon . . ." He also inquired as to whether Jackson had received the volume of Napoleon's *Maxims* that Jeb had recently sent him by way of an orderly for General Winder.[21]

The next day, July 21, Stuart moved his headquarters to Hanover Court House, arriving shortly before dark. He made his headquarters in a grove of about five acres near the courthouse and his brigade pitched their tents nearby. Several thousand men, horses, tents, and artillery pieces were arranged in orderly rows with flags flying. July 22 was taken up with getting moved in and settled.

July 23 was Von Borcke's birthday, and he was presented with a bouquet of flowers by the rest of Stuart's staff. Any expectations they had of another day of relaxation was shattered about 10 a.m. when word was relayed that the enemy was advancing in strength from Fredericksburg, fifteen miles away. A picket several miles from camp was attacked, several men and horses were taken, and by noon Stuart, three regiments, and two pieces of artillery were en route to the scene. When they arrived around dusk, however, it was clear that the Federals were long gone and that there would be no chance of catching them, so Stuart went into camp on a farm belonging to a Mr. Anderson.

The next morning, the 24th, being already well down the road toward the enemy, Jeb decided to press on toward Fredericksburg to see what mischief he might do to the Federals camped there, and by evening he and his troopers were within ten miles of the town. Around 11 p.m. the sky opened up and drenched everyone, which not only dampened plans for an attack, but made Jeb realize he was at risk of being cut off by rising rivers between his men and Hanover. In particular the Matoponi River, which had tributaries named the Ma, the To, the Po, and the Ni, all of which Stuart had forded earlier in the day, were rising steadily, and the Rebels decided to splash back the way they had come. They arrived back at Mr. Anderson's a little after noon, exhausted, and Stuart ordered the column to go into camp while he, Blackford, and Von Borcke climbed onto a railroad handcar hand pumped by two black servants back to Hanover, where they arrived about sunset on the 25th.[22]

Three new members of the cast of players, two mentioned already and all of whom will soon have a larger role to play, should be introduced. They are Captain Norman Fitzhugh, Captain Hardeman Stuart, and soon-to-be Lieutenant Channing Price.

Fitzhugh's background was not as cloudy and mysterious as Redmond Burke's, but it had its share of question marks. His father died when he was four and his mother when he was nine, so that he and his three siblings were raised by either foster parents or in a boarding school. He showed up in Utah in 1859, where he married, prior to which he may have actually been captured by Sioux Indians, possibly even adopted by a chief. In any event, he would occasionally entertain the other members of Stuart's staff with tales of his life among the Indians.[23] He did not enlist until April 1, 1862, in Co. E of Rooney Lee's 9th Virginia, was immediately made a corporal, and two months later, on or about June 21, was summoned to join Stuart's staff as Assistant Adjutant General. He was one of the hardest working members of the staff, and on July 27, 1862, Jeb stood as godfather to his son.[24]

James Hardeman Stuart was from Mississippi, where he studied law and graduated from the University of Mississippi in 1859. When the war broke out he joined a company of infantry, the "Burt Rifles," that became

Company K of the 18th Mississippi Infantry, but when he arrived in Virginia he was assigned to the newly hatched, or struggling to hatch, Confederate Signal Corps. His distant relation to Jeb was probably why Stuart decided to latch onto him. The two families had corresponded before the war, or it may have been Edward Porter Alexander, who was then serving as Beauregard's signal officer, who brought him to Stuart's attention. In any event, as early as December 23, 1861, Hardeman wrote his father that Jeb was going to try to get Alexander to recommend him for a commission. No commission came until June 11, 1862, when he was appointed a captain in the Signal Corps, but within less than two weeks Jeb had him serving as signal officer for the cavalry.[25]

His service with Stuart was brief, from June 26 to August 30, and John Esten Cooke did not meet him until the Peninsula Campaign, but Cooke was so taken with the 21-year-old's charm, spirit, and bravery that after the war he devoted an entire chapter to him in his *Wearing of the Gray,* thus putting him the same category as Jackson, Beauregard, Stuart, Hampton, Mosby, and a small handful of similar luminaries.

Channing Price was the 19-year-old son of a successful merchant with poor eyesight, and therein lay the making of the young man's destiny. Once Channing was old enough to write, his father was no longer able to do so, and he began dictating his letters and other paperwork to the boy. Channing learned to take dictation rapidly and accurately. He also seemed to have a gift for auditory memory, because he could write the letters and other documents accurately and completely the first time, without notes and without revision.[26] Such a gift was invaluable to a Civil War general like Stuart.

Exactly how Jeb discovered the young man's talent is unknown; perhaps it was another example of the General's uncanny ability to sense talent in others. Channing was an enlisted man serving in the 3rd Company of the Richmond Howitzers when Stuart plucked him from the ranks to become first an aide-de-camp and then assistant adjutant general in August, 1862. As Blackford recalled, "Repeatedly I have seen while on a march General Stuart dictate two or three letters to him, giving orders to the commanders of the different columns. Each one of them would state by what places the columns were to move, at what hours they were to leave these places and where they were to concentrate. Price would listen, and without asking him to repeat a single thing, or taking a single note, he would ride out to one side of the road, dismount, take his little portfolio out of his haversack and write the letters ready for the General's signature, and it was rare that any alteration was made when Stuart read them and affixed his signature."[27]

Upon his return to the Hanover camp on July 25, Stuart was presented with a most pleasant surprise—promotion to Major General. General Lee wrote, "It is well-deserved though it has been somewhat tardy." Jackson added, "Permit me to congratulate you upon your well-earned promotion." Lee also let it be known that he wanted Jeb to take command of all the cavalry in the Army of Northern Virginia.[28]

July 26th, 27th, and 28th, being a Saturday through Monday, were spent in relative relaxation in camp and visiting surrounding homes, particular "Dundee," a plantation owned by Dr. Lucien Price, a cousin of Stuart's. It is located a few miles from Hanover Court House and the household included two unmarried daughters, Elizabeth, or "Lizzie," and Ann, or "Nannie." They attracted the attention of many of Jeb's staff officers, and as the romancing sorted itself out, John Pelham became a close friend, if not more, to Elizabeth, while Von Borcke became quite enamored, to the point of buying an engagement ring, of Nannie. Jeb was also fond of Nannie, and wrote many letters to her, some that began "My dear Sweety."

Von's romantic overtures ended in self-imposed misfortune, however. Observing her in conversation on the porch of Dundee with another officer one day, the jealous giant jumped through a window and inserted his considerable bulk between Nannie and his rival. Heated words were exchanged and Nannie ended their relationship. In 1864, when returning by ship to Europe, Von tossed the engagement ring into the sea.[29]

A happier ending attended the romantic experiencee of Col. Tom Rosser. Riding into Stuart's camp at Hanover one day, the handsome officer called to a young boy named Will Winston, eight or nine years old, saying in jest, "Little fellow, if you'll bring me a drink of water, I'll come back and marry your sister." Will dashed off and returned with the water. Several weeks later Rosser was again in the area and although he did not recognize the boy, Will recognized him. Suddenly the Colonel found himself being presented to an attractive 19-year-old young lady. "Sis Betty, here's the man come to marry you," Will announced, and so it came to be. Love developed between Tom and Betty and they were married on May 28, 1863. John Pelham was slated to be the best man, but the young artillerist was two months in his grave by then.[30]

A typical day in camp was occupied by paperwork, riding to surrounding outposts, and tending to other military business. On the 28th, Jeb wrote letters to Channing Price and his battery commander, Capt. Robert C. Stanard, summoning Price to his camp and a lieutenant's commission.[31] When not so engaged the General and his staff were likely to be entertaining visitors or reading in their tents. During the evening after supper, when they were not at Dundee or elsewhere, everyone would assemble around a fire near the large tent fly captured at the White House to listen to Sweeny's banjo, singing, story-telling, conversation, and theatrics.

Von Borcke rivaled Jeb for center stage, as did Lt. Colonel Luke Tierman Brien of the 1st Virginia. Brien, a Marylander, served first as a volunteer aide to Stuart, with no rank, from July to September 1861, then as Jeb's Assistant Adjutant General with a captain's rank, until April 23, 1862, and then received a Lt. Colonel's commission and served as second in command under Fitz Lee after being elected to that position by the men of the 1st Virginia on April 23, 1862. He and Von Borcke became co-authors and producers of various comedy skits during the year of glory, and almost certainly competed with each other and Stuart for laughs and absurdity around the campfire.

Jeb loved to tease, and a person who was the target of his jibes was such only because he had the General's trust. Sometimes he went too far, and when that happened he immediately set about making amends. As Cooke recalled, "Like a child, he must make up with people he had unintentionally offended; and he never rested until he succeeded."

One such prank was observed by an infantryman in Hood's brigade named Val Giles. He was on guard duty where army supplies were warehoused near the Hanover junction when Stuart, John Pelham, and half a dozen other officers rode up. They dismounted and he heard Stuart tell Pelham, "My boy, when I grab him, you swing on too, for he is strong as a young bull." The infantryman watched as the handful of officers approached Fitz Lee, who was waiting to take the train to Richmond. They talked, the train came, mail bags were unloaded, the officers bade Fitz farewell and wished him a good time in Richmond; and as the train began to move, Colonel Lee waved and started to board. Immediately Stuart and Pelham grabbed him and the others closed in. Lee struggled to get away but they held him tight until the train was too far gone to catch. Fitz was not amused, but Stuart and his companions were. "See here young man," Jeb announced, "I'm going to break up this jularky business. You have been gallivanting around about long enough. Possum and taters for dinner at headquarters today. Bring the prisoner along, boys."

They had brought a horse to carry away the kidnapped colonel, and as they mounted Stuart broke into the song *Evelina*.[32] The word "jularky" seems to have been one of Jeb's own design, but its meaning is plain enough.

All of the hi-jinx were performed without the aid of stimulants, at least on Jeb's part. At the age of twelve his mother extracted a promise from him to never drink, and he proved to be a man of his word. It is safe to assume that other members of the campfire crowd made no similar promises, and that flasks or bottles were passed around; but Jeb needed only love of life to inebriate him, and the existence and spirit of those with whom he came in contact.

On Sunday the 26th, Jeb and his staff, including Von Borcke and the newly-minted Signal Officer, Hardeman Stuart, were relaxing at Dundee, visiting Dr. Price's daughters, when they saw smoke and flames issuing from a barn and stables about 500 yards from the house. The servants had the day off, so Stuart and his officers rushed to the scene. Various animals were inside and the men stripped off their coats and spent the next half hour battling the fire into submission. When the danger was passed they returned, sooty and charred, to the veranda, where Jeb entertained everyone with an extravagant description of how he had seen Von Borcke running out of the burning building with a mule under one arm and two pigs under the other.[33]

On the 29th another brigade review was held on a level plain near headquarters and Von Borcke reported that "the whole drill was executed with as much precision as would have been exhibited by regular troops," as opposed to what he considered the Southern volunteers to be. Blackford reported that ladies for many miles around attended, on horseback and in carriages, and that "We of the staff were resplendent."[34] The evening was topped off by a storm that Von Borcke called a hurricane, in which "Thousands of trees were torn up by their roots and hurled in the air. Houses were everywhere unroofed. It may well be supposed that every tent of our encampment was prostrated, and that general confusion and disorder marked the spot."[35]

Von had no advantage to gain by exaggerating the severity of a storm, but it is interesting to note that a book devoted to weather in Virginia during the war records only that July 29, 1862 was "a fine day," near Petersburg, but that there was "a shower at 4:30 p.m. in Richmond."[36]

Channing Price was about to join Stuart's staff as an aide-de-camp, and on July 29 Stuart directed Von Borcke to send Price a letter listing what equipment and clothing he should outfit himself with and the probable cost of each. In what Von headed as "Equipment suitable for an Officer of Cavallerie," he recommended the following, with spelling as he wrote it:

> A good Horse wich can be bot in Richmond or among the Rgt, the cost will be 400-500 Doll.
> A good Jennifer saddle and bridle, wich can be bot at the ordonance for 62 Doll.
> Arms will be sabre & Pistol, wich will cost from 80 to 100 Doll.
> A Uniform trimed with yellow (Cav) or buff (Staff) either coat or jacket 80 Doll to 100 Doll.
> Good Cavalry Boots with Spurs 50 Doll.
> Grey or Black Hat 15 Doll
> Saddle Blanket and other Blanket 20 Doll
> Oilcloth Coat 25-30 Doll
> Several little things not mentioned (little Vallise, Comb, brushe etc. etc.)[37]

The magnitude of the cost of joining the staff can be appreciated when one considers that the pay received by a captain on Stuart's staff was $139 per month.[38]

The next day, July 30, Jeb presented Von Borcke with a commission as a major. Stuart was generous with those whose services he valued, and he sought promotions for them on a regular basis. It was rare, in fact, that he was satisfied with the rank the government agreed to bestow on his favorites—Pelham would have been at least a colonel, Blackford a major, and even Cooke a major if Jeb had his way—but their promotions came slowly or not at all while Von Borcke's seemed ripe for the plucking. His European background may have been at the root of the recognition.

With Jeb's promotion, reorganization of the cavalry was in order. Whereas a brigadier commands a brigade, a major general commands a division, and with the blessing of General Lee and Secretary Randolph, Stuart's command of fourteen regiments was formed into three brigades commanded by Wade Hampton, Fitz Lee, and Beverly Robertson. Including two batteries of artillery, Stuart now commanded a sizeable force. Von put the number at 15,000, but it was closer to a third of that number.[39]

The makeup of the three brigades were: Hampton's, consisting of the

1st North Carolina, 2nd South Carolina, 10th Virginia, Cobb's Georgia Legion, and the Jeff Davis Legion. Fitz Lee's, containing the 1st, 3rd, 4th, 5th and 9th Virginia regiments, and Robertson's, from the Valley, consisting of the 2nd, 6th, 7th, and 12th Virginia regiments, plus the 17th Virginia battalion.[40] United under a single commander, the brigades were not united geographically. Hampton was with the division commanded by D.H. Hill on the Peninsula, keeping tabs on McClellan. Robertson was with Jackson, marching on Gordonsville, leaving only Fitz Lee with Stuart at Hanover.

Wade Hampton was the richest man in South Carolina, owning approximately 12,000 acres and a thousand slaves. He was a notable sportsman, hunter, and horseman, famous for having killed eighty bears by hand, often with a knife after his dogs brought each one to ground, a feat David Crockett would have envied.[41] At the beginning of the war he was a senator in the state assembly, but upon secession he resigned and enlisted as a private in the South Carolina Militia. With the governor insisting he accept a colonel's commission, he raised and financed the equipping of Hampton's Legion, consisting of six companies of infantry, four companies of cavalry, and a battery of artillery. He commanded the Legion at First Manassas, where he was wounded, commanded an infantry brigade during the Peninsula Campaign, where he suffered another wound, and was appointed brigadier in May 1862. Lee, rather than Stuart, selected him to serve as Stuart's senior subordinate, and while he never became close to Jeb, the two maintained a professional relationship and Hampton rarely performed less than superbly.[42]

Beverly Robertson was another matter. He'd served under Jeb's father-in-law before the war, then accepted a captain's commission in the Confederate army and was dismissed from the Union army for disloyalty before he had time to resign. He was elected colonel of the 4th Virginia Cavalry and served under Turner Ashby in Jackson's Army of the Valley until Ashby's death, when he succeeded to command of Jackson's cavalry.[43] Now, consistent with Lee's decision to unite the cavalry of the Army of Northern Virginia into a single division under Stuart, he and the Valley cavalry became the third of Jeb's three brigades. Neither Jackson nor Stuart had confidence in Robertson, however, and he was not destined for either glory or good fortune. Nevertheless, Jeb could not get rid of him.

While Jeb and his buddies were enjoying themselves in and around Hanover Court House, a new Federal army, under Major General John Pope, was preparing for another campaign to crush the Confederate army and capture Richmond. Pope had transferred from the west, where he'd enjoyed an unbroken string of success at New Madrid, Island No. 10, and Corinth. Arriving to take command of the "Army of Virginia," which combined the corps of John C. Fremont, Nathaniel Banks, and Irwin McDowell, and was in the environs of Washington, he delivered a rousing address on July 14, 1862.

> I have assumed command of this army. I have spent two weeks in learning your whereabouts, your condition and your wants . . . and I am about to join you in the field. . . . Let us understand each other. I have come to you from the West, where we have always seen the backs of our enemies. . . . I desire you to dismiss from your minds certain phrases, which I am sorry to find so much in vogue amongst you. I hear constantly of "taking strong positions and holding them," of "lines of retreat" and of "bases of supplies." Let us discard such ideas. . . . Let us study the probable lines of retreat of our opponents. . . . Let us look before us and not behind. Success and glory are in the advance, disaster and shame lurk in the rear. Let us act on this understanding, and it is safe to predict that your banners shall be inscribed with many a glorious deed and that your names will be dear to your countrymen forever."

Stirring but pompous words. Pope did not head up this address with "Headquarters in the Saddle," but "Headquarters, Army of Virginia, Washington, D.C." Still, he prefaced some later dispatches from the field with the former phrase, and Southern wags did not have to hear about it more than once before someone proclaimed that Pope apparently tended to confuse his headquarters with his hindquarters.

Pope was given command on June 26 of the three Federal forces that had tried unsuccessfully to defeat Jackson in the Shenandoah Valley during May and June. Numbering about 47,000 men, the Army of Virginia was initially supposed to protect Washington, hold the Shenandoah Valley, and draw Lee's forces away from Richmond in order to assist McClellan. Now, with McClellan ferrying back north from Harrison's Landing, Pope headed south, striking toward Gordonsville on July 14. Lee, taking advantage of his central position between the two Federal armies, sent Jackson and A.P. Hill to meet him with 24,000 soldiers.[44]

Beginning as a scout on August 4, then a maneuver on the 5th, Stuart took four regiments and a battery of artillery and struck out from Hanover toward Port Royal and Fredericksburg. Their march on the 4th covered twenty miles and they went into camp near Bowling Green. The next day they continued to Port Royal, where they dashed in and captured a detachment of Federal cavalry. Scouts reported a Federal force commanded by Generals Edward Hatch and John Gibbon moving from Fredericksburg on the Telegraph Road and along Massaponax Creek toward Richmond with plans to cut the Virginia Central Railroad.[45] Jeb decided to attack early the next morning.

The Confederates bedded down for the night near Round Oak Church, about twelve miles from Fredericksburg. Von Borcke chose as a pillow a rotting log near the church that he believed was used as a step by ladies in mounting and dismounting. Exhausted, he fell to sleep quickly, but he was awakened by something crawling over his hand. When he shook it off, it commenced to buzz and Von saw in the moonlight that it was a large rattlesnake. He jumped up, seized his long Damascus saber, cut the creature in two, and then continued to whack noisily at the wriggling sections. Jeb and the other staff officers, hearing the ruckus, grabbed their weapons and dashed to Von Borcke's aid, thinking, Von reported, "that not fewer than a hundred Yankees had fallen on me." Once they ascertained the real facts, they broke out in laughter.

They were in the saddle before dawn on August 6 and when within sight of the Federal column on Telegraph Road, they waited until the main body was past and a gap appeared between the marching infantry and the supply wagons bringing up the rear. Pelham then rolled out two cannons, one on each side of the road, and as the bugle sounded for Fitz Lee's brigade to attack, he opened up on the rear of the enemy with canister.[46] Blackford, perhaps with Von Borcke's experience of the night before on his mind, likened the Yankees' reaction to giving "a snake a tap on his tail when he was gliding unconsciously through the grass, making him throw himself into a coil to offer battle, and there remain in a coil as long as danger threatens."[47]

The effect was quite satisfying, but Stuart was outnumbered by at least five to one, and knew better than to throw his mounted troops against infantry in a defensive position, so he contented himself with capturing eleven wagons filled with provisions and more than 100 Enfield rifles, plus eighty-five prisoners and fifteen cavalry horses. Two of Jeb's men were killed.[48]

It was during this small battle that both Blackford and Von Borcke reported seeing, or hearing, explosive minie balls being used for the first and last time during the war in their experience.[49] An artifact found rarely since the war, such bullets contained a powder charge that was ignited when fired and which would detonate after striking a target. William Farley was also known for having captured an English Whitney rifle and a supply of explosive bullets, with which he specialized in killing Federal officers and blowing up artillery caissons.[50]

The Confederates returned to Bowling Green, camped for the night, and on August 7 they started at 9 a.m. and rode back to Hanover Court House, arriving about 3 p.m. Jeb and Blackford were pleased to find that their respective wives were visiting at Dundee.[51] On the 7th a note arrived from General Lee that congratulated Jeb on his recent successes and directed him to make his way to Stonewall Jackson, who had requested his services in regard to Beverly Robertson.

Robertson had commanded Jackson's cavalry for less than two months and had already failed to live up to expectations. Jackson had asked him a week earlier, "Where is the enemy," and Robertson replied "I really do not know." Such a statement is tantamount to a lawyer admitting he or she does not know the location of the courthouse, and Old Jack immediately sent a telegraph to Lee requesting Stuart to inspect Robertson's brigade and provide Jackson with an analysis of Robertson's fitness for continued command.[52]

On the same day Stuart learned he was to join Jackson, Stonewall learned that a portion of Pope's command, about 12,000 infantry under Nathanial P. Banks, was in advance of the rest of Pope's army and potentially ripe for the picking. The result was the Battle of Cedar Mountain on August 9, notable as the only occasion Jackson was seen to pull his sword in battle. Or he at least tried to—from disuse it turned out that his sword had rusted fast to its scabbard, so that he had to unbuckle his belt and wave the entire thing. During the opening stage of the battle the Confederate left—including the Stonewall Brigade—was caught unawares by Federal infantry charging from a woods and briefly gave way. Stonewall himself rallied the troops while Jubal Early in the center held fast and Dick Ewell on the right hammered the Federal left. Finally A.P. Hill's division arrived after a grueling march through brutal heat and, now outnumbered, the entire Federal line gave way. Grumble Jones and the 7th Virginia Cavalry led the pursuit, as the Confederates scooped up about 600 prisoners.

Jackson was still on the battlefield when Stuart arrived on the 10th, and he assigned Jeb, along with Early, to oversee a truce requested by the Federals for the purpose of burying the dead. While the blue-clad soldiers labored in the August sun to place their fallen comrades into mass graves—"kicking them into the pits" according to one Confederate—Jeb met with comrades from West Point and the "old army." They had "a long chat," lunched together, swapped stories, bragged, and Jeb entered into a wager.

One of William Blackford's four brothers, Major Charles M. Blackford, was present, and he overheard Stuart joking with Federal Generals George Bayard and Samuel Crawford. Bayard was a West Point graduate, Class of 1856 (two years behind Jeb), as well as a veteran of Indian fighting before the Civil War, and Crawford was a surgeon who had served in the southwest during the 1850s. The topic was the battle that was fought two days earlier. It was a Confederate victory, but not one as decisive as others of recent vintage, and Jeb asserted that the Northern newspapers would proclaim it a Federal victory. Crawford disagreed, and the old friends bet a hat on the matter. A few days later a package arrived for Stuart from Crawford. It contained a copy of a recent issue of the *New York Herald* and a new hat for Jeb.[53]

August 11th was quiet. On the 12th Stuart inspected Robertson's brigade, then returned to Hanover and penned his report. It wasn't good news for General Robertson. The 7th Virginia, he reported, was "entirely reconciled" to its new commander, Grumble Jones, which may have been the highest praise Stuart ever had for the man. Robertson, "deserves much credit for discipline and instruction in his command," but "[a]warding him full credit for these I regard his transfer to another command as an important measure for the public good. Frankly and fairly he does not possess some of the indispensible requisites of a cavalry commander, particularly on outpost duty," and he "did not for some reason inspire his command with confidence but rather to the contrary." Stuart concluded that it was "important therefore that he should be replaced."[54]

On August 15 Jeb wrote his brother, Alexander, to say they were leaving for the field and that he was about to "bid good bye to Old Hanover with its warm hearts and dear firesides for some time,"[55] and on August 16, Stuart and Fitz Lee's brigade departed for Gordonsville.

Parting from Flora, Little Flora, and Jimmie was not easy. Little Flora climbed onto her daddy's horse, threw her arms around him and gave him "tearful kisses until forced away," an act that would haunt Jeb. It occurred to him they might never meet again, but he was thinking about his own vulnerability rather than hers.[56] Von Borcke probably did not exaggerate when he wrote that Mrs. Stuart made him promise "to watch over her husband in the hour of battle, and do all in [his] power to prevent him from rashly exposing himself to danger."[57]

The brigade moved by "the common road," but Stuart and his staff rode to Beaver Dam Station and boarded a train already so crowded with Longstreet's troops—many of whom were riding on the tops of the cars— that the cavalrymen rode in the tender car.[58] They arrived in Gordonsville on August 17, as the sun was coming up. They had each tried to sleep during the night, but doing so in a car full of firewood located immediately behind a locomotive engine was not particularly relaxing, and when the light grew strong enough to enable them to see each other, they discovered they were each covered with soot that had blown onto them for the past ten or twelve hours. They had, as Von Borcke described, "faces as black as Ethiopia." Once they stopped laughing they spent nearly an hour scrubbing themselves clean, had breakfast, and proceeded by special train to Orange Courthouse, arriving about 11 a.m.[59]

General Lee's new headquarters were also in Orange, nine miles from Gordonsville. When Stuart and his staff arrived they found that everyone's horses except Blackford's had made the journey. Jeb met with the commanding general, and, accompanied by Fitzhugh, Von Borcke, and Dabney, plus a courier, Lt. St. Pierre Gibson of the 4th Virginia, they rode to Clark Mountain, site of a Confederate signal tower, leaving the horseless Blackford behind.

Along the way they ran into John Mosby, almost by accident, and Jeb invited him along.[60] From Clark Mountain they took the Orange Plank Road toward Raccoon Ford, where Stuart had told Fitz Lee to meet him. About nightfall they arrived at the crossroads village of Verdiersville, consisting of one hotel and one residence, popularly known as "My Dearsville." It was directly opposite Raccoon Ford, but Fitz Lee had not appeared. Certain he would arrive soon, Jeb sent Fitzhugh ahead to locate the missing brigade while he and the other four officers arranged to spend the night in front of a two story brick farmhouse belonging to Catlett Rhodes, a few hundred yards from the crossroads.[61]

They bedded down, leaving their horses saddled and tied inside a garden fence behind the house. Jeb lay down on the porch of the house, placing a blanket beneath him and using his cape and his "talma"—a shorter cape that fell from shoulder to elbows—as cover. His hat, gloves, and dispatch case were nearby, and he left his saber, carbine, and revolver on his saddle.[62] The others spread their blankets nearby.

Sometime between 4 a.m. and dawn on the 18th they were roused by the sound of an approaching body of horsemen, and assumed it was the tardy Fitz Lee. The road curved beyond the farmhouse, so the approaching riders were not visible, but the general directed Mosby and Lt. Gibson to mount and ride to meet Fitz. He then strode toward the road, bareheaded, leaving his cloak, hat and dispatch case on the porch.

Hardly had Mosby and Gibson rounded the bend then shots rang out and they came thundering back, leaning low on their horses' necks and shouting "Yankee cavalry!" A squadron of the enemy was visible behind them, galloping in pursuit less than 200 yards away.

Von Borcke, Dabney, Gibson, and Stuart dashed to their horses—Jeb was riding Skylark that day—mounted, and spurred them into action. Skylark and Dabney's horse leapt the garden fence and they raced across a field for the shelter of nearby woods. Von Borcke's black horse began to pitch and rear, so that he wound up mounting without any reins. Mrs. Rhodes came out to witness the action, and she opened the garden gate to allow Von to dash out, practically into the arms of the Yankees. He spurred his horse hard, made a flying leap from a hostile circle of the enemy, narrowly escaped being shot by the leading officer, then dashed up the Orange Plank Road in the direction they had come the night before, still with no reins to guide his charger. The pell-mell flight of the huge man diverted the Federals' attention from Stuart but attracted a flurry of carbine and pistol balls, one of which passed through Von's uniform.[63]

After a mile or so the Federals gave up the chase and Von Borcke was able to reach his reins and get his horse under control. Mosby caught up with him and together they rode back toward the house, where they found Stuart, minus his haversack, cloak, and beloved hat, and Dabney minus all his weapons.

They learned later that Major Fitzhugh had been captured by the same column of Federals. Von Borcke wrote that the major witnessed the entire affair and was amazed at Von's miraculous escape, but Fitzhugh reported that he was at the rear of the column of Yankees, and did not have cause for alarm until he saw a Federal cavalryman wearing Jeb's plumed hat, at which point he demanded to know what became of the man to whom it belonged.

Blackford recorded that the lost hat was the one that General Crawford paid Stuart in regard to the lost wager, whereas Von Borcke said that it was a gift from a lady in Baltimore. Wherever he obtained it, it was lost forever, despite subsequent efforts by Stuart to recover it. The ultimate fate of the hat is as aggravating to admirers of Stuart as its original loss was for Jeb. It was found by Lt. Ford Rogers of the 1st Michigan, who kept it and moved to California after the war with it packed in a trunk. It was smashed flat during the trip, so Rogers took the hat to a San Francisco hat store to be re-blocked. However, the hat's fate did not remain uppermost on his mind, he failed to return to the store "for a long time," and when he remembered to do so, found it had been sold "with a lot of old second-hand hats."[64]

Jeb's chagrin was not lightened by what followed. To the amusement of his companions he tied a handkerchief around his head to ward off the sun, and the little group headed on down the road. Soon they happened upon Longstreet's infantry, which included a Georgia regiment with a well-stocked sutler, and Jeb obtained another hat. The speed of sound being far more rapid than the speed of tired horses, however, word of the loss of the former hat preceded the party of cavalrymen.

"Where's your hat?" was the most common infantryman's call, as well as "Hey Cavalry, why'd you change your hat?" and "Jeb, where'd you get that new hat?" and "I can't tell it's you without no feathers," and similar change-ringing witticisms. As Blackford recalled, "There was a great laugh through the army at Stuart's loss."[65]

The General took the mocking in stride. He had no choice in the matter, for one thing, but while not as experienced at being the catcher as the pitcher in regard to teasing, he knew the rules of the game. He wrote to Flora on August 19 to tell her of the affair, saying, "I intend to make the Yankees pay for that hat."[66] He would get the opportunity.

Fitz Lee's tardiness was due to his having taken a detour through Louisa Court House to collect provisions, thus adding twenty miles, or nearly a full day's ride, to his itinerary. Jeb was not very forgiving, and when he filed his report on the incident more than six months later, he still voiced criticism, saying that Lee had failed to comply with instructions and caused the cavalry to lose an opportunity to "overhaul a body of the enemy's cavalry on a predatory excursion far beyond their lines."[67]

The cavalry and the rest of the army rested on August 19 and moved out early on the morning of the 20th, about 4 a.m., splashing across the Rapidan at various fords and moving north. Fitz Lee was in the advance, followed by Longstreet, with Jackson on his left and Stuart screening their movement on the right.[68]

Lee had learned that Pope was retreating; he had seen it for himself from the signal station on Clark's Mountain. In fact, the capture of Jeb's dispatch case had a lot to do with it—he had been carrying Lee's plan of battle, which involved using Clark Mountain as a screen and falling on Pope's eastern flank, so that capture of the plan alerted Pope to his danger, although the same information had reached Pope via a spy named Thomas Harter.[69] The enemy's departure disappointed Lee, but his comment about it to Longstreet, was "we little thought the enemy would turn his back upon us this early in the campaign."[70]

There were various clashes as the Confederates advanced, none significant in the great scheme of the war, but each as deadly to those involved as Gettysburg. Fitz Lee, supported by Pelham, encountered the enemy at Kelly's Ford, driving them back and capturing several prisoners as well as a Federal cavalry flag.[71] Jeb, riding with Robertson's brigade, found a large body of Federal horsemen near Brandy Station, commanded by George Bayard. The 7th Virginia under Grumble Jones drove them away in two spirited assaults.[72]

Stuart and Von Borcke were in the middle of the action. At one point the Federals concentrated for an attack before Robertson's brigade was up, and Stuart sent several couriers back to urge them along, even recruiting the color-sergeant for that duty. Von Borcke took the battle flag from him, which resulted in several sharpshooters firing at him from 800 yards away. One shot hit the colors, but Jeb took the flag from Von Borcke and sent him off in search of the reserves. This he accomplished, and "occupying the place of honor in front," he led the 7th Virginia in a dash punctuated by a "wild Virginia Yell." The Federals fired a volley, then broke and fled, but not before one trooper brought his carbine to bear on Von Borcke a second too late. The man, according to Von, "at the very moment of firing at me, received my full right-cut on the lower part of the neck, severing his head nearly from his body," after which Von Borcke wiped the blood from his long saber onto his horse's mane.[73]

Blackford was present and witnessed what he described as "a curious thing." A mounted, galloping Confederate trooper was struck in the side just above the hips by a cannon ball that neatly cut away the upper portion of his body while the lower half remained in the saddle, feet in the stirrups, as his horse loped away.[74]

This action, the first significant cavalry battle to occur at Brandy Station, pitted four Confederate regiments against five of Bayard's—the 1st Pennsylvania, 1st Rhode Island, 1st New Jersey, 1st Maine, and 2nd New York. In addition to the 7th Virginia, Jeb sent in the 6th and 12th Virginia plus the 17th Virginia Battalion, all of which had previously served under Turner Ashby. The Southerners lost three killed and thirteen wounded, one of whom was Redmond Burke, shot in the leg, while the Federals lost sixty-one prisoners in addition to a number of killed and wounded. Von Borcke took note that quite a few of the latter were left behind by the retreating Federals, but he also transformed the sixty-one captives into "several hundred."[75]

As had happened during the ride around McClellan and on other occasions, the departure of the Federals and the rearrival of Confederates was met with liberation-of-Paris-type celebration by the local inhabitants. Von Borcke wrote that their joy "cannot be described," and "men, women, and children came running out of all the houses towards us with loud exclamations of delight, many thanking God on their knees for their deliverance from the enemy. A venerable old lady asked permission to kiss our battle-flag, which was borne throughout so many victorious fights, and blessed it with tears."[76]

The massive Confederate advance continued the next day, August 21. Pope was across the Rappahannock, awaiting an assault that Lee had no intention of making. Instead, Lee moved his two corps of infantry upstream to Warrenton, Sulphur Springs Ford, Freeman's Ford, and Beverly's Ford. Jackson crossed the river with eight regiments and two batteries at the former places to threaten Pope's right, while Longstreet repulsed a probing Federal crossing at the latter. Jeb, meanwhile, was planning a raid.[77]

The proposal he pitched to General Lee was to ride around Pope's upper flank and disrupt the rail communications in his rear. So long as Pope was dug in and awaiting battle Lee would not attack him, but a demonstration in Pope's rear might cause him to make a move the Confederates could turn into an opportunity. If nothing else the raid might gather valuable information. It was the sort of action in which Stuart specialized.[78]

Lee gave his consent and Jeb selected 1,500 men from Fitz Lee's and Robertson's brigades. Leaving the 3rd and 7th Virginia regiments, plus all of Pelham's guns but two, they rode upstream to the Waterloo Bridge, crossed the Rappahannock, and moved twelve miles to Warrenton. There they were greeted by another enthusiastic crowd of civilians. Once again they were in the rear of the Federal army, and the column rested for an hour while Stuart gathered information about recent Federal activity. Von Borcke used the time to flirt with the local ladies, and some of Jeb's regimental officers amused themselves by registering as guests at the Warrenton Hotel.[79]

When one of the ladies they met, a Miss Lucas, heard that Stuart was moving toward Catlett's Station, she clapped her hands and exclaimed that the Confederates just had to capture a certain Yankee captain she believed was there. This man, Captain Goulding, Pope's staff quartermaster, had boarded in her family's home during the Federal occupation of the town and he and Miss Lucas made a wager. She maintained that if Pope and Lee fought, Pope would be defeated, whereas he predicted not only that Lee would be defeated but that he, the quartermaster, would be in Richmond within thirty days. They'd bet a bottle of wine, and Miss Lucas saw a marvelous chance to lose her bet but gain much greater satisfaction.

"Oh General Stuart, if you will only capture him, so that he is sent to Richmond, he will win his bet with me, and then if you will bring him by here I will pay him. Won't that be too funny for anything?" she bubbled. Stuart naturally found the prospect enticing, and directed Blackford to take down the captain's name and look for him.[80]

From Warrenton the column rode east seven miles to Auburn, then turned southeast toward Catlett's Station, a depot on the Orange and Alexandria Railroad, Pope's line of rail communication with Washington. The weather was overcast and began to rain. It was also, according to Jeb, one of the darkest nights he had ever seen.

The Confederates persisted through the dark and the rain and captured Catlett's Station, taking a few prisoners and scattering the rest of its defenders. That might have been the end of the raid, but Jeb had a lucky break. Among those captured was a black teamster from Berkeley County who knew Stuart and said that Pope's headquarters, including his personal horses, wagons and staff officers, were just up the road, between the station and Cedar Run.

According to a John Thomason, writing in 1930, the teamster "was glad to see his white folks" and volunteered to show the way.[81] One can speculate about whether a man who'd escaped slavery and obtained a good job driving wagons for the Federal army was glad to see friends of his former master. Blackford reported that the man's presence first became apparent when he was heard singing *Carry Me Back to Old Virginny* and accompanying himself with percussion on a tin bucket, but that when he saw the Confederates he was terrified and rendered speechless. However, he "made a clean breast of it" and agreed to be cooperative. He was mounted behind a trooper with "a guard on each side to insure his fidelity," and told that he would receive "kind treatment if faithful and instant extermination if traitorous."[82]

Without hesitation and with the 9th Virginia leading the way, the gray troopers descended on Pope's headquarters. The commanding general was not there, but several of his staff officers, his headquarters wagon, his dispatch book and other papers, his personal baggage, tent furniture, two headquarters strongboxes, his best dress uniform and a hat were, and all became the property of Jeb Stuart.[83]

There were no keys for the strongboxes and the troopers did not immediately try to break into them, but when an opportunity afforded, Jeb directed some of his men to do so. They hammered away, without result, until Stuart announced, "If nobody can open these strong boxes, we must call on Major Armstrong,"—a nickname he had given Von Borcke—"to assist us." Von accepted the challenge and delivered several "heavy blows upon the safes with a serviceable axe, which laid them open, amid the loud cheers of our soldiers." Inside they found $20,000 in gold, $500,000 in greenbacks, and to Von Borcke's delight, two boxes of Havana cigars.[84] The loss of Jeb's hat was avenged.

For the next few hours, the Southerners rounded up prisoners, hacked down telegraph wires, rifled captured wagons and Yankee tents, burned what could not be carried away, and intended to destroy the railroad bridge over Cedar Run. Accomplishing the latter would have severed Pope's line of supply and might have forced him to abandon his position on the Rappahannock, but the Confederates found it protected by a strong force of infantry and reluctantly abandoned the effort.[85]

The column carried away 500 horses and mules and 400 prisoners, including one who turned out to be a woman dressed in a soldier's uniform. She was disguised to serve as a man—an act repeated at least 400 times during the war—but once captured she elected to reveal her secret and demand to be released. The normally chivalrous Stuart ruled, however, that if she was man enough to enlist she was man enough to go to prison, and she remained with the other captives, "in a state of great indignation."[86]

The Confederates withdrew not long before dawn on the 23rd, marched a few miles and halted for breakfast. Blackford then remembered the Yankee quartermaster captain—Goulding—who made the bet with Miss Lucas. Not expecting to have him, he went to the prisoners, called out his name, and was pleasantly surprised when a "genteel looking young man came forward." Goulding was greatly amused when he heard the reason for being summoned.

Jeb, also amused, directed Blackford to ride ahead to Warrenton to advise Miss Lucas of the loss of her bet and to make certain she had the bottle of wine ready. When the column reached the town, he halted the prisoners in front of her house and called Goulding forward. To the enthusiastic cheers of all in attendance, Rebel and Yankee alike, Miss Lucas presented the bottle of wine to the prisoner. He would indeed be in Richmond within 30 days, there to be processed by the Confederate authorities.[87]

Federals pursued Stuart and his men as far as Warrenton, but stopped there and Stuart's exhausted troopers and horses got some rest further down the road; but after a few hours a battery of Federal artillery began lobbing shells at them. Robertson sent out a squadron to drive them away, but a single shell exploded at the head of the column, killing or wounding fourteen men, and they fell back. Skirmishing continued until nightfall, allowing the Southerners a little more rest, but they were in the saddle before dawn, across the Rappahannock and within Confederate lines by 8 a.m. on Sunday, August 24.[88]

Jeb rode an additional five miles to report to General Lee and deliver Pope's dispatch case and papers. He then had Pope's coat and hat carried to Governor Letcher, in Richmond, and drafted a message to the Union commander to pass through the lines. It said, "General: Your cavalry have my hat and plume; I have your best coat. I have the honor to propose a cartel for the exchange of the prisoners. Very respectfully, J.E.B. Stuart." Before sending it, Jeb shared the message with Stonewall Jackson, who smiled with genuine amusement.

Pope failed to see the humor and did not reply, at least not promptly. Later, following the Battle of Second Manassas, Stuart's chaplain, Reverend Landstreet, was captured and met Pope, who told him that he would send Stuart his hat if Jeb would send him his coat. Stuart declined, writing Flora that he had to have his hat first.[89]

Pope's hat and coat were placed on exhibition in the window of a bookstore on Main Street in Richmond. A card was placed beneath the display reading, "Headquarters in the saddle; the rear taking care of itself."[90] The greater prizes from the raid were, of course, Pope's papers, which revealed his strength, Pope's plans, and most important, the planned movement of additional troops from McClellan's army to Pope's. The latter already had 70,000 on hand, and plans were in the works to swell that number to 150,000. Lee was operating with only 55,000.[91]

The rivers were swollen from the previous night's downpour, Pope was dug in and waiting more reinforcements, and there was no obvious move for Lee to make. He sent word to President Davis on August 23 that he hoped to move the campaign north of the Rappahannock, where the countryside had not been beaten down by passing armies and there were still provisions to be had. The afternoon of the 24th Lee met with Jackson, Longstreet, and Stuart in an open field outside of Jeffersonton. Lee had decided on a new, extremely risky plan.[92]

Early the next morning, August 25, Jackson took his corps, plus Munford's regiment of cavalry, approximately 24,000 men, and moved northwest, up the Rappahannock, crossing the river at Hinson's Mill and marching onward twenty-six miles to Salem. Stuart was kept busy all that day covering river fords and contesting Federal incursions. About 1 a.m. on the 26th he received orders to follow Jackson, which he did an hour later at 2.a.m., although he'd not slept for some time. With the brigades of Fitz Lee and Robertson, plus Pelham's Horse Artillery, he caught up with the rear of Jackson's column at Salem, but the roads were choked with Stonewall's baggage wagons, and rather than try to work through the long lines of infantry, Jeb left his wagons with Jackson's and led his troopers east, knowing he could meet the head of Jackson's column by a longer route covered more quickly on horseback.

Before dawn on August 26, Jackson moved east from Salem with Munford's 2nd Virginia in advance, passed Thoroughfare Gap in the Bull Run Mountains and arrived in Gainesville. Stuart, in the meantime, passed the same mountains farther south and arrived in Gainesville shortly thereafter.

Before leaving to rendezvous with Jackson, Jeb gave Blackford the task of riding ahead to overtake and advise Stonewall of where Stuart planned to meet him, but it became "the most fatiguing and exasperating" ride he ever made. Jackson's infantry completely filled the road so that Blackford could not simply ride past them. The result, as taxing as it was to Blackford, left a particularly rich snapshot of Confederate infantry on the march.

As the captain wrote, "It is almost impossible to pass infantry on the march when going in the same direction. . . . To pass a column meeting you is easy enough, for the men see you and get out of the way, but going in the same direction, you come up behind the men who, with their muskets on their shoulders in every position, completely block the road, and as they are all laughing and talking it is necessary to be continually shouting at them to clear the road; and if an officer loses his patience and they find he is angry they pretend not to hear and keep their muskets crossed from one to another to completely bar the way." Once the infantrymen decided to do so, they got out of the way, apologizing sarcastically, and the rider could advance a few yards before encountering the same situation.

He tried detouring around the infantry by taking down fence rails and riding across fields, but "of course a fence at every field had to be crossed, and no end of ditches and creeks, and occasional swamps and thickets. To leap a horse so often and on such a march was of course out of the question and the fences had to be pulled down, and the watercourses frequently made it necessary to return to the road" so that "[a]fter rapid trotting over rough fields, scrambling through briar patches and letting down fences, I would sometimes find when I went back to the road that the very same regiment was there which I had left an hour before."

The price Blackford paid for being allowed to preserve those then-common; now-extinct images was a ride that would normally take three hours but which took him twelve and, once completed, proved to be useless because Stuart had already caught up with Jackson.

From Gainesville, Jackson's column marched toward Bristoe Station, on the Orange & Alexandria Railroad, Pope's line of supply. Munford, leading, arrived at the station in the afternoon and approached within a hundred yards of the Federals guarding it before they realized they were about to be attacked. The 2nd Virginia swept in, killed two of the enemy, wounded seven, and took forty-seven prisoners. A brigade of Louisiana infantry from Ewell's division was close behind, and no sooner had they arrived then the sound of an approaching train was heard. The Rebels piled rails on the track but the engineer saw the danger. His locomotive was named the "Secretary," and it was empty. It rammed through the barricade and escaped, riddled with bullets.

Seeing another train coming, the Confederates quickly pulled up a section of track and stood back. The second train, hoping to emulate the success of the Secretary, applied full steam, sped past the station, off the track, and into the side of a bank. Close behind was yet another train which piled into the rear of the second with a tremendous crash, scattering cars and their contents in all directions.[93] A fourth train approached but saw what was going on ahead and slowed, reversed, and retired.[94]

Federal prisoners were able to contribute a couple of zingers to the record of Civil War humor while Jackson was at Bristoe Station. The first was heard by Jackson's staff officer, Henry Kyd Douglass, who accompanied Munford and his cavalry into the station in the hope of finding a fresh horse and a new pistol. Several New York infantrymen were captured, who were more vocal about the perceived incompetence of Pope than they were hostile toward their captors. To the contrary, some seemed genuinely impressed by Jackson, and Douglas heard one call out, "What sort of man is your Stonewall Jackson, anyway? Are his soldiers made of gutta-percha, or do they run on wheels?"[95]

The other statement, inspired by similar concern, was destined to become a classic "ring the changes" type of inside joke throughout the Army of Northern Virginia. A Northern civilian on one of the trains that was wrecked suffered a broken leg and was lying on a litter when he heard that Stonewall Jackson was nearby. He immediately pleaded with his captors to be lifted up so he could see the famous general.

Stonewall was not concerned about appearances. He'd worn his blue VMI uniform at Manassas, then before the Valley Campaign he acquired a Confederate officer's frock coat that became, in the words of witnesses, stained and threadbare. It was this same coat that he was wearing at Harpers Ferry. The blue forage cap he'd worn at Manassas and through the Valley campaign was replaced with a gray one, a gift from his wife, and Jackson was destined to trade it for a brimmed hat during the Maryland Campaign, but that had not yet occurred. Kyd Douglass, Jackson's youngest staff member, described his boss's appearance a few days later as "the worst-dressed, worst-mounted, most faded and dingy-looking general . . . ever seen. . . ."[96]

Accordingly, when the accommodating Confederates lifted the injured civilian up to get a look at Jackson, the civilian stared in disbelief, unable to fathom that such a raggedy person could be the legendary Stonewall. Then, with his voice tinted with disgust he cried out: "Oh, my God! Lay me down!"

The story circulated through the ranks quickly, as such stories do, and thereafter, every time something occurred that was not ideal, not intended, not expected, or otherwise surprising, a Rebel was bound to cry out, "Oh, my God! Lay me down!" Whether Jackson ever heard the joke, or had a clue about its meaning, history does not record, but every soldier in his Corps, probably the entire army, understood perfectly.

Jackson had marched his men fifty-four miles in thirty-six hours, but the ultimate prize lay seven miles farther—Manassas Junction, Pope's primary supply depot. Placing Stuart in command, Stonewall directed Brigadier Isaac Trimble to take two regiments of his brigade, the 21st Georgia Infantry and the 21st North Carolina Infantry, and move on the place. They did, and captured the depot, along with 300 infantrymen, eight cannons, and 200 horses, about 2 a.m. the morning of August 27.[97]

All of the cavalry's recent Christmases-come-early experiences—at Tunstall's and Catlett's Station and the White House—were mere trifles compared to what they found at Manassas Junction. Row upon row of stocked warehouses and entire trains of supplies on the tracks; wagons, loaded and parked, covered acres of ground. Here was the larder meant to support an army of 100,000 for a month, and it was now the property of Jeb Stuart and Stonewall Jackson. Once again, Southerners were standing before a cornucopia of equipment, supplies, foodstuffs, and assorted luxuries. Across the century and a half that separates today from then still glows the brightness of that vast treasure. It was, in many ways, the best day of the best year the Confederacy would ever experience.

The graybacks frolicked through the piles of goodies. Barefoot men chose from dozen of styles of shoes and boots. Tattered gray trousers were exchanged for new sky-blue pants. Hats of every style and fashion were tried on, canteens were filled with brandy, or at least some were before the liquor was placed under guard, and men with bulging blanket rolls carried away whole hams skewered on bayonets. Sutlers' stores provided lobster, beef tongue, candy, cakes, oranges, nuts, pickles, catsup, mustard, lemons, potted meats, sardines, and oysters. Jealousy among the branches of the army reared its head when infantrymen observed that cavalry and artillery soldiers were able to carry off more plunder than those on foot.

Even those who arrived late or not at all profited. Jeb assigned a "gaudily-painted" sutler van to Von Borcke to fill and carry to Pelham, whose men were left on the outskirts of the junction. Von first exchanged the four bay horses pulling the wagon with larger, sturdier artillery horses, then had it pulled to Pelham, where the artilleryman emptied it of shirts, hats, handkerchiefs, oranges, lemons, wine, cigars and "all sorts of knick-knacks."[98]

The Confederates spent most of the day looting the depot. At one point an old friend of Jeb's, David French Boyd, spotted Stuart and Jackson on the scene. "I recognized Stuart on the platform, fighting jacket on, black plume in his hat, and literally dancing—as on the old chicken coop years before," with Jackson leaning on a barrel nearby, "his old hat pulled down over his eyes, his arms folded, and evidently in deep meditation. Boyd was a boyhood schoolmate of Jeb's, and the chicken coop incident had occurred some twenty years earlier.[99]

That evening Jackson ordered everything remaining to be burned, and turned his infantry and Stuart's troopers toward Groveton, five miles away, where the Warrenton Turnpike intersected the Sudley Springs Road. Here, on a thickly wooded rise just north of the turnpike, he settled his men in to await Pope's army, which he knew would soon arrive.

Pope had observed Jackson when he departed from south of the Rappahannock. He even understood that it was Jackson, but instead of sending cavalry to investigate and report back, he surmised that the Rebels were enroute to the Valley, perhaps Winchester, and spent his time preparing for an anticipated flank attack by Lee on his left. After observing Lee, he correctly surmised that an assault was not planned from that direction, and that Longstreet and Lee were simply trying to mask an assault on his right. He then swung his army toward Warrenton, shortly after which he received word, via the escaped locomotive "Secretary," that Stuart had attacked Bristoe Station, but he assumed it was only a cavalry raid. It was not until reports of infantry at Bristoe Station arrived, late on the 26th, followed by the discovery that Longstreet and Lee were no longer across the river in his front, that he decided to fall back on Manassas Junction on August 27. By then it was too late.

Lee and Longstreet, meanwhile, with 30,000 men, crossed the Rappahannock three miles above Pope's right flank on the 26th, and followed Jackson's route. As Pope fell back, he unwittingly placed his large army between Jackson and Longstreet with twenty miles separating the two Southern forces, thus acquiring a rare, perhaps priceless opportunity to crush each in turn. Pope was totally confused by the Southerners' movements, however, lacked reliable intelligence of his enemy's' positions, and "threw away his chance for victory."[100] Instead he arrived at Manassas Junction to find it smoldering, with the only Confederates being "a few bloated stragglers" in the ditches and an occasional Rebel horseman on a distant ridge.[101]

In no small part due to Stuart's cavalry screen, Pope "lost" Stonewall Jackson, even though the entire Confederate corps was spread out in a woods just a few miles from Manassas. On the late afternoon of the 28th, Jackson, beginning to fear that Pope was moving for a rendezvous with

McClellan's newly arriving army from the Peninsula, attacked one of Pope's divisions that was marching obliviously down the Warrenton Turnpike. This Battle of Brawner's Farm, or Groveton, saw a fierce head-on clash between the Stonewall Brigade and the Union's Iron Brigade, with John Pelham dashing up on the Rebel right with his Horse Artillery to pour fire into the Federal ranks. Jeb spent the night of August 28 with Jackson in a house at Sudley Mills, and the next morning Stonewall directed him to establish communication with Longstreet, who had just emerged from Thoroughfare Gap. Jeb then stayed with Longstreet to protect his flanks as he marched to join Jackson.

What followed, on August 29 and 30, was the Battle of Second Manassas. Now that Pope had realized where Jackson was, he attacked him with massive strength. Jackson held on, though outnumbered two to one, and around noon Longstreet's men began to arrive on his right. Incredibly, and again due largely to Stuart's cavalry screen, Pope remained igonorant that the full Army of Northern Virginia was now on his front. For his part, Longstreet hesitated to pitch in because Fitz John Porter's corps was hovering off to his right. The Union corps did not join in that day's battle, as ordered, and Porter was later court-martialed; however, he alone among the senior Federal commanders had become aware of Longstreet's presence, and he was paralyzed in part by Stuart's men dragging brush down the roads creating dust clouds to indicate the approach of a gigantic force. After reporting Porter's presence to Lee and Longstreet, Stuart seized some strategic hills facing the Union corps and was quickly reinforced by Confederate infantry.

That afternoon Longstreet was in conference with General Lee when Jeb rode up to report and request further orders. These not being quite ready, he was asked to wait and so he laid down on the grass, put a stone under his head for a pillow, and went sound asleep. "This," wrote Longstreet, "gave General Stuart a half an hour *siesta*. When called, he sprang to his feet, received his orders, swung into his saddle, and at a lope, singing, 'If you want to have a good time, jine the cavalry,' his banjo-player, Sweeny, on the jump behind him, rode to his troopers."[102]

On the afternoon of August 30 Pope's full army, now joined by Porter, renewed its attacks on Jackson. Stonewall was approaching the end of his rope—some of his men, having exhausted their ammunition, resorted to throwing rocks—when at 4:00 Longstreet's entire wing was hurled against the Federal left. The Union flank collapsed, creating for John Bell Hood "the most beautiful battle scene I ever beheld,"[103] and it was only obstinate resistance by some units on Chinn Ridge and Henry House Hill (where Jackson had earned his nickname the previous summer) as well as the approach of darkness, that prevented a disastrous rout. Nevertheless, Pope's demoralized army spent the rest of the night trudging back toward Centreville.

It was during the fighting on the 30th that Captain Hardeman Stuart was killed. He had used his signals for the very first time on the 21st of August, on a hill called View Tree, which overlooks the town of Warrenton. On the 23rd he was directed by Jeb to return to his headquarters when Federal troops were seen advancing on the hill. Once reunited with his cousin, he was sent back with a handful of men to View Hill on the 25th, but he found it occupied. Dismounting, he took off his new captain's coat and tied it to his saddle, then turned his horse over to one of his men so he could scout the enemy's position on foot.

While Hardeman was so engaged, the Federals spotted the other horsemen and attacked. The horse holder fled and the captain's horse and new coat were captured, leaving Hardeman afoot. He began walking in the direction of the army, toward Manassas, and came upon his old regiment, the 18th Mississippi Infantry. They were going the same direction so he fell in with them, and that is where he was on the 29th when John Esten Cooke happened along.

Hardeman called out to Cooke, who recognized his voice but just barely recognized the man. Always "the neatest person imaginable in dress and appearance," young Stuart was now "coatless, unwashed, his looks covered with dust and his clothes had the dingy look of a real soldier. . . . His hair was unbrushed, and hung disordered around his face. . . . (he) had the appearance of a sapper and miner."[104]

Hardeman seemed overjoyed to see Cooke. He told the writer of his adventure, "but seemed to regard the whole affair as an excellent jest, and only the ordinary 'fortune of war.'" Cooke told him to find a horse and come back to Jeb's headquarters, to which Hardeman said he would, and to "tell the General I'll soon be there."[105]

But horses were a precious commodity, and even a captain on Stuart's staff could not simply requisition one. Instead he stayed with his old company, and when they reached the battlefield at Second Manassas, he acquired a rifle and a cartridge box. As God is said to sometimes do, he went in with the infantry and was shot—Cooke said in the heart; another source said the neck—and killed. As an added insult, his body was stripped to his undershirt and drawers "by scoundrels," but the next day some of Stuart's troopers recaptured his horse and coat. They identified them as such because Hardeman's captain's commission was in a pocket.

He was buried where he fell, after which his brother, Edward, spent three days searching for the gravesite. He finally found the spot, marked by a wooden headboard, and erected a rail pen around it. As far as anyone knows, Hardeman Stuart still lies buried on the battlefield.[106]

He was the first of Stuart's military family to go down in history as a lost cavalier in the year of glory. He would not be the last.

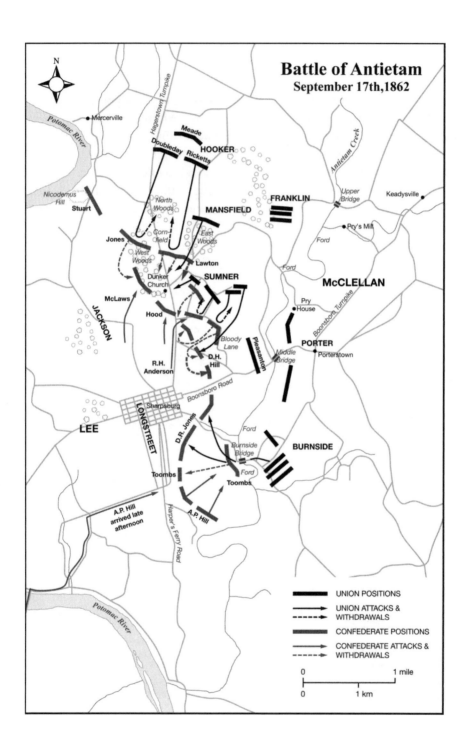

Battle of Antietam
September 17th, 1862

CHAPTER FIVE

TO SHARPSBURG AND BEYOND
SEPTEMBER 1, 1862–SEPTEMBER 27, 1862

I feel secure upon your back,
Maryland My Maryland
When danger howls upon your track,
Maryland My Maryland.
You bore me o'er the Potomac
You circumvented Little Mac,
Oh, may I never know your lack,
Maryland My Maryland.
—Comic parody, written by J.E.B. Stuart to his horse, Maryland

The first day of September found Jeb and his troopers in the saddle, pursuing a thoroughly beaten Pope. It was still raining, which hindered both retreat and pursuit. The Federals had lost nearly 14,500 men, killed, wounded and captured, compared to the Confederates' 9,400, but Lee was not satisfied to simply whip Pope. He hoped to crush him before he could get to the safety of Washington, D.C. and its many forts.

Stuart's men rounded up stragglers, captured wagons, and shadowed the edges of the Union army, searching for weaknesses and vulnerability. Jackson's troops followed, slogging through the mud and covering less than a third of the distance they could travel in dry weather, but ready to take advantage of any opportunity to which Jeb pointed them.

In the afternoon, near the village of Chantilly, Jackson attempted to move around the flank of the retreating Federals, and the division under

A.P. Hill clashed violently with those of Federal Generals Phil Kearny and Isaac Stevens. It was dark, still raining, and the night was filled with lightning and thunder. A rider came toward Confederate lines, but there was not enough light to see who he was. Had it been brighter, the Rebels would have seen a Federal officer with only one arm, his right, riding a light brown horse. They would not have known his name, that he'd lost his arm in the Mexican War, that he'd served in the French army under Napoleon III, or that the horse's name was Bayard. They particularly would not have known that only a matter of moments earlier another Federal officer had warned him to be careful and the officer had replied, "The Rebel bullet that can kill me has not yet been molded."

The Rebels ordered him to stop and surrender. When the rider wheeled about, leaned low over Bayard's mane and galloped away, they shot him. A bullet that had definitely been molded by Rebels struck him in his rear end and traveled up his spine, killing him in an ignominious manner. Stuart and Blackford were two of several Southerners who identified the body of Major General Phil Kearny.

A month later Kearny's widow petitioned for recovery of her husband's horse, saddle, and sword. The Confederates located the items, all still in their possession, and General Lee assigned Jeb to serve as senior officer on a board of survey to determine their value. Then, rather than subject the widow to further bureaucracy and delay, Lee paid the price of the three items to the Confederate government out of his own pocket and forwarded them under a flag of truce to General McClellan.[1]

Stuart and his troopers were occupied on September 2nd, as on the 1st, in roaming the edges of the enemy's lines, picking up stragglers in the Ox Hill and Fairfax Court House areas, but Jeb took time to visit Laura Ratcliffe and Antonia Ford at their home close to Frying Pan, near Fairfax. One need only read a few of Jeb's letters to Flora to appreciate the depth of his devotion to her, and infidelity is a failing totally inconsistent with the man's sense of honor, but if ever he was tempted, it was by Laura Ratcliffe. She was an unmarried, dark-eyed brunette beauty who had come to the cavalry camp in early 1862 to assist at the hospital, and in the months after their first meeting, Jeb wrote four poems to her, gave her a gold coin on a gold chain, a leather bound album, considered having Christmas dinner at her home, and wore a lock of her hair in his hatband. In March 1862, he wrote to her of "that never to be forgotten good-bye."

Antonia Ford, a close friend of Laura's, was also considered beautiful.

She had warned the Confederates of the Federal advance on Manassas in July 1861, and was commissioned "an honorary aide-de-camp" by Stuart, but she did not receive as much of Jeb's attention as Ratcliffe. Nevertheless, Flora knew of both women and perhaps even of her husband's admiration for them. As Henry McClellan, who would become Stuart's chief of staff, wrote, Stuart's "devotion to the society of ladies was one of the noblest and purest instincts of his nature. Towards them he was as naïve and unsuspecting as a child, and as pure in thought and action."[2]

Stuart spent the evening and night of September 2 at what was Camp Qui Vive prior to the Peninsular Campaign, an empty house known as "the Mellon Place," halfway between Fairfax Court House and Centreville.[3] The next day, sunny and clear, he led his column, now joined by Hampton's brigade, toward Drainesville.

Along the way they came to a grey-haired gentleman, mounted, and his three daughters standing beside the road at the entrance to their home. The house was decorated with a Confederate flag and when Stuart and his staff approached the man rode out and asked Jeb where he might find General Stuart. Jeb played with him for a few minutes, pretending not to know, but the man expressed such a sincere desire on behalf of his daughters to see the famous cavalry leader that Stuart revealed his identity, to the thrill of the blushing young ladies, after which he agreed to join the family for lunch.

Traveling a little further, they came to the home of a woman who was standing at the edge of the road with her 15-year-old son. It was her fervent desire that she be allowed to kiss Stuart's battle flag, which he happily permitted her to do, after which she revealed that she had lost two sons fighting for the South, but that she was prepared to sacrifice her last son as well. Von Borcke wrote that tears dripped into his and Stuart's beards as they rode away.[4]

Stuart and his staff then set up their camp in the garden of a hotel located in the center of Drainesville. There the headquarters baggage train caught up with them and they were able, for the first time in three weeks according to Von Borcke, to have a bath and a change of clothes.[5]

Jeb wrote a letter to his cousin, Nannie Price, that evening, and one to Flora the next day, September 4th. That to his wife began, "Long before this reaches you I will be in Maryland." He also sent a set of recommendations for changes in his brigades to Secretary of War Randolph that morning, apologizing for sending them directly but saying that General Lee was too busy and that they applied only to the routine of his command.

On September 5, as the cavalry prepared to cross the Potomac and carry the war into Maryland, Stuart received the welcome news that Beverly Robertson was relieved of command of the cavalry brigade that had once been Ashby's. He was reassigned to the Department of North Carolina. The order broke it to Robertson gently, saying that "his services are indispensably necessary for the organization and instruction of cavalry troops of North Carolina,"[6] Jeb was less circumspect in his reaction, writing, "'Joy's mine.' My command is now okay," to his wife.[7] Colonel Munford was assigned to command of the brigade, which had been Jeb's goal for months.

September 5 was an exciting day for Southerners. After a year and a half of fighting on home soil repelling invaders, they were on the offensive and carrying the war to the enemy's turf. They believed they were about to bring the war to an end, that their ranks would swell with thousands of Maryland recruits anxious to be part of the victory.

Jeb met twice with General Lee that day at the commander's headquarters in the residence of Henry T. Harrison, in Leesburg, and was assigned the task of screening the army's movements by occupying the area between it and Washington, D.C.[8] That afternoon, the cavalry began crossing the Potomac at Leesburg, followed by the rest of the army. Bands played "Maryland My Maryland," and the men cheered when they saw the river, when they entered the water, and when they stepped onto Maryland soil. The Potomac is not a swift or showy river, more rocky and steady, with water up to stirrups, wheel hubs, or waists, depending on one's branch of service. The infantry soldiers pulled off shoes, trousers, and drawers and carried them on their shoulders baring their collective moons beneath the moon. Crossing continued throughout the night and presented a unique sight.

Once in Maryland the Rebels camped at Poolesville, where the soldiers spent most of their money purchasing goods unavailable in Virginia, then Lee and Jackson marched to Frederick while the cavalry veered east and north. This was the first time in the war that all of Stuart's command, some 4,500 mounted men and three batteries of horse artillery, was present in one place and directly under his leadership.[9]

On the 6th, Stuart's cavalry arrived at Urbana and he directed Von Borcke to establish a camp for the division while he rode on to Frederick for a meeting with Lee and his senior officers. There he had an altercation with Captain Elijah V. "Lige" White, commander of a battalion of irregulars known officially as the 35th Battalion, Virginia Cavalry, and familiarly as "The Comanches," that was settled only by the wise intervention of General Lee.

Stuart established his headquarters at Urbana, in the garden of a house belonging to a Mr. Cockey, on the 6th and remained there until the 11th, a time that Blackford called "an oasis in the war-worn desert of our lives"[10] It was here that the single most picturesque, romantic, and *Gone With the Wind*-ish event of the war occurred.

Stuart could spend nearly a week in one place while Lee's army invaded the North because his role was to mask what the infantry was doing. The cavalry was spread in an arc from New Market, Maryland on the left, where Fitz Lee's brigade was posted, to the Urbana/Barnesville area on the right, where Munford's brigade was located, with the center, Hampton's brigade, at Hyattstown. That screen, some twenty-five miles in length, allowed Lee's infantry to move unseen by their enemy toward Federal garrisons located at Martinsburg and Harpers Ferry, and to potentially move further north for an invasion of Pennsylvania.[11]

Jeb's inevitable socializing began in Urbana with an invitation from Mr. Cockey to join his family and visitors, which included "several very charming and pretty young ladies," for a dinner party the evening of September 7. One of the ladies, Anne Cockey, was a relative from New York who was fiercely pro-Confederate, and Stuart christened her the "New York Rebel."[12] The dinner party was followed by "mirth and song," and when Stuart saw that a full moon had risen, he proposed a promenade, so the guests paired off in couples and strolled the equivalent of a block to a large white, two-storied building dominating the summit of a gentle hill. It was the former Shirley Female Academy, now empty and abandoned, and the couples went in and walked from room to room.[13] On the east end of the building was a large auditorium, and when Jeb saw it he turned to Von Borcke and said, "Major, what a capital place for us to give a ball in honour of our arrival in Maryland—don't you think we could manage it?"

Von Borcke took command of arranging the celebration. As he observed, "A soldier's life is so uncertain, and his time is so little at his own disposal, that in affairs of this sort delays are always to be avoided; and so we determined on our way home, to the great joy of our fair companions, that the ball should come off on the following evening."

The party Von planned was christened "The Sabers and Roses Ball," and invitations went out the morning of the 8th to every family in the town and the surrounding area, as well as to the officers of every nearby unit, most of which were in Hampton's brigade. The 18th Mississippi Infantry had a band, whose services Jeb did not have to pull rank to secure so long as he invited the infantry colonel and his staff. The walls of the Academy auditorium were decorated with regimental flags. Sabers were stacked like muskets and roses were placed on every available surface. Hundreds of candles were gathered from the town, and Pelham hung two large, colored lanterns above the entrance doors.[14] The huge building literally glowed.

The party began at 7 p.m. on September 8th. The streets of Urbana filled with arriving guests, "some on foot, others in simple light 'rockaways,' others again in stately family coaches, driven by fat negro coachmen who sat upon the box with great dignity."[15] Ladies wore their finest gowns and officers their best uniforms. Another full moon shone down on the scene as Pelham and his second in command, Captain James Breathed, arrived with the two lovely daughters of Mr. Cockey, Virginia and Martha. Von Borcke escorted the New York Rebel. Horses were picketed outside the building and officers leaned their sabers against the walls.[16]

The band announced its arrival from afar by bugle calls and appeared with the commander of the 18th Mississippi and his staff in the lead, the band playing "Dixie." Stuart welcomed everyone and then announced the Grand March, which he led into the hall. Von, as Master of Ceremonies, had arranged the order of the dances, and had selected a polka as the first. To his surprise and embarrassment, however, the New York Rebel—whom he had selected as "Queen of the Festival"—declined his invitation to the dance floor in order to open the ball. He was not aware until then that the custom in the South was that young, single ladies "did not join in round dances," such as polkas and waltzes, except with brothers or first cousins. They were supposed to dance with strangers only in reels and "contre-dances," being those in which the dancers formed facing lines. "Not to be baffled, however," Von Borcke directed that the music be changed to a quadrille, and soon the room was filled with "many exceedingly pretty women and martial figures of officers in their best uniforms."

The dancing and celebrating continued for another three hours and was at its height, according to Blackford, when a different, non-musical sound reached everyone's ears—"the boom of artillery, followed by the angry rattle of musketry."[17] The band paused, "the lily chased the rose from the cheek of beauty, and every pretty foot was rooted to the floor where music had left it."[18] An orderly covered in dust entered and announced to Stuart that the enemy had driven in the Confederate pickets and was attacking Hampton's camp. "The officers rushed to their weapons and called for their horses. . . . General Stuart maintained his accustomed coolness and composure." Horses were saddled, and the Confederates galloped away, only to find that, "as is usually the case in such sudden alarms, that things were by no means so desperate as they were represented."[19]

Led by the 1st North Carolina and supported by Pelham's guns, the Confederates charged the enemy, which was five companies of the 1st New York Cavalry[20] that had entered Poolsville earlier in the evening, essentially the first resistance of any kind the Federals had shown to Lee's invasion of Maryland. Soon the Yankees were retreating, having lost a handful of killed and wounded, as well as several prisoners. The Confederates pursued them a few miles and the affair was finished before midnight.

The Southern officers returned to the Academy, where many of the women had remained, and to which those who had gone home now returned. By 1 a.m. the band was playing again and the dancing resumed for an hour or more, only to be interrupted again. The lady with whom Blackford was dancing screamed in his ear. She had seen the wounded from the skirmish arriving by ambulance and being carried on stretchers, bloody and moaning, to empty rooms in the Academy building.

The couples rushed outside and gathered around the fallen heroes. Dancing was forgotten and the ladies competed to minister to the needs of the wounded. One of these declared that he wouldn't mind being shot again if it meant he would have such surgeons to dress his wounds. The New York Rebel, with Von Borcke on one side and Blackford on the other, bent over a young man wounded in the shoulder. His jacket was soaked with blood and the young lady started to apply a wet rag to the wound when "her strength broke down and she fainted away." When she awoke a few moments later, Blackford and Von Borcke urged her to return to the Cockey home, but she insisted that she "must first do my duty," which she did by tending to the young soldier's wound.

After the war the Academy, known today as the Landon House, was purchased by Lt. Colonel Tierman Brian, Von Borcke's co-star, who lived there with his wife until 1912. Both the Landon and Cockey houses are still standing, fully restored and in use.[21] One may be confident that for generations after September 8, 1862, people in Urbana referred to aging local ladies with a reverential "she attended the Sabers and Roses ball" as a means of communicating the grand dame's lofty status.

On September 9, after most of the staff slept late, Von Borcke busied himself removing the decorations from the Academy walls, in particular the various regimental colors. More momentous events were occurring at Lee's headquarters in Frederick, where the commanding general met with Jackson and Longstreet to discuss a bold, risky plan. He commanded a force of a little over 40,000, whereas the Federals could bring three times that number to bear if given enough time. Basic, textbook strategy dictated that Lee not divide his army in such a situation but he proposed to not merely divide it, but to scatter it into five segments. His immediate goal was to capture Martinsburg and Harpers Ferry, after which he intended to consolidate his forces at the mouth of the Shenandoah Valley. Supposedly Jackson and Longstreet opposed the plan, but Lee knew his enemy, and wrote later that he was certain that "the advance of the Federal Army was so slow . . . as to justify the belief that the reduction of Harpers Ferry would be accomplished and our troops concentrated before they would be called upon to meet it."[22] The outline of those movements was contained in Special Order 191, issued that afternoon.

Stuart and Von Borcke, meanwhile, had dinner at the home of an Urbana doctor, after which they retired to the veranda. The sound of distant artillery was heard, coming from the direction of Fitz Lee's brigade, skirmishing near Barnesville. The Federals were increasing their pressure on the cavalry screen. Stuart listened but was not alarmed. He and Von Borcke left the doctor's and returned to the home of Mr. and Mrs. Cockey, where they spent another evening, this time calling on Sweeney and his musicians to serenade their friends. The days of relaxation at Urbana were nearly at an end.

The movements of the infantry, pursuant to Special Order No. 191, began the next day, September 10. Lee did not know, and neither did Jeb, that McClellan was finally moving to intercept him. As evidenced by a letter from Channing Price to his family, written that day, Stuart believed that the main body of the Army of the Potomac was still only about ten miles west of Washington, D.C., near Rockville, Maryland. In fact, the Federals were coming through Hyattstown and Buckeytown to New Market, where the left wing of Stuart's screen was commanded by Fitz Lee. Stuart should have been more thoroughly engaged in scouting the movements of the enemy, but he was not.[23]

On the morning of the 11th, advancing columns of Federal infantry were in view and Stuart began falling back slowly. It was raining again, and

Jeb lingered on the porch of the Cockey home until the last possible moment, chatting with his friends as the enemy came nearer, finally galloping away amid scattered gunshots shortly before 2 p.m. Ten minutes later the town was occupied by Yankees.[24]

Jeb led his troopers across the Monocacy River. The Federals remained in Urbana and Stuart and his staff made camp about half a mile short of Frederick at a farm owned by "an old Irishman" with a "buthiful brogue," and at least two pretty daughters—"spirited Irish girls they were"—with whom Von and others "had a lively little dance" that night.[25] Early the next morning, the 12th, the Federals advanced in strength from Urbana toward Frederick. Stuart fell back before them.

The Confederate horsemen rode toward Middletown, a scenic route that afforded a view of the Blue Ridge Mountains and two valleys. After enjoying the scenery, Jeb and his staff made camp at a farmhouse near Middletown. Lee's orders to Stuart were, "I do not wish you to retire too fast before the enemy, or to distribute your cavalry far apart."[26] Jeb was endeavoring to obey, but the enemy was already in Frederick and coming on in force, driving the Confederate horse in different directions.

Dawn on the 13th included the sound of artillery as the Federals moved closer. Hampton's brigade and Pelham's guns slowed them down but the Rebels were outnumbered and the Federals had five or six batteries with which to clear the road. At one point, Stuart ordered Von Borcke to take a mountain howitzer, a small but mobile piece of artillery pulled by two horses, up an elevation to a small plateau, where the gun's crew had a commanding view of the enemy. Von wrote, "The valley beneath, stretching away from the immediate base of the mountain, was literally blue with the Yankees . . . with a waving glitter of bayonets, their numerous bodies of cavalry with 'many a flirt and flutter' of gay flags and pennons, [and] their imposing artillery-trains with the sunlight reflected from the polished brass pieces."[27] Von banged at them for awhile and then descended to rejoin Stuart's retrograde movement.

Lee expected Harpers Ferry to fall by the 12th but it did not happen, with the result that Stuart could not be certain which passage, or gap, in the Blue Ridge most needed defending. Jackson's corps was at Harpers Ferry while Longstreet had two divisions at Hagerstown, and another, D.H. Hill's, at Boonesboro.

Back in Frederick, something more threatening was occurring. A copy of Lee's Special Order 191 was found wrapped around three cigars by an

Indiana private named B.W. Mitchell. It soon worked its way up the chain
of command to General McClellan, and it took McClellan's staff a little
longer to decide it was genuine, but it was and they did.

Who lost the order has been the subject of debate ever since, and
chances are some staff officer carried the memory of those lost smokes and
the shame of what he did to the grave. Had the same thing happened in
reverse, Robert E. Lee would have capitalized on that lightning strike of
good fortune up to and possibly including the final, masterful destruction
of the Federal army. McClellan was not Lee, but even he was capable of
pulling off a tie game when provided with his opponent's playbook.

The Federal commander was engaged in discussion with Frederick
businessmen when he was handed the lost order, and rather than retire to
study the paper and make appropriate plans, he raised his arms in the air
and announced to all that he knew of Lee's intentions. One of the businessmen concluded that McClellan's big news was something General Lee
would like to know, so he rode to Turner's Gap and arrived at Stuart's picket
line about dusk. Stuart immediately sent the information to General Lee,
who issued orders to Longstreet to move in the morning to link up with
D.H. Hill's division at Boonesboro, and to Stuart to hold Turner's Gap "at
all hazards" until Harpers Ferry, which still had not fallen, was in Confederate hands.

McClellan, in the meantime, sent a confident message to Lincoln al-
luding to the lost order, declaring that Lee had made "a gross mistake" for
which he would be "severely punished," and that he was going to move
rapidly after the Confederates and "catch them in their own trap." Then
he did nothing for the rest of the day.[28]

On September 13th and 14th the two armies played a large-scale, slow-
motion game of hide-and-seek at the passes through the mountains between Frederick, on the east side, and Boonesboro and Harpers Ferry, on
the west side of the Blue Ridge.

West of Frederick are Catoctin and South Mountains. Neither comport
with the image of a mountain either in elevation or shape, as neither
are higher than 1,900 feet, with 1,200 being common, and both are long
ridges, fifty and seventy miles in length respectively. Both are extensions
of the Blue Ridge, which is part of the Appalachians, and they run parallel
to each other in a northeasterly direction. Both contain passes where the
elevation is low, and which are wide enough for the passage of traffic,
including armies.

With the infantry of the Army of Northern Virginia on the west side of South Mountain and the Army of the Potomac coming from Frederick at a steady clip, at least by McClellan's standards, and with Stuart's cavalry between the two armies, the question was "which gap or gaps are the Yankees going to try to come through, and where should the most men be placed to stop or slow them down?"

Stuart has been criticized by historians, as well as a few contemporaries, for not doing a better job of predicting the answers to that question on September 13–14, 1862. The Federal approaches ultimately came against Crampton's, Fox, and Turner's Gaps, all of which Jeb covered with troops of one sort or another, but with 20/20 hindsight, had he placed more men in more places at different times, the outcome of the Confederate invasion of Maryland might have been happier for the men in gray.

Turner's Gap is the furthest north. It is located on what was then known as the National Road, which was the first major turnpike constructed in the United States, mostly between 1811 and 1837, and which stretched from Cumberland, Maryland west to Vandalia, Illinois. Today the highway through Turner's Gap is U.S. 40 Alternate. The elevation of the ridgeline above the gap is about 1,200 feet, and the gap is about 400 feet lower, some 200 feet higher than nearby lowlands. It is about 200 feet wide. East of the gap is the Middletown Valley and west of it is the Hagerstown Valley.

A mile south is Fox, or Fox's, Gap. The elevation of the ridgeline and the gap is about the same there as at Turner's, with the same valleys on each side. The road through Fox's Gap is known today as Reno Monument Road. Crampton's Gap lies another six miles south. It connects Burkittsville in the Middletown Valley to the east with Gapland and Rohrersville in the Pleasant Valley to the west.

Stuart's movements and troop placements, after departing Frederick on the 12th were to first direct Fitz Lee to take his brigade, move beyond McClellan's right flank, and operate in his rear. This could have had a marvelous result, disrupting McClellan's advance, delaying him and causing him to send infantry in fruitless chases after men on horses. For the most part, however, it merely took Fitz Lee's Brigade out of the picture for the next two days.

About daylight on the 13th, Stuart placed the Jeff Davis Legion, under W.T. Martin, and a section of Pelham's Horse Artillery in a gap in Cactocin Mountain called Hagen's Gap to slow the Federals as they moved toward South Mountain. There was no expectation that the Legion would be able to hold the gap for any length of time, and by 2 p.m. the advancing Federals had forced Martin out. He fell back toward Middletown, where Stuart and Hampton were.

The bulk of Munford's Brigade was sent south to Crampton's Gap. Hampton's Brigade contested McClellan's advance from Frederick, and was then ordered to Crampton's Gap as well. Stuart, accompanied by his staff, the Jeff Davis Legion, and the section of artillery, withdrew to Turner's Gap, and arrived there about 5 p.m. It was already occupied by a brigade of D.H. Hill's division, under General Alfred Colquitt.[29] The rest of Hill's division was located in Boonesboro, two or three miles up the National Road to the northwest.

While this was going on, Jackson was moving on Harpers Ferry with six divisions. The garrison there, some 13,000 men, was commanded by D.S. Miles, and although Miles' position was untenable, it ultimately took much longer for Jackson to take Harpers Ferry then Lee expected. Longstreet was near Hagerstown, with three divisions, until Lee learned that McClellan had a copy of Order 191, when he ordered Longstreet to join Jackson. Longstreet's other division, McLaws', was north of Harpers Ferry in Pleasant Valley, which connects with Crampton's Gap.

Late on the evening of the 13th, Jeb sent Rosser's 5th Virginia, plus a battery of Horse Artillery, to Fox's Gap. He did not expect the Federals to come in that direction, anticipating their goal would be to relieve Harpers Ferry by moving on Crampton's Gap. Accordingly, he directed Hampton to take his brigade there and, after dark, Stuart rode into Boonesboro, where the rest of D.H. Hill's division was encamped, and where Stuart spent the night.

Early on the 14th Stuart rode toward Crampton's Gap, and along the way he received a message from Rosser that the enemy was advancing on Fox's Gap. In fact, the primary Federal advance was on Fox's and Turner's Gaps instead of Crampton's. However, when Stuart arrived at Crampton's and found the enemy was not there, he surmised that McClellan must be planning to bypass South Mountain altogether and approach Harpers Ferry along the Potomac. Accordingly, he ordered Hampton to cover the river roads while Munford stayed at Crampton's Gap with the majority of his brigade. Jeb also sent a message to McLaws, who was on Maryland Heights overlooking Harpers Ferry, requesting that he send infantry to Crampton's Gap. McLaws complied by sending Howell Cobb's brigade. About noon, Stuart left Munford and rode to Maryland Heights and, predictably, Federals appeared in force at Crampton's Gap shortly after Stuart departed. By the time Jeb arrived at Maryland Heights, he and McLaws could see a significant amount of smoke coming from Crampton's Gap.

Lafayette McLaws was a burly, somewhat irascible, less than brilliant major general who did not like Jeb Stuart. He once commented that Stuart "carries around with him a banjo player and a special correspondent. This claptrap is noticed and lauded as a peculiarity of genius, when, in fact, it is nothing else but the act of a buffoon to get attention."[30] Of events on this day, McLaws would later claim that Stuart tried to talk him out of investigating what was going on at Crampton's Gap, arguing that there was nothing more than a brigade of Federals, and that when Stuart discovered it was a far larger enemy force, he "appeared to be completely dazed."[31]

Considering McLaws would be criticized after the war for not doing more to stop McClellan that September 14, and that he wrote the foregoing statement about Stuart forty-one years after the latter's death, acceptance of his remarks require several grains of salt. They also fail to explain why Stuart had earlier requested that McLaws send infantry to support the defense of Crampton's Gap.

In any event, when Stuart and McLaws rode toward Crampton's Gap they met fleeing Confederates driven out by the Federal Sixth Corps. McLaws, joined by a portion of Richard Anderson's division, made a defensive line across Pleasant Valley to try to stop the Federal advance. Stuart remained there until 10 p.m., then rode to Harpers Ferry.

All the maneuvering and guesswork about which gap to guard was intended to afford Jackson plenty of time to take Harpers Ferry, which finally happened about 9 a.m. on the 15th. The night before the Federal cavalry in the garrison, 1,300 men under Colonel Benjamin Davis, had escaped via a road below Maryland Heights, though Stuart had specifically warned McLaws to block it. Nevertheless, Stonewall accepted the surrender of some 11,500 Union infantry as prisoners, along with seventy-three pieces of artillery, thousands of stands of arms, plus wagons, horses, and other spoils.

The capture of Harpers Ferry was one more in the stream of Confederate seizures of Federal installations going on since June, or earlier if one includes Stonewall's successes in the Valley. This time the big prizes were prisoners and cannons instead of lobster and cigars. The Federal prisoners had not been in the field, and were neither browned nor sunburned as were the Rebels. Seeing how pale they were, one of Stuart's troopers sang out,

"I say Yanks, what sort of soap do you fellows use? It has washed all the color out of your faces." One of the prisoners retorted, "Damn me if you don't look like you have never used soap of any sort." The Confederates laughed and shouted, appreciating a good retort from any source, and the Reb who yelled first responded, "Bully for you, Yank. You got me that time!"[32]

Stuart entered the town about mid-morning and reported to Jackson, who requested he take the news of Harpers Ferry's capitulation to General Lee. Accordingly, leaving his staff to follow, Jeb took one courier and rode the seventeen miles to Sharpsburg.[33] He arrived in the afternoon, reported the Harpers Ferry victory in detail to Lee, and added that Jackson's command would be arriving the next day. Longstreet and D.H. Hill were already at the little village located on Antietam Creek.[34] Stuart and his staff spent the night on and around the porch of Doctor Jacob Grove, and Stonewall's men came swinging in about noon on the 16th.[35] At about the same time, Federal artillery shells began falling in the town and Union cavalrymen appeared across the creek.

The home of Dr. Grove was one of the largest in town, located across from a church, inhabited by the doctor, his wife, and daughters. As soon as shells began exploding, Von Borcke shepherded everyone into the cellar, but as he expressed it, "I had frequent occasion during the war to observe how much stronger is curiosity with women than the fear of danger," and every five minutes one of the ladies would run upstairs to see what was happening, until everyone was in the parlor again, gazing out the windows. Only when a shell hit the roof was he able to convince everyone to return to the cellar. He stayed upstairs, sitting on a sofa and writing in his journal until another shell crashed through the wall above his head and exploded, destroying much of the furniture. When another hit in the courtyard, killing one horse and terrifying the rest, he decided to find a safer place and rode out of town.[36]

The position Lee selected for battle was a hilly area on the west side of Antietam Creek. Lee's right was anchored on the river and extended about two and a half miles farther north. The right was held by Longstreet, the center by D.H. Hill, and the left by Jackson. Hampton's and Fitz Lee's brigades of Stuart's cavalry were on the left, where the Confederate line was weakest and the enemy was expected to strike.[37] Munford's brigade was on the extreme right.[38]

Lee directed Stuart to reconnoiter the enemy's strength and positions—

find out if the enemy had arrived in force or if it was only cavalry—up to and including attacking if necessary. Jeb examined the ground and advised Blackford it was unfavorable for cavalry on the offensive. Instead, he asked his engineer if he could take some couriers and find out what Lee needed to know by stealth. Blackford, who owned a powerful set of field glasses, agreed, took three men, and galloped around the right flank of the enemy. Finding a rise within 150 yards of the Federals, Blackford crawled to its summit and focused his field glasses. Individual enemy soldiers came into sufficient clarity for Blackford to see blue trimmings on their uniforms and bayonet scabbards on their belts—that meant infantry.[39]

After confirming Blackford's report by crawling to the top of the same rise, Jeb rode to the home of Dr. Grove, where Lee, Longstreet, and Jackson were in conference. Stuart's news confirmed what the three commanders had anticipated and the meeting ended. Longstreet returned to his lines and Stuart sent a message to Wade Hampton, who was coming from the direction of Harpers Ferry, to hurry along. Jackson bedded down for the night on a couch at Dr. Grove's house and Jeb spent the night either in the West Woods or on Nicodemus Heights.[40]

September 17, 1862 saw the Battle of Sharpsburg, or Antietam, remembered as the bloodiest day of all wars on American soil. Like Second Manassas it was an infantry/artillery fight, but Stuart commanded foot soldiers as well as cavalry and artillery. Jackson assigned part of his command to Stuart on the 16th, and on the 17th he sent fifteen pieces of his artillery to Jeb to place on Nicodemus Heights, a ridge that ran north to south on the Confederate left, overlooking a twenty-acre field of corn belonging to David R. Miller. Miller's cornfield yielded a harvest equal to two hundred bodies per acre that day, many of whom were scythed by the guns commanded by Stuart and Pelham on the Heights. When the focus of the Federal attacks shifted south from the cornfield to the West Woods and Dunker Church, Stuart shifted the guns, nine from the Horse Artillery and fifteen from Jackson, to a slightly lower rise behind the woods called Hauser's Ridge. At first he was given Early's brigade of infantry as support, and he posted it in the woods, but soon all but one regiment of the brigade was called away to stem a Federal penetration near the church.

When Federals under John Sedgwick attacked toward the West Woods, the twenty-four Confederate cannon unleashed a wall of canister. Stuart's horse was shot from beneath him, a courier was killed beside him, and following the destruction of Sedgwick's Corps—2,200 of his 5,200 men were casualties—Federal gunners spotted Stuart and Lafayette McLaws together and nearly dropped a shell on top of them.[41]

Jackson directed Stuart to take three infantry regiments and twenty-one pieces of artillery, along with three regiments of Fitz Lee's brigade and all of Hampton's, about 4,000 troops, and march a mile along the River Road north of Nicodemus Heights to determine if the Federal right flank could be turned. Jeb left twelve guns on Nicodemus Heights and directed Pelham to place the other nine on a wooded rise about 900 yards from the Federal right flank. There, in Pelham's words, he proceeded to "stir them up a little and then slip away." The stir resulted in return fire from thirty Federal guns that caused Stuart to pull his guns back from the wooded rise and Nicodemus Heights and march back to Jackson's line.[42]

Jeb was busy all day, commanding all branches of combat service, but the Horse Artillery contributed most to the tactical Confederate victory, made hollow by Lee's inability to either whip McClellan or to carry on the Maryland Campaign longer. Pelham's fire was so effective during and between assaults by Hooker's and Mansfield's Corps that one historian declared, "No one movement on either side bore a greater influence upon the final issue of the battle than did the advancement of Pelham's group. . . ."[43]

With both sides having exhausted themselves on the left, the battle switched to the center where horrific scenes took place in a sunken farm-road dubbed "Bloody Lane" before the Federals were finally held. The fighting then flowed to the Confederate right as Burnside's corps forced a bridge across the Antietam and appeared about to cave in Lee's flank. However, at the very last minute A.P. Hill's men arrived from Harpers Ferry and hurled themselves against the Federal ranks, forcing them back to the creek. The day of fighting saw 23,000 casualties between the two sides.

Lee boldly held his position throughout the 18th, essentially daring McClellan to attack again. The Confederate army, barely half the size of McClellan's to begin with, was terribly depleted. Riding along Jackson's line, an officer observed that there was barely one man for every rod—16.5 feet—of ground, giving the impression that a single enemy regiment could break the line essentially anywhere.[44] Nevertheless, according to Blackford, the Confederates were in splendid spirits, ready to renew the fight and "the idea that the battle was over never entered [our] minds."[45]

Someone not in good spirits was Heros Von Borcke. Having found Stuart, he accompanied him to where Stonewall Jackson was located, near some Confederate artillery batteries totaling twenty-five guns. Jackson was drinking a cup of coffee his servant had made him from the contents of a Yankee haversack and he offered some to Stuart, Von Borcke, and, when he arrived shortly thereafter, General Lee.

Leaving "these three great men to their council of war," Von Borcke retired a few yards away, lay down on the ground and gave in to uncharacteristic depression. He knew he was about to die. He had heard and read much, he reflected, both in Germany and elsewhere, of the power of "the presentment of approaching death," and he knew his time had come. He was "taken hold of . . . by the conviction that [he] should be killed before night in the coming battle, and . . . regarded any one as a profane skeptic who had tried to argue [him] out of it, and prove the foreboding nonsensical upon philosophical principles." Sadly, with earnest conviction, he made note of his impending doom in his journal.[46]

Not only did he not die, there was no battle that day. McClellan possessed the men and material to crush Lee, but not the nerve. Von Borcke would live another forty-three years. He recorded his "presentiment" in his journal and later called it the most mournful entry in the notebook, which he could not look at without laughing.

Either during that council of war or later in the afternoon, Lee directed Stuart to undertake another perilous venture. The rest of the army was crossing into Virginia, but Stuart was ordered to take a combined force of cavalry, infantry and artillery, march up the Potomac and occupy Williamsport, Maryland. From there he was to both distract McClellan and threaten his lines of supply and communication.[47]

The principal ford across the river close to Sharpsburg was Boteler's Ford, but it was being used by Confederate wagons and ambulances, and would be used by the infantry on the 19th, so Jeb asked Blackford to find an alternative place to cross. Accompanied by twenty men and not knowing why the ford was needed, the engineer rode along the river after dark, stopping every time the water looked shallow, then riding his horse, Magic, in to find out. Time after time the horse stepped off into water over its head, forcing it to swim and soaking Blackford to his chin, but eventually he found a shallow dam of loose stones designed to trap fish, below which the river was shallow enough to cross.[48]

Jeb had Blackford direct Hampton's brigade to the newly discovered ford. Fitz Lee's brigade was covering the army's crossing of the Potomac, and Stuart and his staff crossed with them at Boteler's Ford. It was late, dark, and raining. Wagons, artillery, and soldiers clogged the roads and fields. Stuart did not get started until 10 p.m., and was in too great a hurry. His shouts were ignored by wagon drivers and soldiers who either did not recognize his voice or did not care. The path to the river was churned, muddy, and so treacherous that anyone on it could barely stay upright. Von Borcke and his mount fell to the ground five times and Stuart at least once, coming close to being crushed by a heavy army wagon.[49]

Things were little better at the fish trap ford Blackford had located. Several Confederate cavalrymen who survived the battle of Sharpsburg drowned in the Potomac because the tail end of their column strayed too far to the left of the narrow passage, where the water was deeper than their horses' heads.[50]

When the sun rose on the 19th Stuart's force of all arms—two regiments of infantry, Hampton's and Munford's brigades of cavalry, and Pelham's horse artillery—were some fifteen miles upstream, near Shepherdstown. After a short rest they continued toward Williamsport, arriving about noon. Here they found a squadron of Federal cavalry that quickly retired toward Hagerstown, six miles away. The Rebels followed for a mile, then went into line of battle to meet the Federals they expected would be returning in force.[51]

Two companies of Confederate infantry threw up breastworks across the Williamsport/Hagerstown road about forty paces from a slight rise in the turnpike. As a result, the Federal cavalry that came galloping down the road to attack the Rebels did not see what lay ahead until they were nearly on top of the foot soldiers. A Rebel captain gave the command to fire and more than a hundred rifles belched smoke and lead in the direction of the blue horsemen, hitting not a single man or horse, the hasty volley going over the heads of the attackers.[52]

The rest of the day and the next witnessed skirmishing back and forth. At one point Von Borcke was nearly captured when he accepted an invitation to share dinner with a local farmer, only to have federal cavalry attack as they were sitting down to the meal. At another point a young lady from Williamsport was allowed the honor of pulling the lanyard and firing one of the guns of Pelham's artillery, earning her the sobriquet of "the girl of Williamsport." That evening Jeb and his staff attended a party at which there was music and dancing.[53]

The 20th saw more skirmishing. Stuart and Von Borcke had a narrow escape when a force of twenty-five Federals used thick underbrush to conceal their movements and managed to get between the pair and their own lines. Von credited their escape to superior horseflesh and horsemanship. Late in the afternoon, the prisoners being taken, which were from different infantry divisions, made it apparent that McClellan had dispatched a sizeable force to dislodge Stuart from Williamsport, which was Lee's original goal. Nevertheless, thinking the enemy was still far away, Jeb ordered Hampton to lead his brigade under cover of darkness to Hagerstown, get in the enemy's rear, and do as much damage as possible. Everyone except Stuart believed the move was a bad idea, so much so that Hampton shook hands with Von Borcke before leaving and told him, "I don't think you will ever see me or a man of my brave brigade again." Before long, however, concentrated fire from Federal artillery and infantry convinced Stuart to reconsider his order, recall Hampton, recross the Potomac, and return to Virginia. By 11 p.m. the gray soldiers were back in the Old Dominion.[54]

Today, 150 years after the battle, Sharpsburg is generally considered a Confederate defeat, the end of Lee's first invasion of the North, the victory that justified Lincoln's issuance of the Emancipation Proclamation. That was not how the Rebels in Lee's army viewed it at the time. The Confederates were ready, as Blackford described, to renew the battle, and that attitude was not limited to uninformed soldiers in the ranks. Von Borcke wrote that "we remained masters of the entire field of battle covered with the enemy's dead and wounded," although "[t]he victory would certainly have been more complete, had not General McLaws failed to obey orders in bringing his division of nearly 7,000 men earlier into the fight, and by the tardiness of his movements to a considerable extent thwarted the combinations of his commander-in-chief."[55] Blackford wrote that when McClellan failed to renew the battle on the 18th that "it was with the belief that we were the victors."[56] Stuart, writing to Flora five days after the fight, said, "We're in Virginia again but only for a short time, we hope to be in Penna. very soon." He acknowledged that the Yankees were claiming victory, but intimated that recrossing the Potomac "was necessary for a different reason," and "[t]he result will show."[57]

On September 21, Stuart and his two brigades continued in the direction of Lee's army, serving primarily to continue screening the army from McClellan. They reached Martinsburg about noon and bivouacked, with Jeb making his headquarters about a mile out of town.

Von Borcke and Pelham visited the home of Captain Ephraim Alburtis that evening. Alburtis commanded the battery in which Pelham served dur-

ing the battle of First Manassas, but had resigned his command due to illness. He was a resident of Martinsburg, and the visit by Von and Pelham
was the equivalent of a modern-day visit from movie stars. They enjoyed
a meal and then sat around the table, with Alburtis's family listening raptly
while Von Borcke regaled everyone with tales of daring and adventure. The
Prussian did most of the talking, but devoted his bragging to events in which
Pelham figured prominently, causing the young artillery commander to
blush so deeply that Alburtis talked about it for years afterward, saying
"good Lord, how he did blush when Major Von Borcke told us all about
him. I never saw anybody get quite so red as that boy, and yet he laughed
about it too." They stayed until late, then departed amidst hugs, handshakes
and tears.[58]

The next day, September 22, Stuart led his men to the village of Hainesville, near Berkeley, Virginia, and made his headquarters in the yard of a
tavern, then dispatched his cavalry to cover a thirty-mile front from Williamsport to Harpers Ferry. The bulk of Lee's army was near Winchester,
but Stuart's supply wagons had stopped at Hainesville and the horsemen
were able to change clothes, reunite with their servants, obtain fresh horses
and restore themselves. Fitz Lee's brigade had rejoined Stuart, and Jeb
placed it near Shepherdstown. Hampton stayed near Hainesville and Munford was sent to Charlestown, opposite Harpers Ferry, where John Brown
had been hanged three years previously.[59]

Jeb wrote two letters to Flora that day, and sent Von Borcke, with half
the staff, to Charlestown to establish a second headquarters there.[60] Pelham
was dispatched to Millwood, where he set up camp at the plantation of
Major George Burwell, called Carter Hall, and there received word of his
promotion to major that day, backdated effective as of August 9.[61] Pelham's
promotion was probably part of a general reorganization of the military
structure of the Confederate armies. On September 18, the Confederate
Congress approved creation of the rank of Lieutenant General, which had
not existed in the Confederate army before and which still did not exist in
the Federal armies. At Lee's recommendation, Longstreet and Jackson were
given the rank, suitable for corps command, and Brigadier Generals Hood
and Pickett were promoted to Major General. Additionally, fifteen colonels
were promoted to brigadier general, including Rooney Lee, who would
soon command a brigade under Stuart.[62]

September 23 through 27 were days of rest for Stuart and his staff. The
army as a whole was recuperating, gathering in stragglers, readjusting from

the Sharpsburg campaign, and preparing for what would come next. Stuart's headquarters were near Hainesville, five miles from Martinsburg, and he was planning a special surprise for his good friend, Stonewall Jackson. Pelham, still near Millwood, was reorganizing the Stuart Horse Artillery. Along with his elevation in rank came more guns and more men, so that he now had five batteries totaling twenty-two guns and 600 men in his battalion. He divided the unit into two sections, the First Stuart Horse Artillery, under the command of Captain James Breathed, and the Second Stuart Horse Artillery, under the command of Captain Mathis Winston Henry, both of whom were promoted on the same day as Pelham.[63]

Only four months, one-third, of the year of glory was behind Jeb Stuart and his companions. Immediately ahead lay a full month of relaxation and much more adventure, overshadowed by a nearing rendezvous with tragedy.

CHAPTER SIX

THE SECOND RIDE
AROUND McCLELLAN
SEPTEMBER 28–OCTOBER 12, 1862

Tis old Stonewall the Rebel that leans on his sword
and while we are mounting, prays low to the Lord.
Now each cavalier that loves Honor and Right,
let him follow the feather of Stuart tonight.

Chorus: Come tighten your girth and slacken your rein;
come buckle your blanket and holster again.
Try the click of your trigger and balance your blade,
for he must ride sure that goes Riding a Raid!

Now gallop, now gallop, to swim or to ford!
Old Stonewall, still watching, prays low to the Lord.
Good-bye dear old Rebel! The river's not wide,
and Maryland's lights in her window to guide.
—Riding a Raid

Autumn—a closing off and a gathering in time—came to the Army of Northern Virginia and to Stuart's cavalry. As John Thomason described the autumn of 1862 in the Valley of Virginia, it "is the loveliest season of the year. The air is like wine, and smells like apples, and in the afternoon the hills lie soft under thin, golden sunlight, their contours molded by the lengthening shadows. Hard outlines lose persistence, and take on a painted quality, and the brooding mountains run off to north and south, unbeliev-ably blue. The grass is green, but the leaves are beginning to turn, so that the wooded slopes look as fine as Persian rugs, with their sharp colors blended to a softness. Ride there, and see why Virginians love Virginia."[1]

On September 28, Stuart moved his headquarters to "The Bower," the plantation home of Adam S. Dandridge, located in Jefferson County near Leetown. The brick house, built by slave labor in 1805, was two and a half-storied with fourteen rooms. It set on a hill overlooking Opequon Creek and had a front porch that faced west toward the sunset and huge oaks, while a second story porch in the rear provided a marvelous view of the Blue Ridge Mountains, particularly North Mountain.[2]

Jeb, his staff, couriers, and servants—about 100 men—pitched their tents in a park-like area a few hundred yards from the house, with Stuart's tent nearer the house, beneath a large tree known thereafter as "Stuart's Oak."[3] Around them the horses, flags, pets, long dining table, desks, camp chairs, stools, firewood, cook fires, forage, pots, pans, skillets, coffee pots, boxes, blankets, cots, weapons, ammunition, saddles, foodstuffs, and equipment of an army were stacked, piled, hanged, and arranged for a lengthy occupation.

Dandridge, in his fifties, owned more than 100 slaves who kept the grounds immaculate. He was related to Martha Dandridge Custis Washington, the wife of George Washington, and he was honored to have Stuart and his men at his home. He and his wife, Serena Pendleton Dandridge, had ten children: five sons and five daughters. The two oldest boys, Adam Stephen III and Edmund Pendleton, were already in the Confederate army, and the next oldest, Lemuel Purnell was a cadet at VMI. The two youngest boys, Phillip Spotswood and Alexander Spotswood were at home. The youngest daughter, Martha Pendleton, or "Mattie," was three and became Stuart's special darling. He often put her in front of him on his saddle as he rode through the camp. The two oldest daughters, Sallie and Serena, a cousin, Lily, and various guests and visitors, were "grown and attractive—some very handsome" according to Blackford, and "exceedingly hand-some" according to Von Borcke.[4] Daughters Mary Roberta and Ann Buchanan were adolescents.

Although The Bower had not been damaged by the war, it was not untouched, and Mr. Dandridge, starting in 1861, kept a record of all horses, hogs, crops, and slaves lost or destroyed by the Union army. A list of accounts due was written in his ledger book under the heading "Abraham Lincoln to A.S. Dandridge."[5]

A historian described Stuart's headquarters at the Bower as "the envy of all commands," and "Half the staff were in love with the Dandridge girls or their visiting cousins," so that "the house was under constant siege."[6] Kyd Douglass, of Stonewall's staff, wrote that "a merry headquarters it was. Mr. Dandridge and his delightful family seemed to turn over the house to the army, and vacant rooms were crowded with young lady visitors who never complained for want of room. The debonair Stuart, the gay cavaliers of his staff, and others of similar tastes, filled the house with a sound of revelry every evening. The sound of Sweeney's banjo and string band, the heavy step of martial heels drowning the soft sound of little feet lightly clad, the musical laughter of the dance, might be often heard late into the night."[7]

Stuart and his entourage remained there a month. The home is still owned by descendants of the Dandridge family and is listed in the National Registry of Historic Places. A one-and-a-half-story gabled roof wing was added on the north side, and a long front porch was added in 1881 (as well as the house's only bathroom). Tragically, a fire gutted the interior in March 1892, but did not damage the walls, and the home was carefully restored.[8]

During the month Jeb and his men were there the first floor of the mansion was open for visits at nearly all times. It contained a "great hall" perfect for musicals, skits, and dances which occurred on an almost daily basis. The members of Stuart's staff were fully aware of the image they presented. "To the eyes of the lovely girls who peeped through the curtains of their chambers in the light of the early morn, we were heroes of romance fresh from the fields of glory—patriots ready and pining to die in the cause of their country," wrote Blackford. "With such prepossessions in our favor it would have been strange indeed if the handsome young men of the staff and the gay and gallant commander of our cavalry had failed to win the friendship of our charming neighbors during the month we spent at the Bower."[9]

As Blackford noted in his memoirs, "This was before wounds and deaths made serious inroads into our military family. Hardeman Stuart . . . was the only one of us who had fallen up to that time, and little I thought how many of those assembled at the Bower would share his fate."[10] Indeed, a time traveler awarded one trip in which to witness the naïve optimism and tunnel-visioned gaiety of the young Confederacy, seasoned with romance, soundtracked with music, and celebrated by nightly dances and balls could select no better site than The Bower during the month of October 1862.

Von Borcke arrived at The Bower on the 28th and had an interesting brush with history of a different kind. A Federal deserter arrived in Stuart's camp claiming to be a former officer of Engineers in the Prussian army so he was turned over to Von to ascertain if his abilities might be put to use in the service of the Confederate cavalry. Von, however, quickly determined that the man was "a great humbug," and got rid of him.

The man was Hans Von Winklestein, aka Henry Van Steinacker. Three years later, during the trial of the conspirators in the assassination of Abraham Lincoln, he would be one of 371 witnesses who testified against the accused, claiming that that while on a horse ride with John Wilkes Booth in the summer of 1863, Booth told him that "Old Abe must go up the spout [be killed], and the Confederacy will gain its independence." At the time Winklestein was imprisoned for desertion and was released shortly after testifying, making his credibility suspect even then. No other witness attributed intent on the part of Booth to do anything to Lincoln earlier than 1864, and his initial planning was to kidnap the president. Accordingly, Winklestein's claims received attention in newspapers in 1865 that Von Borcke read and noted while writing his memoirs.[11]

September 30 was spent squaring away the new camp. Early on October 1 Jeb wrote to Flora telling her of his new headquarters, mentioning bouquets and ribbons girls were "always sending," but assuring her that his heart "ever turns to *my* darling and the loved ones prattling at her knees." He said he would not be able to visit her and expressed the hope she would spend October and November in Staunton with Sandy Stuart, Jeb's nephew. After he completed the letter, pickets reported seeing Federal cavalry across the Potomac, then crossing and advancing on Martinsburg. At Jeb's direction, Fitz Lee's brigade, commanded by Colonel Rooney Lee due to Fitz having been kicked by a mule, and Hampton's brigade went into action.

Arriving outside Martinsburg, they found it in enemy hands, which disgusted Stuart. He quickly made that known to Lee and Hampton, saying, "Gentlemen, this thing will not do; I will give you twenty minutes, within which time the town must be again in our possession."

The roads into town were lined with stone walls, making it impossible to advance in line of battle, so each of two brigades formed in columns of platoons, on separate roads, and charged simultaneously at full gallop, sabers drawn, with Stuart and Von Borcke in the lead while Pelham boomed away with four guns from a nearby hill. The Federals did not wait to give battle but quickly withdrew through Shepherdstown with Stuart and Lee's brigade in pursuit, which was not broken off until the Federals were back across the Potomac.

On the return ride, Jeb and his staff stopped to visit Mrs. Lily Parin Lee, the widow of Colonel William F. Lee, in Shepherdstown. Stuart had served with Lee at Jefferson Barracks in Missouri before the war, and gave him a pair of silver spurs. When Stuart visited Mrs. Lee on this occasion, she insisted that he take the spurs again, which he did. The spurs were silver rather than gold, and Jeb is best remembered for wearing the latter and for adopting the initials "KGS" for "Knight of the Golden Spurs," in connection with spurs that would be a gift from a lady in Baltimore. A year and eight months later, however, Jeb would be wearing the silver spurs at Yellow Tavern, and would direct from his deathbed that they be returned to Mrs. Lee.[12]

Even though it was past dark, the word that the famous cavalry chief was visiting at Mrs. Lee's house spread through town. Soon the house was besieged by what Von described as a mob of squealing young girls, some armed with scissors and all seeking souvenirs. Buttons and locks of hair were snipped from the laughing Stuart. Soon his uniform coat was entirely void of buttons, "and if he had given as many locks of his hair as were asked for . . . [he] would soon have been totally bald." Jeb compromised by insisting that the young ladies be satisfied with a kiss instead, which was as rewarding for him as the womenfolk, although the staff lamented that "this latter favour was unhappily not extended to" them.

It was at Mrs. Lee's house that evening that Jeb wrote three stanzas of parody on the song *Maryland My Maryland*, dedicated to his horse. The group returned to The Bower after midnight and found Mr. Dandridge and servants waiting up with cold ham to make up for the dinner they were denied while in pursuit of the Yankees.[13]

On October 2, Stuart received a packet of documents from Lee that were to be delivered across enemy lines to General McClellan. Jeb decided to assign the task to Von Borcke, and once again Von had a brush with history, although he did not fully comprehend it when it occurred.

Von wrote that "To make a favourable impression upon 'our friends the enemy,' I fitted myself out as handsomely as the very seedy condition of my wardrobe would allow; and as all my own horses were, more or less, broken-down, I borrowed a high-stepping, fine-limbed chestnut from one of my comrades of the Staff for the occasion."[14] Neither Von Borcke nor

Blackford said it, but the high-stepping chestnut had to have been Black-ford's Magic, the "dark chestnut without a white hair," described previously, who suffered from equine A.D.D."[15]

Stuart directed Von to take along some fifty Yankee prisoners for exchange, and Von brought couriers to serve as guards. Another courier car-ried a flag of truce—a white handkerchief on a long pole. The huge Pruss-ian was met by a major who accepted the prisoners and offered to carry the documents to McClellan, but Von Borcke insisted he must see them personally into the hands of a high-ranking officer such as Pleasonton.

As the two majors conversed, "all the Yankee soldiers who were not on duty" came running over to get a look at the "great big rebel officer." So many crowded in that the Federal major had a detail of sentries surround Von Borcke to keep the men back. Waiting for further developments within his cordon of Yankee sentries, Von Borcke was provided with a camp stool, on which he entered into a debate with a group of Federal officers about "who won the Battle of Sharpsburg."

He was allowed to ride with a young officer to the headquarters of Major General Fitz John Porter. He saw that the Federal camp was huge, the soldiers well fed and well armed, and the headquarters tent exceptionally fancy. The more he looked, the more gaudy things appeared. Two regiments of Zouaves, resplendent in wide red pantaloons, short jackets, and fezzes, were drawn up in dress parade. There was a "little town of canvass" sur-rounding the "magnificent marquee" of General Porter. The headquarters flag was unusually large and there was bunting decorating tent fronts. An unusual number of well-dressed sentries were pacing about and a lot of mounted officers, "resplendent with bullion," were galloping about impor-tantly. A hot air balloon was tethered and floating over the camp, and Porter's headquarters was a huge, decorated pavilion, "under which was stretched out a long table laden with luxuries of every description, bottles of champagne in silver ice-coolers, a profusion of delicious fruit, and immense bouquets of flowers." Von Borcke figured out that someone impor-tant was expected other than himself.

The expected visitor was none other than President Lincoln. Near there, at Grove Farm, the famous post-Antietam photos of McClellan and Abe Lincoln were taken, probably the same day. When Von Borcke was finally introduced to Porter the first thing out of the General's mouth was, "You will allow me to express my regret that you have been brought here, and to say that a grave fault has been committed in your coming."

James Ewell Brown ("Jeb") Stuart, commander of the cavalry of the
Army of Northern Virginia and the idol of thousands during his
spectacular year of battlefield success.

A beardless Jeb Stuart (standing) along with West Point classmates Custis Lee,
left (son of Robert E. Lee) and Stephen Dill Lee (no relation), circa 1854.
S.D. Lee went on to become a lieutenant general while Custis served mainly
in Richmond, ending the war as a major general.

Copyright 1914
E. O. Higgins

The Prussian soldier and aristocrat Heros von Borcke became one of Stuart's closest aides during the Civil War, though at six-foot-four and 240 pounds, it was inevitable that a Yankee bullet would eventually find him.

Thomas J. ("Stonewall") Jackson was hardly known for the sartorial splendor this painting suggests. However, at the Battle of Fredericksburg he did show up in a brand new uniform, given him by Jeb Stuart, much to the amazement of onlooking Confederate troops.

Von Borcke and Porter exchanged a few words and Von was hastened on his way, but not detained. He paused long enough to write a note to a major serving on McClellan's staff who was from Prussia, then accompanied the same young officer who had brought him to Porter's headquarters. He arrived back at The Bower and the inevitable, ongoing dance about 10 p.m. and gave a full report to Stuart, who told him, "My dear Von, you shall have thirty minutes dancing, and then a fresh horse shall be saddled for you, and you must be off at once to make your reports to Generals Jackson and Lee." Thirty minutes later, Jeb cut in as Von was dancing with "a very pretty girl," and said, "Be off, my dear fellow; I will do your duty here." Both performed accordingly.[16]

The next several days were quiet in a military sense and busy in regard to socializing. The talents of Sam Sweeney and his band of musicians were fully utilized, in addition to which the staff contained a "capital band of singers."[17] They played, sang, and danced every evening, according to Blackford, and Von wrote that Sweeney played "sentimental, bibulous, martial, nautical, [and] comic songs out of number," "assisted by two of our couriers who played the violin, musicians of inferior merit," and that Sweeney's "chief reliance was in Mulatto Bob, Stuart's servant, who worked the bones with the most surprising and extraordinary agility, and became so excited that both head and feet were in constant employment, and his body twisted about so rapidly and curiously that one could not help fearing that he would dislocate his limbs and fly to pieces in the midst of the breakdown."[18]

Stuart was at the center of the celebrations, being the "noisiest of the party," who "did not like it at all if any one of his Staff officers withdrew himself from these innocent merry-makings, after the fatigues of the day, to seek an early rest, and would always rouse him from his slumbers to take part in the revelry."[19] Music and dancing were not the only diversions. The great hall was the scene of skits and comic theatrics as well. Von Borcke was a primary, if not dominant, contributor to these productions, but he had an ally in Tierman Brien, even though the former staff officer and Lt. Colonel had officially resigned his commission.

In one of Von's and Brien's productions, a sheet was stretched across the hall, lit with lamps from behind, and the two men occupied the area between the screen and the illumination so that their shadows provided the performance. The scene opened with Von Borcke wearing "Mr. Dandridge's capricious nightshirt," stuffed with pillows so that he appeared even more huge than normal, stretched out on a table attended by a nurse and doctor, the latter being Brien. The doctor was wearing "an old mashed stovepipe hat, huge spectacles, an old-fashioned swallow-tailed coat of some Dandridge of past generations" and carried a battered umbrella.

Von groaned in agony and the doctor produced a bottle of "physic with a streaming label attached to the neck," from which a large dose was administered amidst a stream of medical jargon, after which the doctor took a swig himself. The patient, still moaning, began to twitch while simultaneously describing to the doctor that he'd attended a dinner party and consumed a ludicrous number of items, including oysters, cabbage, venison, beef, and other foodstuffs. Doctor Brien examined him, took his pulse, and pressed on the patient's mountainous stomach, causing Von Borcke to cry "Mein Gott! Mein Gott! Doctor!," after which the doctor forced his arm down the patient's throat and began, "with great effort of muscular power expended in jerks and tugs," pulling out and holding up for inspection a set of antlers, a pair of cow horns, a complete cabbage, a whole watermelon, handfuls of oyster shells, stalks of corn, and finally a pair of boots. As each item, or its shadow, was removed from the patient's gullet, the nurse, or a hidden assistant, removed a pillow that comprised the huge belly until a complete cure was accomplished. Doctor and patient then polished off the rest of the physic, became tipsy, and concluded the performance with a silly dance.

The audience regarded the performance as hilarious. Blackford wrote that it was a performance "I have rarely seen equaled and its effect on the audience was convulsive. All the negroes on the place were allowed to come in to see it and their intense appreciation of the scene, and their rich, broad peals of laughter added no little to its attractions."[20]

Von and Brien ventured into theatre again on October 7, when a "grand ball" was held at The Bower, to which Mr. Dandridge invited families from Martinsburg, Shepherdstown, and Charlestown, as well as Stuart and his staff. No theatre was on the agenda but the two clownish officers prepared a secret pantomime that Von called "The Pennsylvania Farmer and his Wife."

Colonel Brien portrayed the farmer, with pillows stuffed beneath a large greatcoat. Von wore an old ball gown belonging to Mrs. Dandridge that "was enlarged in every direction," and his hair was "sweetly ornamented with half-a-bushel of artificial flowers."[21] The pair waited until the ball was "quite en train," then entered the great hall.

Mr. and Mrs. Dandridge were the only ones who knew in advance what would take place. The two officers' absence was just being noticed when they appeared, although supposedly no one recognized them immediately. "Von Borcke was transformed into a blushing maiden weighing two hundred and fifty pounds and six feet two and half inches tall; a riding skirt . . . supplemented by numerous dainty underskirts and extended by enormous hoops according to the fashion then in vogue, hung in graceful folds to conceal the huge cavalry boots the huge damsel wore. Her naturally ample bosom palpitated under skillfully arranged pillows, and was gorgeously decorated with the Dandridge family jewelry and ribbons, while 'a love of a bonnet,' long braids of hair, and quantities of powder and rouge completed her toilet."

They promenaded among the guests, Von flirting "coquettishly" and using an enormous fan to hide his whiskers, while Brien made humorous remarks to which Von responded "with a simpering affectation that was irresistibly ludicrous." Their appearance and costumes were a surprise to everyone, and before the laughter and delight had subsided in the least, the band struck up a waltz and they took to the dance floor. "Round and round the couple went, faster and faster went the music, and faster and faster flew the strangers. It was not until in a fury of the whirling dance, with hoop skirts flying horizontally, that twinkling amid the white drapery beneath, the well-known boots of von Borcke betrayed the first suspicion of who the lady was." Then as suddenly as they had come they vanished, waltzing out through the open door followed by convulsive roars of laughter from the delighted audience.[22]

The next day, October 8th, Stuart gave Von Borcke another assignment, partly official but mostly not. He'd arranged a gift for Stonewall, one he'd planned for weeks—a new uniform coat. It isn't clear when Jeb had it made, and considering his correspondence with Flora about his own jackets and trousers, it seems likely that he would have arranged the order through her, but if so that correspondence has been lost. In any event, the coat was magnificent, a fine example of a tailored general's frock complete with four rows of gold braid on each sleeve, three stars in an oak leaf cluster on each side of the collar, and double rows of gilded brass buttons. It is the coat he wore in the best known of his photographs.

Von Borcke found Jackson "in his old weather-stained coat, from which all the buttons were clipped long since by the fair hands of patriotic ladies, and which, from exposure to sun and rain and powder-smoke, and by reason of many rents and patches, was in a very unseemly condition." Jackson acted appreciative, but barely touched the coat, telling Von, "Give Stuart my best thanks, my dear Major, the coat is much too handsome for me, but I shall take the best care of it, and shall prize it highly as a souvenir. And now let us have some dinner."

He attempted to fold up the gift and put it away but Von protested, telling Jackson that Stuart must know whether the coat fit and that he, Von Borcke, could not return without having an answer, so Stonewall finally agreed to put it on for dinner, which was served at a table outside. When Jackson's staff saw him they "were in a perfect ecstasy at their chief's brilliant appearance, and the old negro servant, who was bearing the roast-turkey from the fire to the board, stopped in mid-career with a most bewildered expression, and gazed in wonderment at his master as if he were transfigured before him." Word of the remarkable development spread through the army camp and soon soldiers "came running by hundreds to the spot, desirous of seeing their beloved Stonewall in his new attire."[23]

Stuart, that same day, was planning a new, unusual raid. In fact, of all the various excursions, forays, and campaigns that Stuart made, this may have been his most remarkable. It would be the single raid his granddaughter, in a memoir of the Stuart family published in 2012, selected as the one that best demonstrated the daring and the accomplishments of her grandfather.[24]

It was actually Robert E. Lee's idea, although Stuart had told staff members on more than one occasion that he wanted to "visit" Pennsylvania. The details of the raid were kept secret until the day it began, and considering the content of Jeb's letter to Flora on September 22, when he said they would be in Pennsylvania soon, it may have been hatched immediately after Sharpsburg, when Lee sent Stuart on the feint to Williamsport, Maryland. Final orders for it were issued by Lee on October 8.

The raid had two principal goals, two ancillary goals, and several potential benefits. The primary goals were to ascertain the location of McClellan's army and destroy the railroad bridge over the Conococheague Creek at Scotland, near Chambersburg, Pennsylvania. The Cumberland Valley Railroad used the bridge to carry supplies to Hagerstown for McClellan's army, and if destroyed would leave only the Baltimore and Ohio line as a Federal source of supply.[25] The secondary goals were to collect horses for the cavalry's use and to capture governmental officials to use as exchange for "our own citizens that have been carried off by the enemy," as Lee put it.[26]

The Confederates' acute need for horses was recently made worse by an outbreak of disease and diarrhea among Southern livestock. The direction regarding captives was uncharacteristic of the chivalrous Confederate leader and was in response to the imprisonment of civilians accused of disloyalty to the Union and incarcerated by the Federals. The practice began early, with Lincoln's suspension of habeas corpus in 1861, and was invoked with a particular sense of vengeance under Pope.[27] Southerners were imprisoned but potentially available for exchange. The military exchange rate being an officer for an officer and an enlisted man for an enlisted man, the Confederates also needed human currency to exchange civilians.

The additional, beneficial effects of the raid were the securing of military supplies, the destruction of what could not be carried off, and the creation of a diversion that would keep the Federals from reinforcing the Kanawha Valley of West Virginia so that Confederates might take possession of valuable salt mines in that area.[28] The fact that the raid would be great fun and, if successful, would enhance Jeb's reputation were additional incentives.

A total of 1,800 cavalrymen were selected, 600 each from Stuart's three brigades. W.E. "Grumble" Jones, promoted to Brigadier on September 19, was given command of the detachment from Munford's brigade. Hampton would lead his 600 and Rooney Lee would command those from Fitz Lee's brigade. Pelham would bring four pieces of artillery, two each from Breathed's and Hart's batteries, along with sixty men.[29] A principal condition for each man's selection was the condition of his horse, and this is what probably led to the exclusion of Von Borcke, although he recorded that "it was yet necessary that I should remain, to fill his place in [Stuart's] absence, to act for him in case of emergency, and to keep up frequent communications with General Lee."[30]

After another ball on the evening of October 8, ending about 11 p.m., Stuart and his staff returned to their tents and spent two hours preparing. Then Jeb reassembled his staff, as well as Sweeney and Bob, a violin player, and returned to The Bower "and gave a farewell serenade to the ladies."[31]

The troops from Lee's brigade mustered at The Bower at 8 a.m. Orders for the raid were issued as Order No. 13, dated October 9 and signed by Lt. Channing Price, saying in part that horses were to be seized and one-third of the troopers were to be assigned as horse leaders, three horses to a man, placed in the center of each brigade. All horses were to be receipted in the name of the Confederate States, but no private property was to be touched in the state of Maryland, still considered a Confederate ally. The public functionaries of each town were to be taken prisoner but treated kindly. No straggling, looting, or foraging was allowed.

The 1,800 rendezvoused near Darksville on the afternoon of the 9th and moved twelve miles north toward McCoy's Ford, near Clear Springs, Maryland at the mouth of Black Creek. After dark, in order to conceal their approach from a Federal signal station on the Maryland side of the river they approached Hedgesville and went into a fireless bivouac. Stuart had prepared an address that was delivered that evening:

> Soldiers! You are about to engage in an enterprise which, to insure success, imperatively demands at your hands coolness, decision and bravery; implicit obedience to orders without a question or cavil; and the strictest order and sobriety on the march and in bivouac. The destination and extent of this expedition had better be kept to myself than known to you. Suffice it to say that with the hearty cooperation of officers and men I have not a doubt of its success— a success which will reflect credit in the highest degree upon your arms. The orders which are here published for your government are absolutely necessary and must be rigidly enforced.[32]

Jeb probably did not actually speak the words but had them printed for distribution, and there can be doubt that many of the 1,800 burned to know their destination, while a few more wondered exactly what "cavil" meant.[33]

Stuart and Hampton rode to the ford to decide their approach. Hampton selected twenty-five men from his brigade under the command of Lt. H.R. Phillips of the 10th Virginia, and Col. M.C. Butler added seven more from the 2nd South Carolina, one of whom was an experienced scout, Lt. Robert Shiver. These thirty-two soldiers crossed the river about 3 a.m. in order to surround and capture the Federal pickets on the other side. The rest of the men turned in for as much sleep as they could, knowing it might be their last for awhile. Jeb and his military family, including Pelham, caught a little rest in a haystack , or "hayrick," in an open field.[34]

The command was in the saddle before daylight on the 10th, and upon hearing shots they splashed across the Potomac. Phillips and Shiver did not succeed in capturing the pickets, but they drove them away from the main body of their troops. One of the enemy was wounded and several horses were captured.[35]

The entire command was soon across and on the National Turnpike heading toward Mercersburg. Luck was with them, as a heavy fog obscured their movements. They soon discovered that an entire division of Yankee infantry, under Major General Jacob Cox, was moving on the turnpike ahead of them. Cox had been promoted to major general only four days earlier, and his first accomplishment at that rank was to lose ten stragglers from the tail of his command to the 2nd South Carolina. Cox turned off toward Hancock, oblivious to what lurked behind, while the Confederates proceeded on the turnpike.[36] Citizens reported that Cox's men consisted of six regiments of Ohio troops on their way to the Kanawha Valley. This was exactly the type of information the raid was intended to provide, and Stuart sent word of Cox's movement to General Lee by telegraph at his first opportunity.[37]

Twenty Rebels were dispatched to capture the signal station near Crystal Springs, at Fairview, and they managed to get within a hundred feet before being spotted. The two officers at the station fled, leaving two privates, equipment, and papers to be captured.[38]

The Federals learned of Stuart's presence by at least 5 a.m., when a citizen reported to a captain in the 12th Illinois Cavalry that they were crossing at McCoy's Ford. By 7:30, the news had reached Brig. Gen. John R. Kenly, at Williamsport, and by 10 a.m. word was forwarded to Brig. Gen. William Brooks, at Hagerstown, that Stuart was headed to that place. Both of these men commanded infantry, whereas cavalry were needed to intercept the raiders, so the Confederate horsemen were temporarily free from pursuit.

As the Rebels neared Pennsylvania, the men "became wild with enthusiasm, and eagerly watched for the line so the fun would begin."[39] Once across the state line the rule against taking private property would no longer be in effect. The column was already in position for the all-important task of rounding up horses, which was accomplished in two ways. The first approach was for the 600 men of the front brigade to serve as advance guard and the last 600 as rear guard while the middle 600 spread out and rounded up animals from nearby fields and led them back to the column. Within the center division, groups of six to a dozen soldiers and one officer operated together, dashing out to round up horses whenever they were seen or suspected.

This second approach was facilitated by the weather, which was rainy, so that the Pennsylvania farmers were in their barns threshing wheat, using machines powered by horses. Each time a thresher was heard, a group of cavalryman would ride over, knock on the barn door with the hilt of a saber, and then relieve the farmer of his horses. A great many of these were large Conestogas, not suitable for cavalry but ideal for artillery, and when these were found the Rebels led them away in the same harness they wore in the threshers, partly for convenience but principally because the animals were too large for collars used by Confederate batteries.[40]

Sometimes the Confederates were mistaken for or would identify themselves as Federal soldiers conscripting horses for the Union. This elicited a string of vindictives and cursing of the army, the Federal government, the war in general, and Lincoln in particular, which the Rebels found highly amusing. "After allowing the farmer to air his patriotism for awhile," Blackford wrote, "our men would admit they held the same unfriendly opinion of Lincoln, and then tell the astounding fellow who they were. Generally he would not believe the statement at first and the expression on his face, and the faces of the men working with him, as the truth broke upon them, was very amusing.[41]

Of greater interest were the pantries, in which "there was no end to the stores of good things they had on hand." Blackford went along on several of the horse roundups and had a great time, being rewarded in every case by amusing scenes. Altogether the raiding parties gathered so much bread and baked goods that all 1,800 men were fully supplied.

At one house visited by men of the 9th Virginia, all of the menfolk had fled, leaving only women and babies. The troopers asked for food but were told there was none. Pretty certain that was not true, a lean Rebel fixed the ladies with a wolfish grin and declared, "I'm hungry enough to try one of them babies if there's nothing else to eat." A meal was quickly provided.[42]

The first town they came to in Pennsylvania, about noon, was Mercersburg. Local militia fired a few shots, melted away, and the Confederates rode in. Blackford was informed that a map of Franklin County—a valuable prize—was located at the home of a citizen, so he called on the house to obtain it. The door was answered by a lady, or at least a female, there being only womenfolk in the house, all of whom Blackford described as "rough specimens." His request for the map was refused, so he pushed by the infuriated ladies and found the map hanging on a wall. He took it and retreated, observing that, "Angry women do not show to advantage, and [the] looks of these were fearful."[43]

The column was on the move again by 2 p.m. and a lady flagged down some of them outside town and asked if there was any "news from the Rebels." The Southerners exchanged amused glances and proceeded to tell her the Rebel army was met and destroyed, and that they were "on the way back from whippin' 'em now." The lady, greatly relieved, asked, "Would any of you good Union boys like some good brandy? It's good and old. I've been saving it for some Union soldiers." The Rebs accepted and she poured it into canteens before the troopers rode on. One, however, could not resist turning and calling back that, oh by the way, "We're Jeff Davis guerilla boys." The lady was last seen throwing her hands over her head and dropping her reading glasses.[44]

Five miles out of town they paused to feed their horses with corn taken directly from surrounding fields. Chambersburg was twenty miles away, rain was falling, and the roads were muddy. Pelham's guns and men had become so dirty and "grotesque," that upon riding past the little battery, Stuart asked the young major, "Where did you get all the farmers?" The artillerymen present called themselves farmers thereafter. The going was difficult, but an advantage of having hundreds of spare horses was that as soon as one tired, cavalry or artillery, it could be exchanged quickly for a fresh animal.[45]

The next towns up the road were Campbellstown and St. Thomas, where Stuart's men encountered local militiamen who fled after firing a few shots, making their presence known so briefly that Blackford reported "not a shadow of opposition" during the entire day.[46] The job of rounding up horses continued, but Stuart ordered that horses ridden or driven by women were to be left alone.[47] One elderly lady the Confederates encountered at a farmhouse came out to the barn from which a string of horses was being led and asked that they not take the animal she used for her buggy, as she had owned him since he was a colt and he was now thirty-five years old. Blackford found that claim difficult to believe, as it would mean the animal was the equivalent of 125 in human years. However, upon examining the animal and noting its gray hairs and teeth worn down to the gums, he directed that the animal be returned to her.[48]

At dark on the 10th, with light rain still falling, the column reached a hill near Chambersburg about 8 p.m., having covered forty miles. Not knowing whether the enemy occupied or might soon occupy the town, Stuart decided to secure the place before going into camp. He did not know that two men had arrived earlier to warn the city of the approaching Rebels, so that local officials had fled, the bankers hid the cash, stores were locked up, and a band of militia had formed to defend the town.[49]

Chambersburg was one of the few Northern cities that saw a healthy share of war, but this was its first such experience, and the Confederates heard drums beating the long roll, calling out its defenders. Stuart had Pelham place two of his guns on the hill and sent nine men under a flag of truce to demand unconditional surrender.

With no town fathers to make a decision, the colonel of the local militia, A.K. McClure, decided to speak for the town, but he first took the precaution of putting on civilian clothes and posing as a citizen.[50] His concerns about being recognized and taken prisoner were both complicated and alleviated when he realized that he knew one of the Rebel scouts, Hugh Logan. Logan was indebted to McClure for professional services prior to the war, and rather than threaten the colonel, he told him to go home and remain quiet in order to escape arrest. He also said that if McClure was taken prisoner, he, Logan, would attempt to secure his release. This piece of good luck convinced McClure, instead, to "share the fate of his fellow citizens," and along with two others, he went forward to meet the Rebels.[51]

McClure "modestly suggested that there might be some United States officers in the town in charge of wounded, stores, or recruiting offices," and asked what would become of them. He was told they would be paroled, unless there was some special reasons for not doing so, and that such officers should not leave town. McClure worried. What if there was some "special reason" he would not be paroled? He felt like he still had "ample opportunity" to leave, but that would mean violating his agreement to stay, which might put his family in danger. Of particular concern was the fact that he had "sixty acres of corn in shock . . . three barns full of grain, excellent farm and saddle-horses and a number of best-blooded cattle." This property was "worthy of a thought," the Yankee surmised, and he devoted greater detail in his memoirs to his property than to his family. In the end he decided to surrender the town, stay, be bound by the terms of the surrender, and take his chances on discovery and parole. He then made a beeline for his farm, expecting it "to be overrun . . . and to find the place one scene of desolation," but in the meantime he nobly decided to "destroy all the liquors about the house."

Soon his farm was crawling with Rebels. All ten of his horses were taken and pickets were posted on the road in front of his home. After midnight one came into the yard, bowed, and politely asked for some coals to start a fire. After he was supplied, the "mild-mannered villain" stripped off fence rails for the fire. Then another came and asked for some water and, after being "piloted" to the pump, thanked McClure profusely. Thereafter a parade of Confederates came into the yard for the same purpose, but each asked permission before drawing water, each thanked him for it, and each left his yard without further disturbance. McClure was "somewhat bewildered by this uniform courtesy," but decided it must be "a prelude to general movement upon anything eatable in the morning." He then calculated what he might lose to the Rebel's breakfast table, particularly the mountain trout in his spring and the blooded calves in his yard.

His fears seemed to be coming true at 1 a.m., now October 11th, when half a dozen officers came to his door and asked if he would make them some coffee, promising to pay in Confederate money. This prompted McClure to negotiate a "treaty with them on behalf of the colored servants," whom he expected to be seized and taken into slavery, but the Rebels agreed to accept bread instead. However, upon seeing a fire in the fireplace, they asked to enter and warm themselves while the coffee was being made. McClure reluctantly invited them in, and soon they were seated around the fire discussing "politics, the war, the different battles, the merits of generals of both armies, etc." McClure had a cup of coffee with them, and found most of them to be "men of more than ordinary intelligence, and culture, and their demeanor was in all respects eminently courteous."

The officers relished the coffee and discussed its scarcity before asking if there was any more. Upon being told there was, they asked if a few more officers and "a few privates who were prostrated by exposure" could come in for a cup. Deciding the others "were as welcome as those present," McClure acquiesced and the Rebels "came in squads of five or more, until every grain of browned coffee was exhausted." They then requested tea, and another twenty were served with that beverage.

An officer then asked for bread, which led to more men being supplied, at least a hundred in all, and when one noticed a box of Killickinick tobacco on the mantle he asked if they could fill their pipes. McClure said smoking was not offensive in his home, which led to another hour of conversation and "free talk on matters generally." At 4 a.m. a bugle blew and the Rebels left, thanking McClure for his hospitality, having not made a "single rude or profane remark."[52]

While McClure was having his excellent adventure, Stuart rode to the town square and gave orders for the Provost Guard to protect private citizens. Then he and his staff rode back to the toll house on the edge of town, had coffee, and tried to sleep on the kitchen floor.[53]

Rebels cut the telegraph wires, but not before the local marshal got off a message to Governor Andrew Curtin.[54] Curtin wired the news to Secretary of War Stanton, saying "the people have surrendered Chambersburg." Stanton contacted McClellan at 9:10 p.m., telling him, "Not a man should be permitted to return to Virginia. Use any troops in Maryland or Pennsylvania against them." McClellan wired back that "Every disposition has been made to cut off the retreat of the enemy's cavalry."[55]

True to his word, Hampton paroled wounded Union soldiers in the local hospitals, a total of 275 men.[56] Colonel Butler visited the bank but found the cash missing. Typically, there were a few citizens who came out and spoke kindly to the invaders, even bringing them food, while others huddled behind locked doors and missed out on a significant brush with history.[57]

Stuart gave Grumble Jones the responsibility of burning the railroad bridge at Scotland, one of the major purposes of the raid. Soon, however, Jones' detail returned with discouraging news—local citizens said the bridge was made of iron. Stuart included this disappointing news in his report to General Lee, and it was repeated down the years by chroniclers of Stuart, including the folks who wrote the historical marker that was erected there in 1947.[58] In fact, Jones and his men were duped. The bridge was made of wood and would be burned by Confederates the following June during the Gettysburg campaign, but patriotic, or crafty, citizens fooled Jones or some other officer who wasn't anxious to spend the night trying to light a bridge in the rain. No one was sent to the structure to verify the story, which was fortunate for Jones considering that Jeb would not have let such a major error by anyone go unpunished, particularly someone he already despised.[59]

Back at the toll house on the edge of town, Blackford was unable to get much sleep, being uncomfortable from wet clothes and having his equipment buckled and belted on. He reflected, "It doesn't look as if it ought to take any time to buckle on a saber and put on a field glass and haversack, but when suddenly called to arms in the night it is very distracting and something is apt to be left behind . . ." so that he "always slept completely equipped when on active service, and slept sounder for feeling ready for any emergency."[60]

Stuart slept more poorly. Three times during the night he roused Benjamin White, the scout who was his principal guide, and asked if the rain was likely to make the fords back across the Potomac impassable. White was from Montgomery County, Maryland, and he assured the general they would be able to get back safely.[61]

Channing Price and Chiswell Dabney left the toll house early, in the dark. It was raining but they needed to do some shopping. They procured numerous items, almost identical in character based on the lists each sent home—black overcoats, blue trousers, wool socks, a pair of boots, a bridle, canteens, bleached castle soap, teaspoons, a pocket book, several small booklets containing U.S. postage, and "various other little things as much as I could carry."[62]

Before dawn on October 11 the rain stopped and the sky cleared, to everyone's relief. Stuart sent word to the citizens that they should gather in the town square, where his cavalry was already in position. Colonel Mc-Clure arrived about 7 a.m., and saw Stuart and his staff. Squads of troopers leading captured horses were still coming into town. He described the famous general as being "of medium size" and having "a keen eye, and... immense sandy whiskers and moustache . . ." with the "demeanor to our people . . . of a humane soldier."

McClure observed that several Confederates were arrested by the Confederate provost for taking private property, although most of the shops and stores were closed and undisturbed.[63]

There was, however, a Federal army depot located near the train station, and everything therein was fair game. It contained "mountains of clothing" plus 5,000 rifles and hundreds of pistols and sabers. The Southerners exchanged their worn-out gear and clothes, caring little they might be mistaken for Yankees.[64]

With troopers and citizens in earshot, Stuart announced that the next stop would be Gettysburg. Pelham shouted to his gunners, "You're to have the first whack in Gettysburg to make up for being late in Chambersburg." The column of riders, led horses, and cannons then trundled out of town east, toward the little crossroads town destined to become legend nine months hence. Butler's South Carolinians, previously the advance guard, stayed behind to destroy the Federal depot and follow as rear guard. Rooney Lee's men took the lead. The last of Butler's men, plus a detachment of the 1st North Carolina, set a slow fuse and rode to the edge of town to observe. The explosion came as the last of the Rebels departed the town at 9 a.m.[65]

In fact, Jeb had no intention of going to Gettysburg, and as soon as they were out of town, he called to Blackford, asked him to ride ahead to be out of earshot of everyone, and told him something that Blackford said "made an indelible impression on me, and is now as fresh (some thirty years later) as if it had occurred yesterday."

Stuart paused and then said, "Blackford, I want to explain my motives to you for taking this lower route and if I should fall before reaching Virginia, I want you to vindicate my memory."[66] Stuart was obviously worried, and his "unusual earnestness" worried Blackford. Jeb took out a map and explained that Cox, whose infantry they'd passed when the Federals turned toward Hancock, was behind, making it impossible to return the way they'd come. They were then at the top of a loop, directly north of McClellan's army, which was concentrated around Hagerstown, Mechanicstown (modern Thurmont), and Frederick. Ahead lay Cashtown and beyond that, Gettysburg. He planned to turn south at Cashtown. The Maryland line and Emmitsburg were then dead ahead but the Federals would be positioned so that the Confederates would approach from their rear, where they were not expected and for which Jeb believed no preparation to meet them had been made.

The problem was they would have to cover a great deal of distance without being located, which would require quick marching and precautions against information being communicated to the enemy. In effect, without premeditation, Stuart was proposing to again ride completely around McClellan's army, in a sort of "fool me once" situation for the Federals, who were likely in turn to regard it as "try to fool me twice and you're dead."

"You see," Stuart said, "the enemy will be sure to think that I will try to recross above, because it is nearer to me and further from them. They will have all the fords strongly guarded in that direction, and scouting parties will be on the lookout for our approach, so that they can concentrate to meet us as any point. They will never expect me to move three times the distance and cross at a ford below them and so close to their main body, and therefore they will not be prepared to meet us down there."[67]

Jeb asked Blackford if he understood and considered the plan sound. What Stuart was proposing would take the Confederates within ten miles of McClellan's entire army, would mean that for most of the day they would be passing near enemy camps, and that they would be trying to accomplish the longest non-stop march he or anyone in the command had experienced. The engineer stretched things a bit and told Stuart he believed the plan was a "wise movement," and that if Jeb did not return that he, Blackford, would make certain his motives were made clear to those in Virginia. It was a solemn moment. Jeb Stuart did not tend to talk about his own death, and Blackford was "touched by this mark of confidence." Both men's eyes filled with tears.[68]

The Federal pursuit was led by the Confederates' old acquaintances from the Peninsula, Colonel Rush's Lancers of the 6th Pennsylvania Cavalry. Rush's command was split between several locations, but some were behind the Rebels near Chambersburg. Telegraph wires that had not been cut were abuzz. Governor Curtin wired McClellan that "latest advices say they are moving in direction of Gettysburg, thence by Emmitsburg, to destroy Government stores at or near Frederick. These statements are mere conjectures, given to you as received." General Pleasonton, in command of McClellan's cavalry, believed Stuart would retrace his steps and cross the Potomac at or near where he had first entered Maryland, so he started in that direction before receiving an order from McClellan's chief of staff, R.B. Marcy, that the Rebels were heading for Gettysburg and that "Mr." McClure, of Chambersburg, reported they would be crossing the Potomac by way of Frederick and Leesburg, which was fairly accurate. Accordingly Pleasonton headed for Hagerstown and Mechanicstown, and sent scouts to Gettysburg and Emmitsburg, so that "they should not be allowed to escape unharmed."[69]

The Confederates reached Cashtown, turned south, passed through Fairfield, and re-entered Maryland. While in Adams County, where Gettysburg was the county seat, the Rebels collected over eighty horses and roughly fifteen hundred dollars worth of supplies. In Cashtown, twenty-two dollars worth of goods were taken from the Williams Ruff store and ten dollars worth of goods from Captain Mark's Store. At Fairfield over a thousand dollars worth of hats, shoes, and clothing was taken from the Paxton and McCreary store and two hundred dollars worth of merchandise from Sullivan's store, along with thirty stands of arms from the Home Guard Armory. They also seized thirteen prisoners.[70] The Federal officer who calculated and recorded these details, Lt. Colonel Jacob M. Sheads, also noted that a resident of Adams County named Warren Danner was seen riding with Stuart's cavalry.

Shortly after the Confederates crossed into Maryland, a courier carrying dispatches from Frederick to Colonel Rush was captured, and Stuart learned the enemy still had no idea of his location, that Rush had enough men in Frederick to protect the city, that four companies of his Lancers were headed for Gettysburg, that another 800 men under Pleasonton were hurrying to Mechanicstown, four miles from Stuart's position, and that the railroad crossing on the Monocacy was occupied by two brigades of infantry.[71]

Stuart's men arrived at Emmitsburg about sunset on the 11th, having covered thirty-one miles from Chambersburg.[72] The column and its horses stretched over five miles, and moved with three videttes in the lead, followed at 150 yards by one squadron of the 1st Virginia, followed at another 200 yards by the rest of that regiment and by the 600 of Rooney Lee's brigade, followed by a section of Breathed's battery, followed by 600 horse leaders from Jones' brigade, followed by Hampton's 600-man rear guard and Hart's section of artillery, with another squadron 200 yards behind them and three more videttes 150 yards further back.[73]

Emmitsburg contained a mix of northern and southern sympathizers, and some of the latter reported that 140 of Rush's Lancers had passed through the town an hour earlier, on the hunt. Stuart ordered that anyone attempting to leave town should be overtaken and captured, as they might be trying to notify the enemy. Accordingly, when the advance squadron saw a young lady dash out of town they gave chase. Their horses were tired and hers was not, but they were not going to shoot at her. When two Rebels finally overtook her after a mile, they learned she had mistaken them for Yankees and was hurrying to her home outside of town. This was an amusing tale, and the Confederates escorted her back to the house from which she had come.[74]

On the column rode through Emittsburg to Rocky Ridge, where, about 9 p.m., the advance guard met a scouting party of General Pleasonton's cavalry, which turned immediately toward Mechanicstown. The Rebels continued to ride. Out of the dark came a lone buggy that pulled to a stop when it met the Confederate advance guard. Inside was a lone Yankee officer.

"Move aside, men, move aside," the officer ordered. The troopers did not.

"I'm an officer of the 79th Pennsylvania on recruiting service and I must get on," the man shouted. The Southerners grinned.

Stuart rode up and the Federal yelled, "Are you the officer in command?" "I am."

"Then be good enough to order your men to make way. I'm a Pennsylvania officer on recruiting duty, and it is important for me to get ahead." "Very well," Jeb replied, and then he said something in low tones to one of the troopers, who dismounted and climbed into the buggy.

"What do you mean to do sir?" the officer demanded. "Nothing." "Who are you?" "Nobody."

"Who is that officer?" "General Stuart." "What General Stuart?" "Jeb Stuart, Major General of Cavalry, Confederate States of America."

"Oh my God, I'm procured."[75]

At half past 10 p.m. a company of the 6th Pennsylvania Cavalry saw General Stuart's column going toward Woodsboro, the next town south after Rocky Ridge, and reported it to Colonel Rush and General Pleasonton, who was a few miles away at Mechanicstown, but Pleasonton did not receive the message until past midnight.

On the column rode through Liberty, New London, and New Market. The soldiers had had very little sleep, but were told they must keep moving all night and cover the remaining forty miles to the Potomac. Along with the clopping of hooves and the jangle of equipment came loud snores from men asleep in their saddles. As Blackford recalled, "During the day there is always something to attract the attention and amuse, but at night there is nothing. The monotonous jingle of arms and accoutrements mingles with the tramp of horses' feet into a drowsy hum all along the marching column, which makes one extremely sleepy, and to be sleepy and not to be allowed to sleep is exquisite torture. Only thirst, with water in sight but out of reach, is so bad."[76]

Blackford rode Magic for the entire expedition, afraid that if he traded her for another mount she might get loose, and even though she was a high-stepping, high-strung animal, he could not bear losing her. He would sometimes dismount and walk beside her, taking ears of corn from fields they passed and breaking them into pieces to feed her.

While doing so the column passed a house protected by a large bulldog that targeted Blackford for attack. He charged and Blackford defended himself with his saber, inflicting a wound on the animal's shoulder that infuriated it more. He began circling Blackford and Magic, growling savagely and looking for an opening. Stuart witnessed the scene and helpfully shouted "Give it to him, Blackford," roaring with laughter. Wishing he could shoot the animal, but knowing they were too close to the enemy to do so, Blackford endured the attack until the dog's owner finally came out and called it off. Blackford identified himself as a Federal officer and asked if any other of "our" troops had passed by recently, but was told that none had.[77]

At New Market citizens provided the disconcerting news that General George Stoneman with 4,000 to 5,000 men were at Poolesville, and that his men were spread along the river guarding the fords.[78] A little south of

New Market, Stuart did something phenomenal. Of all his exploits, it may one of the most telling.

It was nearly midnight. The Union army might show up any moment. They'd been under tremendous strain all day and faced a similar day on the morrow. The soldiers were worn out and barely able to stay in the saddle, at which point Jeb rode up to Blackford, laughed, and said, "Blackford, how would like to see the New York Rebel?"

They were within a few miles of Urbana, where the Sabers and Roses Ball was held and where Mr. Cockey's house of young ladies resided. Urbana was southwest, toward McClellan's army, but Blackford was game. "I'd be delighted," he said. "Come on then," replied Stuart.

Off they went, Stuart, Blackford, a few other staff officers and a few couriers, about a dozen men. One can imagine the shame and ridicule that would have followed if the Federals had attacked and captured or destroyed the Confederate column while Stuart was on this lark, but as Blackford said, "The night was light enough to see very well and the roads were perfectly familiar to us . . . so there was really no danger of capture even if we had fallen in with a force of the enemy, for we could have scattered and rejoined the command."[79]

They arrived at the home of Mr. Cockey a little after midnight, dismounted, and knocked on the door. A woman's voice came from upstairs, "Who is it?"

"Jeb Stuart and staff." There was a pause, and then, "Who did you say it was?"

This time Jeb shouted and laughed, "General Stuart and staff, come down and open the door!" Amid squeals and pounding footsteps on stairs, the doors were unlocked and thrown open. For half an hour the friends laughed and joked, then Stuart and his men mounted and rode southeast to intercept the column further south from where they had left it.[80]

Jeb would not discover it until later, but during his absence the biggest tragedy to befall him on the raid occurred. His servant, Bob, was caring for Jeb's spare horses, Skylark and Margrave. He may have been drinking, but sheer exhaustion was just as reasonable an excuse, and he fell asleep beside the road and did not wake until prodded by Federal cavalrymen. When released the next month, Bob obediently returned to Stuart, but without the horses.[81]

When dawn finally came on Sunday, October 12, the Confederate troopers arrived at Hyattsville, having covered sixty-five miles since Chambersburg. They still had twelve miles to go, and the Federals were in a dither, determined to bring them to ground. McClellan telegraphed Washington that "Cox's division is loaded in cars in Hancock, with cavalry well out toward the Pennsylvania line, and if the Rebels attempt to cross below Hancock, I have infantry at or near all the different fords. . . . I have six regiments of cavalry now up the river between Hancock and Cumberland . . . . I have given every order necessary to insure the capture or destruction of these forces, and I hope we . . . teach them a lesson they will not soon forget.[82]

McClellan had, indeed, covered the fords ahead with infantry, and Pleasonton's cavalry was coming from the rear. Pleasonton's failure to catch Stuart thus far was not due to lack of effort. In the preceding twenty-eight hours his men had covered seventy-eight miles. He had lost hundreds of troopers to straggling, but still had some 4,500 to throw at Stuart's 1,800. He expected Stuart to try to cross at the mouth of the Monocacy, where it flowed into the Potomac, and by 8 a.m. he was nearly there.[83] Stoneman's cavalry was east, near Poolsville, and a Federal signal station on nearby Sugar Loaf Mountain was certain to spot the Rebels. The Federals had troops in front of Stuart and were closing in from three sides.

Stuart, however, had a secret weapon in the form of Captain Benjamin White, the Marylander who'd assured Jeb in Chambersburg that rain would not prevent them from crossing the Potomac. Now he showed his general that Yankees could not prevent them from doing so either. He'd lived in the area all his life and knew the back roads and rarely-used river crossings.

White led them toward Poolsville, in plain sight of the signal station and in Stoneman's direction. A squadron of Federal cavalry appeared, the first enemy the Confederates had encountered other than militia, but they were only a scouting party that scattered when the Rebels charged. On they rode, nearly a mile and a half, seemingly straight into the enemy's jaws, and then suddenly they turned right, south, down a seldom-used cart trail toward a crossing called White's Ford.

Nevertheless, the enemy was there—infantry, possibly a regiment, dug in on the Virginia side of the river along a wooded bank, with the entire crossing in their field of fire. Even if the Rebels could overwhelm them, the Federals would buy time for Pleasonton, Stoneman, and other infantry units to hasten to the site.

Rebels dismounted and prepared for battle. Pelham wheeled guns into position. Rooney Lee sent a flag of truce to inform the Federals that Stuart's entire force was up and would attack in fifteen minutes unless they surrendered. There were actually less than 200 Federals, of the 99th Pennsylvania Infantry, but the Rebels did not know that. One of them recorded, "The moment seemed to be a critical one indeed, but General Stuart remained perfectly composed."[84]

The fifteen minutes expired without a surrender. Skirmishers under Colonel Wickham went forward and Pelham opened fire. Rooney Lee's brigade advanced . . . and found the Pennsylvanians had fled.

Pelham now turned his guns in the direction of approaching bodies of Federals coming from two directions, less than a quarter of a mile away, while the cavalry and led horses splashed across the river. The horses had been without water so long that a major threat to the Southerners' safety was that they would all stop to drink and create a giant traffic jam at the river, so Stuart sent Blackford to tell each company commander that no man was allowed to water his horse.

The long files of men crossed the river and the last were nearly across when Stuart's calm composure broke. He approached Blackford almost in tears and said in a choked voice, "Blackford, we are going to lose our rear guard." "How is that, General," Blackford responded. "I've sent four couriers back to Butler to call him in, and he is not here," Jeb replied. "You can see the enemy closing in on us from above and below."

Butler's South Carolinians were the first to cross the Potomac on the raid and would be the last to recross it, if they crossed it at all.

"Let me try it, General," Blackford said. Stuart paused, then extended his hand and said, "All right, and if we don't meet again, old fellow, goodbye." As Blackford rode away, Jeb called after him, "Tell Butler if he can't get through to strike back into Pennsylvania and try to get back through West Virginia. Tell him to come in at a gallop."

One can imagine Blackford's feelings, which he described as making "a strong impression." With all his various deliveries of orders and extra excursions, Blackford had ridden Magic nearly 100 miles in two days, but she responded with a characteristic snort, toss of her head, and burst of speed. They passed Pelham and one cannon staying behind to slow the enemy, firing rapidly, and then they were alone on the road, galloping hard. From ahead came one of the four couriers. He had not been able to find Butler.

Blackford rode on and met another, and another, each delivering the same dismal report. Blackford knew Magic would run until she died, and thought that was a possibility if they went much further. He reached the place where he hoped to find the South Carolinians, but no one was there. On he pushed, one, two, three miles swept by and still no Butler.

Coming around a sharp bend, he nearly collided with Butler's men. They were facing to the rear and standing fast.

Blackford pulled Butler aside and explained the situation. They had to move quickly, but it would not be good to panic the men. The rear guard mounted and moved out at a trot, then a gallop. Word came that one of Pelham's other two guns, of Hart's battery, was falling behind, its team exhausted. Blackford told Butler to abandon it if necessary, but the horses held out.

Pelham was still banging away at the river, and Butler ordered his men into line of battle, expecting they would have to cut their way through. Sabers were drawn and the 600 came on like the Light Brigade.

When they came in sight of the ford, however, Pelham was right where Blackford had last seen him and the crossing was still open. They flew into the river and Pelham limbered up and followed. When they were halfway across the Federals arrived, almost exactly as they had done at the end of the first ride around McClellan. Bullets flew over their heads and splashed around them, but then guns opened up from the Virginia side, significantly squelching the enemy's fire, and soon they were safe on Virginia soil.[85]

They rode to Leesburg and went into camp that afternoon, "as weary a set as ever dismounted," according to Blackford. Some of the troopers literally fell off their horses and went to sleep where they landed.[86] Stuart and his staff went to the home of Dr. Jackson where they were welcomed and given genuine beds in which to sleep.[87]

The raid was another amazing success, just what Southern spirits needed, something that put "ride" back into "pride." Blackford calculated that they had destroyed a quarter of a million dollars worth of supplies, brought off nearly 1,500 horses, captured numerous prisoners and paroled hundreds more.[88] They'd ridden 126 miles in three days and eighty in twenty-seven hours, non-stop, all within spitting distance of the enemy, and the totality of their loss was one man wounded.[89] Two more were reported as having fallen out of line and were presumably captured. That did not coincide with Federal Colonel Rush's report, in which he claimed to have taken twelve prisoners, even naming one, "a very intelligent young man, Jonathan Scott, of the First Virginia Cavalry," who supposedly ticked off the identity of eight regiments and two legions involved in the raid, a force "between 4,000 and 5,000 strong, and . . . [which] entered at Dam Number 5, and were to leave at Edwards Ferry."[90] Never mind that intelligent young Mr. Scott failed to mention that only a few dozen men came from each regiment and that the Confederate column entered and exited Maryland at different places than Dam Number 5 and Edwards Ferry.

In addition to Jeb's two horses, lost with Mulatto Bob, the Confederates abandoned sixty others that became lame or disabled, but they brought in nearly forty civilian prisoners—mayors, postmasters, and other town officials—to use as currency for imprisoned Southerners.[91]

On the Northern side the predictable finger-pointing, justifying, explaining, and excuse-making began. Colonel Rush explained that "with the small and crippled force at my disposal near this town (seven companies, of about 275), it has been impossible for me to do more than I have done to check this unfortunate raid." Major General John Wool, commanding the Federal Eighth Corps, concluded his report with, "From want of cavalry, we could not follow the enemy, as he, from reports made to me, kept continually on the trot, and sometimes even galloped his horses."[92] General McClellan wired General Halleck on October 14 to whine that "with my small cavalry force it is impossible for me to watch the line of the Potomac properly or even make the reconnaissances that are necessary for our movements. This makes it necessary to weaken my line very much by extending the infantry to guard the innumerable fords. . . . My cavalry force, as I urged this morning, should be largely and immediately increased."[93] He also wrote, "I did not think it possible for Stuart to recross, and I believed that the capture or destruction of his entire force was perfectly certain."[94]

Lincoln received the news of this latest embarrassment while on a boat in the Potomac with friends and some army officers. When asked what he thought of the news, he looked thoughtful, then took a stick and drew an imaginary circle on the deck. "When I was a boy," he said, "we used to play a game—three times around and out. Stuart has been around McClellan twice. If he goes around him one more time, gentlemen, McClellan is out."[95]

As it turned out, the third time around McClellan by Stuart that put McClellan out of command occurred only on paper, as part of the exchanges between Lincoln and McClellan at the end of the month. The general repeatedly, in long, exhaustive letters to Washington, described how woefully undermanned his army was, particularly the cavalry, saying at one point that it was necessary to use all of his cavalry against Stuart and that "this exhausting service completely broke down nearly all our cavalry horses and rendered a remount necessary before we could advance on the enemy."[96] Lincoln wrote from the White House on October 26 to say:

> Of course you know the facts better than I; still two considerations remain. Stuart's cavalry out-marched ours, having certainly done more marked service on the Peninsula and everywhere else. Second, will not a movement of the army be a relief to the cavalry, compelling the enemy to concentrate instead of forarying into squads everywhere?

McClellan finally moved his army, but the only thing that kept him in command at the end of October and beginning of November were the Congressional elections scheduled for November 4, 1862. Lincoln knew the Democrats were likely to gain seats in the House and did not want the removal of McClellan, a Democrat, to add fuel to the political situation. When the votes were tallied the Democrats picked up thirty-one seats, but not enough to gain a majority, and on November 5 Lincoln drew up orders for Little Mac's removal.[97] Stuart's third ride around him was only symbolic, but the second ride around him certainly played a significant role in sealing McClellan's military fate.

There were critics of Stuart's raid in the South, of course, in that it involved too much risk for too little gain. Stuart had failed to burn the railroad bridge, too many of the horses he brought back were suitable only for artillery instead of cavalry, and while he brought in information about the disposition of McClellan's army, it consisted principally of the news/no news that "Little Mac" had not done much of anything since the Battle of Sharpsburg. Jubal Early called it "the greatest horse stealing expedition that . . . annoyed the enemy." Confederate General Dorsey Pender wrote his wife that "Beaut is after a lieutenant generalcy," and one of the troopers who participated in the raid described it as "horse stealing . . . [and] abuse of old folks."[98] For the most part, however, all concerned were amazed at what Stuart had accomplished between October 9 and 12, 1862.

Stuart could not know it, nobody could, but he had reached an apex of his career and a zenith of his own joy. Immediately ahead lay a few days of basking in the afterglow, and beyond that lay more balls, more battles, more victories, and more glory, but within little more than three weeks his world would be turned upside down, and he would be gut-slammed in a manner he had never known before. Soon a process of whittling away would begin on both of his little families, real and military, and even his reputation. He would never be as complete, as capable, as close to his dreams and as untouched by loss as he was that autumn afternoon.

CHAPTER SEVEN

THE BOWER AND BEREAVEMENT
OCTOBER 13-NOVEMBER 16, 1862

The dew is on the blossom
and the young moon on the sea.
It is the twilight hour,
the hour for you and me.
The time when mem'ry wanders
across life's weary track,
when the past floods up before us
and the lost comes stealing back.
When the past floods up before us
and the lost comes stealing back.
—*The Dew is on the Blossom,* a Serenade, by "Amelia" (1850)
(One of Stuart's favorite songs)

About noon on October 13, Stuart and his column headed back toward
The Bower. They reached Snickersville, at the foot of mountains dividing
Loudon and Jefferson Counties, at dark and the troops went into camp
while Stuart, Channing Price, Chiswell Dabney and a handful of aides rode
ahead. After seven miles they stopped to feed their horses and get a little
sleep at the home of a Mr. Castleman, then started again at midnight and
rode the remaining fifteen miles. As they neared The Bower before dawn,
they announced their approach by first having a bugler, Private George
W. Freed of Company E of the 1st Virginia, play a single bugle call,[1] then
having Sweeny break into song on his banjo.[2] Lamps and candles were lit.

Mr. Dandridge put coffee on to boil and brought out food. The ladies of the house got up to welcome them back.

Von Borcke was tail-wagging happy to see Stuart, saying, "Our delight in being again together was unspeakable." Stuart had personally selected an "excellent bay horse" for Von Borcke from among those captured, to Von's further joy. After greetings and a bite to eat, Price and Dabney headed for bedrooms and went straight to sleep, two very tired young Rebels.[3]

During Stuart's absence, Frank Terrill had joined the staff as inspector and Major Norman Fitzhugh had returned from being a prisoner, following his capture near Verdiersville. He had been kept in the Old Capitol Prison in Washington D.C., but the ordeal was made bearable due to its briefness and because the occupant of the adjoining cell was the spy, Belle Boyd, who was arrested on July 29, 1862. Only eighteen, she'd gained fame, or infamy, by shooting a Yankee who cursed her mother on July 4, 1861, then by smuggling messages to both Turner Ashby and Stonewall Jackson.[4] Fitzhugh's cellmate was a staff officer for General Ewell,[5] and the three made the most of their imprisonment. Boyd and Fitzhugh were taken from prison on August 29, 1862, put aboard the *Juanita*, and transported south for exchange.[6]

Stuart, Blackford, Pelham and others had tales of their adventures to share, and the next day, October 14, Jeb wrote a lengthy, detailed report of the expedition to General Lee, which concluded with a footnote stating, "I marched from Chambersburg to Leesburg, ninety miles, with only one hour's halt, in thirty-six hours, including a forced passage of the Potomac—a march without a parallel in history." Boastful as this statement was, Jeb's ninety miles in thirty-six hours was a little less impressive than the eighty miles in twenty-seven hours claimed by Major McClellan.

The prisoners taken during the raid, civilian and military, were gathered at The Bower and sent to Richmond under a detachment commanded by Captain Benjamin White. About forty were civilian officials and the same number soldiers.[7] Channing Price sent a long letter to his mother along with White for delivery, in which he gave a full account of the expedition and ended by saying that General Stuart had received the message from Ellen, Channing's sister and Jeb's cousin, and that he was directed by Stuart to tell Ellen she was still his sweetheart. Enclosed with the letter was a leaf from the Blue Ridge which Jeb sent to Ellen as a memento of the raid, and a "little pocket book for stamp currency," one of those from Chambersburg, that Channing sent to his mother to keep for him.[8]

Another ball was held at The Bower on October 15. Von Borcke recorded that "the ladies of the neighbourhood were brought to the festivity in vehicles captured in the enemy's country, drawn by fat Pennsylvania horses." He also reported that "Stuart was, of course, the hero of the occasion, and received many a pretty compliment from fair lips," and "[y]ielding to the urgent solicitations of the ladies and the General, Brien and I again produced our popular extravaganza, which was received, as at its first representation, with the greatest applause."[9]

Another incident that may have occurred at this ball was that Stuart was presented with a pair of golden spurs, a "token of appreciation" from "the ladies of Baltimore," in response to which Jeb began signing his letters with "KGS" for "Knight of the Golden Spurs."[10] Von claimed he presented the spurs to Stuart but Jeb wrote a letter on December 5 saying they arrived while Flora was there and "she buckled them on."[11] Flora did not arrive at Stuart's camp until November 13, nearly a month after the ball.

Von Borcke was not the only person to whom Jeb gave a horse that month. The other was Robert E. Lee. During the Sharpsburg campaign, Lee's best-known mount, Traveler, set back, or reared, while being held by the General, with the result that Lee was pulled down and forced to catch himself with both hands, severely injuring, or breaking, both wrists and forcing him to ride in an ambulance. Stuart decided he needed a less-spirited horse. Accordingly, Jeb negotiated the purchase of a five-year-old sorrel mare named Lucy Long, after a popular song, from Mr. Dandridge and presented it to the General. Lee kept her most of the war and rode her often, until she got with foal during the Petersburg Campaign. She was stolen shortly before the end of the war, but Lee's youngest son, Captain Robert Lee, found her in the eastern part of the state and brought her to Lee's home in Lexington. She lived there the rest of her life, outliving both the General, who died in 1870, and Traveler, who died in 1871, reaching the venerable old age of thirty-three before passing away in 1891.[12]

The rest and relaxation did not last long. On October 16, news came early that two columns of the enemy—infantry, cavalry, and artillery—were crossing the Potomac and advancing. One, about 6,000 infantry, 500 cavalry and six pieces of artillery, was commanded by General A.A. Humphreys and the other, 4,500 infantry, 2,000 cavalry and four guns, by General Winfield Scott Hancock.[13] Humphreys marched from Shepherdstown toward Smithfield and Hancock from Harpers Ferry toward Charlestown. The advance had all the markings of a general offensive and was treated as such by the Southerners.

Stuart opposed Humphreys with Fitz Lee's brigade, skirmishing and falling back. The Federals came uncomfortably close to The Bower.[14] It began to rain heavily, which may have been why they unexpectedly called off their advance and went into camp. Stuart posted double outposts and two of Pelham's guns to watch the Federals, then returned to headquarters.[15]

There he found two visitors from England, Francis Lawley and Frank Vizetelly. Lawley was a former member of Parliament and private secretary to the Chancellor of the Exchequer. He had resigned and moved to the United States in 1856, after a scandal broke in which it was revealed that he was using insider information gained in his governmental position to speculate on stocks in order to pay off gambling debts. He was then, in 1862, serving as a correspondent for *The Times*, a London daily newspaper, covering the war from the Southern side. Vizetelly was a correspondent and combat artist for the *Illustrated London News*. Both men had been at Lee's headquarters and wanted to spend a day with Stuart.

Jeb wrote a letter to Flora that evening, telling her of the latest ride around McClellan, proclaiming it to her as he did to General Lee, "without a parallel in history." He devoted a good portion of the letter to explaining why he was unable to secure a silk dress for her, as she had requested, attributing the failure to the "bad management" of an unnamed member of his staff to whom he had assigned the task while he tended to the "dangers, hardships, anxieties, and cares of my position."

With regard to that day's fighting, he told her that Porter and Sumner's Corps (of which Humphrey's and Hancock's divisions, respectively, were parts[16]) advanced with 20,000 men about eight miles from Charlestown and the Bower, "but went back in a hurry before we could attack them." This is curious, both for the inflated numbers and the claim they had retreated. He closed by saying he had sent "a trophy" for "La Petite," one his names for little Flora."[17] It would be his last gift to the little girl.

The Yankees resumed their march the next day, October 17, causing Stuart to conclude that he could no longer stay at The Bower. He ordered tents struck and wagons loaded, bid farewell to the Dandridge family, apologized to the two Englishmen, and rode away to do battle. Lawley and Vizetelly promised to return for a longer visit later.

Arranging Pelham's guns on a semicircle of hills in advance of the enemy, he fell back, hoping to draw them in and then halt or seriously impede further encroachment. General Lee arrived with A.P. Hill's division at about 9 a.m., musketry and artillery fire were exchanged, and the situation took on the trappings of a significant battle. Then the Federals stopped, turned around, marched back to the Potomac, and recrossed that night. Apparently the entire affair was simply a "reconnaissance in force" for the purpose of ascertaining whether Lee's army was in the Valley or elsewhere.[18] Stuart directed his staff to return to The Bower and re-establish headquarters, to everyone's satisfaction.

The week that followed was one of calm and relaxation, punctuated by merry evenings. Vizetelly returned but not Lawley, who was in Richmond filing his report to *The Times*. Von described him as "an old campaigner" and Blackford declared him "the most interesting narrator I have ever listened to around a campfire." Considering some of the men with whom Blackford usually shared a campfire, that was a high compliment indeed. There was supposedly "not a disreputable or reputable place of prominence in the civilized world that he did not know all about," and Jeb's military family sat late into the night listening to his tales.[19]

Stuart spent a portion of the week writing letters to his real family and reports about his military family. On the 22nd he wrote his cousin, Nannie Price, a chatty letter. On the 24th he wrote letters to General Samuel Cooper, the adjutant and inspector general and highest-ranking officer in the Confederacy, to urge that Pelham be promoted to Lt. Colonel. The same day he wrote General Lee urging that Colonel Munford be promoted to brigadier and be put in command of what was previously Robertson's brigade but which now appeared destined, contrary to Jeb's wishes, to be commanded by Grumble Jones. Jeb did not mince words or cloak his feelings about Jones, saying he was not a fit person to command a brigade of cavalry, that if put in command it would result in opposition, insubordination, and inefficiency, and that he "must beg the Commanding General to avert such a calamity from my division."

He also filed returns for his three brigades with Brig. Gen. R.H. Chilton, in Cooper's department, urging Munford's promotion and proposing the formation of a fourth brigade to be commanded by Tom Rosser, whose promotion to brigadier he also requested. On the 25th he penned another letter to General Cooper requesting that William Farley be given a major's commission and be put in command of a unit of sharpshooters.[20]

On an unspecified day that week, Stuart and Pelham rode to Jackson's camp at Bunker Hill, arriving past midnight. Pelham, who Kyd Douglass described as Jeb's "artillery pet," bedded down in Douglass's tent and Stuart bedded down in General Jackson's, which led to one of the rarest events of the Civil War—Stonewall Jackson cracking a joke.

Douglass wrote that Jackson was asleep when Stuart arrived and that Jeb removed only his saber before crawling into bed—probably a pallet on the floor of the tent—next to Stonewall. The night was chilly and Jeb "unconsciously . . . began to take possession of blankets and got between the sheets." Discovering himself the next morning to be "in the full panoply of war," Jeb crawled out of the bed and went outside to join others standing around a fire. When Jackson emerged, Jeb greeted him with "Good morning General Jackson, how are you?" Old Jack passed his hands through his uncombed hair, rubbed his leg, and in tones as comical as he could muster, said, "General Stuart, I'm always glad to see you here. You might select better hours sometimes, but I'm always glad to have you. But General, you must not get into my bed with your boots and spurs on and ride me around like a cavalry horse all night."[21]

The idyllic time at The Bower was approaching its end, but one more scene worth describing is the romance between John Pelham and Sallie Dandridge.

There is an enduring legend that three women donned black to mourn John Pelham after he was killed, but there is no reliable record about who they were or whether any of them had a colorable claim to being Pelham's sweetheart. One possible claimant was Belle Boyd. She met him in 1861 while he was a lieutenant in the Alburtis Battery, training at Winchester, Virginia. She found him "irresistible," and in November gave him a Bible inscribed "To John S. Pelham from Belle. With the sincere hope he will read carefully and attentively for his own if not for her sake." Deeper in the text she wrote a poem:

I know thou art loved by another now
I know thou wilt ne'er be mine.
But take from me still my heart's pure vow,
I ask thee not now for thine.[22]

However smitten Belle may have been, she obviously considered Pelham to be out of her reach, although it is not known who she believed it was who had his heart.

Another candidate was Bessie Shackleford of Culpeper, who was the last girl Pelham courted, or at least visited. They were definitely close, but when she wrote of him in later years, it was as an admirer rather than lover, calling him "fascinating," and "a splendid boy."[23]

If the legend of the three women in black is true, the identity of two is not known, but one was almost certainly Sallie Dandridge. Sarah Pendleton Dandridge was one year younger than Pelham. She had dark brown eyes, wavy auburn hair, and an attractive figure. Her photograph reveals a handsome woman, perhaps not beautiful by current standards, but striking, with a high forehead, full lips, and an aquiline nose. She was said to be both reserved and vivacious, with many suitors. The other staff officers at The Bower, Blackford, Von Borcke, and Cooke, wrote of Pelham's romance there with varying levels of detail, mentioning they would often walk hand in hand in the garden, that Pelham was sometimes absent from parties because he was alone with Sallie, that they sometimes took moonlight boat rides on the Opequan, and that they would go for rides in a yellow army wagon captured from the Federals that served as an all-around utility vehicle during Stuart's stay on the estate.

Apparently their romance was more than a flirtation, and involved discussions of marriage, up to and including correspondence between Pelham's father, Dr. Atkinson Pelham, and Sallie's, Stephen Dandridge, with the latter expressing delight at the prospect of his daughter's engagement.[24] It was not to be. Pelham had less than five months to live, and Sallie's additional seventeen years would contain more than its share of tragedy. Of the five Dandridge daughters, she was the only one to marry, to a lawyer named Blackburn Hughes, after the war. The couple lived in Martinsburg, possibly at The Bower, and she delivered "several stillborn children," dying herself in September 1880 while delivering the last of these at age 40.[25]

On October 26, a Sunday, a review of Hampton's Brigade was held in a field near The Bower. It was another spectacle, attended by all the ladies from the region, held on a pleasant but overcast autumn day. After the review, there was a demonstration of a small, one-pounder gun, which impressed no one, after which the field and staff officers competed in rounds of horse racing and fence jumping.

Jeb wrote a letter to Flora that day, reporting that it was a "rainy dreary Sunday," giving her a status report on his staff ("Von Borcke is one of the noblest fellows I ever met . . . Fitzhugh and all are devoted to me . . . Price is a ready & correct writer . . . Hairston worried my life out with his wretched spelling . . . Chiswell is improving."). He wrote of his devotion to her, lamented that Cousin Nannie Price was sick, enclosed $200, reported the loss of one horse but the acquisition of Lilly of the Valley, which he thought would suit Flora, and added a foreshadowing request: "You must send me La Pet's daguerreotype . . . I want it to look at."

Word soon came that the enemy was moving east, so that The Bower could no longer serve as headquarters. The young ladies who were guests of the Dandridge family began to depart. The 29th of October dawned hazy and rainy. A member of Stuart's staff observed that "nature wept in sympathy with us at the separation." The halcyon days were four years behind him when Von Borcke wrote of their final departure: "With heavy hearts indeed, we left the beautiful spot, and bade adieu to its charming, kindly inhabitants. Silently we rode down the hill, and along the margin of the clear Opequon stream, musing on the joyous hours that had passed away, hours which those few of our dashing little band of cavaliers that survived the mournful finale of the great war, will ever hold in grateful remembrance."[26]

General McClellan, who did not know he had less than two weeks left to command the Army of the Potomac, had finally acquiesced to President Lincoln's entreaties that he do something with his army. On October 26 he crossed the Potomac with two divisions of the Ninth Corps, plus Pleasanton's cavalry, and pushed back the Confederate pickets at Snicker's Gap. Lee's army responded, and soon both behemoths were in motion. On October 28, Longstreet's Corps marched toward Front Royal while Jackson remained in the Valley.[27]

On the 29th Stuart's men rode from The Bower with Fitz Lee's brigade, commanded by Colonel Wickham due to Lee's mule kick injury, and six of Pelham's guns, followed by Hampton, toward the Blue Ridge and Snicker's Gap. The weather was rainy and cold, but the men were in good humor, and when they reached the town of Smithfield in the afternoon, Von Borcke saw to it that Sweeney and his musicians performed a serenade for a widow he'd met there on the 17th.[28] They halted near Berryville and camped for the night about two miles out of town. Von Borcke wrote, "We were invited to supper by a prominent citizen, at whose pleasant house we greatly enjoyed a warm cup of tea, a capital old Virginia ham, and afterwards a pipe of Virginia tobacco before a roaring wood-fire." During the night everyone was awakened by a loud crash, which turned out to be a large hollow tree that had begun smoldering from a nearby campfire and which was blown over by the wind.[29]

When they awoke on the 30th there was frost on the ground, and as Stuart and his staff were shivering and getting a fire restarted, a nearby planter showed up to invite them to breakfast, which they did not hesitate to accept. It turned out that the man had a quantity of hams and bacons he was willing to sell, and Dr. Eliason, the staff surgeon, purchased a wagon load. About two hours later the contents of the wagon disappeared, a theft Von Borcke attributed to "rascally negro camp-followers."

They rode all day through the gorgeous Blue Ridge countryside. Snicker's Gap was occupied by a regiment of Marylanders who had fought an engagement with Federal cavalry the day before, and dead bodies of men and horses still littered the sides of the road. They moved into Loudon and Fauquier Counties, neither of which had been significantly affected by the war. The Federals, in the vicinity of Leesburg, put forth no resistance.

Major McClellan recorded that they bivouacked that night at Bloomfield[30] and Von Borcke said it was near Upperville.[31] The two towns are about eight miles apart and they were probably strung out on the road between. Dr. Eliason was from Upperville and he invited Stuart and Von Borcke to his home, which soon filled with visitors desiring to see the famous cavalry leader. Dr. Eliason's daughter was ten, and blind, and she and Von Borcke became fast friends. "With the most eager interest she listened to the words of the foreign soldier, whom she required to give her an exact description of his personal appearance; and I was deeply touched as I looked into those tender, rayless blue eyes which gave back no answering glance to my own, and which were yet bent towards me with such seeming intelligence." Neither of them could know that Von Borcke would return to her home in a few months, on the edge of death.

During the night Stuart was informed that Federal troops were at Mountville and on the morning of the 31st he sent Wickham there and, in a charge by the 9th and 3rd Virginia, he surprised the 1st Rhode Island and 3rd Indiana Cavalry regiments, capturing between fifty and one hundred of them and driving the rest toward Aldie.[32]

Von Borcke and Farley, riding together, gave chase to a Federal officer. They called for him to surrender but he refused, spurring his horse harder and occasionally firing at them with a revolver. Von Borcke finally gained on him and was preparing to slash him with his huge saber when Farley shot him from the saddle. Leaving the officer in the dust, they continued after the retreating Yankees but soon gave up and returned. The Federal officer, a captain, was lying against a fence, in agony and delirious. Von stopped and tried to help, giving him a drink from the officer's canteen and sending for Dr. Eliason. The wounded Federal was not appreciative, and called out to everyone that the Rebels who had killed him were about to rob him as well, then emptying out his pockets and throwing his money, watch, and other possessions into the road. When Eliason arrived he examined the man and declared his wound mortal, but added that the man's delirium was not due to being shot but to being drunk. Von sniffed the man's canteen and found apple brandy. The man was taken to a field hospital where he died the next morning. The personal possessions he had scattered in the road were mailed to his family in Indiana.[33]

Stuart began to follow the enemy toward Aldie, but received information that Federal troops had reoccupied Mountville and so returned there, only to find the information was incorrect. He then moved toward Middleburg where he planned to camp for the night.[34] Von was sent ahead to find food and forage, but was soon mobbed by ladies who had heard that Jeb was nearby. When Stuart caught up he found Von "attended by a staff of fifty or sixty ladies, of various ages, from blooming girlhood to matronly maturity." Stuart agreed to stay for a little while and he was soon surrounded by women anxious to hear him speak. Some had tears in their eyes and some began kissing the skirt of his uniform coat and his gloves. Stuart told them that "your kisses would be more acceptable to me if given upon the cheek." The ladies hesitated for a moment, until one of the most elderly in the crowd, "breaking through the ranks, advanced boldly and, throwing her arms around Stuart's neck, gave him a hearty smack, which served as the signal for a general charge. The kisses now popped in rapid succession like musketry, and at last became volleys, until our General was placed under as hot a fire as I had ever seen him sustain on the field of battle. When all was over, and we had mounted our horses, Stuart, who was more or less exhausted, said to me, 'Von, this is a pretty little trick you have played me, but in future I shall detail you for this sort of service.' I answered that I would enter upon it with infinite pleasure, provided he would permit me to reverse his mode of procedure, and commence with the young ladies."[35]

The next three days, November 1 through 3, were filled with cavalry skirmishes. D.H. Hill's infantry division, of Jackson's Corps, advanced through Ashby's Gap and headed for Paris and Upperville, towns not quite four miles apart and a little more than eight miles from Middleburg. Stuart covered Hill's front and, in compliance with orders from General Lee to "get exact information of the strength and movements of the enemy," constantly sought out and received reports of Federal activity he forwarded to the commanding general.[36]

The evening of November 1, Stuart went into camp about a mile beyond Union, then accepted a supper invitation at a "Mr. C.'s" plantation, dining on a saddle of mutton.[37] Fighting on November 2 was heavier than on the 1st, with a great deal of artillery dueling and skirmishing from behind stone walls. One of Pelham's caissons received a direct hit, causing the loss of several men. Another battery lost fifteen men killed and wounded in a half hour.

With Federal infantry arriving, Stuart fell back through Union with the enemy close behind. Captain Bullock of the 5th Virginia was riding within fifty yards of Stuart when his horse was shot and Federals swarmed over him before he could get to his feet. Ignoring a demand to surrender, Bullock shot two of the enemy with his revolver and took off running with the Yankees close on his heels. Stuart led a handful of couriers to the officer's rescue.

To add to the confusion, numerous cattle, oxen, and sheep were pastured in the area and they stampeded about, mixing in with dismounted cavalry, riderless horses, cannons, firing soldiers, and the dead and wounded. One shell landed in the middle of a herd of sheep and exploded without killing any of them. A herd of oxen was running back and forth near one of Pelham's batteries when a young bull suddenly leaped into the air, turned a complete somersault, and fell to the ground, seemingly dead. In a few seconds he staggered to his feet, wobbled about, regained his senses and ran away, a victim of "windage" from a passing artillery shell.[38]

As hot as the action was, Jeb had another concern. He'd received two messages from his brother-in-law, Dr. Brewer, who was with Mrs. Stuart in Lynchburg, attending four-year-old Flora, who had contracted typhoid. The second message, received the 2nd, stated that the little girl's "case was doubtful," and asked him to come to Lynchburg to be with his wife. Jeb replied in words that sound as much designed to convince himself of his duty as to convince others:

> I was at no loss to decide that is was my duty to you and Flora to remain. I am entrusted with the conduct of affairs the issue of which will affect you, her, and the mothers and children of our country much more seriously than we can believe. I wonder if Dr. Brewer really thinks with you that I ought to leave my post under existing circumstances. . . . If my Darling daughter's case is hopeless, there are ten chances to one that I would get to Lynchburg too late—if she be convalescent why should my presence be nec-

essary. She was sick nine days before I knew it. . . . My darling let us trust in the Good God who has blessed us so much, to spare our child to us—but if it should please him to take her from us let us bear it with Christian fortitude and resignation. It is said that woman is better at bearing misfortune than man—I hope you will exemplify it. At all events remember that Flora was not of this world, she belonged to another and will be better off by far in her heavenly habitation.[39]

Stuart continued falling back, steadily contesting the enemy's advance, which sometimes consisted of double and triple lines of infantry. Their advance was discontinued when dark approached and Stuart bivouacked about a mile from Upperville.

The Federal infantry renewed its advance on November 3, a Monday, crossing the fields and steadily driving the dismounted troopers of Fitz Lee's brigade before them. Hill's infantry had not yet arrived, although they were only a few miles away. Colonel Wickham, temporarily commanding the brigade, was wounded in the neck by a piece of shrapnel, and command evolved to Colonel Rosser.[40] A minie ball passed through Blackford's boot and gave him a flesh wound in the leg. He recalled that the wound was not serious enough to cause him to leave the battlefield, but that the nervous shock of it caused him to throw up. At various times during the war he had three horses shot from beneath him, had men killed by his side or while in conversation with them, and had bullets pass through his clothing a dozen times, but this was his only wound.[41]

Before abandoning Upperville, Stuart sent a telegram to Flora saying, "I have come through four days hard fighting unscathed. How is my little Flora?"

Continuing their grudging withdrawal, Stuart and Von Borcke were the last to ride out of Upperville, with enemy cavalry riding in front of pursuing infantry, and artillery shells raining down about them. A shell hit a house and toppled its chimney, sending bricks flying and nicking both men. Despite the danger and explosions, a few young ladies of the town—dedicated Stuart fans—came outside to wave farewell to their hero as he left the village.[42] Stuart went into camp that evening on the heights near Ashby's Gap.

Late that evening, before midnight, Stuart roused Dr. Eliason, Von Borcke, and several couriers in order to ride to Jackson's headquarters, which was about twelve miles away, near Millwood, leaving Rosser in command.

The weather was extremely cold and windy, made worse when they found the ford across the Shenandoah, past the town of Paris, so swollen it was necessary for their horses to swim. The men's wet clothing froze and icicles formed on boots and horses' bellies. They arrived at Jackson's camp about 2 a.m. The General and his staff were asleep, and planning not to rouse anyone, the little group built a fire and gathered around it "with teeth chattering like castanets."

Jackson awoke at dawn on the 4th and ordered breakfast for the shivering group, which turned out to be coffee and a haunch of cold venison a neighboring farmer had provided. Daylight and the food restored Stuart's good humor, and as soon as he completed his military business with Jackson, the little group of companions began joking and teasing each other at the breakfast table. This resulted in Von Borcke providing Jeb with a new joke from which he might ring many changes. Intending to say about Stonewall, "It warms my heart when he talks to me," the Prussian said in his awkward English, "It gave me heartburn to hear Jackson talk."

The little group—all except Jackson—roared with laughter, and Stuart immediately began finding ways to make Von's mistake more hilarious with jibes such as "at least he doesn't give you a stomach ache as well." Stonewall, however, pressed his hand over Von Borcke's on the table and said, "Never care, Major, for Stuart's jokes; we understand each other, and I am proud of the friendship of so good a soldier and so daring a cavalier as you are." This flustered Von Borcke more, as he idolized Jackson and Stuart, and was filled simultaneously with deep embarrassment and swelling pride to be the focal point of their intense but opposite attentions. Stuart slapped him on the back, a little embarrassed himself, and shouted "Hurrah for old Von! And now let us be off," and soon they were mounted and riding back the way they had come.[43]

They crossed the Shenandoah again, at a more shallow ford, went through White Post and stopped at noon at a planter's home for a hasty meal. There Von purchased two live turkeys that he attempted to carry across his saddle with their legs tied, but found this unmanageable and turned the birds over to a courier who simply cut off their heads with his pocket-knife.

The son of the planter served as their guide for a quicker route back to Ashby's Gap and their camp. They were in heavily wooded, mountainous terrain that was impenetrable except by hidden bridle paths. They heard gunfire ahead and, arriving at a summit, saw several thousand Federal infantry below, on the far side of which Rosser's horsemen were firing and retreating. Stuart said aloud what each was thinking: "The Yankees have taken Ashby's Gap. Rosser is retreating, and we are completely cut off."

They were stuck. Stuart needed to return to his command quickly, but doing so without the gap in the mountains would require a circuitous ride of nearly sixty miles. It was almost dark and they finally decided their best course of action would be for Stuart to remain there to watch the enemy's movements while the rest of the party split up to find a local resident who could guide them across by some little-known route. After agreeing on a particular whistle as a signal to reunite around Stuart, they spread out and began moving through the woods.

Someone—Von claimed it was he—discovered a raggedy native in the brush who agreed to cooperate when a revolver was pointed at him, and once the group reunited, Stuart told the man that if he could get them over the mountains to Barber's Cross Roads, where he believed Rosser would be, he would be rewarded, but if he betrayed them he would be shot. This elicited promises of cooperation and the man led them to a narrow, boulder and bramble-strewn path that finally emptied out near the village of Macon, around which were numerous campfires that indicated an army camp. Approaching cautiously, not knowing what color uniforms might be around the fires, they were relieved to discover soldiers of D.H. Hill's division. Stuart gave the man a fifty-dollar bill.

They were still several miles from Barber's Cross Roads, and did not arrive until midnight, only to find that Rosser was seven miles further, near Orleans. In a bad humor, Stuart ordered Von Borcke to ride to Rosser's camp and bring him back immediately, with orders for the brigade to follow and give battle to the enemy at daylight.

As ordered, Fitz Lee's brigade arrived at dawn on November 5 and, to everyone's surprise, Hampton's arrived soon thereafter from a different direction, having been on detached duty with the infantry for the previous week. With Hampton on the right and Rosser on the left, an artillery duel began. In addition to Pelham's six guns, Hampton provided two fifteen-pounder brass cannons the South Carolinian had purchased when he formed the Hampton Legion. The guns were too large to be used as horse artillery, but were reliable and accurate for long-range work. Shells whistled back and forth, one of which struck a locust tree about twenty yards from

Stuart and his staff, a fragment of which struck Von Borcke's horse in the right rear leg. Skirmishers and sharpshooters advanced, a barricade was erected in the road, and a Federal cavalry attack was repulsed, but the enemy was reinforced and Stuart began retiring toward Orleans. As they were falling back one of the Confederate troopers was hit in the brain by a bullet and killed instantly, but instead of tumbling from the saddle his nervous system caused his body to stiffen and he remained upright on his horse for several moments.

At Orleans the Southerners halted and caught their breath. Stuart and his staff were invited to dinner at a country house half a mile from the village belonging to a "Mrs. M." The retreat then continued toward Waterloo Bridge over the Rappahannock, near Warrenton, which they reached after dark. A mile further on they went into camp at the house of a "Mr. M." where Von's two turkeys were cooked and served.

The reason for Von Borcke's reluctance to name the citizens who were kind to Stuart may be illustrated by the fact that the homes of both "Mrs. M." and "Mr. M." were, within days, robbed and burned by Federal troops. He kept a journal in which he wrote only their initials, knowing it might fall into enemy hands any time.[44]

That night, past midnight, a telegram was delivered and a staff member awakened the general. It was from Dr. Brewer. Little Flora was dead. She was ten days short of her fifth birthday. The news devastated Stuart. His staff gathered around him and he wept, saying, "I will never get over it—never!"[45]

It was true. For weeks thereafter, once the day's business was done and orders for the next day issued, it was not unusual for his staff to see him with his head on his arms at his desk, his shoulders shaking, the sound of sobs audible. Every little girl with blond hair he saw reminded him of her, and even the sight of light blue flowers recalled the color of her eyes. He frequently talked to Von Borcke and others about her, telling John Esten Cooke, "I shall never get over it. It is irreparable." On the Gettysburg campaign the following July he sent his wife pressed blue flowers in honor of the little girl, and on his deathbed he would whisper to Von Borcke, "My dear friend, I shall soon be with little Flora again."[46]

For the time being he could only write to Mrs. Stuart, saying:

Waterloo Bridge, Near Warrenton
November 6th, 1862

My Dear, Dear Wife,

The affliction fell at last and its intelligence reached me this morning. I was sometime expecting it and yet it grieves me more the more I think of it. When I remember her sweet voice, her gentle ways and strong affection for her Pa, and then think she is <u>gone</u>, my heart is ready to burst. I want to see you so much and to know what her last words were. She is better off, I know, but it is a hard blow for us. She is up in Heaven where she will still pray for her Pa and look down upon him in the day of battle. Oh, if I could see her again. No child can ever have such a hold on my affection as she had. She was not of earth however . . . .

God has shielded me thus far from bodily harm, but I feel perfect resignation to go at his bidding, and join my little Flora.

I cannot write more. Your loving husband, J.E.B. Stuart[47]

The rest of the morning passed quietly. The enemy did not press the attack for a few hours, during which time a Confederate patrol captured a Federal supply wagon containing, among other things, cigars and bowie knives. Both were appropriated by Stuart's staff, who smoked the former and carried the latter in order to cut beef.

Shortly after noon the enemy attacked again, driving the Confederates. A battle raged around Waterloo Bridge, and as evening approached the Southerners fired the bridge and turned toward Culpeper Court House, eight miles away, where they went into camp after dark. It snowed that night, and Stuart and his staff found shelter in an empty house, where they built smoky fires in its two tumble-down fireplaces, but the windows were broken and the weather so cold, wet, and windy that no one was able to sleep.

The next morning, November 7, the Federals were on the offensive by 10 a.m., and the Confederates continued retreating. Things were getting desperate. They'd not eaten anything since the turkeys, and the roads were so muddy it became necessary to bury two artillery pieces their teams were unable to pull further. By evening they had fallen back to the Hazel River.

Stuart's command was no longer a proud band of cavaliers. So many horses had been killed or broken down that nearly 500 were part of "Company Q," which was under the command of Fitz Lee's quartermaster, Major Mason. Food was so scarce that persimmon trees along the road had been stripped of their fruit. At dark they went into camp in a forest of oak and pine. It was snowing again and the men shivered in their blankets and, for those fortunate to have them, overcoats. Von's servant, William, managed to forage some potatoes, which he roasted, and the evening was made somewhat more pleasant by the arrival of a courier from Culpeper with mail, including letters to Von from Europe. He became so absorbed reading them, sitting near the fire, that he did not notice when sparks set his blanket on fire until Stuart called out, "Von, what are you doing there? Are you going to burn yourself like an Indian widow?"[48]

It is likely that Stuart obtained two new members for his military family while at Culpeper, being Setter puppies he named "Nip" and "Tuck." The historical record is sketchy, with occasional references to the animals, the most descriptive being that "he had brought [the dogs] out of Culpeper, on the saddle, as he fell back before the enemy."[49] How and why General Stuart would have the opportunity or inclination to carry two Setter puppies—they could not have been grown and carried on his saddle—with him during these strenuous days is a mystery, and perhaps it occurred at another time. There may be a heart-warming story about the dogs but it is lost to history. As with the "paragon of coons" tethered to the artillery piece in front of Stuart's headquarters during the Peninsula campaign, what became of the dogs is either lost or undiscovered.

The bedraggled Confederates did not know it yet, but something else momentous had occurred that day—McClellan was replaced in command of the Army of the Potomac by Ambrose E. Burnside.

The next day, November 8, Stuart and part of Rosser's command recrossed Hazel River to see what the enemy was doing. They found them in camp near Jefferson, inactive, so they returned after posting pickets two miles beyond the bridge in the direction of the enemy.

Longstreet's Corps, including General Lee, arrived and went into camp not far from Culpeper Court House, and Jackson was following with all of his corps except D.H. Hill's division, which was left at Front Royal. Jeb sent a telegram to Flora, asking her to bring Jimmie and come to Culpeper. The cavalry headquarters baggage wagons arrived as well, so the staff pitched theirs and the General's tents, thinking they would be in the vicinity for several days. The new camp was christened "Camp No Rest."

General Lee's reaction to the appointment of Burnside as the new commander was to send word to Stuart that, "I am in doubt, whether the change from him [McClellan] to Burnside, is a matter of congratulation or not. I have some acquaintance with McClellan and knew where to place him. Burnside has to be studied." Accordingly, he directed Stuart to "ascertain the position of the enemy," which Jeb set about doing immediately.[50]

The next day, November 9, Stuart rode to Brandy Station to reconnoiter while members of his staff and Pelham constructed a fireplace and mud chimney for the headquarters tent, using the yellow wagon to transport materials. Jeb returned that evening after stopping at Lee's headquarters and receiving orders for a "reconnaissance in force" the next day. Supper was "slender," consisting of coffee and baked potatoes.

On the 10th Stuart took Fitz Lee's brigade, a battery of horse artillery, and a regiment of infantry, crossed the Hazel River at 8 a.m., and headed toward the enemy's camp near Jefferson. By 10 they made contact with Federal cavalry, a squadron of the 5th New York, which stood its ground until attacked by most of a regiment. Federal artillery arrived and a duel of cannons commenced, after which the Confederate infantry came up and drove the enemy back.

But soon Yankee infantry arrived and drove the Confederates back in turn, to Stuart's chagrin. Thinking he would punish them for what he called their "impudence," he gathered about thirty infantrymen and posted them just inside a stand of woods, telling them to hold their fire until the Federals were within two hundred yards. Jeb then stayed in sight, sitting on his horse in an open field near the woods, intentionally exposing himself to lure the enemy. Staff officers protested, but Jeb told them to leave if it was too hot for them. He was not in a good humor, and was probably filled with gloomy thoughts about his lost daughter. Von Borcke was standing in front of a tree at the edge of the woods, but decided to take shelter behind it instead. Soon shouts of Federal officers could be heard, some saying, "Kill that big rebel colonel." Three bullets hit Von Borcke's tree at a height lower than his head. Then Stuart jumped and put a hand to his face.

Von Borcke ran to his side, fearing the worst, but upon looking at Stuart's face, broke into laughter. One of the enemy's bullets had clipped off half of the General's moustache as neatly as a barber might do with scissors.[51] Jeb retired from his exposed position, the Rebel infantrymen indeed punished the impudent Yankees, and the Confederates continued falling back toward the river. Von Borcke was dispatched to deliver the information gained from the reconnaissance to General Lee, but he could not resist stopping at cavalry headquarters to tell his comrades of Jeb's new moustache style and to inform the commanding general of the development. Everyone had a laugh at Stuart's expense.

There was other bad news awaiting Jeb—decisions about his requests to reorganize his command submitted to Richmond and General Lee on October 24 and 25. Grumble Jones would still assume command of Robertson's brigade, and no promotion came through for Pelham. In fact, the Horse Artillery was to be reduced in size from five batteries to four. This was offset to some degree by the announcement that a new brigade was assigned to Stuart's command, but to be commanded by Rooney Lee instead of Rosser, who also was not promoted. Stuart's command now consisted of 603 field officers, 30 staff, and 8,551 enlisted men.[52]

Mrs. Stuart and Jimmie arrived on the 11th. She tried to retain her composure, but it was obvious she had been crying. General Lee came to Jeb's camp to convey his sympathy to Flora, and seven of Stuart's staff officers presented her with a letter in which they said, "We feel that the right to call ourselves friends has been given us by both yourself and the General. Your kindness has proven it and we cannot but feel individually bound to him who daily manifests his friendship to one and all of us. As friends we desire to express to you our sincere condolence with you and to assure you that our prayers shall ascend to a kind Providence that he will give both of you and our General strength to bear this heavy blow."[53]

Only the three-year-old boy, who was passionate about horses, was immune from sorrow, and if left unguarded he would make a beeline for the nearest horse. Von Borcke and other staff officers entertained him with rides and attention while Jeb consoled his wife.

A telegram arrived from Richmond from Frances Lawley that he was going to complete the visit he attempted on October 16. Von Borcke went to the train station at Culpeper to pick him up, substituting one of the carriages appropriated in Pennsylvania for the yellow wagon used for most errands. On November 12th Stuart took Lawley and a portion of Fitz Lee's brigade on another reconnaissance to stir up the Yankees and to let the Englishman see cavalry fighting up close. Von Borcke remained at headquarters and was pleasantly surprised when both Colonel Brien and Vizetelly arrived, barreling into camp singing a new, made-up version of *Dixie* that Vizetelly had composed for the occasion.

Stuart returned in the evening, bringing with him thirty prisoners, and at dinner Jeb and Lawley took turns recounting the adventures of the day, which included another escapade by William Farley. The scout was riding alone in a forward position and came within sight of a regiment of Yankee infantry on the road ahead. Watching them from concealment he saw the colonel and one of his staff leave the road and detour for some reason to a nearby plantation. As soon as the pair dismounted and before they could enter the house, Farley rode up with drawn pistol and said, "Gentlemen, you are my prisoners; make the least outcry to your men for assistance and I will blow your brains out." The pair and their horses were among the prisoners that accompanied Stuart back to his camp. One can imagine what confused speculation and theorizing buzzed through the regiment of Yankees about the fate of their Colonel and his adjutant.[54]

The next day, November 13, was quiet. Jeb, Flora, and Jimmie spent time together and that evening Von Borcke and Captain Fitzhugh walked to General Pickett's camp, about two miles away, to dine with a mutual friend, Captain James Dearing, who commanded a battery of artillery. There they found little to eat—a small piece of pork—but a canteen of apple brandy that made up for some of what was missing. Soon they were joking and singing, and after someone suggested that a courier be sent to Stuart's camp for Sweeney and his banjo, the musician arrived in less than an hour. The rest of the night was spent singing, watching the black servants dance, and making the night ring until, borrowing horses for the return trip, Von, Fitzhugh, and Sweeney returned to Camp No Rest. Captain Dearing was later promoted to colonel and placed in command of a regiment of cavalry. In April 1864, he became a brigadier general and, on April 6, 1865, was mortally wounded at High Bridge on the Appomattox, thus acquiring the distinction, on April 23, of becoming the last Confederate general killed in the war.[55]

The 14th was another quiet day at the cavalry camp, so much so that Stuart directed Von to accompany Lawley and Vizetelly to Richmond to tend to various matters of business. While there he outfitted himself with new boots, coat, hat, socks, and enjoyed a succession of dinner parties and social engagements at which he was the center of attention.

On the 15th, General Burnside obtained permission from President Lincoln to change the Army of the Potomac's direction of approach to Richmond and move toward Fredericksburg. He planned to steal a march on the "Old Gray Fox," Robert. E. Lee, and he nearly succeeded.

On the 16th, Stuart wrote a letter to Lily P. Lee, the widow of Col. William Lee with whom Jeb had traded the silver spurs. The letter began, as one might expect, with discussion of the "affliction . . . laid heavily on me in the loss of my darling little daughter whom I loved too well." After admitting that it made him "weep like a child" to think that "a child . . .

who loved her Pa like idolatry is now lifeless clay," he reported that whereas Mrs. Stuart was near him, "she is not herself since the loss of her little companion." The remainder of the letter mentioned their common friends in the army, Redmond Burke, Von Borcke, and Pelham, and ended abruptly with, "I want a pair of *very* high top Russian leather boots No. 9. Can you go into as extensive a business as that?"[56]

On or by the 17th, Stuart reported to Lee that Burnside was moving toward Fredericksburg[57] and Lee promptly put Longstreet's Corps in motion from Culpeper.[58] A month or so later, when Lee filed his report regarding the actions of this period, he wrote, "To the vigilance, boldness, and energy of General Stuart and his cavalry is chiefly due the early and valuable information of the movements of the enemy."[59]

Stuart's personal battle flag, sewn by his wife, Flora in 1862. It accompanied most of the campaigns of the Year of Glory, but accidentally fell into a fire at Stuart's headquarters and was damaged. Sent home for repair, it was still in Flora's possession when Stuart was mortally wounded. She displayed it at the Virginia Female Institute in Staunton (now Stuart Hall) while she was principal there after the war, and it was donated to Stuart

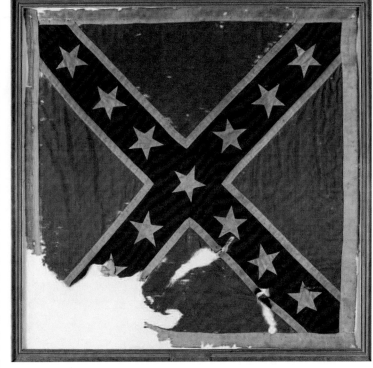

Hall by the family in the 1960s. In 2006 it sold for $956,000. *Courtesy of Heritage Auctions, Dallas, Texas, and the Texas Civil War Museum, Fort Worth, Texas*

The uniform of 1st Lt. (later Major) Philip Preston Johnston, of Stuart's Horse Artillery, worn during the Year of Glory. Johnston served under Pelham, distinguished himself at Brandy Station, and was wearing the uniform when wounded at Spotsylvania, the bullet entry hole and blood stains still being visible. *Courtesy of Wallace Johnston Jammerman, Gr. Grandaughter, and Ronald Cleveland*

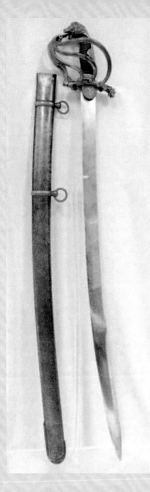

Believed to have been crafted by Harry McArdle of the firm of Mitchell and Tyler in Richmond, Virginia, this saber was given to Stuart by Heros Von Borcke, although its presentation was not described in Von Borke's memoirs. *Courtesy of Heritage Auctions, Dallas, Texas, and the Texas Civil War Museum, Fort Worth, Texas*

Above: Stuart's gold mechanical pencil and gold cuff links.

Right: Stuart's field glasses and case.

Both images courtesy of Heritage Auctions, Dallas, Texas, and the Texas Civil War Museum, Fort Worth, Texas

Above & Right: Stuart's compass. *Courtesy of Heritage Auctions, Dallas, Texas, and the Texas Civil War Museum, Fort Worth, Texas*

Right: Stuart's gold pocket watch. Stuart's initials are engraved on the case within a Scottish belted buckle motif. *Courtesy of Heritage Auctions, Dallas, Texas, and the Texas Civil War Museum, Fort Worth, Texas*

Below: Case for Stuart's gold spurs (see next image) with leather straps and buckles rolled and inserted at left. *Courtesy of Heritage Auctions, Dallas, Texas, and the Texas Civil War Museum, Fort Worth, Texas*

Above: Stuart's golden spurs, given him in the fall of 1862 by an anonymous lady in Baltimore. He thereafter used the initials "K.G.S." in letters to a few close friends and family, standing for "Knight of the Golden Spurs." *Courtesy of Heritage Auctions, Dallas, Texas, and the Texas Civil War Museum, Fort Worth, Texas*

Left and above: Stuart's gold watch fob with three hunting dog motifs, possibly a West Point graduation present, as he is clearly wearing it in a photo of him taken in 1854 standing between Custis Lee and Stephen D. Lee. *Courtesy of Heritage Auctions, Dallas, Texas*

Below: Three views of Stuart's ring, a gift from his parents upon graduation from West Point and engraved inside with his name and June 1854. It contains a green stone depicting the West Point insignia and was worn by Stuart from 1854 until his death. The ring shows extensive wear from the rubbing of reins, and was likely removed by his wife on May 12, 1864. *Courtesy of Heritage Auctions, Dallas, Texas*

Right: Signatures of Stuart and his staff from his "Common Book." Stuart carried a 8" by 11" book in which he kept personal recollections, verses and letters, the first page of which is dominated by this collection of autographs by Stuart and nine of his staff officers. *Courtesy of the Virginia Historical Society*

Center: Autograph of Stonewall Jackson in Stuart's autograph book. The book contains the signatures of 30 Confederate generals as well as six European visitors and two of Stuart's staff. All of the autographs were signed directly on a page of the book except three, like Jackson's, which were clipped from another document and pasted onto a page. One suspects that Stuart wanted to capture and preserve Jackson's inscription of "your much attached friend." *Courtesy of the Virginia Historical Society*

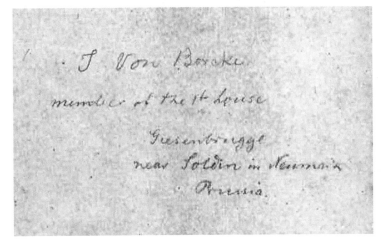

Left: Autograph and inscription of Heros Von Borcke in Stuart's autograph book. *Courtesy of the Virginia Historical Society*

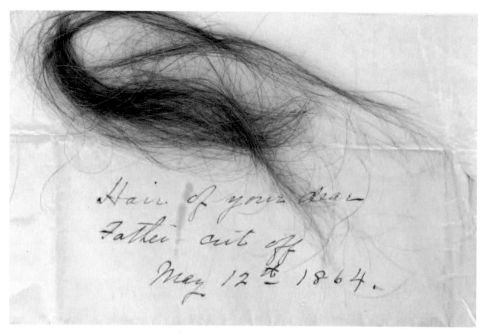

A lock of Stuart's hair snipped from his head by his wife, Flora, after Stuart's death on May 12, 1864. *Courtesy of Heritage Auctions, Dallas, Texas, and the Texas Civil War Museum, Fort Worth, TX*

Telegram sent by Jeb Stuart to his wife Flora on December 14, 1862 following the Battle of Fredericksburg. "We were victorious yesterday. Repulsing enemy's attack in main force with tremendous slaughter. Gen. Jno. R. Cooke (Flora's brother) was wounded in the forehead. Is in no danger & receives all the attention that a mother or sister could give if here. I got shot through my fur collar but am unhurt. JEB Stuart" *Courtesy of Virginia Historical Society*

The Bower. Stuart and a portion of his cavalry camped around the home of the Dandridge family from September 28 to October 29, 1862, and held balls, skits, and charades in its "great hall" almost nightly. It was described as "a merry headquarters" that was "the envy of all commands." *Courtesy of Louise McDonald and the Dandridge family descendants*

Dundee, in Hanover County, home of Dr. Lucien Price and his daughters, Elizabeth and Nannie, site of the marriage of Elizabeth and Dr. John Fontaine on January 20, 1863, attended by Stuart, Von Borcke, and Chiswell Dabney. Frequently visited by Stuart, who wrote a poem about the home and considered it to be the most lovely place on Earth.
Courtesy of Richard Barrett

The ballroom of the Shirley Female Academy, or the Landon House, where the Sabres and Roses Ball was held on September 8, 1862, interrupted when Federal cavalry attacked Confederate pickets, resumed after the attackers were driven away, and interrupted again by the arrival of Confederate wounded from the skirmish. *Courtesy of Kevin Dolan*

The Shirley Female Academy, now known as the Landon House, in Urbana, Maryland, site of the "Sabres and Roses Ball" on September 8, 1862. *Courtesy of Kevin Dolan*

Ordnance Rifle No. 194, one of only four surviving cannons known to have been in the Stuart Horse Artillery. A three-inch ordinance rifle, it was delivered to the Federal army in January 1862, captured by the Confederates, most likely at 2nd Manassas, and used by the Horse Artillery until re-captured at the Battle of Tom's Brook on October 9, 1864 by 3rd Cavalry Division forces under Custer. *Courtesy of Ronald Cleveland*

CHAPTER EIGHT

FREDERICKSBURG AND THE DUMFRIES RAID
NOVEMBER 17, 1862–JANUARY 1, 1863

Last of all the brave Burnside
with his pontoon bridges tried
a road no one had thought of before him.
With two hundred thousand men
for the Rebel slaughter pen
and the blessed Union flag waving o'er him;
but he met a fire like hell,
of canister and shell,
that mowed his men down with great slaughter.
'Twas a shocking sight to view,
that second Waterloo,
and the river ran with more blood than water.
—Richmond is a Hard Road to Travel, *as sung by Sam Sweeny*

Lead elements of the Federal army were in Falmouth, directly across the Rappahannock River from Fredericksburg, by November 18. Burnside might have seized the city immediately had he not decided to wait for pontoon bridges before trying to cross the river. These did not arrive until the 25th, and by the 22nd Longstreet's Corps had occupied the high ground west of the old town called Marye's Heights. The stage was set for another colossal battle.

Stuart and his troopers shadowed Burnside as soon as it was evident he was moving, battling near Warrenton and collecting prisoners as they moved.[1] Jackson's Corps left Winchester on the 22nd, heading for Fredericksburg, and arrived there on the 30th. Along the way, on November 28th, Jackson's wife gave birth to daughter Julia, Stonewall's only child.

Stuart established headquarters in a pinewoods about five miles from the town, on the Telegraph Road to Richmond, christened Camp No Camp. His exact, day-by-day movements during these last days of November are difficult to pinpoint. He and his men were probably in the saddle from November 17 to the 22nd, and once located in Fredericksburg, Jeb's attention turned to Port Royal and whether Burnside might attempt a crossing there. Port Royal is about eighteen miles southeast of Fredericksburg, where the Rappahannock was navigable by gunboats. It is not known whether Stuart obtained intelligence that gunboats were on the way—they were—or whether he simply anticipated they might appear, but he sent Pelham's artillery there and then joined him to locate the best places to post guns.

Another tragedy visited Stuart on November 25, this time to his military family, when venerable Redmond Burke was killed, or murdered, near Shepherdstown. The night of November 24, Burke and his three sons, Edward, John Redmond, and William, or "Jug," were returning to Shepherdstown for the night, planning to join Stuart in the morning. However, their presence was communicated to Federals on other side of the Potomac by Union sympathizers, who then guided a company of the 2nd Massachusetts Infantry across to surprise Burke's party at the home of a friend. Local legend said Burke dismounted at the house and handed the reins of his horse, a gift from Stuart, to Jug and walked toward the house. Before he reached the door, one of the civilian guides stepped forward, placed his pistol against Burke's chest and fired two shots, killing him instantly. If true, he was not given a chance to surrender and was killed in cold blood. The Union version of the story differed, reporting that Burke's death wound came as he attempted to flee after being called on to surrender.[2]

Stuart's two most faithful chroniclers, Blackford and Von Borcke, were on leave during those days. Blackford obtained a twenty-day furlough on or about November 10th, to spend time with his family in Abingdon. Von Borcke was sent to Richmond on the 14th and by the time both returned, Stuart was established near Fredericksburg.

When Von Borcke returned he found the general was in Port Royal, and he reported being joined by Vizetelley and Lawley the same day or the next, for whom a tent was pitched near Stuart's.[3] Hitching up the yellow wagon, he hauled the two Englishmen to a high point from which they could view the enemy on the other side of the river. Vizetelley made a sketch that later appeared in the *London Illustrated News,* after which Von Borcke carried them to the headquarters of General Micah Jenkins for dinner and then back to their tent, where Von tried unsuccessfully to convince them to go on a possum hunt.[4]

On the 27th Wade Hampton took 208 men, crossed the Rappahannock at Kelly's Ford, and went by back roads to a point two miles from Hartwood Church, where he attacked a camp of two squadrons of the 3rd Pennsylvania Cavalry at 4 a.m. on the 28th, wounding four Federals and taking eighty-two prisoners, five of whom were officers.[5]

Stuart was in Port Royal by the 28th, and visited the home of the Bernard family, Gay Mont, near where he erected a signal station on a hill to observe enemy movements. He returned on November 30 with Pelham, Will Farley, Major Andrew Venable, and Lt. Walter "Honeybun" Hullihen. The Bernard family offered their home for his use, but Stuart declined, saying it "was unsoldierly to sleep in a house."[6] He nevertheless returned often and considered the family to be good friends, sometimes sneaking into their home unannounced, then making his presence known by playing the "music-box" in the library.[7]

Stuart spent November 29 in the company of General Lee, scouting the river in anticipation of the arrival of Federal gunboats. On the 30th he returned to Port Royal, but before leaving directed Channing Price to send a telegraph to Flora in Lynchburg to inquire about Jimmy. Having not heard anything from her and still haunted by the loss of La Pet, he was uneasy that his son might also become ill. Price sent the telegram, and wrote to his mother on the 30th that he planned to go down to the river to see the Yankees on the Falmouth side. He had heard that "you can go down to the river bank & talk to them across the river."[8]

On either November 30 or December 1, Mulatto Bob arrived with Jackson's corps and returned to Stuart's headquarters. Missing since getting captured on the second ride around McClellan, he reported leaving Jeb's two horses at the house of "a good Southern man near Hyattstown, Maryland," and that they would be brought to Leesburg as soon as possible.[9]

On December 1, Jeb sent sixty men of the 9th Virginia, under Major T. Weller, across the river to capture prisoners from whom intelligence might be gained. They returned with two Federal officers and forty-seven men.[10] On December 2, Stuart wrote to General Chilton in Richmond to report the death of Redmond Burke and pay him homage, declaring that "his gray hairs have descended in honor to the grave."[11]

That evening the Bernards hosted a dinner for Stuart, as well as Pelham, Rooney Lee and various aides and staff officers. The lady of the house, Helen Bernard, did not feel as warmly toward Stuart as he did toward her family. She wrote that he "does not impress me so favorably, a bold dashing soldier, he doubtless is, but without the striking marks of high breeding which distinguished Gen. [Rooney] Lee." Of the latter she wrote that he was "[t]all, robust, athletic, yet polished, courteous and with a gentleness of manner almost like a woman's." Of Pelham she said he "pleased us extremely, a mere youth apparently, beardless and slender almost to a fault, but quick and energetic in his movements and with an eagle eye that shows his spirit."[12]

While dinner was underway, Stonewall Jackson arrived at the signal station looking for Stuart and was told, erroneously, that he was not nearby. Inside the house, Stuart, Lee, and Pelham discussed whether the family was in danger with the enemy. Lee opined that the Bernards should leave, but Jeb said "he thought we need not be in a hurry, as if it became necessary to put troops around the house and there was danger of the house being knocked to pieces, we might still escape or take refuge in the cellar." Lee told Pelham he would depend on him to provide artillery and he would place sharpshooters along the river that night.

The three officers may have been goading Helen. With her concerns about "striking marks of high breeding," she must have been visibly snobbish, such that the three young men delighted in speculating that her grand house might be "knocked to pieces" and she would be forced to cringe in the cellar. When a soldier came to the door to report that Jackson had come and gone, she became more anxious, recording that "We are inclined to think that when 'Old Stonewall' appears upon the field, the time for action has come."

Another tragedy befell Jeb that day. His nephew, Sandy Stuart, son of William Alexander, died of whooping cough. The loss was particularly hard on William, whose wife had died the previous July. He said of the boy, "He was my favorite."[13]

On December 3, D.H. Hill's division occupied Port Royal. There was an expectation that Burnside would try to force a crossing nearby under the protection of gunboats. Hearing they might attempt to put a pontoon bridge at a particular spot, Stuart and his staff rode there and found a Federal engineer officer on the opposite side of the river sketching. Stuart and his party drew up in a line on their side of the river and watched until the engineer finally noticed them and "bundled up & travelled off, looking like a dog caught in the act of sheep killing."[14]

Stuart, Pelham, Von Borcke, Dr. Eliason, and Ben White were all in Port Royal on the 3rd, leaving only Channing Price and Major Fitzhugh at headquarters. Price wrote his sister to say it was dreadfully lonesome there and that he wished he was with the General, "as I have found that I am always happier when with him than anywhere else in this life we are now leading." In regard to the death of Redmond Burke he wrote, "the Genl exhibits great feeling on the subject & cries almost every time an allusion is made to it."[15]

On the 4th the speculation about Federal gunboats became reality when the *Jacob Bell, Currituck, Coeur de Lion,* and *Anacosta* steamed into sight and began lobbing shells into the town. A battery from Alabama, plus Hill's infantry, returned fire, which did little damage to the gunboats but convinced them to move out of range. Pelham, however, was waiting downstream with two three-inch rifled cannon, and the gunboats were only three hundred yards away when he opened fire, scoring direct hits on one ship with his first two shots. The gunboats returned fire and managed to take away the leg of one of Pelham's gunners, but Pelham had the advantage of elevation and the gunboats steamed away.[16]

It snowed that night. Pelham and Rooney Lee returned to Gay Mont for the evening, but Jeb did not accompany them. On the 5th Burnside attempted to cross the river at a place called Skinker's Neck, which was unoccupied the day before but which was now, to Burnside's disappointment, crawling with Jackson's infantry.[17]

On December 5, snowball fights began in the Confederate camps. Hood's and McLaws' divisions of Longstreet's Corps were camped next to each other and an open field lay between their camps and Stuart's headquarters. After a few hundred of McLaws' men attacked Hood's camp, Hood's entire division fell into battle line with colors flying and officers leading. They drove the assailants back to their camp, where they were reinforced and a counterattack was made. "Sharpshooters" took position behind cedar trees and bushes along Telegraph Road and "the air was darkened with the snowballs" as the fight moved back and forth across the field. Stuart and his staff mounted boxes to view the battle but attempted to remain neutral, even raising a white flag at one point, which was completely ignored by the combatants. They could not refrain from shouting commands and encouragement, but were frequently the targets of snow-balls from both sides. Hood's division was relentless, and was in the process of driving McLaws' men out of their camp when Rebel Yells were heard on the right and two brigades of Anderson's division charged in to reinforce McLaws. This turned the tide and Hood's men were driven back to their own camp. Casualties for the day included a broken leg in Hood's division and the loss of an eye in McLaws'.[18]

That same day Stuart wrote a poem to a "Miss Bell Hart" and signed it "James Elder Brother Stuart." Jeb had six sisters—Ann Dabney, Bethenia Frances, Mary Tucker, Columbia Lafayette, Virginia Josephine, and Victoria August—so the exact identity of Bell Hart is a bit of a mystery. Interestingly, however, the poem was one that Stuart sent to at least four different women over the course of ten years.[19] He also wrote a letter to Lilly Lee, lamenting the death of Redmond Burke and vowing to put a monument over him "if I live." He also mentioned both the silver spurs her husband had worn and his new gold ones.[20]

On December 6, Stuart and some of his staff braved the icy weather and returned to Port Royal where they dined again at Gay Mont. Pelham, whose artillery was still at Port Royal, attended, and after discussing how the gunboat threat had abated but a buildup of troops was occurring at Fredericksburg, Stuart directed him to take his artillery there.[21]

That evening Captain Lewis Guy Phillips of Britain's Grenadier Guards arrived at Camp No Camp. His regiment was in Canada and he'd obtained leave in order to observe the war.[22] Blackford wrote of Phillips that he "was a fine fellow whom we all liked," who wanted to see everything, and that during the upcoming battle he "went under fire freely and showed perfect coolness, though it was his first experience."[23]

That a large battle was going to be fought in and around Fredericksburg was obvious, and on December 8 General Lee issued a circular urging the citizens to leave the city before Burnside began shelling the place. The frozen roads out of town soon filled with women, children, and old people in all kinds of wagons, buggies, and carts, many with no place to go but the surrounding woods.[24]

On December 9 one of Stuart's couriers, Private Thomas F. Chancellor, whose family lived six miles out of the city, invited Stuart and his staff to attend a party there the following evening.[25] Jeb gave it careful thought but decided the battle was so imminent that he should decline. He did not restrain his staff, however, and after supper on the 10th Blackford, Sweeney, two fiddlers, Pelham, Von Borcke, Dabney, Captain Phillips, and Major Frank Terrell piled into the yellow wagon, pulled by four mules, for the trip. Mulatto Bob followed on horseback, leading another horse in case the ride became too rough for Captain Phillips. The roads were icy and rough, the mules high-spirited, and Von Borcke was driving. Blackford, anticipating a mishap, lowered the tailgate and sat with this legs dangling out the back, thinking that if the overcrowded vehicle tipped over he would leap away.

They jounced merrily along, singing loudly, so that infantrymen came out of their tents and shouted or cheered. After two miles, Major Terrell offered to drive and Von agreed, wanting to "unite in the animated conversation and merriment going on behind." Terrell picked up the pace and everyone was enjoying the excitement until, with a crash, the rear axle snapped and a rear wheel flew off. Blackford dropped straight down. Mercifully his legs were not caught beneath the wagon bed, but when his feet hit the road he was pulled out on his back. He still would have been okay, but the wheel landed on his head, gashing it and knocking him out.

They patched him up, but the yellow wagon had delivered its last ride. The bed was completely detached from the front wheels, which were still hitched to the mules by the axletree. Glum, with four miles to go and nobody to assist, they did the best they could. Blackford recalled riding the rest of the way sitting on the front axle, while Von wrote that he, Phillips, and Dabney rode there, the musicians rode the two horses, and the other men rode the mules.

The party at the Chancellor home was another extravaganza under the stars, in a candlelit mansion with music from banjo, bones and violins, Virginia reels, and beautiful women. Blackford retired early and spent the night, but the others partied late, then borrowed a wagon from their host and returned to headquarters shortly before dawn on the 11th.[26] The revelers were able to get very little sleep before being awakened by cannon fire. The Federals were laying pontoon bridges across the river, an artillery duel had commenced, and Barksdale's brigade of Mississippians was in the town of Fredericksburg to contest their crossing.

Stuart was up at the first sound of the guns, and with members of his staff he rode to a hill near Telegraph Road where General Lee had his headquarters and where Jackson, Longstreet, and other generals commanding infantry divisions were gathered. The hill offered a view of the plain and the city and was known thereafter as Lee's Hill.

Blackford, awakened by the cannonade, rode into town and joined the others. He was from Fredericksburg and was anxious to know what was occurring in the town, so with Stuart's permission he took three couriers and rode to where Barksdale's men were battling the enemy, who had suspended their efforts to lay bridges and were crossing in boats to drive the Rebels out. He returned to Lee Hill and at 10 a.m. the Federals began shelling the city with over 100 pieces of artillery. Citizens who had not already abandoned their homes choked the roads out of town, although some insisted on remaining.

About 2 p.m. Lee ordered Barksdale to retire, and the Federals completed their bridge building and began crossing. After sending Blackford into the city to crawl into the home of a former neighbor to observe the enemy laying a bridge near the house, with columns of infantry waiting to cross, Stuart spent the day watching, then returned with his staff to their tents.

Early on the 12th they returned to Lee's Hill as "interminable columns of infantry, blue in colour, and blurred by distance, flowed towards us like the waves of a steadily advancing sea. On and on they came, with flash of bayonets and flutter of flags, to the measure of military music, each note of which was borne . . . by the morning breeze."[27] At about 11 a.m., Stuart and Von Borcke rode out to examine the enemy's activity on the Confederate right, where most of the cavalry were posted. They passed long lines of Confederate infantrymen waiting for what was to come, lying behind or improving their earthworks, cooking, or engaged in conversation. The Federals fired a large shell occasionally, which the Rebels called "Yankee flour barrels," and they cheered the explosions, most being harmless.

It was foggy, and near Deep Run Creek where Hood's and Early's divisions were posted, Stuart and Von Borcke took a bridle path away from the earthworks, believing it was a short cut to the far right of the line. They'd not ridden far when they came upon a line of horsemen ahead in the fog, most of whom were wearing brownish, dust-colored jackets over their uniforms. Believing they were Confederates returning from a patrol they continued riding toward them until, at about forty yards distance, the horsemen opened fire and a dozen or more charged, demanding that the Rebels surrender. Stuart and Von Borcke wheeled and galloped back to their lines, where some of Early's riflemen opened fire on the enemy. They failed to leave, however, until Hood rode up, took in the situation and summoned a contingent of Texas marksman who crawled to within eighty yards of the horsemen, opened fire and drove them away.

Stuart continued further, passing A.P. Hill's division and coming at last to the position of the cavalry on the Port Royal road. They were skirmishing with Federal horseman and were in good spirits. Stuart, knowing the terrain was not favorable for mounted combat, but anxious to find a role to play, rode forward into a field that seemed to offer an arena for cavalry action, but found the ground too soft.

About 2 p.m., he decided to ascertain what the enemy was doing between Fredericksburg and Hamilton's Crossing. Tying their horses at a small barn, he and Von crept along a ditch to an elevation a few hundred yards from the enemy and trained their field glasses. They saw several thousand infantry, significant works under construction, and at least thirty-two pieces of artillery. Stuart sent Von Borcke to report this to Lee and rode over to talk to A.P. Hill. Von Borcke found Lee with Jackson, who heard Von's report, then rode to the barn and went on foot to observe, while Von worried for their safety.

After returning from the barn, Stuart joined them and all but Jackson, who returned to his command, rode back to Lee's Hill. There they found that a 32-pounder Parrot guns had burst a few moments earlier, not killing anyone but coming close to injuring Captain Phillips, who was nearby. At dusk Stuart and his staff returned to camp and spent the evening with their English guests, discussing the latest developments.[28] Pelham and Phillips stayed up late, discussing artillery tactics, possible English recognition of the Confederacy, and the coming battle.[29]

A bugle called Stuart and his staff to horse at dawn. The day of battle had arrived and they would spend it on the right of the line. Captain Phillips opted to return to Lee's Hill, believing it would afford the best view, but before departing he gave a narrow red and blue striped ribbon, the colors of his regiment, to Pelham and asked if he would wear it that day as a good luck charm and as a souvenir Phillips could keep. Pelham, blushing, took the ribbon and tied it around his cap.[30]

The field was covered with fog again and Burnside delayed his attack, originally planned for dawn. A little after 9 a.m., with most of the fog burned away, the Federals began an artillery barrage that opened one of the bloodiest, most fruitless infantry assaults of the war. As soon as the Federal "Grand Division" commanded by Gen. William Franklin in front of Jackson commenced to move, Stonewall said, "I am glad the Yankees are coming," and penned a note to Stuart to have Pelham open fire. Mere moments before, Jeb had sent a message to Lee saying, "I am going to crowd them with artillery."

George Gordon Meade's division of 4,500 men was leading. They crossed the Richmond Stage Road and were in the process of realigning when artillery fire came from their left, causing a halt. It was Pelham, with a single twelve-pounder Napoleon originally captured from the Yankees at Seven Pines. He was only a few hundred yards from Meade's left, so close that the Federals first thought they were receiving friendly fire. In fact, Pelham was so far in front of his own lines that the Federals might have rushed and captured him. Instead they milled about while Meade called for assistance from the nearest Federal guns, Battery A of the First Pennsylvania Artillery. As it rolled forward Pelham scored a direct hit on one of its guns and knocked it out of action.

Pelham fired, moved, and fired again, sending shells into the enemy's ranks so rapidly that they believed they were receiving fire from two complete batteries. Within twenty minutes, five batteries of Yankee cannons, thirty to thirty-six guns, plus some of the twenty pounder Parrots on Stafford Heights across the river were raining shells on Pelham. He was so well positioned, however, in low ground and behind the cover of a hedge, that most of the shells missed completely. Pelham did not even dismount, although he ordered his men to lie flat on the ground when the enemy fire became heaviest, and one of his men was struck in the head and killed in that position.

When enemy fire slackened, Pelham's gunners jumped up and fired back, sending solid shot into the massed infantry and blowing up an artillery caisson. The Federal assault was stalled, and nearly every eye in the Rebel army, including General Lee's, was on the spectacle.

Stuart first sent dismounted sharpshooters from the 9th Virginia Cavalry to assist Pelham, then summoned John Esten Cooke, who began the war as an artilleryman, to bring up a Blakely rifled cannon and its crew. He did so, but fired only a single shot before Battery A of the Federal Maryland Light Artillery scored a direct hit on the gun, killing two of its gunners.

Pelham continued to fire, relocate, and fire again for over an hour, delaying the Federal advance, and allowing the Confederates to ascertain where their artillery batteries were located. Stuart sent him a message asking "How are you getting on?" and Pelham answered, "I am doing first rate." Only when he ran low on ammunition, after Stuart sent three messages telling him to withdraw, did he do so. He'd had two gunners killed and another mortally wounded, three seriously and five slightly wounded, and fourteen horses killed. Later that day Lee told Jackson that "you should have a Pelham on each flank," and Jackson thanked Pelham three times for his accomplishments. Pelham did not file an official account of the action, but in his battle report General Lee referred to him as "the gallant Pelham," which was how he was remembered from then to the present day.[31]

The events and outcome of the battle are well known, and not being a cavalry fight, most of Stuart's activities consisted of gathering and relaying information. His men engaged in various harassing attacks, and at one point a bullet hit the fur collar of Jeb's red-lined cape, handmade by Flora, and tore it away. Blackford and Von Borcke were together part of the day, and their respective accounts of an incident illustrate the convenience of memory. Blackford wrote that while watching the battle, "Von Borcke became so excited that in spite of all I could do to prevent it he stood up and of course drew upon us a severe shelling. One of these shells passed right between our heads as we sat on a lot on the rear slope of a hill . . . [and] Von Borcke dodged so that he lost his balance and rolled down the steep slope, to our great amusement." Von's account of the same incident was that "a shell passed so near to our heads that my gallant friend and myself were precipitated headlong by the force of windage at least fifteen feet down the hillside, where we both lay motionless for a brief space, and then rose in a fit of uncontrollable laughter as we looked each in the other's blank and astonished face."[32]

Stuart and his staff returned to headquarters late. Captain Phillips was there, having had a magnificent view of the battle from Lee's Hill. Pelham returned the regimental ribbon to him, "its gay colours just a little blackened by powder-smoke." Also present were Lt. Thomas B. Turner and Lt. Walter Hullihen, who had just returned from an expedition behind enemy lines to rescue Mary Lee, the commanding general's daughter.

She had become trapped at the home of friends when Burnside advanced, and the two officers volunteered to bring her back. After sneaking across the river and through enemy lines, they arrived at the place, Cedar Grove Plantation in King George County, but Mary's friends convinced her it was too risky to accompany them to her father's army. This turned out to be sound advice. Turner and Hullihen attempted to recross the river on a raft held together by their suspenders, but it fell apart. Returning to the Yankee side of the river, they were picked up by a cavalry patrol whose commander believed their story of being stragglers and sent them with a single guard toward the Federal camp. Distracting the guard by examining and admiring his horse, Hullihen made a grab for his pistol but missed and was nearly killed when the guard fired three times at nearly point blank range. Turner then grabbed the trooper's carbine and fired. The trooper wheeled his horse and galloped fifty yards before falling or jumping from the animal. The two young officers did not take time to investigate. The home of a relative of Turner's was nearby, where they were able to obtain a canoe and get back to safety.[33]

The next day, December 14, was one of waiting, with the Confederates expecting Burnside to renew his offensive. Stuart spent most of the day at Jackson's headquarters and on the Confederate right with his cavalry. Other than skirmishing and artillery dueling, however, combat was not renewed. Jeb sent a telegram to Flora informing her of the previous day's victory, the wounding of her brother, John R. Cooke with a non-life-threatening head wound, and the shot he'd received in his fur collar.[34]

The 15th was another foggy day, and Stuart sent Blackford to scout the enemy's activities. Riding between the lines he came upon a battalion of Confederate sharpshooters that included his brother, Eugene. They shared the same type of assignment and fell in together. When they arrived at the enemy's rifle pits they found them empty, and Blackford sent a courier to report this to Stuart. Continuing into the city, they found Federal stragglers sleeping or hiding in houses, but rather than place them under guard they told them to double-quick to the Confederate lines or be shot. In town, they found another brother, Charles, a captain in the 2nd Virginia Cavalry, on the same type of scouting errand, so they decided to visit their old home.

It had been used as a hospital and was in shambles. The room in which all three were born had been an operating room and the floor was half an inch deep in clotted blood. The walls were splattered with blood, and severed arms, hands, legs, and feet were scattered about. Their uncle, an old bachelor named John Minor, had lived in the house until his death a few months earlier, and what remained of his library and collection of fine art was torn and broken up. An artillery shell had passed cleanly through the house, entering a window, passing through a wall and bookshelf, and exiting out a panel door. They did not know it then, but the house also contained the body of a dead Union sharpshooter killed in the attic that would not be found for weeks.[35]

About noon on December 15 a squad of mounted Federals approached Jackson's headquarters under a white flag carrying a request for a truce in order to bury the dead and tend to the wounded. Jackson examined the document but returned it, saying he could agree only if it was from the commanding general. The squad went back, returned two hours later with Burnside's signature, and the truce was allowed.

Von Borcke was one of several Confederate officers assigned to oversee the truce. The Federals came in columns of 200 and 300 men and gathered first the wounded and then the dead. The work progressed steadily for half an hour, until several Confederate enlisted men came forward to help and a Yankee battery of artillery opened fire. Shouting "treason" and similar comments, the Rebels dove back into their breastworks, but the firing ceased and the Federals explained it was all a mistake, after which work resumed.

Von became engaged in searching for the body of Union General Conrad F. Jackson, who commanded the Third Brigade in Meade's division and was killed leading an attack. He was found in a small ravine, lying next to his adjutant. The general rode a gray horse during the battle that attracted the Rebels' attention. It lay nearby, pierced by several bullets.

Those wounded on the 13th and still alive on the 15th were in pitiful condition. The men from the two armies talked, and many of the Federals spoke of Burnside with contempt, saying he was not capable of commanding an army.

Channing Price wrote that Stuart spent the day "on a high hill near the R. Road."[36] He observed the burial parties, going down at least once to visit with Federal officers, but was in a foul mood because he wanted the Confederates to take the offensive and go after Burnside while his army was huddled with its back to the river. Shifting his chagrin onto the burial parties, he mumbled that "These Yankees, have always some underhand trick when they send a flag of truce, and I fear they will be off before daylight."

In the evening the Federals delivered a demand for the surrender of Port Royal, which made no particular sense, but Lee directed Stuart to ride there in the morning and see what was happening. Before he left he discovered that his prediction about the Yankees had indeed occurred, as they had slipped out of their earthworks in the dark and sneaked, from his point of view, back across the Rappahannock. Any opportunity to destroy the Federal army or drive it into the river, as both Stuart and Jackson wanted to try, was lost. One Yankee regiment did not get the message. Camped a distance from the rest of the army, no one bothered to rouse them during the night when everyone slipped away. They were still asleep when a regiment from Mississippi came along and took everyone prisoner.[37]

Jeb sent Channing Price to Fitz Lee, who was back in command, to tell him to take the Horse Artillery and his brigade and pursue the enemy. Then, with Rooney Lee's brigade, he rode to Gay Mont to see if the Federals were occupying or about to invade Port Royal. There was no enemy to be seen and he concluded that the demand for the town's surrender was a ruse to divert attention away from Burnside's retreat—more underhanded trickery.[38] Jeb was not the only officer disgusted. Major Phillip H. Powers, another of Stuart's staff, wrote home saying that he had ridden over the battlefield after the Yankees left and found 200 to 300 of their dead still lying about unburied. In one place he counted eighty-five bodies, frozen and nearly naked, who were carried to a place for burial but then abandoned when their "inhuman friends had left that duty unperformed and under cover of the truce flag evacuated their position."[39]

Jeb dispatched Chiswell Dabney to Lynchburg that day to escort Mrs. Stuart to Fredericksburg in order to be with her wounded brother.[40]

On the 17th, Jeb allowed his staff to sleep late, then called them together for breakfast in his tent at mid-morning. Captain Phillips of the Grenadier Guards was joined by another member of his regiment, Captain Wynne, who came from Canada with Phillips but took ill in Richmond and missed the battle. In the afternoon, Stuart met under a flag of truce with Colonel Joseph H. Taylor, Federal Major General Sumner's chief of staff. Taylor was at West Point after Stuart, but the pair met on the frontier, and they discussed various matters. The subject that interested Stuart most concerned another West Point graduate, William T. Magruder of Maryland, who was close behind Stuart at the academy. Magruder had the rare distinction of serving as both a Federal and Confederate officer during the war, first as a Federal until October 1862, when he resigned and went south. He received a captain's commission and was on the staff of Confederate Brigadier Joseph R. Davis, who commanded a Mississippi brigade.

Taylor told Stuart that Magruder went to Lincoln to request a brigadier's commission, carrying with him letters that attested to his loyalty to the United States, but resigned and joined the Confederate army when the general's star was not forthcoming. Stuart had heard a similar story about Magruder the previous summer, before his resignation, from a Federal non-commissioned officer of cavalry taken prisoner near Hanover.

Stuart sent Wade Hampton to harass the enemy, and he captured a cavalry picket of forty men, a stand of colors, and twenty wagons, then continued to the Occoquan and captured thirty more wagons and nearly 150 more prisoners.[41]

The next day, the 18th, Stuart wrote a letter to Custis Lee to tell him what he had heard about Magruder, adding that Taylor said that Magruder should be kicked out of the Confederacy. Jeb asked Custis to relay this information to President Davis, but Magruder's immediate superior, General Davis, was the president's nephew, so the captain was safe from censure. He continued to serve as a Southern officer until he was killed in Pickett's Charge at Gettysburg.[42]

Jeb opined to Custis that the victory at Fredericksburg was the "neatest and cheapest of the war, adding with typical fanfare that "Englishmen here who surveyed Solferino and all the battlefields of Italy say that the pile of dead on the plains of Fredericksburg exceeds anything of the sort ever seen by them." Jeb had four Englishmen available to render such opinions, but Vizetelley was the single most likely candidate to have viewed Solferino and the battlefields of Italy. Solferino was a battle between the French, under Napoleon III and the Austrians under Franz Joseph, fought June 24, 1859, and involving some 300,000 troops.

During the end of December the Confederates settled into winter quarters. Longstreet's Corps stayed around Fredericksburg while Jackson camped along the road to Port Royal. Stonewall's headquarters were in an office in the rear of Moss Neck, the palatial home of the Corbin family, where he established a famous relationship with the family's five-year-old daughter, Janie, as he waited to see his own daughter for the first time. The woods around these places were filled with the sounds of axes as the soldiers constructed rough cabins, sheds, and stables. Among the staff, Pelham and John Esten Cooke moved in together, building a hut with a wood floor and a fireplace.[43]

The army's animals suffered from low temperatures, scant forage, and an outbreak of Mud Fever, which caused the loss of a fourth of the army's horses and mules. Von Borcke described the symptoms as becoming "first visible just above the hoof, whence it gradually extended, eventually involving the entire limb." The infection was brought on my wet, muddy conditions and was particularly common for animals wintered outside. The legs swell up, become painful, and render the animal lame. Treatment is bathing the animal's legs in hot water to remove scabs, keeping it dry and clean, and use of antibiotics, all of which were unlikely or impossible for Civil War soldiers living in wet winter woods.[44] Von reported that his mule, Kitt, came through the winter fine, looking "as gay and sleek as ever," and attributed her good health to having an "omnivorous appetite." "All was fodder to her impartial palate," he wrote, "from pine-leaves to scraps of leather, and even the blankets with which I covered my horses were not safe from her voracity."[45]

The morning of the 20th, anticipating his wife would arrive at any time, Stuart sent Channing Price to find suitable quarters for her near where her brother was convalescing at the home of a Mrs. French. He found a room nearby at a home belonging to a Mrs. Alsup. Hampton returned from his raiding that day. Among his captured prizes were boxes of champagne, claret, cheese, and 300 pairs of new boots, one pair of which he sent to Stuart.

On December 21, Custis Lee visited Stuart's camp to view the battle-field. More English visitors showed up during the Christmas and New Year's holidays. Captains Phillips and Wynne departed, but Spencer Compton Cavendish, the Marquis of Hartington and eighth Duke of Devonshire, arrived, accompanied by Colonel Leslie of the British army. Cavendish, generally referred to as Lord Hartington, was on a holiday tour of the American war and had visited both Lincoln and Davis. Lincoln was impressed by him and predicted he would have a distinguished political career, but the Lord's sympathies were with the South.[46]

Lawley was still on hand, and having two members of Parliament of differing ages at the same table for meals required a degree of Victorian etiquette not discarded even in a muddy army camp. Blackford reported that it was his first time in contact with "civil rank" and admitted to making "a little mistake at table as a consequence." He recalled that "At our mess table, the General sat at the head and I usually at the foot. Mr. Lawley, who was past middle age, sat next to me and Lord Hartington next to him. In carving I passed the plate to Mr. Lawley first as the oldest guest but with a polite bow he handed it to Lord Hartington, who was quite a young man. After that I always helped 'my Lord' first."[47]

Nevertheless Blackford considered the guests to be "unassuming," even to the extent of enlisting their confidence in a small prank concerning Stonewall Jackson. He took the Englishmen to Moss Neck and told them on the ride over of a habit of the General's, which was to insist on taking everyone's hat, even though he had no place to put them. "In a tent or in a room with only camp furniture there was no place, of course, to hang them," so that everyone who entered would simply hold their hat in their hand. Jackson, however, "would jump up and collect them all with 'let me have your hat, sir,' and then would realize that there was no place but the floor to put them." Blackford wrote that upon being introduced to the English Lord, Lawley and the rest, Jackson "went through his performance," and that the guests "could scarcely keep their countenances."[48]

Flora Stuart arrived at Jeb's headquarters on the 23rd, and Channing

Price took the general and Flora to Mrs. Alsop's, where they had dinner before going to Mrs. French's to see her brother, Brig. General John Cooke. They found him sitting in the parlor with "a piece of plaster on his forehead," looking pale but seemingly improved and hoping to return to the field soon. In the afternoon, Jeb sent Price to Lee's headquarters to deliver a report of Hampton's recent raids, as well as the captured Federal flag taken on the 17th. Lee was not there, however, and he left the flag and report with Brig. General Chilton.[49]

Stuart spent the night of the 23rd with Flora at Mrs. Alsop's, which was only about three-fourths of a mile from his headquarters. She had brought him a new pair of boots, probably the ones he had requested of Lily Lee in his letter of November 16, but they were not as nice as two pairs captured from the enemy, one by Hampton and the other by Lt. Colonel James Corley, that were given him. Accordingly, Jeb gave away the pair from Flora.[50]

December 24 was filled with preparations for a Christmas Eve celebration in Stuart's large tent. Couriers were sent out to round up food, which included thirty dozen eggs, sweet potatoes, butter, and twenty turkeys. Everyone joined in the efforts for a feast, including Mrs. Stuart, Von Borcke, staff officers, couriers, and servants. Mulatto Bob was appointed "majordomo and body-guard of the household and its inmates," which turned out to be no small challenge. Texans from Hood's brigade got wind of the turkeys and made more than one raid.

Officers in their finest uniforms, a few wives, and various guests came together that evening. In addition to the roasted birds they had hams, chickens, breads, apple brandy, and whiskey. Von Borcke acted as master of ceremonies and read Dickens' *A Christmas Carol*, which he acted out and made more humorous with Prussian mispronunciations.[51]

The next morning, Stuart traveled to Jackson's headquarters for Christmas dinner with Stonewall, General Lee, General Pendleton, and others, prepared by one of Jackson's aide's, Lt. J. P. Smith. The brick office building Jackson used as his headquarters had hunting scenes on the walls and was decorated for Christmas. The guests were impressed, particularly Lee, who remarked on how stylish Jackson was becoming, with a dining room servant wearing a white apron. Mrs. Corbin sent over butter cut into pads stamped with a rooster, and when Stuart discovered this he could not resist teasing Jackson, saying the rooster was apparently Stonewall's coat of arms but that having it stamped on the butter was a clear sign of moral degeneracy. The evening was filled with more joking and laughter, with Stuart displaying the characteristic boyish charm and good humor he had lacked of late.[52]

On the afternoon of the 26th, after visiting Flora and her brother at Mrs. French's, Jeb, Price, Pelham, Dr. Eliason, Dabney, Farley, Hullihen, and Turner joined 1,800 men from the brigades of Hampton, Fitz Lee, and Rooney Lee, plus a battery of Horse Artillery, and crossed the Rappahannock and the Rapidan for another foray into Yankee-held territory, remembered as the Dumfries Raid.[53]

Jeb's plan was to divide his force and strike the Telegraph Road, a major line of communication and supply for Burnside, at three points between Aquia Creek and the town of Occoquan, then reunite at a point north, depending on what the events of the day determined. After spending the first night at Bristersburg, the commands separated early on the 27th, with Fitz Lee aiming for the road north of Chopawamsic Creek, Hampton toward Occoquan, and Rooney Lee for Dumfries.

It took most of the day to get into position, as each command had to travel about twenty miles, but late in the afternoon Fitz Lee hit the road at his destination, captured wagons and prisoners, and rode toward Dumfries, where Rooney Lee had captured several pickets but found the town heavily defended. When the two brigades united, Jeb first planned to attack, but prisoners informed him that a strong force of infantry and cavalry was there and that the Rebels were in danger of being overwhelmed. Accordingly, Jeb had Fitz Lee make a demonstration with a portion of the 5th Virginia, as if preparing to charge, while the rest of the brigade and Rooney's rode on the Brentsville Road toward Cole's Store. The men of the 5th carried out the ruse, attacking first on foot, then in a mounted sweep that drove back the enemy's skirmishers and in which eleven of the enemy were captured. When almost dark the Rebels disappeared, joined the rest of the two brigades, and spent the night near Cole's Store.

Hampton, meanwhile, reached Occoquan about sunset on the 27th, charged into the town, which was occupied by a detachment of the 17th Pennsylvania Cavalry, captured eight of their wagons and nineteen prisoners, and drove the rest away. He then withdrew and headed to Cole's Store, where the wagons and prisoners were united and sent back to Lee's army under a squadron of the 9th Virginia.

On the 28th, Stuart led the column to Greenwood Church, where he stopped and dispatched 150 men of the 2nd South Carolina, under Col. M.C. Butler, to go to Bacon Race Church to capture a force of the enemy believed to be there. Butler encountered enemy pickets within a mile of the church and drove them in, but found a large force of cavalry and two pieces of artillery. Thinking the rest of the command was coming to his support, Butler held his ground under fire from the Federals, but was unaware that shortly after leaving Stuart at Greenwood Church that Stuart and Fitz Lee had become occupied with a force of 150 men of the 2nd and 17th Pennsylvania Cavalry who were in search of the Rebels who attacked at Occoquan.

When they ran into Fitz Lee's brigade a battle ensued. The 1st Virginia charged and the 2nd Pennsylvania fled. The 17th put up a little resistance but soon the entire force of blue horseman was fleeing with Confederates close on their tails. After a chase of two miles about thirty-five of the Yankees were able to cross the Occoquan River at Selectman's Ford, but the remaining 115 became prisoners of the Rebels. The Confederates continued their pursuit until they captured the enemy's main camp, which was filled with supplies.

Butler, meanwhile, was taking a beating from the enemy's artillery and advancing cavalry, and decided it was time to retrace his steps toward the main command, which apparently wasn't coming to his rescue. He traveled only a short distance, however, before finding the enemy across his path in numbers greater than his. He detoured, chased by Yankees while the rest of Stuart's command were chasing other Yankees. After covering three or four miles he eluded his pursuers and joined Stuart at Selectman's Ford.

After more skirmishing, and the capture of another wagon and a few prisoners, Stuart had his men burn the enemy supplies they could not carry, and turned north toward Burke's Station. It was dark but Jeb planned to spend another full night in the saddle.

At Burke's Station he surprised and captured the telegraph operator, then turned the key over to his own telegrapher, Private Sheppard, who spent two hours intercepting messages from General Samuel Heintzelman and others concerning Stuart's raid. The Federals were in great alarm, and orders were going out to destroy everything if attacked. While this was going on, Stuart's men tore up railroad tracks and destroyed the railroad bridge over Accotink Creek. Once he believed they had accomplished all they could do, Jeb had Sheppard send a message that was one of the war's classic examples of high jinx. Addressing it to Quartermaster General Montgomery Meigs of the Federal army in Washington, he wired, "Gen. Meigs will in the future please furnish better mules, those you have furnished recently are very inferior, which interfered seriously with our moving the captured wagons.—J.E.B. Stuart."[54]

He then cut the telegraph wires and headed toward Fairfax Court House, where he hoped to surprise another force of the enemy. Before leaving he had his men build campfires to convey the impression that they had gone into bivouac, which attracted enemy artillery fire.[55] With the shells exploding behind them, the Confederates rode through the dark several miles, but found Fairfax occupied by a brigade of infantry under Brig. Gen. Edwin Stoughton. They turned away and finally halted at dawn on the 29th at Frying Pan and the home of "a good Union man" named Barlow, near Chantilly. The troopers caught some badly needed sleep, but Jeb took time to visit Laura Ratcliffe, who lived nearby. About 11 a.m. the march resumed up the Little River Turnpike to Dover, which they reached at sunset. They spent the night there, with Stuart and Channing Price accepting an invitation from Colonel Hamilton Rogers for supper, and the night, at his home, Oakham.

The next morning, the 30th, John Mosby came to Stuart's room shortly before dawn. He had been with the column since it left Fredericksburg, but he now asked to be left behind with nine men. He had long agitated for independent, irregular command, saying he would "rust away my life" otherwise. Stuart approved, and when the column rode away from Dover, Mosby and his men dropped out at Middleburg to commence a career that would become legend.[56]

From Middleburg Stuart and the two Lee brigades continued south to The Plains, in Fauquier County, while Hampton rode from Dover to Haymarket. Stuart and the Lees spent the night at The Plains, departed at 7 a.m., and rode thirteen miles to Warrenton, which they believed was held by a strong force of the enemy. Fitz Lee detoured around the town but the enemy cavalry had departed, so Rooney Lee proceeded into the town and Fitz turned back and joined him.

Hampton's brigade rejoined the other formations at Warrenton, and on the 31st Stuart rode thirty-five miles to Culpeper Court House, where he spent the night and saw in the New Year. On the first day of January the column returned to the army around Fredericksburg.[57]

Stuart had captured about 250 prisoners, an equal number of horses, twenty wagons filled with equipment, numerous small arms, and a bounty of food such as coffee, cheeses, cakes, nuts, oranges, and lemons, all with the loss of one officer killed and twelve men wounded. Nevertheless, he was not as pleased with the results as he had anticipated, stating in his report that he regretted not capturing Dumfries or achieving more on the Telegraph

Road. Nevertheless, he had destroyed enemy railroad facilities, cut Burnside's communications link with Washington, caused the enemy to think he was making another raid into Maryland, and generally disrupted their lives across Northern Virginia.[58] It was something he did well.

CHAPTER NINE

THE LONG COLD WINTER
JANUARY 2, 1863–FEBRUARY 28, 1863

For I'se gwine home to Dinah,
Yes, I am gwine home.
Den I ain't got time to tarry,
I ain't got time to dwell,
I'm bound to de land of freedom,
oh, niggars! fare you well.
—Ain't Got Time to Tarry, *by Dan Emmett (1859)*

The first two and a half months of 1863 were a trial of endurance for Jeb and his cavalry. In addition to cold weather, they dealt with shortages in food, blankets, clothing, and even firewood. Their daily activities were either monotonous in camp or strenuous on long patrols of the Rappahannock. Stuart sometimes went on patrols, but generally left it to his brigade commanders to plan and execute them.

Flora stayed in Fredericksburg until mid-February, living in Mrs. Alsop's house, tending her brother, and enjoying the longest simulation of domestic life she would have with Jeb for the rest of their lives. Little is recorded of these days, but it's likely that Jeb, Flora, and Jimmie spent many of them as would any small family living in close quarters. One gauge of the attention Jeb paid them is the lack of letters to friends and other relatives he wrote during this period. Jimmie was ill with an unstated ailment, but he improved significantly by the second week of the month.

When not with Flora, on a patrol, or inspecting his outposts, Stuart spent time writing reports of the cavalry's actions of the previous nine months and shoring up the organization of his division. Whenever possible, he visited Jackson's headquarters at Moss Neck, although it was a day's ride each way. He also spent time talking, laughing, and joking with the members of his military family and visitors.

Jeb slept at Mrs. Alsop's regularly and had his office in his tent. It was large, with two fireplaces, a wooden floor and reinforced walls. A long table that would seat numerous guests was in its center, his field desk was in one corner, and on other sides were smaller tables and camp equipment for the use of staff, particularly Channing Price.

Von had a Sibley tent, designed by Henry H. Sibley, a Mexican War veteran, Indian fighter, and Confederate Brigadier. The tent was circular with a tall conical top that served as a chimney for the Sibley stove, also round and designed to sit in the tent's center, radiating heat in all directions. Von laid planks on the floor and covered them with a square of old canvas. His bed was constructed from a large packing case for saddles, and he constructed an "easychair" out of a whiskey cask by sawing one side off to within a foot of the floor and stuffing the bottom with blankets so that the other vertical side of the barrel served as a backrest.[1]

Pelham and John Esten Cooke were next door to Blackford, who had a large tent to himself.[2] Stuart was not able to bear being away from Pelham, as the fact that the major moved in with the staff rather than camping with his artillerymen illustrates. Blackford recalled that he and Pelham became closer than ever before during those winter months, not only living next door to each other but building a set of stables to accommodate their horses, Pelham's three and Blackford's five. Blackford's extras were for pulling the engineer equipment wagon driven by. his servant, Gilbert.[3]

Letters home were filled with war news, family gossip, and requests for items the officers could not otherwise obtain. Channing Price asked his mother for gray cloth to make a pair of pants and a vest. His saber had rubbed a large hole on the left side of his trousers and he was unable to find either cloth or replacement pants nearby. The cloth he received and turned into a vest must have caught Stuart's eye, as Price asked in a letter dated January 28th for more to make one for Stuart. Blackford needed blankets, as his best one was stolen from the back of his horse by "some rascal" while tied in front of General Lee's headquarters, of all places.[4]

The stockpile of food gathered for the Christmas Eve dinner carried over for awhile into January, but Texans continued to try to steal the remaining turkeys, which resulted in an alarm being raised by Mulatto Bob and "many a hurried night chase" by Von and others. Once the last turkey was eaten, decent food became scarce. Servants went out daily to buy or forage what they could find, but they regularly came back to report there was nothing to be had. When they could find anything, it often consisted of "beef so tough or bacon so rancid that only the sharpest pangs of hunger could induce a human being to tackle it as food." Von cut minie balls into small pieces for birdshot and went after whatever was flying in the woods, usually returning with nothing but a few blackbirds, robins, and sparrows. Often the staff had only four or five of these small, normally inedible creatures to divide equally among twelve or more hungry men.[5]

The lack of food and the cold weather did not prevent the Confederates from having fun. Many regiments had a band, and one or more played every evening. In a day before radio, phonographs, and television, songs were sung rather than simply listened to, and the sound of singing and laughter from numerous quarters was commonplace. Enterprising soldiers erected a theatre and took turns performing. Negro minstrels were a popular entertainment, plus a great many skits, plays, readings, poetry recitations, and other talent demonstrations.

The hunger was made more unbearable by the existence, nearby, of a flock of sheep whose owner demanded such exorbitant prices that no one could purchase any. All attempts at negotiation failed, but the couriers assigned to headquarters came up with a plan. The sheep sometimes strayed, attracted by the cavalry horses' fodder. One suspects a trail of fodder from flock to camp may have been laid, but it wasn't mentioned. Instead, the owner of the sheep was told he must keep his sheep away from the horses' feed and to ensure this occurred, the couriers dug a deep trench across the paths by which they normally came and covered it with pine branches and straw. Some of the sheep fell in the trench and did not escape because of "such injuries as necessitated their immediate slaughter." The owner of the sheep was notified and he, unable to make use of the animals thus lost, agreed to sell the "greater part of the meat" at a reasonable price.[6]

On January 12, Stuart wrote a letter to Colonel J.F. Gilmore, Chief of the Confederate Engineer Corps, requesting that three lieutenants of Engineers be assigned to the cavalry division. Blackford was the staff engineer, but more could be put to work. Besides, Jeb had an ulterior motive—he wanted to bring Channing Price's older brother, Tom, and Frank Robertson into his military family.

Thomas Randolph Price was another of the odd and interesting persons with whom Stuart surrounded himself, but he was not an engineer. He was a scholar, or more particularly, a Philogist. He studied ancient languages such as Sanskrit, Latin, and Greek, and the history, literature, and archeology of the people who spoke those languages. He traveled in Europe after graduating from the University of Virginia in 1858, living in Berlin in 1859, Greece in 1861, and Paris in 1862. He'd only recently returned to North America, running the blockade on Christmas Eve. He wanted to become involved in the war, and made an application to the Engineer Corps. It isn't clear whether he believed he had engineering experience or, more likely, that Channing Price lobbied Stuart and Jeb suggested the Engineer's Corps as the most likely avenue for adding him to the staff. Stuart's letter to Colonel Gilmore stated that he would like to have three engineer lieutenants and that Thomas R. Price would be "very acceptable" to him.[7]

Jeb devoted a good deal of time on January 13 and 14 to catching up on paperwork, writing four letters to General Samuel Cooper in Richmond. The first was about the make-up and command of the 11th Virginia Cavalry, and the second letter contained recommendations for filling a vacancy for major of the 15th Virginia, plus another urging of promotion for Pelham, this time to full colonel. He also repeated his request that William Farley be commissioned a Major of Sharpshooters, as he'd done October 25th. The third requested formation of a new brigade and promotion of Tom Rosser to command it. The fourth letter, on the 14th, was a recommendation for Captain John Blair Hoge, who began the war in the 1st Virginia but who resigned due to illness and became a quartermaster.[8]

Stuart also wrote on the 14th to Wyndham Robertson, former governor of Virginia, 1836–37, and father of Frank Robertson. The Robertsons were the type of family for which "FFV" (first families of Virginia) was coined. They could trace their lineage to the first settlers of the colony, one grandmother being Pocahontas. Frank's mother, Mary Frances Trigg Smith Robertson, was an heiress to a fortune in land in Virginia and Louisiana.

Frank was a brother-in-law to Blackford, who lobbied Stuart to add him to the staff. Frank had itched for military service since before the war, having helped form a military company in December 1860 while attending the University of Virginia. Like many others, he did not favor secession but was determined to follow his state, Virginia, and when she seceded the company, called the "Sons of Liberty," shouldered flintlocks and marched to Harpers Ferry to seize the Federal arsenal. They were too late. Federal troops set the arsenal afire to keep it out of Southern hands, and the governor of Virginia ordered the company back to the university. Frank then tried to join the Richmond Howitzers, the elite unit to which John Esten Cooke belonged, but Frank's father heard and forced him to withdraw. Undaunted, he obtained a lieutenant's commission in the "regular army of Virginia," which entitled him to be trained at the Virginia Military Institute, but after two months there, terrified the war would end before he saw action, he resigned and joined the 48th Virginia Infantry. He became a first lieutenant, but fell ill with pericarditis, a painful infection of the sac with encloses the heart. While recuperating at home, Stuart visited Blackford at the Robertson home and met Frank.

He had been recuperating ever since, but was ready to return. He'd written a letter to Stuart to offer his services, and Blackford tried to convince Jeb to bring him on. The problems were (1) Stuart already had more staff officers than most generals; (2) he was constantly being petitioned by friends, family, and strangers to add others; (3) no funds were available to pay new staff officers; and (4) Stuart had a rule not to accept volunteers who would serve without pay. He made exceptions to this latter rule, but he'd adopted it to avoid being overrun with young gallants willing to serve for free who might create more havoc than assistance.

The letter to Frank's father explained that he, Stuart, had an "avowed determination" to not take on additional volunteers other than those already on his staff in order to avoid "objectionable" persons whom he could not refuse if they were willing to serve without pay. He suggested, however, that if Frank could obtain an engineer's commission he believed he might be assigned to the cavalry division, which Jeb said he very much desired.[9]

Stuart may have been thinking about bringing Frank onto his staff because that day he received the resignation of Major Samuel Harden Hairston, the division quartermaster. Sam was the brother of Watt, whose rheumatism and health problems would lead him to resign as well, but Sam's reasons for leaving are not known. He'd been on the staff since May 1862 and served as quartermaster since June. There was no indication that Jeb was dissatisfied with Hairston's performance and the letter simply said, "I have the Honor respectfully to tender my resignation as Major and Quartermaster of the Cavalry Division, and request that it may take effect immediately." Jeb tried to talk him into staying, and tried three months later to have Hairston appointed to an "able and working military court." Hairston stayed on for a while, receiving a thirty day furlough on May 2, at the end of which his resignation was accepted.

Of the many ways members of Stuart's staff met their end, Sam Hairston's was unique. After the war he was at the state capitol building in Richmond on April 27, 1870 to hear the Court of Appeal's decision in an important case. The building was crowded with spectators, lawyers, legislators, reporters, police officers, and other officials, and about 11 a.m., as the court was convening, a girder supporting the second floor gallery of the courtroom collapsed. Those in the gallery fell to the first floor, along with tons of debris. Hairston was among the dead.[10]

Around January 15 another visitor from the Grenadier Guards arrived from Canada, Lt. Col. T.H. Bramston. Bramston was a lieutenant until the previous June when, customary in the British army, he purchased a Captain's and then a Lt. Colonel's rank when its previous holder, C.G. Ellison, retired.[11] He shared Von Borcke's tent, but had only a very few days' furlough.

On January 17, an invitation came to Stuart and Von Borcke from Dundee, in Hanover County, near where Stuart made his headquarters the previous July and where Von became enamored with the flirtatious Nannie Price. Her sister, Elizabeth, was to be married to Dr. John Fontaine, surgeon for Fitz Lee's brigade, on January 20.[12] Fontaine was part of Stuart's military family and would join the General's staff in the near future. He would be the first doctor to examine Stuart's mortal wound at Yellow Tavern, and would tend him until his death. Von Borcke was not merely agreeable, but desperate to attend the wedding.

Stuart attended a review of Rooney Lee's brigade the day of the wedding, at which Generals Lee, Longstreet, and Jackson were present, but as soon as it was over, he rode to the lovesick Von Borcke and called, "Well, Von! How about the wedding? Shall we go?" The ceremony was scheduled for seven p.m. and was nearly 35 miles away, but when Von pointed this out to Stuart, he responded, "Oh, that's nothing. Let's be off." Away they went at a gallop, or what Von recorded as ten miles an hour. They changed horses at Bowling Green and rode through the entrance to Dundee as the clock struck 7, splashed with mud and hardly presentable to the fashionable men and elegant ladies dressed in their finest.

After the wedding they enjoyed the reception, which included music, songs, and a game similar to charades, "tableaux vivants," in which players assumed the positions of a well-known painting, image, saying, or other scene. In one of these Von and Antoinette Price, another cousin, portrayed the coat of arms of the State of Virginia, which depicts the Goddess of Liberty standing on a tyrant and uttering the state's motto, "Sic Semper Tyrannus" ("thus be it ever to tyrants") which John Wilkes Booth would make infamous. As Von pointed out, the Latin phrase was commonly translated by soldiers as "Take your foot off my neck." Stuart was charmed by their performance and demanded several encores.

Chiswell Dabney showed up, unexpected. He was on furlough visiting his parents, but was delayed returning and, already three days late and technically AWOL, he ran into Captain John Fontaine at Hanover Court House. Fontaine and his wedding party were headed for Dundee and insisted that Dabney come along. Deciding that "a miss was as good as a mile," and that he would get in no more trouble for being four days late than three, he accepted the invitation, only to be surprised to find Stuart and Von Borcke there ahead of him. The handsome eighteen-year-old was so popular among the ladies at the wedding party that they banded together to "espouse [his] cause" to Stuart, first begging forgiveness for Dabney's tardiness and then pleading that he be allowed to stay longer. Like an overly indulgent father, Stuart did both, giving Dabney permission to stay an incredible eight more days.[13]

The party lasted all night without giving Von the opportunity to be alone with Nannie. Unbeknownst to him, Nannie's father had let her know that a foreigner such as Von was not a suitable candidate for marriage, regardless of whatever European titles and personal charms he possessed, and Nannie was not inclined to be rebellious, particularly when there were so many other fishes in the sea.[14]

Stuart was ready to return to his command as soon as the party ended, but it began raining and he delayed the ride back a few hours. As soon as the rain stopped, after dark, he exercised what Von called his "iron will" and they took leave of their hosts just as they were about to turn in for the night. Halfway back to headquarters, they were intercepted by a courier reporting that Burnside was attempting what became known as "the Mud March." Not knowing that rain and cold would turn the Union maneuver into a debacle, Stuart urged Von into a quicker pace and they were back at headquarters early on the 22nd.[15]

The Mud March began on January 19, when Burnside issued orders to his commanders to prepare to march the next day with three days rations. They assembled in weather that, while cold, was dry and clear. Burnside's goal was to salvage his and his army's reputations for the blunders and slaughter that comprised the Battle of Fredericksburg. His original plan was to send his cavalry twenty miles downstream to Kelly's Ford, where they would cross and sever Lee's line of supply and communication, while his infantry and artillery crossed between Kelly's Ford and Fredericksburg to attack Lee's right flank.

Some of his commanders considered this risky and leaked word to Lincoln, who agreed, so Burnside scrapped the plan for a move in the other direction. Under this approach he would march upstream ten miles to the United States Ford while feinting to the left as though intending to cross the river with two corps near Fredericksburg. His commanders signed on to this strategy and it became a reality on the 20th. For one day.

On the 21st, Burnside's engineers were supposed to lay five pontoon bridges and then two Grand Divisions of two corps each were to dash across the river in four hours or less and attack without mercy. Instead, the skies opened up, the wind began to howl, and rain began to pour. Even if the weather had cooperated, Lee became aware of what was going on and moved troops to his left to meet the threat. He didn't need to bother.

The storm was not merely wet, cold, and miserable, but as one correspondent said, "Shocking." The roads became a sea of mud. The army was trying to move ponderous pontoons that composed five bridges, plus150 pieces of artillery and the wagons, ambulances, blacksmith forges, limbers, caissons, and other vehicles that made up the Army of the Potomac. All sank into the sodden, clinging soil of Virginia.

Double and triple teams of horses and mules were attached to wagons and caissons. Soldiers heaved on ropes, put shoulders to wheels, pushed, pulled, fell, struggled, shivered, and cursed. Wagons sank to their hubs, cannons to their muzzles. The wind whipped and tore. Exhausted horses floundered and fell, covered in mud. The men were soaked and each sodden step sucked at shoes and, if not successfully pulling them off, added what seemed like fifty pounds to each man's foot. Even Burnside was seen "completely covered with mud, the rim of his hat turned down to shed the rain, his face careworn . . . ."

By nightfall the pontoons had still not reached the river. The rain did not cease. At least 150 horses and mules died in the mud and were often buried by it. Burnside pressed on the next day, ordering food for two more days and issuing a whiskey ration for the army. It was no use.

The Rebels were no help. From across the river they watched and shouted taunts, then erected signs with messages like "Burnside stuck in the mud," "Yanks if you can't place your pontoons, we'll send help," and "This way to Richmond."

Burnside finally managed to get fifteen pontoons into the river, about five short to complete one bridge, and placed artillery to cover a crossing, but the rain did not relent and Lee's army not only moved into place to meet him but thoughtfully plowed up the ground between their lines and the river to make it more difficult to cross. Finally, on the 22nd, Burnside ordered his army of thousands of miserable, indistinguishable mud men back to their camps at Falmouth. On January 26, Burnside leveled charges against officers he claimed had conspired against him or, alternatively, he offered to resign. Lincoln chose the second option and the inventor of the Burnside Carbine and the man for whom sideburns are named became the shortest-tenured commander of the Army of the Potomac.[16]

On January 26, John Esten Cooke recorded that he had dinner with Lt. Hullihen, Captain Farley, and a friend named Tom, after which he visited with General Stuart in the latter's tent. They had obtained newspapers telling of the Mud March, and Jeb remarked, "They are sticking in mud now, the rain of Tuesday stopped them." He returned to his tent and wrote a paragraph in his journal, noting that the army's artillery had returned and that there would not be a fight, adding, "What does that mean? One more fight, and I hope we will have them." He concluded his short entry by noting a commonplace occurrence in Stuart's camp: "Darkey singing 'Ain't got time to tarry! Banjo.'"[17]

About the 28th another visitor from England arrived, Captain J. William Bushby. Little is known about him, but he came over on a blockade runner to Charleston and arrived in Virginia bearing gifts for Generals Lee, Jackson, and Stuart. For Lee he brought a fine English-made saddle. For Stuart he brought a modern breech-loading, bolt-action carbine now, in the Museum of the Confederacy with Stuart's hat, saddle, LeMat revolver, French saber, saddle, gauntlets, and lesser treasures. The gift for Stonewall was an "India rubber bed."

It snowed on Wednesday the 28th, completely covering the army camps and inspiring more snowball fights. Stuart enjoyed watching the fun and circulated among his staff, taking dinner in Chiswell Dabney's tent and visiting briefly with John Esten Cooke. The General's mess, or eating arrangements, had up to recently been a group affair at the long table in his tent, attended by Fitz Lee, Von, Blackford, Pelham, and others, but not Cooke. However, it had proven too daunting to try to feed so many people at one time in one place, and accordingly, the "mess . . . split to pieces from overbulkiness."

Snow was still falling, but after dinner and while the evening was still early, Jeb mounted and rode to Mrs. Alsop's to spend the night with Flora, singing *Ain't Got Time to Tarry* as he rode away for the five mile trip to town.[18] After the General left, Channing Price, Dabney, other staff members, and their friends moved into Stuart's roomy tent, summoned Sweeney and his musicians and had "an uproarious time with the banjo, violin, and tambourine," in the midst of which Price found time to write home to his mother.[19]

January 29th dawned still and white, the snow being eight to twelve inches deep. Stuart's staff officers stayed in the tents where it was warm and dry, reading, napping, talking, or writing letters. Stuart spent the day at Mrs. Alsop's with Flora and Jimmie. From the infantry camps could be heard the shouts and noise of more snowball battles, and a band was playing. Hood's Brigade of Texans and Georgians, camped near Lee's headquarters, took the field and routed the South Carolina brigade of Micah Jenkins, camped not far from Mrs. Alsop's.

After dinner Cooke rode to Mrs. Alsop's to see Flora, but she was out and he visited with Jeb instead. Stuart, knowing Cooke kept up on the latest newspapers, asked what he heard was going on in the North and Cooke told him he thought there would be a "thundering Spring campaign and then it will end." Jeb opined that if there was a spring campaign it would last through the year and thereafter, to the end of Lincoln's first term. They agreed that Lincoln had a great deal of muscle and an iron will, but Stuart said he was not a man of much ability.[20]

On January 30, Hood's Brigade, flushed with its snowball victory over Jenkins the day before, took the field and with flying guidons and mounted officers advanced in line of battle on William Wofford's brigade, snowballs flying. It was camped in a pine forest near Camp No Camp, so Stuart and his staff came out to watch. Dabney mounted up and joined Hood's Brigade, reporting later to his mother that it was "very amusing I can tell you," but that being on horseback made him "quite a target" and he "like to have had my head knocked off."[21] Cooke decided the battle was worth a newspaper article and wrote a six-page account for the *Whig*.

That day, the 30th, Von Borcke escorted the English Captain Bushby to Jackson's headquarters to introduce him to the General and to deliver the India Rubber Bed. Along the way he impressed the captain by shooting a buzzard out of the sky with his revolver, admitting that in doing so he "astonished himself not a little." When they arrived at Jackson's headquarters, they were received by the General with "all his usual affability." He was "much pleased with the present, promising to use it regularly."

Captain Bushby asked Jackson for his autograph and he agreed at once, but when writing a blot of ink fell on the paper and Jackson threw it to the floor to do another. Bushby picked it up and put it in his pocket, and Jackson, seeing this, said, "Oh Captain, if you value my simple signature so much, I will give you a number of them with the greatest pleasure." He then filled a large sheet with his signature and presented it to Bushby.[22]

That evening Cooke and Farley rode to Mrs. Alsop's to visit Flora and arrange for Miss Nannie Alsop to bake some cakes and puddings for them. Before leaving Cooke stopped in at the General's tent and Stuart pulled out the carbine that Captain Bushby had given him, saying "Look what my English friend brought me. That shows what they think of me in London."

Cooke was quick with a comeback, "What? That you are a breech-loader?"

Saturday the 31st saw more of the same, with snow on the ground, visits among the officers, and such entertainment as could be found. A copy of *The News* arrived, containing an article Cooke had written about Jackson. He and others went to Stuart's tent in the evening and chatted with the General, Von Borcke, and Captain Bushby, the primary subject of conversation being Stonewall. Sweeney played *The Old Gray Horse, Jine the Cavalry*, and other favorites. One of his cousins joined in on the violin and as dark approached Stuart mounted to ride to Mrs. Alsop's, shouting "Good Night!" to all as he departed.[23]

February 1st was still lazier. Flora had a late lunch, about 2 p.m., with a Mr. Garnett, John Esten Cooke, and friends. Jeb was on his way to "Fonthill" in Essex County, the home of Robert M. Hunter, former Confederate Secretary of State, now a Confederate senator. Much of the dinner conversation centered on debate between Cooke and Garnet about whether "the Essex girls" would allow Stuart to kiss them. These were Pink and Iday Hunter, the senator's daughters. Garnett asserted the girls never kissed people but Cooke claimed "they had honoured me with that mark of affection on sundry occasions," which "dumbfounded" Garnett.[24]

Kisses, particularly who kissed Jeb Stuart and who he kissed in return, was a popular topic. Earlier that month Stuart accompanied Robert E. Lee to visit William P. Taylor, an elderly former Congressman, at his home

"Hayfield," in Caroline County. Staying with the Taylor family were two great nieces, 13-year-old Fannie and 14-year-old Bessie Gwathney. General Lee, upon being introduced to the girls, told them he had brought kisses from another of their aunts and asked if he could deliver them. He then proceeded to kiss each girl four times on the lips, twice for the aunt and twice for himself. Stuart, looking on, said "General, I don't think it fair for you to get all the kisses. I would like to kiss these little girls too." Fannie Gwathney responded, to everyone's amusement, with "General Stuart, I would love dearly to kiss you but I just can't let anyone take General Lee's kisses off my lips."[25]

On February 2, Von Borcke inspected the horses of Hampton's Brigade, which was performing arduous patrol and picket duty along a forty-mile stretch of the Rappahannock. Mud Fever and the lack of forage were taking a terrible toll on the animals, and Von wrote, "It was a mournful sight to see more than half the horses of this splendid command totally unfit for duty, dead and dying animals lying about the camps in all directions."[26]

Cooke visited Colonel John B. Baldwin of the 52nd Virginia Infantry. Baldwin was a former member of the Virginia Legislature who met with Lincoln just prior to the firing on Fort Sumter. In Cooke's words he was "a man after [my] own heart . . . [because he] likes to take a long time in dressing, and to do it lazily. Puts one boot on, and then lights his pipe and studies the fire!"

On February 3, Stuart tried to improve the condition of his larder and accepted an offer from Chiswell Dabney for a "firkin" of butter, which is a wooden tub equal to a fourth of a barrel. Stuart sent the servant, Gilbert, to retrieve it. When Von Borcke heard about it he said he would take a little as well.[27]

Nannie Price visited, and Cooke saw her on the 4th, after which he "dined solus as usual." Stuart spent the evening in his headquarters tent and Cooke stopped by for an hour, saying they recalled old battles. Before retiring he wrote that Stuart's "resemblance to Longstreet is very striking; and his gayety amazing."[28]

On February 5 it snowed all day. Stuart renewed his efforts to rid his division of "Grumble" Jones and get Rosser, preferably, but either Munford or Wickham, alternatively, promoted to brigadier and put in command of Jones' brigade. He sent a letter to Gen. R.H. Chilton in Richmond, beginning, "A trial having shown that Brigadier General W.E. Jones does not possess the qualities essential to a successful Cavalry leader and commander, I beg leave to request that . . . either Munford, Wickham, or Rosser replace him."[29]

Cooke and Stuart chatted again that evening. Stuart predicted there would be a fight within a week, but not at Fredericksburg. The discussion drifted to the John Brown raid on Harpers Ferry, in which Stuart was a significant player and Cooke an observer with the Richmond Howitzers. Cooke closed his journal entry by saying he would write out Stuart's narrative about John Brown fully.[30]

In Richmond on February 5, Robert E. Lee's oldest son, Custis, wrote Stuart in response to Stuart's letters about Captain William T. Magruder, the promotion of Pelham and Blackford, and other matters. Lee said there should be no difficulty about Pelham's promotion, but that there were no vacancies in the Engineer Corps that would allow Blackford to advance. In regard to Magruder, he said, predictably, that he did not wish to trouble the President about the matter, but had passed the letter on to General Davis, who passed it on to Magruder, who wrote a response that Lee enclosed to Stuart but which has not survived. One suspects Stuart read it, wadded it up and threw it in one of his two fireplaces.[31]

Stuart took Jimmie riding on the 7th. Flora was in better spirits. Her despair over the loss of little Flora, coupled with the worry over her brother's wound was somewhat relieved because General Cooke was mending. During the recent visit by Captain Phillips of the Grenadier Guards, Phillips had presented Jeb with a walking stick of Canadian oak. Stuart said it was a "great comfort" to him, and he rode with it crooked in his arm. As he, Jimmy, and Cooke rode, probably with the little boy on the saddle in front of his father, the conversation drifted to what they hoped to do once the war ended, and Stuart said he wanted to travel to Europe . . . but hoped to make the trip alone.[32]

February 8th and 9th, a Sunday and Monday, passed quietly. Cooke asked Stuart to be allowed to inspect Rooney Lee's artillery, his real goal being the equivalent of a furlough. Stuart was not fooled, but told Cooke he could go to Hunter's, where Rooney Lee's brigade was camped, which was exactly what Cooke had in mind. William Farley went with him.

Flora's time near her husband was drawing to a close. The weather was still good, and when not with her or tending to military affairs, Jeb was at his tent, visiting with others or playing with the half-grown dogs, Nip and Tuck. A blanket was spread on the floor of the tent for them near one of the fireplaces. When Stuart tired of writing and was not engaged in serious conversation, he would "throw himself upon his blankets, play with his pets, laugh at the least provocation, and burst into gay song."[33]

On the 9th, Stuart's military family was joined by Channing Price's older brother, Tom. Jeb's request to Colonel Gilmore of the Engineer Corps of January 12 was approved, and Tom took the train from Richmond to Hamilton's Crossing wearing a new uniform, saber, and pistol. On arriving, he found no one to meet or convey him across the "lake of mud" between there and Stuart's camp. After sending a courier and waiting several hours a wagon arrived and carried him to Camp No Camp. There he introduced himself to Stuart, Major Fitzhugh, and Lt. Dabney, and tried to settle in. His first real taste of what it was like to be a member of Jeb Stuart's staff came about midnight, when Stuart rode into camp singing and shouting. He then proceeded to have "a great romp" with two of his aides, probably Fitzhugh and Dabney, and managed to rouse everyone in the camp from their beds.[34]

This minor incident, recorded by Tom Price in journal he had just started about his military experiences, captures Stuart's exuberance, boyish relationship with his staff, and his ability, without the aid of alcohol, to get everyone up and frolicking in the middle of the night. It also describes behavior that is a bit surprising. That night was the next to last Flora would be nearby, but instead of spending the night with her, Jeb chose to romp off to his army camp in a mood of monumental glee. Along with his recent comment to Cooke about visiting Europe alone, it suggests that while he was devoted to Mrs. Stuart, he was also happy to be away from her. He may well have found her gloominess oppressive.

February 10 was another quiet day. Food supplies were still low, the only items available being heavy biscuits and molasses.[35] Stuart wrote two letters to General Cooper, one about a Captain Collins in the Engineer Corps, assigned to the 15th Virginia, and another attempt to get Pelham promoted. Everyone, particularly Stuart, was mystified at the failure of the army to make the promotion official. The young artilleryman had made such a name for himself he was nationally famous, and he had the backing of Generals Lee and Jackson as well as Stuart. Jeb closed his letter with emphasis, saying:

It has been alleged that he was too young. Though remarkably youthful in appearance, *there are Generals as young* with less claim for that distinction, *and no veteran in age has ever shown more coolness and better judgment in the sphere of his duty*.[36]

On or about the 11th, after running the blockade, a six-pounder Whitworth cannon arrived for the Horse Artillery. The Whitworth was an English gun, particularly accurate, that fired a unique, spiraled projectile that fit the rifling inside the tube precisely. Pelham turned it over to the command of William Hoxton, who'd recently been promoted to lieutenant.

On February 12, Stuart, Flora, and Jimmie departed for Richmond, where she would stay with her sister, Maria, and Dr. Brewer, and Jeb caught up on a few matters of personal business. Tom Price was given his first engineering assignment—tracing a map of Spotsylvania and Caroline Counties. He'd been in the army three days and was already longing to be back in Europe doing what he loved, writing: "Oh to be back at my favorite studies! Oh! For Berlin, or Paris, or Athens. I long so to hear again literary conversation, and have my thoughts once more directed to agreeable topics."[37]

Stuart was in Richmond the morning of the 13th but returned by evening. Pelham wrote two letters, one to Lt. Llewellyn "Lou" Hoxton, who was at West Point with him, to assure his old friend that brother "Willie" was not merely doing well, but was gallant, noble, and courageous. He added that he was anxious for "Fighting Joe" Hooker to come over for another battle, as the Army of Northern Virginia was "invincible," and once Hooker was willing to live up to his nickname, it would add another name to the army's long list of victories. His other letter was to 1st Lt. Phillip Preston Johnson, of Breathed's battery, directing him to prepare papers to pay a blacksmith named Andrew Connor and to get some cloth for an overcoat, which Pelham would arrange to have sewn by a lady near Fredericksburg.[38]

Tom Price dined with Stuart that evening, his first time, and was disappointed to find the fare not much better than anyone else's. They had meat Jeb called "stalled beef."[39] This was classic Jeb Stuart wordplay humor. Beef was typically issued to soldiers either fresh or preserved by salting—"salted beef." The meat that Stuart and Tom Price dined on was from oxen that became ill or too exhausted to work and were confined in stalls until they recovered, died, or were put down, thus falling somewhere between being butchered intentionally and being salvaged, or preserved, thereby becoming "stalled beef." This and similar puns show up in Stuart's letters and the recollections of others about him, tickling some acquaintances and causing others, like Tom Price, to roll their eyes. One suspects that the child's joke, "What did the fast tomato say to the slow tomato?—Catchup!" would have sent Jeb into gales of hilarity.

Von Borcke's report on his inspection of Hampton's horses at the beginning of the month convinced Stuart that the South Carolinians needed relief from their patrols on the Rappahannock. He ordered Fitz Lee to replace Hampton, and made plans to go with several of his staff to inspect both brigades. On February 17 it snowed again, but Stuart directed Von Borcke, Tom Price, and Pelham to go a day earlier than the rest, so after breakfast they set off to Culpeper.

They rode across country to the main road at Chancellorsville. The snow was nearly a foot deep, there was nothing to eat, and they were literally in the Wilderness, as the region was known. At dark they stopped at the house of a free black named Madden, their horses nearly exhausted, and asked to spend the night. From the door they could see a fire going, but when they made their request Madden slammed the door, declaring, "he would have 'nothing to do with no stragglers'."

Stunned, they stood in front of the door in silence, not knowing what to do next, then Pelham had an idea. "This won't do at all," he told his companions. "We can't possibly go on; to remain out of doors in this terrible weather is certain destruction; and as we are under the obligation of preserving our lives as long as possible, for the sake of our cause and our country, I am going to fool this stupid old [negro], and play a trick off on him, which I think quite pardonable under the circumstances."

He pounded on the door until Mr. Madden opened it, when Pelham launched into an explanation. "Mr. Madden, you don't know what a good friend of yours I am, or what you are doing when you are about to treat us in this way. That gentleman there," pointing to Von Borcke, "is the great General Lee himself; the other one is the French ambassador just arrived from Washington, and I am a staff officer of the General's, who is quite mad at being kept waiting outside so long after riding all this way on purpose to see you. In fact, if you let him stay any longer here in the cold, I'm afraid he'll shell your house as soon as his artillery comes up."

Madden listened to this tall tale and invited them in, apologizing profusely, took the trio's horses to his stable, and fed them corn while the trio dried out before the fire. He then came back in and prepared a hot meal. Pelham continued the ruse until the next morning when they "paid him a liberal indemnity" and "endeavored to undeceive him," unsuccessfully, as Madden "continued to inflate himself with a sense of his own importance at having been honoured with a visit from such distinguished guests."[40] A story may have passed down from generation to generation of

Maddens of the night General Lee stayed the night at granddad's house.

On the 18th the snow became rain. Stuart set out for Culpeper, which Pelham and the others reached about noon. Hampton's headquarters was on the main street, and the weather had turned the red clay soil into gumbo. Stuart, other staff officers, and Sweeney and Mulatto Bob arrived before dark. Fitz Lee's officers had put together a minstrel show, which Sweeney and Bob joined, and gave a performance Von claimed could rival any in London.

Jeb and his officers stayed in the Virginia Hotel while their horses enjoyed a dry stable. The lady who owned the hotel had a son in Fitz Lee's brigade and she seemed determined to make the General's stay comfortable. The next day, February 19, Stuart and all but Von Borcke and Pelham rode on to Richmond.

The main street in Culpeper was so muddy it was unusable. Carriages and wagons could not navigate it and pedestrians could not cross, so Von Borcke and Pelham gathered planks and large stone blocks and constructed a bridge. This allowed them to gain access to the home of Bessie Shackleford, one of Pelham's female friends. The home contained four other daughters, Lucy, Georgia, Kate, and Shirley, which made it a target for visiting Southern gallants. One, Major Eales of Rosser's regiment, was in Culpeper after release from a Federal prison but while still on parole, meaning he could not take up arms again until exchanged. He was as drawn to the Shackleford home as were Pelham and Von Borcke.

The Shackleford girls were more free-thinking and intellectually stimulating than the Scarlet O'Hara/Melanie Hamiltons of the world. They were raised to voice their opinions on religion, politics, literature, music, and the arts, and were a magnet for men like Pelham. The three officers and the Shacklefords "relished the gaiety of [each other's] society with peculiar zest." It did not detract from the girls' charm that they were attractive, particularly Bessie, who had blue eyes, long black hair and a milky complexion. No one could know that in a month Pelham would die in their house and that in almost exactly four months, Von Borcke and Eales would be shot on the same day, Eales being killed and Von Borcke so seriously wounded it would mark the end of his days in Stuart's command.[41]

While in Richmond on the 20th, Stuart visited the Confederate Senate and the Virginia House of Delegates. He was symbolically offered a seat in the House of Delegates, and spoke a few words of thanks before being introduced to individual members, one of whom was a relative of Chiswell

Dabney's named Peter. When introduced to him, Peter said that the General ought to know him and Stuart "I suppose you should as you married my old sweetheart." The identity of that old sweetheart is a mystery.

Stuart and most of those who accompanied him to Richmond, including Channing Price, returned to Camp No Camp on February 21, but everything was "dull and quiet." Chiswell Dabney went to Richmond with Stuart but did not come back with him as he was supposed to do, choosing instead to make a side trip in order to "see the girls." Once again it made him absent without leave, and this time Stuart was not as lenient as at Elizabeth Price's wedding. When Dabney returned, Stuart stunned the eighteen-year-old by having him arrested and confined to quarters for eight days. Dabney employed the verbal charm and wheedling that worked on Stuart before, and after half a day Jeb relented and released him from confinement. Still, the lesson to Dabney was accomplished. He was so embarrassed by being arrested that he delayed telling his mother several days, and was not AWOL thereafter.[42]

Pelham and Von Borcke remained in Culpeper the rest of the month. The telegraph wires were down on the 20th but were restored by the time Jeb returned, and Cooke reported he seemed happy to see his staff. Rumors were running about the camp that two of the Federal army's "Grand Divisions" had withdrawn from their positions across the Rappahannock and that the Confederate army would soon be moving as well. Neither rumor was exactly true, but not completely inaccurate. The evening was spent in conversation among Stuart, Fitz Lee, Colonel Wickham, and Cooke in the General's tent.[43]

It rained on the 22nd and everyone stayed indoors. Stuart spent a portion of the day drafting a letter to Secretary of War James E. Seddon regarding his recommendations for a five-person panel of judges for an upcoming military court and writing out the qualifications of each of the officers he recommended.[44] He had labored through the winter on his reports of the campaigns of the previous six months, but as of the 22nd was still only as far along as the raid on Catlett's Station, which occurred during the ride into Maryland.[45]

Among Stuart's less-than-critical, but still very important issues during these days was the fact that Colonel Munford and the 2nd Virginia Cavalry were fed up with the absence of Sam Sweeney. He was still on the roster of Company H as a private. There was no allocated slot on the staff of even a Major General for a banjo player, and his regiment wanted him back. Having a talented, famous musician to play the latest songs was the zenith of 1860s' entertainment. Jeb tried to deflect Munford's legitimate request for Sweeney's return as long as he could, but he was wearing down and told Flora that "I think I will let him go for a while if not altogether."[46]

It snowed again, and Jeb and his officers focused on smoky chimneys that needed remodeling, Channing Price accidentally putting on and leaving with his brother's cap, snow being a foot deep on the ground, whether jackets and other items requested from home were ready, who was going where and when, and what they would be delivering or picking up when they did. Dabney, like Pelham and Von Borcke, was not at headquarters, and Blackford was preparing to leave. Blackford's wife was living in a house in Fredericksburg, and he spent as much time with her as possible, neglecting to keep a record of his military life.[47]

On February 23, Stuart received orders from General Lee to send a portion of Fitz Lee's brigade across the river to conduct a reconnaissance in force. Federal pickets above Fredericksburg had been withdrawn, and it appeared the Army of the Potomac was moving. Upon receiving Lee's directive, Stuart went to his headquarters "in a great bustle," then dispatched Major Fitzhugh to United States Ford to observe Federal activity. He had Channing Price send both a telegram and a courier to Fitz Lee, at Culpeper, telling him to conduct the mission even though he, his uncle, and everyone were aware of the obstacles—snow, swollen river, rain, mud, distance, and "impracticable" roads.

Fitz selected 400 troopers from the 1st, 2nd, and 3rd Virginia regiments, crossed the river at Kelly's Ford the morning of the 24th, moved down river, and, early on the 25th met Federal troops near Hartwood Church, about eight miles behind Falmouth and the main body of the Federal army. The Rebels charged, drove the 3rd and 16th Pennsylvania Cavalry from their positions, took 150 prisoners plus horses and equipment, and returned to Culpeper in the rain on the 26th.[48]

Stuart took a few other staff officers and followed Major Fitzhugh to United States Ford, where he spent nights in Fitzhugh's tent and tried during the days to ascertain if the Federals intended to cross the Rappahannock or move in another direction. He wrote Flora on the 26th to say he had "been absent several days up the river, and returned this afternoon wet as a submerged rat," then told her about Fitz Lee's "brilliant success," He also reported that at this time Rooney Lee attacked two gunboats with a section of Horse Artillery near Tappahannock, which was near the coast, and put them to "ignominious flight."[49]

Since departing from her husband and brother, Flora had sunk back into despair over the loss of her daughter and worry about the future. Jeb tried to prop her up, saying she "must be brave and not give way to gloomy forebodings," and to remember that "fortitude is woman's specialty, and patience her most shining virtue." He completed his letter of February 26 by telling his wife to fill her scrapbook with articles and cuttings that Jimmie would prize in "after years," and to collect *carte de visites*—inexpensive cardboard photographs—for her album. In particular he asked her to get one of "one of my best of friends, Joe Johnston."

The evening of February 27, Jeb invaded the tent of one of his staff officers and began wrestling with them, tickling them, and throwing them down in the mud. Tom Price watched and recorded the scene in his diary with slight disdain. When the frolicking was over, they had hard boiled eggs and talked about their campaigns, with Stuart proclaiming the first ride around McClellan as the "most perilous and most successful of all." With regard to the second ride around McClellan, Jeb declared that if he had been prevented from recrossing the Potomac by either the enemy or depth of the river, he would have turned back into Pennsylvania and wandered about until he could return to Virginia. In fact, he hoped to get permission from General Lee and the Secretary of War to try such a raid again if they would give him 10,000 men.[50] His words, with no foreknowledge of Brandy Station or the Gettysburg campaign, were noteworthy.

As February drew to a close, Jeb telegraphed Pelham and Von Borcke to come back to Camp No Camp, and then returned to working on his reports. He was still only as far as Second Manassas. Von Borcke wrote, "We felt very sad at leaving pleasant old Culpeper and the hardships and monotony of our camp life fell on us the more heavily after an interval of comparative ease and abundance. The remnant of February and a part of March dragged slowly by, so dull and eventless that existence was scarcely tolerable, and we looked forward to the commencement of spring and the reopening of the campaign with intense longing."[51]

Had he known what awaited, or had a mere inkling of the tragedy and sorrow that would occur in but a few days, weeks, and months, or had he known who would no longer be among their gallant little band of companions by the time spring became summer, he might have elected to remain in those days of eventless existence forever.

CHAPTER TEN

IRREPARABLE
MARCH 1, 1863–APRIL 16, 1863

Just as the spring came laughing through the strife,
*   with all its gorgeous cheer,*
in the bright April of historic life,
*   fell the great cannoneer.*

A clang of sabres 'mid Virginian snow,
*   the fiery pang of shells,—*
and there's a wail of immemorial woe
*   in Alabama dells.*

From *The Dead Cannoneer,*
by James Ryder Randall (1839–1908)

One may argue whether March 1863 came to Virginia like a lamb or a lion. The sun rose at 6:25 a.m. on Sunday, March 1, and by 7 a.m. the temperature was forty degrees.[1] It was not snowing or raining, but recent rains and snow melt were causing flooding in various places, including the North Anna River, where the railroad bridge washed out, severing communications between Lee's Army and Richmond.[2] At 9 p.m., three and a half hours after sunset, the temperature was forty-five.[3]

Stuart spent the day relaxing and reading. He'd recently acquired a copy of *Practice of War* by Antoin-Henri Jomini, a French general considered to be a great Napoleonic strategist, and whose theories were taught at West

Point.[4] Jeb was so impressed that upon finishing the book he wrote a letter to its publishers, West & Johnson of Richmond, saying, "It should be the pocket companion, inseparable from his Prayer Book, of every officer in the Confederacy."[5]

Stuart also acted on a difficult decision that day—asking for the resignation of Major James "Watt" Hairston. Watt was a cousin who'd provided good service as an Assistant Aide-de-Camp and Assistant Adjutant General since September 1861. However, the same good service was repeatedly interrupted by health problems, and his rheumatism was particularly bad that winter, so Jeb "felt it due to the country & to myself to ask him to resign,"[6]

Stuart worked on his reports on March 2nd and 3rd, straining to be accurate and colorful, never failing to praise officers and men of his command whom he believed performed admirably. He relied on and received considerable assistance in their preparation from Channing Price.

The afternoon of the 3rd brought another flurry of snow and gusts of wind. It also brought a new member to Stuart's staff—Frank Robertson. A direct descendant of Pocahontas and subject of Stuart's letter of January 18, 1863 to Frank's father, Robertson had joined the engineer corps and been assigned to Stuart's staff. He now had the three engineers he'd wanted, one of whom, Blackford, was actually an engineer instead of a philologist or a favored son and future farmer. Unlike Price, Robertson was glad to be there, and promptly wrote his father on March 3, "For the first time in 16 months I feel comparatively happy." He moved in with Blackford, met other staff officers, and was welcomed by Jeb, about whom he wrote, "I thought from what he said that he got me the position more as a means of getting me on his staff than for any assistance I might give the Engineer Corps." As for Tom Price, he made the quick deduction that, "He seems to know very little more about it than myself."[7]

Blackford and Pelham were reading aloud to each other during the winter months, and were then taking turns reading *History of the War in the Peninsula*, by General Sir William Francis Patrick Napier, an account of Napoleon's campaigns in Spain and Portugal, written by one of Napoleon's officers in the late 1820s and published in 1851. Their reading was interrupted, on or about March 3, by the arrival of a present for Pelham and Stuart. It was homemade candy, sent by Nannie Price, who was at Orange Court House visiting a friend. The note accompanying the gift said, "Dear General, we had a little candy stew last night and knowing your fondness for 'sweets' of all kinds, I send you some of it this morning. Miss Brill sends some of it for the 'Gallant Pelham,' which you must be sure to give him. If you could see the burns on our fingers I am sure it would be much sweeter."[8] Wheels began turning in Pelham's head about how he might visit her at Orange, not knowing the candy would lead indirectly to his death.

On March 4 Stuart called Tom Price to his tent. He'd seen Price reading *The Fairy Queen*, a "semi-opera" written by Henry Purcell in 1692 based on Shakespeare's *A Midsummer Night's Dream*. Jeb either did not consider it appropriate reading material for a member of his staff, or genuinely thought that Price would prefer some good "war literature." Accordingly, Stuart gave him the copy of Jomini's *Practice of War* he'd just finished, plus an article about the previous summer's campaign in Virginia written by Prince de Joinville, translated from French.

Price was not impressed. He sniffed to his journal that evening that he had already read the article and that while the writing was clear, de Joinville's opinions were "hopelessly biased and incorrect." It isn't clear how Price felt himself an expert considering he was in Europe at the time of the battles. He then wrote a sentence that would haunt him and embarrass Jeb Stuart: "Gen. Stuart was with us and prattled on all evening in his garrulous way—described how he commenced the war by capturing 50 of Patterson's advance guard on the day preceding Bull Run."[9]

Stuart had a better surprise for Channing Price, who had proven to be a dream adjutant. His ability to hear a lengthy verbal order and then reduce it to flawless writing, plus his dedication to Stuart and willingness to do the work of three men made him a rare prize. Whatever one might say about Stuart, it could never be that he didn't try to reward those who did good work. In this case it was a promotion of Channing to major.

He showed up at the door of Price's tent the evening of the 4th and had Price's orderly take and then hand a paper to him. It was dated that day and addressed to General Samuel Cooper, saying, "I have the honour to request that R. Channing Price, my present valued and efficient Aide-de-camp be commissioned as Major, AAG on my staff vice major J.T.W. Hairston whose resignation on account of ill health has been already forwarded. I desire the appointment to take effect Mar. 1st." Price was thrilled, and wrote his parents to tell them the good news.

Stuart wrote a letter to Flora that evening, telling her of Watt's resignation, saying that Channing Price deserved to be "Chief of Staff," that Major Fitzhugh was on thirty day leave, that Frank Robertson had joined the staff, that Lt. Hagan was going to Richmond, that he was "messing alone" but that someone always dropped in "for sociability's sake," and asking that she send him a *carte de visite*—"yours full length—bless that pretty figure—the pattern of grace." He closed by saying he was saving some candy for Jimmie.[10]

His headquarters camp was located at the same site all winter, and would remain there until April 9, but there was some confusion about the correct name of the place. John Esten Cooke consistently headed his journal entries as from "Camp No Camp," and Dabney called it the same as early as November 26, 1862; but Stuart penned a letter to Flora on March 6, 1863 and headed it as "Camp Cross-Sabres."[11] The letter was brief and contained no war news.

On Sunday, March 8, Pelham made a trip to the camp of some Alabama friends, particularly Colonel Edward A. O'Neal of the 26th Alabama Infantry. There he received an unusual and cumbersome gift. A "Miss Moore" in Alabama had sent him a note and a 12-pound Yankee cannon ball. Although it is not certain, the young lady was probably the daughter of Alabama's first wartime governor, Andrew Barry Moore, who held office from 1857 to 1861.[12]

It seems unlikely that anyone would lug a cannon ball from Alabama to Virginia when it was not particularly challenging to find one in Virginia, but the context of the sparse historical record about the incident suggests that was the case. Apparently the roundshot had been fired by Federals in Alabama and had come into the possession of Miss Moore, who decided its highest and best use would be to have the current hero of Alabama fire it back at them. On March 9, Pelham wrote a note to her saying that their mutual friend "Sam," at O'Neal's camp, had given him the note and cannon ball, and "If he had known with what pleasure I would receive it, I think he would have sent them to me sooner." He then wrote, "I promise faithfully it shall be returned to its former owners with all the bitterness and force you could desire and with all the accuracy my limited experience will permit. . . . I will reserve it till we get to 'close quarters'. . ." He promised to send her an official report on the success or non-success of that one shot.[13] The fate of the cannon ball is unknown.

On the night of March 8–9, John Mosby pulled off the trick that made him a legend. With twenty-nine men he slipped into the Federal army camp at Fairfax Courthouse. There was still snow on the ground and it was drizzling. The sky was overcast and it was so dark that at one point as the mounted raiders penetrated the enemy lines they got separated and had to circle around looking for each other for two hours. Mosby told only one of his companions where he was taking them, so they were nearly as surprised as anyone when they found themselves on a street in Fairfax at two a.m. with Federal picket fires burning ahead but the pickets gazing into the dark in the opposite direction.

The Confederates were in gray uniforms, but they wore rain gear and it was too dark for anyone to see. The raiders split into squads of four or five men, took the pickets prisoner, collected the local telegraph officer, and moved to the headquarters of the Federal commander, Brig. General Edwin H. Stoughton. There, accompanied by five men, Mosby knocked on the door and announced he had dispatches for the general. When the door opened, Mosby seized the general's aide. Lt. Sam Prentiss, who was wearing only a dressing gown, and told him to take them to the general's bedroom. There, with two men holding pistols on Stoughton, Mosby pulled down the covers and shook him awake.

The popular story is that Stoughton woke up and asked, "Have you captured Mosby?" to which Mosby replied, "No, but he has captured you." In reality Stoughton saw the three strangers and said "What do you want?" to which Mosby replied, "You are my prisoner," and then tried to bluff Stoughton into believing that Stuart had captured all of the Federal camps in the area. Stoughton was a prisoner but not a fool, and he dismissed Mosby's story, saying, "I think you are a raiding party and a small party at that. Is Fitz [Lee] here?" When Mosby said he was, Stoughton said "Take me to him. We were classmates."

As Stoughton dressed, Mosby took a piece of coal from the fireplace and wrote "Mosby" on the wall of the bedroom. They then rode out of Fairfax, taking the general, a captain, the telegrapher, thirty enlisted men, and fifty-eight horses.[14]

When Stuart heard of the raid, he declared it to be "unparalleled in the war." Robert E. Lee said that "Mosby had covered himself with glory," and made certain that he received a captain's commission. Mosby gave General Stoughton's saddle to Stuart, who authorized him to make his organization of irregulars, or "partisan rangers," a permanent outfit, even though Lee did not support the idea. After the war Mosby would write of Stuart, "He was the best friend I ever had and made me all that I was in the war."[15]

On March 8, John Esten Cooke returned from two weeks leave in Richmond, "a little blue." Stuart came to his tent and chatted, causing Cooke to record in his journal that evening, "He is charming when he throws off business." Jeb was still thinking about little Flora, and told Cooke he could not get over it: "It is irreparable." Cooke noted that he had never spoken of her death to him but once before.[16]

Cooke and Stuart talked more on the 9th, particularly about their mutual relative in the Federal army, Phillip St. George Cooke. Jeb believed that Cooke had done his best to catch him and his command during the first ride around McClellan, whereas John had heard through the family grapevine that upon receiving the order to pursue his son-in-law, General Cooke's hand trembled so bad he could not read it and that he had his men prepare slowly while he had a leisurely dinner. Stuart responded that "General Cooke was a man who would do his duty up to the handle," to which John Esten wrote in his journal, "Granted, but he was a poor cavalry officer if he couldn't find the backs of 1,500 cavalry in a big road, and catch them ten miles off in 12 hours!" He said that Stuart and General Cooke were devoted to each other before the war, but that now Jeb "seems to think bitterly of him."[17]

On March 12, Blackford and Frank Robertson rode to Fredericksburg to see the battlefield. Robertson found the town "more shattered than I anticipated," with some houses "mere wrecks," and at least fifty with an average of fifty cannonball holes each. After viewing the panorama from Lee's Hill, they rode to the river where they could see Federal pickets on the other side. Blackford was wearing a blue Federal overcoat and one of the Yankees shouted, "Hey, did you pay for that coat?" Blackford replied, "Yes, I bought it with a bullet."[18]

John Pelham had another matter on his mind, and was conspiring with Blackford during that first week in March about how he might escape to Orange Court House to visit Nannie Price. He knew his recent absences from headquarters, coupled with prospects of an upcoming campaign and Stuart's desire to keep him close, made it highly unlikely he would be given a furlough if he requested one; and by requesting it and being denied, he would be in clear violation of orders if he left camp. The goal, then, was to obtain Stuart's approval for some sort of duty-based travel, so the pair decided the battery of Horse Artillery commanded by Captain Marcellus Moorman, camped near Orange Court House, needed inspection.

On or about March 13, possibly before, Pelham casually asked for Stuart's written consent to inspect the battery. Such an inspection was routine. Pelham was Moorman's commander, and Pelham did not suggest he was going to accomplish the task immediately. Stuart approved the request and had Major Fitzhugh write the order.

The next morning Pelham was in the saddle before dawn, knowing that if given time, Stuart might change his mind or events could give rise to new orders. He knew Jeb well, as the former proved to be the case. Stuart breakfasted with his staff that morning, probably because he was departing for Culpeper to testify in a court martial. Seeing that Pelham was not present and upon learning the young cannoneer was on the way to Orange, he countermanded his consent, and had Fitzhugh dispatch a courier to bring Pelham back.

Pelham had too great a head start, and was at the outskirts of Orange the evening of March 15 when the courier overtook him. He took the note ordering him to return, smiled, and told the messenger, "Sergeant, I'm certain that General Stuart would not want me to wear out my horse by riding over those roads tonight. I'll return first thing tomorrow." He then rode into Orange, cleaned up, had dinner with Nannie Price and her friend, then escorted the ladies about town with one on each arm.[19]

The court martial in Culpeper was the culmination of a battle of words, resentments, charges, and counter-charges between Tom Rosser and Henry Clay Pate that had erupted the previous July over command of the 5th Virginia. Stuart was called as a witness. He went by train with a stop in Richmond.[20] Mosby met Stuart at the railroad station when he arrived in Culpeper, flush with the story of his capture of General Stoughton.[21] The two men, who were becoming wartime heroes of epic proportion, laughed and cavorted like schoolboys over the escapade. It is probable that it was then that Stuart received Stoughton's saddle.

On the 13th, Jeb wrote Flora to say he was in Culpeper at Mrs. Hill's, the wife of Major Hill. This may have been Henry Hill, with whom Stuart served on the frontier prior to the war, or it may have been a relative of Gen. A.P. Hill, who was born at his father's estate, Greenland, outside of Culpeper. That the latter might be the case is suggested by the fact that Stuart wrote General Hill a letter shortly before leaving for the town, and he received a reply from General Hill dated March 14, while there, suggesting they corresponded about where Jeb would stay.

The letter from Hill is short, but it contains two comments that make it clear that, however much Stuart admired Stonewall Jackson, Hill did not. With regard to his winter camp, Powell wrote Jeb, "I suppose I am to vegetate here all winter under that crazy old Presbyterian fool." With regard to the recent promotion of Elisha "Bull" Paxton, a major on Jackson's staff, elevated by Jackson over the heads his regimental commanders to the rank of brigadier, Hill wrote, "How do you like *Paxton* Brig. Gen! The Almighty will get tired, helping Jackson after awhile, and then he'll get the damndest thrashing—and the shoe pinches, for I should get my share and probably all the blame, for the people will never blame Stonewall for any disaster."[22]

March 15th was a Sunday and the court martial did not meet. Stuart attended the Episcopal service in Culpeper and heard what he considered to be "a first rate sermon." It was raining hard and he wrote Flora later, answering her letter of the 12th, which contained more expressions of sadness and worry. The loss of Flora made her more afraid she would lose her husband as well, and Jeb tried to comfort her with reverse psychology, writing, "My Dear One, as Providence has so placed our lives to be much separated, it is due to me & to yourself that you should endeavor to be cheerful & contented, if you dote on me too much I will be taken from you—think of me as the *hard case* you know I am and then you won't miss me so much."[23]

Things were quiet back in Camp No Camp, particularly with the General absent in Culpeper. On the 15th, John Esten Cooke wrote the following in his journal: "Day follows day, without much difference. This is my routine. Wake about 8—find my fire burning and boots, cleaned with real Day & Martin, setting by it. Dress leisurely, gazing into the fire with one boot on or cravat in hand—an old weakness."[24]

Henry Pate hated Stuart and could not have been encouraged by learning that Jeb would testify at the court martial. Stuart had once stated that Pate "could not be a corporal in the Missouri army" and had lobbied long and hard for the promotion of Rosser—Pate's accuser—to brigadier. Nevertheless, the court martial did not have as its goal the dismissal of Pate, and while Rosser's side of the story was sustained, Pate was soon back in the saddle. When Rosser was later promoted to general, Pate received command of the 5th Virginia. It would be in that position that he and Stuart would see each other last—at Yellow Tavern—where Pate would be killed and Stuart mortally wounded.

The morning of March 16 before Pelham departed Orange, a locomotive arrived carrying some of Fitz Lee's troopers and information that Federal cavalry were moving toward Kelly's Ford on the Rappahannock, apparently intent on crossing the river and moving on a principal Confederate line of communication, the Orange and Alexandria Railroad. Fitz

Lee sent the troopers to Orange to bring ammunition back from a supply depot, with orders to return immediately. Pelham could not resist. He had seen no action since his grand performance at Fredericksburg, and he rationalized that Stuart would want him to travel to the place where he might do some good if the General knew all the facts. Accordingly, he boarded the train with Fitz Lee's troopers when they steamed back to Culpeper.

He was surprised to find Stuart already there. Once again, Pelham had analyzed his chief correctly, for Stuart was happy to see him rather than upset he had not returned to headquarters. It is possible, even probable, that Stuart teased Pelham that his real reason for coming to Culpeper was in order to continue visiting young ladies, in this case Bessie Shackleford.

Shackleford would be the last close woman friend of Pelham, whose death was a day away. She may have donned black for him, but it is unlikely. She wrote about him after the war and after losing her own husband, Charles Harris Lester, a former Federal captain, in 1899. Her recollections were clearly affectionate, but are more the words of an admirer than a lover. "One could never forget him. A boy, and yet a man, that was Pelham. . . . He spoke gently and moved quietly. He was quick, though—oh so quick!— just as quick as I was. He would answer a question before you had it half spoken and if there was a joke to be played on someone—well you had to jump faster than you ever jumped before to get ahead of Major Pelham. Sometimes I used to sit and just look at him and wonder if it could be true that he was the man they were all talking about, the man who could aim those guns so that they would kill and kill and kill. He didn't look as though he could ever order anybody to be killed. . . . I used to say to myself, 'A man like that—this boy?' That is really what he was, you know—a boy, a splendid boy."[25]

The news Stuart relayed to Pelham about the Federal incursion was sketchy. He thought they were dealing with a raiding party, when in fact it was 3,000 horsemen and six guns. Fitz Lee was deploying to meet them with the troops he could pull together, which was not a lot. He had 1,900 men in his brigade but only 800 had serviceable horses. By 6 p.m. the blue troopers were at Morrisville, six miles from Kelly's Ford, and Fitz reinforced the pickets near the ford with sharpshooters, but they totaled only sixty men. The Federal commander, Gen. William Averill, could have ridden over the handful of Rebels, but he went into camp on his side of the river.

At Culpeper, fifteen miles away, Stuart was not alarmed. Whether he did not know the size of Averill's force, believed Fitz Lee had more men available, or was simply confident that one of his men could whip four of the enemy, he decided to go with Pelham and visit the Shackleford home instead of riding toward the battle that was likely on the next day.

It was a night of innocent fun, made poignant by the events close on its heels. Bessie and her sisters gathered around the family's piano with the two Confederate officers. First Bessie played classical pieces, then everyone joined in to sing modern favorites—*Dixie, Bonnie Blue Flag, Lorena,* and *The Yellow Rose of Texas.* Afterwards they had refreshments and Stuart and Pelham took their leave, Pelham promising Bessie to see her the next day and wish her a happy St. Patrick's Day.[26] They then went to the Virginia Hotel and ran into Captain Henry Gilmor of the 12th Virginia Cavalry.

Gilmor, like John Mosby, operated as a partisan. He'd performed some feats of derring-do under Turner Ashby and Stonewall Jackson in the Valley Campaign, but enroute to Sharpsburg in September he had been captured and was not released until February. He was then without a command and he asked Stuart the evening of the 16th if he could be of temporary service. Jeb consented.

Gilmor wrote that he, Stuart, and Pelham went to a hotel room occupied by Col. Richard Welby Carter of the 1st Virginia Cavalry, and were joined by six other officers—Col. Tom Rosser, Col. Solomon Williams, Maj. John William Puller, Capt. A. Rogers, Col. James Henry Drake, and none other than Col. Henry Clay Pate. It seems remarkable that these ten men (particularly Stuart, Rosser and Pate) would crowd into the same hotel room for conversation and sociability in the middle of Pate's pending court martial. While the topic of Averill's incursion must have come up, Gilmor wrote that it was "a jovial party."

They would have been less jovial had they been able to fathom their fates. John Pelham and Major Puller would be killed the next day and Tom Rosser would be seriously wounded. Colonel Williams would be killed at Brandy Station in June, ten days after his wedding. Colonel Drake would be killed the following summer at Shepherdstown, Pate and Stuart would fall at Yellow Tavern. Only Gilmor, Rogers, and Carter were not marked men, and it was the former who recorded the occasion.[27]

The next morning, March 17, Pelham woke early and sent a message to Moorman's battery, telling the captain to "Be on the alert. Large force of cavalry between Morrisville and Bealton Station. If everything is quiet here I will be at Rapidan Station tomorrow." It was his last written order. He joined Stuart for breakfast in the hotel dining room, where they decided to ride toward Kelly's Ford. Horses were a challenge, as both came to Culpeper by train, but Sweeney's black mare was in Culpeper and, although "raw-boned," she was acceptable to Pelham. Stuart, of course, had no difficulty requisitioning a horse from anyone to whom he made a request. He probably used General Stoughton's saddle.

Averill's Union cavalry and artillery were up early as well, preparing to force a crossing at Kelly's Ford. It was not a simple matter of splashing across. In addition to the Confederate riflemen in pits and houses on the Confederate side of the river, there were felled trees along both banks, the branches of which were cut and sharpened, forming an abatis. The river was high from recent rain and snow melt, and Averill was turned back more than once before gaining the far side and taking twenty-five of Fitz Lee's men prisoner.[28]

Gilmor slept in, but when word spread that Stuart was planning to ride to the scene of the action, Major John Puller roused him. Gilmor dashed to the stable for his horse and, with Puller, caught up with Stuart and Pelham as they were passing the Shackleford house. Bessie was on the front porch waving a white handkerchief at Pelham. Gilmor doffed his hat as he passed.

They traveled east, with Stuart and Pelham making note of suitable artillery positions in the event the enemy pushed toward Culpeper. The first Confederate force they met was the 5th Virginia, Puller's regiment. He stayed but shouted to Gilmor, "Harry, leave me your haversack if you get killed." Gilmor, Pelham and Stuart rode on and found Fitz Lee.

Fitz was watching an enemy line of battle facing his brigade about a mile west of Kelly's Ford, in position behind a stone wall. Lee could not see their entire force and did not know he was outnumbered. The 3rd Virginia Cavalry was ready to attack, and Breathed's Battery of Horse Artillery—four rifled Blakely guns—was on its way. Lee pointed toward the enemy and said to Stuart, "General, I think there are only a few platoons in the woods yonder. Hadn't we better take the bulge on them at once?" Stuart looked at the enemy position with field glasses and replied, "By all means."

Hearing an attack was planned, Pelham turned back to find and hurry along Breathed's Battery. Fitz did not wait for the guns to come up, however, and ordered a squadron of the 3rd Virginia to proceed on foot toward the enemy. When the Rebels got within 200 yards of the Federals, they met a withering fire from cavalrymen behind the wall and four pieces of Yankee artillery hidden from sight. The Rebels quickly turned back, but before they went more than a few dozen yards, Stuart was in the middle of them, waving his hat and telling them to hold their ground unless "they would leave him by himself."

Gilmor witnessed this and wrote, "Never did I see one bear himself more nobly. I stopped to gaze upon him, though I expected every moment to hear the dull thug (*sic*) of a bullet and see him fall. 'Confound it, men' said he, 'come back;' and *they came.*"

The dismounted troopers of the 3rd Virginia took cover behind a sod fence, and the remainder of the regiment, mounted in columns of fours, charged out with sabers and pistols drawn. Several saddles were emptied before they reached the wall, and those who did so were unable to get through or over. They exchanged shots and slashed with sabers, but to no avail. Rather than turn and run, the 3rd moved left, toward the home and icehouse of C.T. Wheatley, on the Rappahannock. Two regiments of Federal cavalry headed in the same direction to cut them off, whereupon the 2nd Virginia Cavalry galloped into the fight. For several minutes the blue and gray cavalry hacked at each other until the 1st Virginia arrived and drove the Federals back.

Still not realizing how large the Federal force was, Lee decided to deliver a final blow. He ordered the 5th Virginia, under Rosser, to attack the enemy's right flank, get in their rear, and cut them off from escape back across the river. Gilmor was told to find Rosser and deliver the order. He did so and Rosser's regiment began moving. The river was on their left, and the stone fence that had stopped the attack of the 3rd Virginia ended about forty yards to their right. As they attempted the move, Federal riflemen opened on them with enfilading fire. Several troopers were hit and the size of the enemy's force now became apparent. The Confederate advance stalled and troopers seemed about to break and run.

Rosser tried to rally them, shouting and encouraging, and saw Major Puller sitting calmly on his horse, doing nothing. "Major Puller, why in the name of God don't you assist me in rallying the men?" Puller, who had awakened Gilmor that morning, said only, "Colonel, I am killed," and toppled from his horse. He was shot through the breast and died in moments.

Rosser extricated his regiment and continued fighting, receiving a severe wound in the foot later in the day. The battle went back and forth, with each side attacking and counterattacking, but neither gaining ground.

Meanwhile, Pelham rode three and a half miles before finding Breathed's Battery. He urged them forward at a gallop, and they were on the field in thirty minutes. Pelham helped Breathed find the best location for the guns and they opened fire. Pelham watched for a while and it seemed the enemy's fire was slacking, indicating either that the Rebel guns were doing damage or were keeping the enemy from being able to serve their pieces. Telling Breathed to "not let your fire cease; drive them from their position," he rode to the main part of the battlefield.

There are different versions of what happened next, but Gilmor was closest and in the best position to know. He recalled being on the extreme right of the 3rd Virginia, about half an hour after the mortal wounding of Major Puller, when Pelham rode up beside him. The men of the 3rd were preparing to attack again, and artillery shells from the enemy's guns were falling nearby. Gilmor and Pelham were watching and Fitz Lee rode up. He had not yet been wounded, but he'd had two horses shot from beneath him.

"Keep cool boys," he said to the troopers. Then gesturing toward the exploding shells, he said, "These little things make a deal of fuss, but don't hurt anyone." The men of the 3rd cheered and Lee rode on. The regiment moved forward in column and as it was about to pass him, Pelham drew his saber and spurred his horse into a gallop, moving diagonally across an open field toward the head of the column, his reins in one hand and his saber in the other, shouting, "Forward, forward!" The stone wall that had previously deterred the Rebels was ahead, but an opening—either a gate or a breach—had been located and the troopers were funneling through.

Pelham stopped at the opening, stood in his stirrups and waved his saber over his head, telling the men to "Hurry, hurry!" A shell, probably a Hotchkiss, exploded overhead. Pelham dropped his saber and fell from his saddle, landing on his back, his blue eyes open, appearing more stunned than mortally wounded. The black mare trotted away. Someone, probably Captain James Bailey, shouted, "My God, they've killed poor Pelham."

Gilmor, Bailey and one of Fitz Lee's staff officers, Charles Minnigerode, dismounted, lifted Pelham onto the back of Gilmor's horse, and led it to a safer area. Upon examining him, they found only a small wound in his head but it was bleeding steadily. The black mare was caught and Pelham was laid across her back, hands dangling on one side and feet on the other. Two dismounted troopers were put in charge of the body and told to find an ambulance and a doctor. Gilmor rode away to report the incident to Stuart.

As Gilmor rode up, Stuart saw blood on his uniform and asked if he was hurt. Gilmor replied, "It's not my blood, but that of poor Pelham, killed a few moments ago. I've brought his body from the field." Stuart stiffened and a look of distress and horror came to his face. Before either man could say more, however, they realized that Federal cavalry were closing in and they galloped away to avoid capture. When safe inside a stand of trees, Stuart reined in and demanded the details. When Gilmor finished telling what he had seen, Stuart lowered his head to his horse's mane and wept, muttering, "Irreparable, our loss is irreparable."

The two men dispatched to find an ambulance were not successful, but instead of continuing the search they led the black mare with Pelham lying across her back in the direction of Culpeper. Gilmor found them an hour to two later walking unhurriedly, having covered four miles from the site of Pelham's wounding. Gilmor was indignant, and shouted at the men, ordering them to remove Pelham's body and lay it in a grassy fence corner until an ambulance arrived. Then he made a startling discovery—Pelham was alive. He was covered with blood that was clotting around his wound, but he was breathing.

This time an ambulance found them. Stuart had directed one of his couriers, Private Joseph Minghini of the 12th Virginia, to find Pelham and remove him from the battlefield. He located an ambulance and upon arriving he also found Pelham breathing shallowly. He assisted in placing the major in the ambulance, then sent word ahead to the Shackleford family that they were bringing him there. On the way to Culpeper the ambulance stopped at the home of Dr. William A. Herndon and summoned him to the Shackleford home as well.

The Shackleford family prepared to receive the wounded man in their parlor. A bed was set up, near which was a basin of hot water, cloths, bandages, flannel, and a bottle of brandy. Stuart, hearing his friend was still alive, rounded up two more doctors so that three were on their way. When Pelham arrived, they laid him on the bed, removed his uniform, and began washing the blood and mud from his body. They wrapped his hands and feet in flannel, poured brandy down his throat, and the doctors examined the wound. They found that a piece of shell "not larger than the end of my little finger," according to Gilmor, had "entered just at the curl of the hair on the back of the head, raked through the skull without even piercing the brain, coming out two inches below where it entered. The skull was badly shattered between the entrance and exit of the shell." All three physicians agreed there was no hope of Pelham's recovering.

The doctors removed some of the pieces of Pelham's skull, but could offer no more medical assistance and soon left. Bessie Shackleford and Gilmor were in charge of the dying man, and Gilmor took one of the small pieces of Pelham's skull as a memento. Visitors came and went and Pelham continued breathing until about 1 a.m. on the 18th, when he opened his eyes, gazed at Gilmor "with an unconscious look," drew in a long breath, exhaled it slowly, closed his eyes, and died.

Stuart arrived at 2 a.m. hoping his friend was still alive, but he took in the scene and knew what it meant. Holding his plumed hat in one hand, he stepped to the side of the bed and gazed down at the young man he loved like a brother, then leaned down and kissed his forehead. A loud sob broke from Stuart and a tear fell from his eye onto Pelham's cheek. The General stood and, borrowing a pair of scissors, cut a lock of Pelham's hair, then turned away and uttered one word, "farewell," before leaving the house.

The battle at Kelly's Ford continued to rage after Pelham's wounding, and Fitz Lee gamely continued to attack, finally massing all five of his regiments and launching them against Averill. It was a terrific gamble. Had it failed Averill might have crushed Lee's entire brigade, as there were no troops in reserve to come to the Rebels' rescue. The gamble paid off, however, just barely, and with the aid of bad intelligence. The Federals were pushed back, their cannons almost taken, and their field hospital nearly overrun. The Virginia regiments withdrew and reformed to attack again. In the meantime Averill received a report that Confederate infantry was advancing on his right and trainloads of reinforcements were coming up in Lee's rear to join the battle. The reports were inaccurate, but at 5:30 the Federal commander needed to decide to continue the contest, attack, or withdraw. Claiming in his report that the mission was a success but that his horses were exhausted, he chose the latter option and left the field in the hands of the Confederates. Averill reported total casualties, killed, wounded, and missing, of eighty. Lee reported eleven killed, eighty-eight wounded, thirty-four missing, and the loss of 170 horses. He'd taken twenty-nine prisoners.[29]

Gilmor stayed with Pelham that night, sleeping on the floor. In the morning the body was placed in a wooden coffin and sent to Richmond via Gordonsville and Hanover Junction, a trip of nearly 100 miles. Stuart wired Von Borcke to meet the train at Hanover, take charge of the remains, escort them to Richmond, and arrange to have them sent to Pelham's family in Alabama.

The news of Pelham's death arrived at Camp No Camp by courier—probably Private Minghini—on the 18th. The members of Stuart's military family, including the servants, were overwhelmed with sorrow. Blackford recorded that the day Pelham left for Orange Court House he had marked the place in Napier's *History of the War in the Peninsula* where he and Pelham were reading and that, some thirty years later, he had never "had the heart to read more in it since."[30] Von Borcke wrote, "One after the other, comrades entered my tent to hear the confirmation of the dreadful news, which everybody tried as long as possible not to credit. Couriers and negroes assembled outside, all seemingly paralysed by the sudden and cruel calamity; and when morning came, instead of the usual bustling activity and noisy gaiety, a deep and mournful silence reigned throughout the encampment. I was much touched by the behaviour of Pelham's negro servants, Willis and Newton, who, with tokens of the greatest distress, begged to be allowed at once to go and take charge of their master's body—a permission which I was, however, constrained to refuse."[31] Cooke wrote, "It cast a shadow over me I could not dispel, and is a mournful thought still. He was a brave, noble fellow, and I had learned to love him. So we pass."[32]

Von Borcke was at the depot when the train arrived at Hanover early on the 19th. Pelham's coffin was not the only one being transported but it was the only one with a teary-eyed member of the Horse Artillery in attendance. He provided Von with more details of Pelham's death, and Von boarded the train for the remainder of the trip to Richmond. He wired ahead to have a hearse waiting at the station but found none when he arrived and "was obliged to remove the body into the town in a common one-horse wagon."

The wagon and its sad contents arrived at the Governor's Mansion, and Governor Letcher, who knew Von Borcke, directed that the body be placed in a session room in the State Capitol, where it was draped with a flag of Virginia and an honor guard was put in place. The next day Von Borcke "procured a handsome iron coffin, and with my own hands assisted in transferring the body to its new receptacle. I was overcome with grief as I touched the lifeless hand that had so often pressed mine in the grasp of friendship. His manly features even in death expressed that fortitude and pride which distinguished him. By special request I had a small glass window let into the coffin-lid just over the face, that his friends and admirers might take a last look at the young hero, and they came in troops, the majority being ladies, who brought garlands and magnificent bouquets to lay upon the coffin."

The casket was moved to the center of the capitol, near a giant statue of George Washington, where it remained for thirty-six hours. Although numerous participants wrote in detail about Pelham's death and the days following, no one mentioned whether his body was embalmed, and it likely was not. Being then three and a half days dead, the body's condition for viewing seems dubious, but viewing through the small window continued.

John Esten Cooke was among the hundreds who paid their respects. He noted that someone placed an evergreen wreath, intertwined with white flowers, on the coffin. A friend of Pelham's identified only as Evelyn, from Alabama, wrote, "With moistened eyes a little party of Alabamians gaze upon it. The flag is removed, and there—dear God! I can hardly write it for the blinding tears—there is the body of my darling friend—noble noble Pelham! Stiff and stark in death, the loved face white and cold, the same sad smile lingering upon his beautiful lips."[33]

Hundreds paid their respects, and one reporter claimed the coffin was visited by most of the ladies in Richmond. Others, such as Sallie Dandridge, came from other parts of the state. The longstanding account of his death causing three women to don mourning clothes, which originated from another correspondent's report, is probably accurate in the sense that at least three women in black came to pay their respects as he lay in state. However, it is unlikely that any of them did so out of a belief that she was engaged or betrothed to Pelham. Even the leading candidate—Sallie Dandridge—was denied as a possible contender for that honor by Pelham's niece, Emma Pelham Hank, who lived to be 100 and was interviewed in 1984.[34]

Stuart remained in Culpeper until the 20th. He wanted to go to Richmond for Pelham's rites but as in all things, he considered military duties his top priority. Instead he wrote letters about his feelings for him. To Alabama Congressman J.L.M. Curry he wrote on the 18th that "he was beloved, appreciated, and admired, let the tears of agony we have shed, and the gloom of mourning throughout my command bear witness. His loss to the country is irreparable." To Flora he wrote on the 19th, "You must know how his death distressed me." To Nannie Price, at Dundee, he wrote, "To behold that calm sweet face that so quickened at the battle cry in its last moments of consciousness now cold in the sleep of death, wrings tears from the most obdurate." To his division he issued General Order No. 9 on the 20th, a long, stirring announcement of Pelham's death, a directive that all members of the Horse Artillery and division staff wear a badge of mourning for thirty days, and saying, "The memory of 'the gallant Pelham,' his many manly virtues, his noble nature and purity of character, are enshrined as a sacred legacy in the hearts of all who knew him."[35]

At 5 p.m. on the 20th, Pelham's coffin was taken to the Richmond depot with full military honors, a battalion of infantry as escort, and a long procession. There it was loaded on a railroad car to begin a journey to Alabama through four states, hundreds of miles, for two days on nine different trains. At the border of Pelham's home state it was transported by ferry, by wagon, and by another train to Montgomery, where it lay in state on the second floor of the Supreme Court chamber. It was covered with an Alabama flag and large quantities of flowers, after which a long line of people filed past until March 26. On the 27th the casket was taken down the Alabama River to Selma by steamboat, where a crowd that included family and pallbearers took it to the railroad station and mourners gazed through the glass window at Pelham's face. Nine days dead, the face was described as "statuesque and unharmed," with "a lovely smile around his lips and the half-opened eyes." At every station along the line to Blue Mountain, the depot nearest his home, crowds met the train carrying flowers. The casket arrived at Blue Mountain at 10 p.m. on the 28th and was transferred to a hearse pulled by four white horses for the final seven miles to the Pelham home.

His mother was standing on the front porch when her son arrived, and John's sister-in-law noticed that in addition to the white horses, the pall bearers had white hair, the casket was covered with white flowers, and a full white moon was shining, so that it seemed "a Company 'all in white.'" His mother must have noticed too, for as he was carried into the parlor she said quietly, "made white in the blood of the lamb." It was evening, and not light enough in the parlor to see through the little window. Mrs. Pelham directed that the casket be placed so that the first sunlight the next morning, a Sunday, would fall on his face.

The body remained in the family parlor through March 29 and hundreds more came to see the "quiet face so like life, asleep." On Monday, March 30, a committee met to plan the funeral, and on the 31st the body was transported by wagon to Jacksonville, nine miles away, where the services were to be held in the Presbyterian Church. However, the crowd gathered was the "the largest body of people ever seen together in Jacksonville, Alabama," and the funeral was moved to the larger Baptist Church. Finally, that afternoon, the casket was lowered into a grave in the Pelham family plot in the city cemetery. Before it was covered with dirt, local school children covered it with lilac blossoms.[36]

Stuart left Culpeper on the 20th, but did not return immediately to headquarters. He wrote a wrote a long letter that day to Flora from "near Fredericksburg," but at Camp No Camp Cooke wrote in his journal that day that Stuart had not returned. Channing Price wrote a letter home from headquarters on the 21st saying he hoped the General would come that day, as a telegram addressed to him at Culpeper was delivered the night before.

Stuart's letter to Flora on the 20th addressed other topics besides Pelham, particularly his continuing efforts to prop her up, as she was still depressed. In the classic style of husbands and wives, he brought up past disagreements as examples of how his position in such matters had proven best—in Wytheville at the beginning of the war she had accused him of loving his country better than his wife, and later while visiting Dundee she had discovered his valise was locked and demanded that he open it, which he declined to do because it contained sensitive military information. He explained that time had proven his actions correct in both instances, and wrote sweetly and chauvinistically, "Now Dearie, let us gather wisdom to let old hubbie manage his matters and when he withholds be satisfied there is reason for it, and submit without question or complaint."

Stuart went to Richmond on the 21st and stayed with his brother, Alexander, with whom he sat up visiting until past midnight. Von Borcke was still in the city, and he noted that Stuart was "still deeply affected by the loss of his young friend, and greatly grieved that he had not been able to attend the funeral ceremonies."[37] Stuart's principal reason for being in the city was official business, at the office of Secretary of War James Seddon, with whom he had made an appointment. Upon arriving, an aide to the secretary ushered him into Seddon's office and announced him as "General Stuart." Seddon was at his desk, reading or writing, and he did not look up or say anything. Stuart stood for a few moments, then stepped forward and spoke. As soon as he did, "up bounced the Secretary, all confused, and stammered out that he had taken him to be the other Gen. [George H.] Steuart, of Maryland." Jeb found the incident greatly amusing, more for the deference the Secretary of War showed him than the lack of deference he showed General Steuart.[38]

On Sunday, the 22nd, Jeb attended services at St. James Episcopal Church and listened to a sermon by Dr. Joshua Peterkin.[39] In a little less than a year and two months, Dr. Peterkin would preside over Stuart's funeral service in the same church.

He returned to his headquarters on the morning of the 24th, carrying a great deal of paperwork for Channing Price. Price's promotion to major was official and Stuart gave him a set of stars to put on his uniform jacket. Price was honored, but not as elated as he had expected to be. His being brought out of the ranks and made lieutenant was still more of a thrill for him, and he fretted that he did not know any lady in the neighborhood whom he could ask to sew on the stars, which meant he would "have to get some bungling hand to do it for me." He was also uncomfortable when the clerks in his office greeted him "in a rather low voice" as "Major." Price had not told other staff officers he was recommended for promotion, but Jeb made certain everyone knew by "calling in a loud voice several times to-day, when something required my attention for Major Price."[40] This must have startled the other rank-conscious staff officers who were not expecting it, but Cooke, at least, thought it was "an excellent appointment."[41]

Jeb wrote Flora again on the 24th, having received a letter from her dated the 16th. Their exchange and receipt of letters was out of synch, so that he was reading things she had written before she had received his latest letter. From the content of his to her it is obvious that she was still worrisome and fretful, probably even jealous, to which Jeb wrote, "and so like Thomas you are beginning to doubt & question, well I could give your doubts & questions a decided quietus if like Our Savior did Thomas I could thrust your hand into my side and bid you test there the pulsations of a heart that for nearly eight years, been, & is *yours*," and "Do not torture your mind with such things. Be cheerful, confiding and true & you will not be wanting in *happiness*. Dismiss the apparitions of the past, cease to conjure up the hobgoblins of future trouble, and take hold of the present with a firm hand and stout heart, and thus mould under Divine Providence a future of contentment and peace."

However much Jeb wanted to bolster Flora's flagging spirits, this letter must also have been verbalization of the thoughts and philosophy he was preaching to himself since the loss of Pelham.

On the 25th, Stuart breakfasted with Tom Price. They were alone and Jeb was talkative, recounting the amusing incident in Secretary Seddon's office on the 21st. Later that day Stuart received a visit from Stonewall

Jackson, who had moved his headquarters from Moss Neck on March 16 to a place about two miles from Stuart's headquarters.

When Jackson arrived he went straight to Stuart's tent but found it empty, and Channing Price scrambled to find him, which he did in the tent of another staff officer. Price made a small witticism by telling Jeb that he was "surprised" by Jackson, after which the two commanders dined together and Jackson returned to his headquarters.[42]

On the 26th Stuart spent more time tending to paperwork. He prepared a letter to Colonel J.F. Gilmor, who headed the Confederate Corps of Engineers, to report favorably on the work of Blackford, Frank Robertson, and Tom Price, suggesting they each be promoted. He then prepared a letter to General Cooper asking that Major R.F. Beckham be appointed to replace Pelham as commander of the Horse Artillery.[43]

The selection of Beckham must have been a surprise to the Horse Artillery and Stuart's staff. Rather than selecting one of Pelham's battery commanders, like Breathed or Moorman, who were familiar with the operations of Stuart's flying artillery, he selected a stranger with limited artillery service. Beckham was an 1859 graduate of West Point who began the war as an engineer. He was then commissioned a lieutenant and put in charge of Groves' Culpeper Battery, which he commanded at First Manassas and where Stuart saw and was impressed by his conduct. In January 1862, he joined the staff of Maj. Gen. Gustavas F. Smith as an side-de-camp and served there a year, being promoted to major before Smith resigned at the beginning of 1863, leaving Beckham without a command. He applied for a commission as major of artillery, which is where he was when Stuart tapped him to replace Pelham.[44] Subsequent campaigns and events would prove, again, that Jeb had an eye for talent.

On the evening of the 26th Stuart stopped in at the tent of John Esten Cooke with a copy of Order No. 9, regarding the death of Pelham, and read it aloud, his face flushing and his voice catching as he did so. Cooke announced the order "excellent; terse and eloquent: in a style which the Gen. is best hand at, of any one I ever knew"—positive praise indeed from a novelist.

Stonewall showed up for dinner again, and Cooke ate with the generals. Stuart told Jackson he had gone to Culpeper three times recently, "with his satchel and spy glass," expecting the enemy to come in that direction and still believing they would do so. Cooke marveled at Jackson's eyes, calling them "curious" and "brilliant as a diamond!"[45]

President Davis proclaimed Friday, March 27, 1863, as a national "day of humiliation, prayer and fasting."[46] It was observed in the army camps and Stuart's headquarters. Major Fitzhugh was assigned the task of finding black crepe for the staff to wear for thirty days in honor of Pelham, whose loss continued to eat at them. Channing Price wrote on the 30th that "I declare, nothing has happened in the progress of the war which I have felt more keenly than his death," and then echoed the same type of sentiment that Stuart, Von Borcke, Cooke, and Blackford had—"he was sincerely attached to me, I think, & I loved him almost like a brother."

Paperwork continued on March 27 and 28. Stuart needed a new aide-de-camp since the promotion of Channing Price, and he offered the position verbally to a private named Robert H. Goldsborough of Co. B of the 39th Battalion of Virginia Cavalry, which was serving as an escort for Maj. Gen. Richard S. Ewell.[47]

On the 30th, Stuart sent a letter to Thomas R. Price, Sr., the father of Channing and Tom, asking if he would serve as a surety on the official bond required of Major Norman Fitzhugh now that he was the Cavalry Division Quartermaster. Two sureties were required and Jeb had asked his brother, Alexander, to serve as the other. While at it, Stuart could not resist some light-hearted wordplay with the elder Price. "I wonder how you all can keep your heads above water when the whole country is crying 'Down with the *Prices*, "he wrote. "It must be consoling to the financiers to observe that the *Price Sterling* (a play on the name of Confederate General Sterling Price) is not as much above the *Price current*, as before Channing's promotion." Probably chuckling at his own wit, he closed by saying, "I will spare you any further affliction now but I must have my joke, 'No rose without its thorn, *nary Jeb without his joke*.'"[48]

However light-hearted he tried to be, however much he was trying to take a firm hold on the present and be content, Stuart gave thought to paying further respects, in verse, to Pelham that same day. He wrote two poems, one about Dundee and the other about Pelham, then went through the rain to Cooke's tent carrying both verses and Pelham's saddle. He gave the saddle to Cooke as a memento of their mutual friend. Cooke was honored, and wrote he would cling to the saddle. Jeb read him the poems, and asked him to write an obituary for Pelham and send it to *The Sentinel* for publication.

Chiswell Dabney left on the 30th to inspect the 10th Virginia Cavalry, which was camped between Fredericksburg and Beaver Dam. Beaver Dam was the home of the Fontaine family and the site of what Dabney recalled as the most marvelous week of his life. Neither Jeb nor any of his staff doubted that young Chiswell would mix pleasure with business and visit his friends and relatives at Beaver Dam. Thus it was amusing when, shortly after Dabney departed, Dr. John Fontaine arrived and said that nobody was home at Beaver Dam. The staff had a laugh at Dabney's expense, and when he returned on April 1, he told Channing Price that he was "mad enough to have killed somebody" when he found the house empty on the 31st.[49]

The month of March ended with more rain. It fell, pooled on the already sodden soil, then soaked under the bottoms of the tents and huts of the staff, covering the floors of some.[50]

April began. Stuart and his staff had nine more days in the camp near Fredericksburg before the Spring Campaign would begin. Channing Price and Stonewall Jackson had a month to live. Von Borcke would be with his hero, Stuart, for less than three more months. The war would last another twenty-four months and Stuart would see thirteen of them.

The weather continued to be awful. Besides rain, it was so cold nobody wanted to venture out, but so windy it was difficult to keep fires going inside and smoke would not vent from makeshift chimneys, backing up inside instead. Cooke kept to himself and wrote sketches and pieces about whimsical things such as "Some (smoking) Pipes I Have Known." Channing Price tended to paperwork. Von Borcke whiled away the hours as best he could. Blackford continued to tutor his two assistant engineers.

Stuart received word from Flora that she would be back in Richmond at the end of March, which coincided with the reconvening of the Pate court-martial on April 2. Stuart did not have to testify, but he either needed to attend or did so as an excuse to see Flora, and the evening of April 2 he went there hoping to see her. He was disappointed again and after visiting the Brewers, Mrs. Robert E. Lee, and Dundee, he returned on the 3rd.[51]

April 3 was Good Friday, and upon returning to Camp No Camp, Jeb attended church services in the city and "heard a fine sermon to a crowded congregation." The weather had finally improved, and he pronounced it "beautiful." In fact, the weather made him want to go with Flora to the Dan River and gather violets on the hills. In his letter to her that evening, he told Flora of an opportunity for her to obtain a room in Fredericksburg at no cost, and said he "would certainly advocate acceptance if there was the slightest certainty of my own movements. If the roads dry up hastily, I shall not be here."

Flora sent him a *carte-de-visite* of herself, but Jeb told her it made her look "so sad, and I am told you are extremely sad nowadays." Once again he inserted advice into his letter to bolster her sagging spirits, which clashed with his own natural buoyancy. "This war is not over," he reminded her, "and you must nerve your heart for its trials, its griefs, and its woes, and let me ask you now my dear one, partner of my joys and sorrows, not to take from me that confidence I feel I deserve, that love of which I have been so proud, and that firm support which woman knows so well how to give or withhold."

There is another, very valid reason for Flora's moodiness—she was pregnant.

The child would be a little girl born October 9, 1863, after Jeb's year of glory, having been conceived while Flora was staying in Fredericksburg at Mrs. Alsop's. Stuart would see his baby daughter no more than four times between her birth and his death, but she partially filled the ragged hole in his heart from the death of little Flora.

Discussion of her condition did not show up often in Stuart's letters. He occasionally mentioned to friends that Flora was "indisposed," and in one letter he addressed the topic all expectant parents discuss, usually at great length—what to name the new baby. For Jeb the choices were clear— if a boy, I will have an heir named John Pelham," if a girl, "Maria Pelham Stuart."[52] Perhaps Flora did not want to honor her own sister so, or perhaps Jeb decided his native state should be honored more. The little girl's name would be Virginia Pelham Stuart.

On April 4, Stuart was in camp and Tom Price was present when an un-named captain stopped by to chat. Stuart and the captain agreed that the next time the Federal army attempted to cross the Rappahannock, it would be at United States Ford, and Stuart made the remarkably accurate pre-diction that the next battle would be fought near Chancellorsville. The cap-tain is unnamed because Tom Price either forgot his name or because, when the *New York Times* published the diary entry on May 21, 1863, it elected to not identify the officer.[53]

On the 5th Stuart and his staff woke to falling snow. Tom Price and Frank Robertson were supposed to ride to Germana Ford on the Rapidan River near Stevensburg for a week's work, but seven inches of snow on the ground distressed the unsoldierly Tom, so they delayed their trip for a day.[54] The purpose of Price's and Robertson's expedition was to help oversee the reconstruction of a bridge, which was definitely engineering work. They were not being sent because they had accumulated genuine engineering skills, but because Blackford was given a twenty-day furlough in which to recover from his illness. Together the two assistant staff engineers might possess enough training to at least appear that they knew what they were doing, but the real engineering would come from Captain Charles Collins of the 15th Virginia Cavalry who was going with them, in command. Collins started his Confederate career in the artillery and then transferred to the cavalry, but his value was that he was an 1859 graduate of West Point who served two years in the U.S. Army Corps of Engineers before the war.[55]

Stuart was walking around with a photo of Nannie Price in one pocket and a photo of her sister Ellen in another. He was happy to display them to anyone who might be interested, and Channing observed that the photos seemed to make him feel "well fortified." Jeb had also picked up presents of sweets at Dundee: candy for Channing, a cake for Tom, and cake and pies for the rest of the staff. The evening of the 5th he invited those of his military family who were not away from camp to his tent to enjoy them.

Stuart wrote Flora on the 6th in response to letters he'd just received from her. Apparently her two letters did not contain anything to make him believe she was still feeling blue, as his was chatty and devoid of husbandly or philosophical advice. He discussed changes on his staff and plans for reorganization and acquisition of new appointments. One person he had his eye on was "Cousin of Little Mac," Henry B. McClellan. He also described his belated wedding present to Elizabeth Price and John Fontaine— a special, Jeb Stuart-designed set of two silver tumblers, on which was "a device representing a Fountain" with two cavalry sentinels mounted on each side, with the motto "nous defendrous La Fountaine" (we defend the fountain) and the initials "K.G.S." (Knight of the Golden Spurs) above. He considered it "quite unique and appropriate," and the wordplay connecting the groom's name and a fountain was pure Jeb.[56]

On April 5 the sun came out and melted the snow, giving rise, by the 7th, to expectation that the roads might become dry enough to break camp. The news that a move was coming circulated, and last visits were made to friends. John Esten Cooke went to see Mrs. Alsop and her family on the 8th, "truly sorry to leave those kind friends all."

On the 6th, Jeb wrote a letter to General Cooper to request that Robert Goldsborough be commissioned a 1st lieutenant and assigned to his staff as an aide-de-camp to replace Channing Price, who was promoted to Assistant Adjutant General, asking that his commission become effective on April 1.[57]

Jeb wrote another letter to Flora on the 8th. He was upset because he had learned that a previous letter to her was mistaken by Jeb's mother for one to her, and she had opened and read it. Considering that letters from Jeb to his mother either did not survive or were sparse, one cannot blame the lady for being anxious to hear from her famous son, but Stuart was not amused. "I don't know what I wrote," he told Flora, "but I certainly did not write for her to see." Another couple of sentences were devoted to Pelham: "He was noble in every sense of the word; I want Jimmie to be just like him." He told her to keep and re-read "those advice letters" he'd sent previously, and then began a new section of the missive with a centered, underlined title of "Strictly Private," wherein he addressed the previously alluded to question of "What shall it [the new baby] be named?"

After inviting her to exchange ideas for the name, he made his pitch for John Pelham or Maria Pelham, saying the latter would "combine two lovely natures in the name of our little one." He rejected "Rachel," Flora's mother's name, saying he didn't like the name and that if Rachel Cooke said anything about the baby not being named after her, Flora should say "Ma, you were not with us," an expression of Jeb's resentment toward his father-in-law than criticism of his mother-in-law.

The actual orders for the move came on the 9th, which Von Borcke met with "intense relief." The camp was dismantled and tents and other baggage were loaded on wagons and taken to the train station. Stuart found time amidst the turmoil to write a letter to General Chilton in Richmond recommending a change to the law authorizing military courts, probably prompted by the Pate proceeding, which had dragged on for months and was still pending

The new headquarters was to be near Culpeper, and Stuart assigned Chiswell Dabney and John Esten Cooke the task of seeing that everything was wrapped up and loaded, while he, Channing Price, Von Borcke, and Major Beckham boarded the train at Hanover and rode first to Gordonsville and then to Orange Court House. The trip was uninteresting, but a Miss Lee and a Miss Pearce were on board, riding from Green Springs to Orange. Their company helped pass the time and may have became fodder for generations of family lore in the Pearce and Lee families, in which a simple train trip became a life-changing romance.

When Stuart arrived in Culpeper he and Beckham went to the homes of friends while Price and Von Borcke stayed at the city's one hotel, the Virginia House. If the friends with whom Jeb stayed were not the Shackleford's, he certainly made a visit there. His last appearance, on March 18, was one of the most painful experiences of his life, but when John Esten Cooke caught up with him there the afternoon of Saturday, the 11th, he found Bessie Shackleford joyful and the home lavish. Thoughts of Pelham were still on their minds, and Cooke began his next diary entry, on the 22nd, with "Poor, poor Pelham!"

On April 11, Jeb received an "intimation" about Brig. Gen. Isaac Trimble's report concerning the capture of Manassas Junction the previous August 27. Approaching the junction, Jackson had put Stuart in command of its capture, turning over two regiments of Trimble's brigade to him for that purpose. Perhaps Trimble did not know this, or forgot during the months before he wrote his report, because he reported that "I had no assistance from artillery or any part of General Stuart's cavalry," and "General Stuart did not arrive until 7 or 8 o'clock in the morning," after which his cavalry engaged in "an indiscriminate plunder of horses."[58]

Trimble's men, about 1,000, were more than enough to take the junction. Most of the enemy either fled or were captured. The fact that cavalrymen went after the horses indiscriminately is not exactly a surprise, considering they rode horses and Trimble's infantry did not, and no matter what time Jeb arrived in person, his report of the affair was that the capture was accomplished "with . . . little difficulty." Accordingly, Trimble's old maidish rant (he was twice Stuart's age) smacks more of resentment than objective reporting. Predictably, it set off a war of written opinions in which Jeb and Trimble attempted to pencil whip the other into submission over the next several months.

April 12 was a Sunday and Stuart and his staff attended the Episcopal Church in town, heard Reverend Cole preach, and took Communion. Once again the Pate Court Martial re-convened, again in Culpeper and now on a Sunday, for the purpose of receiving the testimony of Fitz Lee, who was in town for that purpose.

Tom Price and Frank Robertson had arrived at Germana Ford for their bridge rebuilding duty to find a group of eighty "mechanics" gathered from various infantry units to do the manual labor under the command of a Captain McTier and two other officers. They had worked about a week when Vespacian Chancellor, a Stuart courier and member of the family that founded Chancellorsville, came in with a report. An elderly citizen had arrived from across the Rapidan with news that a large force of the enemy was coming their way along the plank road.

Captain Charles Collins opined that if the tale was true the Rebel cavalry pickets would have reported the enemy's movement. Chancellor responded that that might be so, but the citizen was a sensible old fellow who "knew a Yank when he saw him." Robertson volunteered to take Miranda and check out the report. Collins agreed.

Robertson forded the river and told the Confederates working on that side, cutting wood for the bridge, to make certain their weapons were loaded. He rode a mile, saw nothing, and was beginning to think it was a false alarm when he came to a cabin with another elderly gentleman in its doorway. Robertson started to talk to the man but he shouted, "Look, look!" and pointed up the road. Seventy-five yards away and coming fast was a squadron of enemy cavalry.

Robertson straightened, wheeled, and spurred back the way he'd come, hearing shouts of "Come here, Johnny," and "Stop, you damned Reb," mixed with several carbine shots from behind. Miranda proved fast enough and he shouted warning to the Confederates on that side of the river before splashing across to where Captain Collins and Tom Price were watching.

The Federal cavalry were close on Robertson's heels, and the entire force of wood cutters, forty men, were captured before they could cross the river. The other forty, on the Confederate side, took cover in a deep cut leading to the ford, and Collins directed Robertson to ride to the top of a knoll to see what the enemy would do.

No one yet knew that an entire Federal infantry corps was following the cavalry. Robertson galloped up the hill, drawing fire, and tried to watch their movements. He was the only Confederate in sight and a lot of bullets were sent his way, so he rode Miranda back down the hill to a small cabin and tied her to a poplar tree behind it. He then dashed out to a foot-high rock wall in front and tried to conduct his reconnaissance from there. The Yankees had seen where he went, however, and continued shooting at him, one bullet coming so close he was temporarily blinded by flying rock dust.

When he was able to look again, he saw the forty captured Confederates being marched away, the forty hiding in the cut, and a regiment of enemy cavalry riding toward the unfinished bridge. They did not know there were still forty Rebels to contest their crossing until a well-aimed, well-timed volley swept away the front of the Federal column.

This was Robertson's first sight of men being killed in battle, and he was impressed both with the skill of the mechanics-cum-rifleman, and the "realization of the tragedy of war." The enemy did not try to cross again for several hours, during which time thousands of infantry and several pieces of artillery came down the road and spread out on the hills opposite the little band of Rebels. When they had approximately 5,000 men in position, they demanded surrender of the men in the cut. They had little choice, as they would have been shot if they tried to flee.

There were four other Confederate mechanics with neither of the groups, three cutting wood further back and one close to where Robertson was hiding. This man came around the corner of the cabin and told Robertson they were surrendering. Robertson was crestfallen, particularly at the thought of a Yankee taking Miranda, so he decided to see if he could at least turn her loose so she might escape. He went to her, hung his saber and pistol on the cantle of the saddle, and started leading her up the hill, intending to release and drive her. It was 250 yards to the crest and he expected to be shot, but no firing came. He wrote later that "the absolute quiet seemed to urge me to go with her," so he rebuckled his sword belt. The lone Rebel at the cabin stepped out and asked him what he planned. Robertson said, "I'm going to try to get over the hill. I'll not surrender."

The soldier looked at him in an appealing way Robertson never forgot. He was "also crazy to get away," but he had no horse and offering to let him ride double on Miranda would get all three of them killed. Robertson mounted and the infantryman began running up the hill. They made it nearly a hundred yards before the Federals fired. Robertson lay flat across Miranda's mane and spurred. He saw bullets kick up dust and heard a cry from behind. His companion was killed.

Only Collins, Tom Price, Robertson, and the three other woodcutters escaped capture. Robertson returned to Germanna Ford three weeks later and talked to a woman who lived across the river. She told him the Federals buried ten men killed and that she and her husband buried the lone Rebel who tried to escape with Robertson. He was hit three times in the back. Robertson counted twenty-nine bullet holes in the little cabin.

At Culpeper, the train carrying the staff's baggage arrived the evening of the 12th, and on the 13th the staff and their servants began the laborious task of pitching tents and setting up camp. The site, selected by Von Borcke, was half a mile from the court house on a wooded hill—pines and cedars— next to the road leading to Orange Courthouse, "commanding a view of the village and the surrounding country." It was christened "Camp Pelham."

It took most of the day to get the camp set up, and Stuart found time to write a letter to Lieutenant Henry B. McClellan, adjutant of the 3rd Virginia Cavalry, telling him that due to the young man's "patriotism, fidelity and ability," he desired that he be commissioned a major and come to Stuart's staff as an Assistant Adjutant General.[59]

Everyone turned in tired, but about midnight Stuart was roused by a courier. Pickets reported a large force of enemy cavalry moving on the other side of the Rappahannock in the direction of Culpeper. Jeb had Channing Price awakened and brought to his tent, where Stuart dictated orders to Fitz and Rooney Lee to put them on alert, plus wrote a dispatch to General R.E. Lee about the enemy's movements. He then gave Channing directions for getting headquarters in motion the next morning and let him go back to his tent for a couple more hours of rest.

Only the brigades of Fitz and Rooney Lee were at Culpeper at the time. The sad condition of horses in Hampton's brigade had necessitated leaving it behind while many of its troopers went home—some all the way to Mississippi—to procure new animals. While the dismounted troopers were thus engaged, each regiment of the rest of the brigade sent representatives home to attempt to recruit more men.

On the morning of the 14th, Lt. Hagan roused the staff and they joined Stuart in an unhurried ride to Brandy Station to see what the enemy might be doing. Rooney Lee's brigade was there, waiting to see where it was needed most. He, one regiment, and one gun from the Horse Artillery had ridden to Kelly's Ford, where they repulsed a few attempts by the Federal cavalry to cross. At 11 a.m., however, news came that the Federals had forced a crossing at the nearby railroad bridge and that more than a regiment were on the Confederate side of the river. Stuart, the 9th Virginia, and Beckham's guns headed that way "at a quick trot." Jeb was determined "to jam them right into the river." When they arrived they found that most of "the scoundrels had cleared out," except for a few stragglers who were hurried along by artillery shells. Rooney Lee's adjutant, Captain William T. Robins, took a party to reoccupy the bridge, which was accomplished, but Robins' horse was shot and its leg broken, so the animal had to be put down.

Rooney Lee returned from Kelly's Ford to report that all was secure there. An artillery duel then commenced, with the Rebel guns lobbing shells across the river and the Federals replying in kind. Stuart, Channing Price, Tom Price, Rooney Lee, Benjamin White, and Captain James L. Clark, an aide-de-camp, dismounted to watch the show. The spring weather was greening up the grass and the horses wanted to graze, so the officers tied or picketed their horses to allow it, and sat or lay down in an open field below and about fifty yards from Breathed's guns. Channing Price stretched out on his side, propped up on one elbow. Captain White removed his gloves and Captain Clark seized them to use as a pillowcase, with Channing's knee as a pillow. As they watched, one or two voiced the idle opinion that it was odd the Federals did not fire at the little group, considering they were lower and closer than the Confederate cannons. Channing's horse was tied to a bush, and it managed to get itself twisted around, so Price got up to untangle its reins, and just then he and some others spotted the Federals moving and training a gun directly at them.

Everyone jumped. White snatched his gloves from the ground, but moved only a couple of steps before the shell landed exactly where he and the gloves had been seconds before—in the middle of the knot of men. All should have been killed, but miraculously the shell did not explode, merely splattering them with dirt. Tom Price called it "the narrowest escape," and Channing "the most wonderful escape I ever knew."[60] The officers separated so as to not continue to be an inviting target, and the sight of a Confederate limber on its way to resupply Breathed's guns diverted the Yankees' attention, and soon the shooting ended.[61]

About the time the artillery shower ended a real one began, and they returned to camp. There they were dismayed to find Camp Pelham completely dismantled, loaded up and hauled to the rail station in anticipation that the enemy was going to force them to move again. The rain stopped and word was sent to bring it all back, but the wagon supposed to be carrying the staff's baggage tipped over in the muddy road, which delayed its return by hours. When it finally arrived, it contained only General Stuart's tent and baggage. Everyone crowded into his large tent, wet and supperless, and lay down to sleep. It began raining again and continued all night.

The next morning, April 15, it was still raining, and Stuart and his staff set out in different directions to find something to eat. The large amount of rain made Stuart think the river would rise sufficiently to prevent another attempt by the enemy to cross, but that was not the case. A courier arrived to report that Federals had crossed before the river got too high, so Stuart and his men mounted up and returned to Brandy Station with rain still falling in torrents.

Nobody was in a great mood, but Stuart was now hoping to find a sizeable force of the enemy on his side of the river, so that he could engage them with a swollen, uncrossable stream at their backs. At Brandy Station he learned the crossing had been made at Beverly's Ford and hurried in that direction. As he came in sight of the ford, he saw eight or ten men standing in the road about fifty yards ahead, but could not tell if they were friend or foe. Rooney Lee and Colonel John Chambliss, commanding the 13th Virginia, rode forward to find out. Stuart decided they were the enemy and ordered a charge. The dismounted men, definitely Yankees, ran.

The Federals were recrossing the rising river while they could, but two squadrons of the 3rd Indiana Cavalry were still on the Confederate side, serving as the rear guard. They opened fire and fell back. There was a mill race, or creek, between them and the river that was so flooded that four or five of the Federals fell and drowned trying to cross it. When the Rebels reached the stream, they found it could only be crossed at one point, single file, and the Indiana troopers were able to pick off one Confederate as they did so. The 13th Virginia finally got enough men across to rush the enemy, capturing twenty and wounding five.

Stuart had not allowed Von Borcke to join the charge, so he went about a hundred yards to the right where Federal sharpshooters where firing, hoping to capture or shoot some. He rode to within forty yards and shouted at them to surrender. There was a swollen stream, probably the same mill race, between him and the Federal rifleman who "in the fancied security offered by the broad foaming stream," responded by firing at Von. One bullet nearly cut off a lock of his hair, so he spurred his horse and tried to leap the stream. He got about half way across and sank nearly out of sight. Luckily, his horse was able to keep its head, swim the rest of the way and scramble up the steep bank, where a corporal and a private of the 3rd Indiana were fumbling to reload their weapons. They'd not expected Von Borcke to do an impression of a flying amphibian, and when the huge Prussian rumbled into their midst with his LeMat pistol pointed at them, they dropped to their knees and begged to be allowed to surrender.

Von Borcke was not particularly sympathetic, considering he'd given them that opportunity and they'd elected to shoot at him instead, but he compromised by ordering them to swim the flooded stream to the Confederate side, where a courier waited to take them prisoner. Stuart had witnessed Von Borcke's latest adventure, and was gleeful when the soaking, muddy giant lumbered back. He told Von he didn't expect to see him emerge after his plunge, and that when climbing the bank on the far side, he looked like "a terrapin crawling out of the mud."[62]

Beckham brought up his guns and rained several shells onto the enemy, but they were intent on withdrawing, and merely fired a few rounds back before disappearing. The loss on the Confederate side was one man mortally wounded. They returned to Camp Pelham, upon which the rain ended, and they were able to get some supper and then some sleep.

The next day, the 16th, was quiet. Chiswell Dabney rode to Nelson County to inspect Hampton's Brigade. Major Fitzhugh was preparing to take the train to Richmond and then Fredericksburg to tend to some staff business. Channing Price received a letter from his sister, and sat down that evening to write a long one to his mother about his recent adventures. It would be his last letter home.

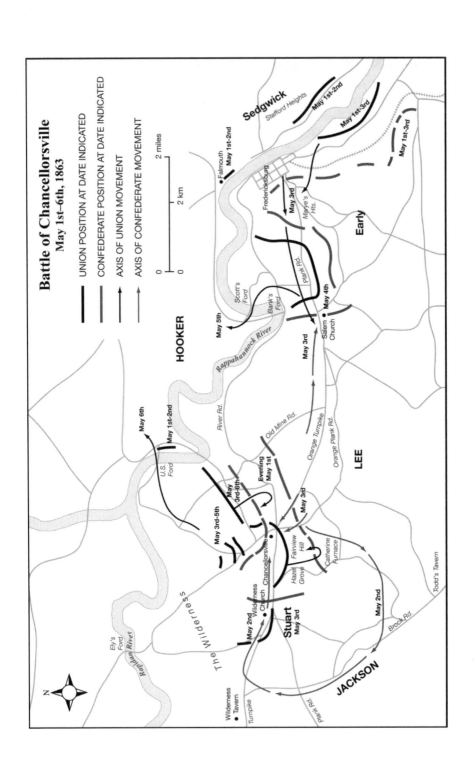

Battle of Chancellorsville
May 1st–6th, 1863

	UNION POSITION AT DATE INDICATED
	CONFEDERATE POSITION AT DATE INDICATED
	AXIS OF UNION MOVEMENT
	AXIS OF CONFEDERATE MOVEMENT

0   2 km
0   2 miles

Sedgwick
Stafford Heights
May 1st-2nd
May 1st-3rd
May 1st-3rd
Falmouth
May 1st-2nd
Fredericksburg
May 3rd
Marye's Hts.
Early
Scott's Ford
Bank's Ford
May 5th
May 3rd
May 4th
Salem Church
Plank Rd.
HOOKER
Rappahannock River
River Rd.
Old Mine Rd.
Orange Turnpike
Orange Plank Rd.
LEE
May 6th
May 1st-2nd
U.S. Ford
May 3rd-5th
May 3rd-6th
Evening May 1st
May 3rd
May 3rd
The Wilderness
Ely's Ford
Rapidan River
Hazel Grove
Fairview Hill
Chancellorsville
Church
Catherine Furnace
May 2nd
Wilderness Church
Stuart
May 3rd
Wilderness Tavern
Turnpike
Plank Rd.
Brock Rd.
Todd's Tavern
JACKSON
May 2nd
N

CHAPTER ELEVEN

CHANCELLORSVILLE AND THE SECOND CORPS

APRIL 17, 1863–MAY 31, 1863

Ol' Joe Hooker, won't you come out of The Wilderness?
Come out of The Wilderness, come out of The Wilderness?
Ol' Joe Hooker, won't you come out of The Wilderness?
Bully boys, hey! Bully boys, ho!

—*Verse to* Jine the Cavalry, *added by*
Stuart at the Battle of Chancellorsville

April 17 was another uneventful day, but speculation was growing about when and where the Federal army and its new commander, Joe Hooker, would begin the next campaign. John Esten Cooke predicted he would not come before May, and that the current reports of activity were "only feints all along from U.S. Ford up, to keep us off his rear." Supplies and ammunition arrived by train, and Cooke took the General and Von Borcke for supper to his cousin Jack's house a mile from Culpeper.

On the 18th, about 2 p.m., a citizen of Culpeper named Fayette Spillman reported to Charles Latham of the "Black Horse" cavalry that enemy horsemen had crossed at Hart's Mill and Waterloo Bridge. Stuart had Channing Price prepare a dispatch to Fitz Lee to find out whether the report was accurate, but he added a note that it might only be a rumor, which it was.

There was at this time a visitor on his way to Stuart's headquarters who would provide some of the most entertaining developments of the year of glory, possibly the entire war. His name was Justus Scheibert. He was 31 years old, from Pomerania, where the Von Borcke family had an estate, and like Von, he'd joined the Prussian army and been commissioned a captain. In January 1863, he was ordered by the Prussian Engineer Corps to go to North America and observe the latest developments in warfare, particularly with regard to the construction of fortifications, Scheibert's specialty. Rifled cannon were being used by both armies and Scheibert was to study their effect on different fortifications—masonry, earth, wood, and armor—on land and at sea.

He was a large man, but more in the sense of being overweight than tall like Von Borcke, and like Von, he considered himself a man of the arts. He was a talented musician, an artist, and would author more than one book. He was full of energy and excited to be on the great adventure, which would last for seven months. He spent most of that time in the Eastern Theatre of the war, even though he intended to spend it in the West because he believed that was where the war would be decided. More to the point, he expected Vicksburg, a large river fortress, to come under siege, making it an ideal site for studying the effect of rifled cannon fire on fortifications.

On March 15, 1863, he was aboard a blockade runner that came into Charleston through fog and dark of night, pursued by and fired on by a Federal gunship. Scheibert kept a journal of every development, and he was keenly observant in a wide-eyed tourist manner. He knew where he was going and how the war was progressing, but to actually see the people and places was quite exciting, so that his accounts are fresh and filled with detail.

He was warmly received by General Beauregard and remained in Charleston for two weeks before traveling to Richmond. He had a letter of introduction from James A. Mason, the Confederate Commissioner to the United Kingdom and France, to Secretary of War Seddon, and after arriving in the capital he visited battlefields of the Peninsula Campaign near Richmond. A year had passed since the battles, but the debris of war— knapsacks, broken weapons, leather and an "unpleasant miasmata"—lay everywhere. Pigs wandered about, rooting at shallow graves and gnawing on bodies that stared out with terrible distorted, expressions.[1]

From Richmond, Scheibert traveled to Lee's headquarters near the Rappahannock, consisting of five plain tents with chimneys, grouped around a Confederate flag, arriving on April 9, 1863. Lee was ill, so he did not meet the commanding general immediately, but was escorted through the army camps by Major Charles Venable of Lee's staff . He wrote of his impressions of each branch of the army, commenting on the infantry's uniforms and manner of drill, the types of cannon, and his belief that the cavalry sabers were too light. He was generally quite impressed, noting however that strict discipline was not to be seen in camp life. Near the camp of the high-spirited but valorous Texans, for instance, no one considered it insubordination that every stranger who passed by, from private to general, was pelted with snowballs.

On Sunday, April 12, he attended an outdoor church service near Lee's headquarters, with about 600 soldiers who listened reverently to Dr. B.T. Lacy. He saw several ladies in attendance and was struck by the appearance of one man sitting on a log. His face was delicate and nearly covered by a full black beard, and he exuded devoted reverence. While watching the man Venable whispered in his ear that he was looking at Stonewall Jackson.

Venable took Scheibert to visit the battlefield at Fredericksburg, where he found Federal dead half-buried and glaring out of shallow graves with repulsive expressions, sometimes with both hands above ground and fists clinched. The city was in ruins.

When Scheibert had arrived at Lee's headquarters, the general, although too sick to see him, sent a message that he should use his tent and remain there until they could get acquainted at which time he should find other lodging. In other words, Scheibert had a place to stay as long as Lee was unable to use his tent, but once Lee was back on his feet the visitor would need to find another place to stay.

Lee's illness had commenced in late March. On March 27, he'd written to Mrs. Lee, "I have felt so unwell . . . as not to be able to go anywhere." He called it a heavy cold, and on April 5 he wrote her that while he still considered it a "bad cold," the doctors thought it was some "malady which must be dreadful if it resembles its name, but which I have forgot." The symptoms were "a good deal of pain in my chest, back and arms. It came on in paroxysms."[2] He was, historians have concluded, suffering not from a cold but a heart attack. It may have been mild in comparison to the one that would take his life twelve years later, but it rightfully alarmed his doctors, who "have examined my lungs, heart, circulation . . . and have been tapping me all over like an old steam boiler before condemning it."

Lee felt ill for most of Scheibert's stay, but was able one day between April 14 and 17 to leave the house in Fredericksburg where he was recuperating to visit his headquarters. Scheibert was awed to meet the victor of so many battles (he included Sharpsburg in his list), particularly because

he was a former engineer, as Scheibert still was. Physically he found him
tall with white hair, dark eyes, high boots, simple coat, big felt hat, a look
of kindness for everyone and an impression of a "man of affairs" instead
of a soldier. Lee even found time and energy to play chess with Scheibert,
and felt well enough to both beat the Prussian and to tease him for the loss.
The underlying thought in Scheibert's mind, however, was that he needed
to find someplace else to stay. Just then Von Borcke arrived.

It is not possible to pinpoint the exact day the two Prussian officers met
the first time, but it was about April 17. Von Borcke first mentioned Scheibert on April 21, by which time they'd already been introduced. Scheibert
left Lee's headquarters for a trip back to Richmond on April 19, and wrote
of their first meeting as occurring shortly before then, saying that the tall
major rode up just as he was taking leave at Lee's headquarters. They were
introduced but Scheibert failed to catch his name, and it wasn't until Von
began speaking that he realized he was a fellow countryman. Von spoke
Pomeranian, to Scheibert's joy, and Von probably saw their meeting as a
chance to show someone from back home what a big splash he'd made in
the Southern Confederacy. He asked Scheibert to come meet Stuart and
Scheibert accepted without hesitation, riding out the next day.

He found Stuart in his tent/office, and was impressed by Jeb's youth,
flashing eyes, full beard, gray jacket, and gray trousers tucked into high
boots. Stuart greeted him warmly and told him that if there were any more
like Von Borcke in Prussia to send them all over. Before Scheibert left,
Stuart invited him to come spend a long visit at his headquarters, which
was, of course, just what Scheibert was hoping for, and he accepted grate-
fully. Scheibert traveled to Richmond on the 19th to tend to unidentified
business, then arrived at Camp Pelham on April 21.

The 19th was a quiet Sunday in Stuart's camp. The weather was beautiful, in Jeb's opinion, and he wrote a letter to Flora that morning to tell
her that he pined for her. He also described Camp Pelham as beautiful,
lamented that he'd not heard from her since the 7th, and devoted most of
the letter to discussion of where she was and where she ought to stay. He
was still seething that his mother had read his previous letter, and sulked
that nobody "wants his letter to his wife read by others," an ironic declara-
tion considering those letters have been published in book form, today on
the internet, and have been read by thousand of "others."

Before he sent the letter, one from Flora arrived dated the 17th. Jeb
was glad to get it, but it caused him more concern that some of his letters

were not catching up with her, particularly the one in which he had enclosed $120. He urged her to write a letter of condolence to Pelham's mother in Alexandria, Alabama.[3]

On April 20, Stuart took care of some staff business, writing a letter to General Cooper to request that Henry B. McClellan be appointed Assistant Adjutant General, with the rank of major, to replace Major Norman Fitzhugh, who was now the cavalry division quartermaster.[4] He had written McClellan about the position on April 13, requesting a prompt reply from him, which had apparently been received.

McClellan, a genuine first cousin of the former commander of the Army of the Potomac, was born in Pennsylvania in a family that had its roots in Connecticut. He was descended from General Samuel McClellan, who commanded Connecticut troops in the Revolutionary War, as well as William Bradford, the first governor of the Plymouth Colony in Massachusetts. His father was a doctor, and he graduated from Williams College in Williamstown, Massachusetts, at age 17, and intended to study for the ministry. A friend, Dr. Mark Hopkins, persuaded him to wait a few years and found the young man a teaching position in Stony Point Mills in Cumberland County, Virginia. Thus the stage was set for "a pure-Dee Yankee" to become a Rebel.

It is not abundantly clear how or why this New England-educated, aristocratic Northerner developed a quick and genuine fondness for the South, but by 1859 he was writing a college friend that "I have learned to eat bacon and greens, corn-field peas, shoat, and many other delicacies you fellows who have never been south of the Mason and Dixon's line don't know anything about." He was teaching in a rural, mountain school with a class of "eleven of the future Presidents and Presidentresses under my charge" and "I am comfortably situated in every respect," and hoping that "all my classmates have had as pleasant times as I have had."

When war broke out he did not vacillate long or hard about where his loyalties lay. On June 14, 1861 he enlisted as a private in Company G of the 3rd Virginia Cavalry, and was then appointed adjutant of the regiment on May 18, 1862. His background and ties to the family came to the attention of the Confederate high command, and President Davis received a letter dated November 25, 1861 about the situation, in which the writer reported that McClellan "was among the first to rush into the ranks" of the Confederate army. Nevertheless, he wasn't singled out and made famous for propaganda purposes. Instead, at the Battle of Kelly's Ford he came to the attention of Fitz Lee, who commended his gallantry, and that brought him to the attention of Stuart, who probably could not resist the idea of adding one more interesting character to his staff of interesting characters.[5]

Von Borcke wrote that during this time period, on both sides of April 20, he and others enjoyed "visits in the neighbourhood and pleasant horseback excursions in the company of our lady acquaintances." It is highly probable that one such excursion included Tom Price and that they rode to the Chancellor House, which has been remembered by history as Chancellorsville. There is only a little evidence for this, being principally an article in the *New York Times*, published May 21, 1863, that began "At the time of the arrival of our army at Chancellorsville [on May 1], among other things found in the Chancellor house was a diary of an officer on the staff of Gen. Jeb. Stuart." That officer was Tom Price and the last entry in the diary, or at least the last one published in *New York Times*, was dated April 19. It told of the extremely close brush with death that Stuart and his staff experienced on April 14, when the Federal shell landed in their midst as they were lounging and observing an artillery duel.

When Scheibert arrived at Camp Pelham on the 21st, he found Stuart and his staff doing what they did on many evenings—sitting on logs around a campfire and singing. The song of choice that night, as on many occasions, was Stuart's personal favorite, *Jine the Cavalry*, and Scheibert wrote down the words as he heard them:

Bully Boys ruche, Bully Boys ruche,
will you see joy, join the cavalry
join the cavalry, etc.

The weather was warmer, but not much dryer. It had continued to rain frequently, keeping the Rappahannock high and the Yankees on the far bank, but a new enemy had invaded camp—pigs. Then, as now, pigs that escape the sty became feral, living in the woods and, as Von described "exploring and devouring everything that fell under their snouts." They would even come into the tents, and on at least two occasions they "set their fancy" on Von's large cavalry boots, dragging them into the woods so that Von and his servant had to hunt for them.

Scheibert moved in with Von Borcke in his Sibley tent, which was something Scheibert had not seen. He said that it had holes in it like a sieve and that every morning a puddle formed in its center. He was loaned an old black horse by Von Borcke named, appropriately, Old Black. Scheibert was accustomed to riding in carriages or on trains, and was not an accomplished horseman, which Stuart's staff took amused note of immediately. He nevertheless took a great liking to Old Black and wrote admiringly of the animal's stamina.

He and Von went on hunting trips, Von Borcke riding his mule, Kitt, which Scheibert identified as Katy. Von wrote frequently of Kitt and her personality, and Scheibert was impressed with the mule's antics and ability to perform exceptional amounts of hard work. Despite the abundance of pigs, or perhaps because of it, they were not successful hunting, and things were dull during the last of April. Von took advantage of having a countryman in his captivity and read to him out of the diary that would become his memoirs, the adventures in which made Scheibert envious.[6]

Indeed, Von did not have to strain the slightest to impress Scheibert. On one occasion shortly after Scheibert arrived, he was walking with Stuart when the General nodded toward Von and called him a splendid proud fellow. Additionally, everywhere Scheibert went he heard tales of Von's accomplishments, and everyone seemed anxious to consider him a friend.

On the 21st, John Esten Cooke had dinner with the Shacklefords, and on the 22nd he wrote in his journal of recent events, particularly the actions at Kelly's Ford and the railroad bridge, and closed by lamenting the fact that there was no literature to read in the new camp. He'd recently received a letter from a friend in the Shenandoah Valley and he longed to be there. The lack of literature meant he should write, but then he decided to go to town, after which he decided to stay in his tent and smoke. Outside his tent the previous evening he'd heard his black servant, Lige, singing, "Jeff Davis, he got a pretty young wife; Old Abram, he got none."

In the evenings, including many from the 23rd through the 27th, Stuart, Von, Scheibert, Channing Price, and other members of the staff (but not Blackford, who was still on furlough) went to town and visited friends, particularly the Shacklefords. There, at the same piano on which Bessie had entertained Stuart and Pelham the night before the latter's death, Scheibert impressed everyone with his playing, and with, as Von Borcke described it, "his original practice with the idiom and pronunciation of the English language."

Jeb's cousin and principal flirt, Nannie Price, sprained her ankle sometime during the week after Stuart arrived at Camp Pelham. She was in the greenhouse at Dundee and took a "false step," with the result that she was unable to walk on it. She and her sister each wrote Jeb and Channing Price a letter apiece, and Stuart told Channing he could read the one he'd received from Ellen. However, in another case of people reading the wrong mail, Channing thought it was okay to read the one to Jeb from Nannie as well. Stuart was, in his own words, "furiously indignant," and made Channing promise to never do such a thing again.

Stuart then wrote Nannie a five-page letter but only one page survived. Its exact date is unknown, but its content put it in the week of April 20–27. With regard to Channing's indiscretion, he told Nannie that he hoped his reading the letter "gave him one fourth the ecstasy it gave" Stuart. One wonders what kind of things Nannie wrote and what kind of ecstasy the written words imparted. Whatever it was, that and a comment about the misspelling of a soldier's name in the newspaper, caused one of Jeb's wordplay synapses to fire off flaccidly, viz "While in the subject of spells I take occasion to remark that you, little enchantress you, whether with the aid of a gazette or a gazelle, have woven, wrought or cast (according as you are a weaver or an ironmonger) a spell around me (I mean me myself) which is nonetheless sweet because it is a mis-spell."[7]

On April 25 a former member of Stuart's staff was killed. Tom Turner, the young man who had gone with "Honeybun" Hullihen to rescue General Lee's daughter prior to Fredericksburg, had transferred to Mosby's command in March. After dark that day, Turner and some other Rangers were at the home of Charles H. Utterback, about three miles from Warrenton, when a squadron of the 8th Illinois Cavalry commanded by Captain Elon J. Farnsworth, attacked. Farnsworth was a former quartermaster and a future brigadier general. He would gain fame for carrying out the equivalent of the Charge of the Light Brigade at Gettysburg on July 3, 1863, when he obeyed foolish orders from his commander, Judson Kilpatrick, to attack Rebel infantry behind a stone wall. He did his duty, but was shot five times and killed.

On April 25, however, he personally and mortally wounded Tom Turner by shooting him in the left shoulder and a lung. Turner, partially paralyzed, was carried from Utterback's house to one belonging to a Mr. Skinker, and from there to Turner's home, "Kinloch," in Fauquier County. There the Yankees came again on the 28th, found the wounded Rebel, accused him of only pretending to be seriously wounded, and roughed him up. He died the next morning, nine days short of his 20th birthday.[8]

On the 26th, Stuart sent a dispatch to Mosby, whose partisan rangers were watching for enemy activity along the Orange & Alexandria Railroad. "Information on the movements of large bodies is of the greatest importance to us just now. The marching or transportation of a Division will often indicate the plan of a campaign. Be sure to give dates & numbers & names as far as possible."[9] It wasn't long before such information began flowing in.

On April 28, an air of excitement and anticipation stirred Lee's army. Scheibert saw several couriers arriving at and being dispatched from Stuart's tent. He gave Scheibert a map of the nearby area and asked him to put his engineering and artistic skills to use by copying it into a smaller version. All the staff seemed occupied, and Scheibert thought Stuart had a pensive look.

What transpired was that three corps of Hooker's infantry—more than 40,000 men—were observed on the march, heading toward crossing points on the Rappahannock and Rapidan on Lee's far left flank. The Rebels did not know what "Fighting Joe's" plan was, but they knew the Federals' long-awaited, rain-delayed offensive had commenced.

Hooker's plan was to send those three corps—the Fifth, Eleventh, and Twelfth—to threaten Lee's left, while the First and Sixth Corps marched downriver, crossed, and threatened Lee's right flank. His other two infantry Corps, the Second and Third, would be held in reserve for use as needed, while his cavalry, six brigades under Stoneman, would launch a deep-penetration raid against the railroad lines connecting Lee's army to Richmond. Hooker believed Lee would have to either abandon his position around Fredericksburg and retreat, or stand and give battle to nearly 135,000 Federals with a force of only about 53,000. It was a good plan, and might have succeeded but for that indefatigable team of Bobby Lee and Tom Jackson.

By the time reports began pouring into Stuart's headquarters on the 28th, the three corps moving on Lee's left were bivouacked across the river at Kelly's Ford. Despite the seemingly dire situation, Stuart accepted an invitation, through Von Borcke, to have dinner that night, along with other members of the staff, at the plantation home of an elderly widow whom Von had befriended and who he identified only as "Mrs. S." The lady was "a poetess" who had previously written verses glorifying Generals Lee and Jackson. Accordingly, when she asked permission after dinner to read her latest poem, everyone expected it was going to be General Stuart's turn in the spotlight. With her guests paying rapt attention, she rose and began to read stilted and stylistically heavy-footed rhymes that described adoration for . . . Von Borcke!

Von was astonished, as Stuart probably was, and he claimed to be embarrassed by "her eloquent and touching . . . flatteringly sounded" verses, such that he sat, "blushing and transfixed to [his] chair with stupefaction." When she finished, Stuart and the rest of the staff broke into applause and the huge Prussian, "at a loss how to behave," rose from his chair, advanced on Mrs. S., knelt before her on one knee, took her hand and kissed it. "That won't do, Von," shouted Stuart, who stepped up and delivered a "hearty kiss on the old lady's cheek." Mrs. S. laughed and told him with self-deprecating good humor, "General, I have always known you to be a very gallant soldier, but from this moment I believe you to be the bravest of the brave."[10]

At 5 a.m. on the 29th, Stuart came to the tent occupied by Scheibert and Von and shouted that everyone was to be in the saddle in a quarter of an hour. Almost at the same instant, a bugle began to blow, followed by the sounds of men rising, fumbling for clothes and weapons, pausing to urinate, yawning, griping, and shouting, directing servants to saddle horses, fix coffee, or help locate items in the dark. Stuart told Scheibert to come to his tent and the portly European hustled in. The eastern sky was showing the faintest traces of light and Stuart was all bustle and business. He handed Scheibert a double set of three bars, indicating the rank of a captain, and pronounced him an honorary member of the staff. By affixing the bars to his collar, Stuart said, he might hope to be exchanged if he was taken prisoner, whereas if the enemy thought him a spy they would convene a hasty court and hang him.

Scheibert was honored and a little horrified, but was given no time to ponder the situation. More than one passing staff officer advised him, sotto voce, that a big fight was coming. Von Borcke rummaged about, found an old uniform coat for Scheibert, who sat down to sew the captain's insignia to its collar. Stuart and the others did not wait for him, and rode away while he was still sewing.

Shortly after Stuart returned from dinner with Mrs. S., a courier arrived with word that the enemy was approaching the river at numerous points with forces of all arms. Rooney Lee's brigade and two batteries of the Horse Artillery were already near Brandy Station, watching and prepared to contest a crossing. Fitz Lee's brigade was soon in the saddle and following Stuart.

Scheibert got his insignia sewn and was in the saddle, he believed, in not more than ten minutes after Stuart rode away. However, upon going a third of a mile he found himself in the rear of Fitz Lee's brigade. Scheibert had no idea where Stuart was and rode about asking directions in broken English, which led to a small adventure. Six little girls, aged about four to eight, were standing beside the road, and when he approached the oldest stepped forward and called out "Halt!" They were carrying garlands of roses and, apparently believing him to be an important officer, they promptly decorated his horse.

Scheibert continued to flounder and search, a fat man on a skinny black horse bedecked with red roses, who rode awkwardly and whose speech could hardly be understood. He fell in behind a wagon train for a while, but was told after a few miles that it was moving in the opposite direction from the rest of the cavalry. He turned and rode back toward the Rappahannock, slightly panicky about his inability to fulfill his new military station and worrying about Yankees with lynching ropes jumping out and taking him prisoner. Luckily he was headed where he needed to go, and he caught up with Stuart and his staff on a hill above Kelly's Ford about noon, at which time he was able to deliver the garlands of roses to their intended recipient.[11]

Stuart's immediate goal was not to necessarily resist the enemy's advance, but simply keep track of his movements and keep Lee informed of them. The weather was not cooperating. It was overcast and drizzly, and a blanket of fog covered the river. That, plus the heavily wooded nature of the terrain, made it nearly impossible to ascertain the enemy's activities. Before long Rooney Lee's pickets fell back, reporting that a large body of enemy cavalry was across the river and that it sounded like pontoon bridges were being placed so that infantry and artillery could cross.

The dense fog was of no advantage to the enemy, however, and soon Rebels brought in prisoners who stumbled into their hands. One approached between two troopers, trying desperately to make himself understood by speaking in a foreign language. Von and Scheibert perked up and came forward. After a little experimentation, they discovered that French was a common tongue and that the opposite of Stuart's warning to Scheibert had occurred—a Belgian artillery officer observing on Hooker's staff had blundered into the Rebels and been captured.

The Belgian was indignant. He was in full Federal uniform, but he declined to tell the Confederates any information about the enemy's plans or strength, shrugging his shoulders instead and saying, "Gentlemen, I can only give you one piece of advice—that is, to try and make your escape as quickly as possible; if not, your capture by the large army in front of you is a certainty." Von told him they tried to make it a habit of fighting first before retreating, then informed the man he would be sent to Richmond as a prisoner of war. This got him quite worked up, and he argued that Belgium was a neutral country and he claimed his country's privileges, to which Von pointed out that his wearing a Federal uniform rather than a Belgian one left the Rebels no choice—he would be a prisoner until duly exchanged.[12]

By 4 p.m. the fog burned off and the enemy could be seen, which turned out to be something unexpected. The Federal troops in the immediate front were only cavalry. The infantry had crossed the river and turned to march in the direction of the Rapidan. Stuart knew what they had planned. Leaving one regiment behind to track and resist the enemy's cavalry, he took the rest of the two brigades toward Stevensburg and the Germanna Ford on the Rapidan, certain the enemy was planning to cross the recently reconstructed bridge there and march toward Fredericksburg.

Stuart had divined the enemy's plan, but the fog and deception by their cavalry made him too late to get in front of them. When he reached the road intersection near the home of Mr. Madden—for whom Pelham had put on a show on February 17—the Federals had already passed by. Their rear guard was only 300 yards down the road. Stuart ordered an attack with dismounted riflemen and artillery, which caused immediate chaos in the enemy's rear. Instead of turning to fight, their infantry stampeded forward at the double-quick.

As soon as they were out of sight, Stuart advanced and captured several dozen stragglers who'd fled into the woods and become lost. From them he was able to identify the three corps, learned their destination was Chancellorsville, and that Stoneman's cavalry was on its way toward Culpeper Court House. He directed Rooney Lee to take the rest of his brigade, the 9th and 13th Virginia, plus six pieces of artillery, and go after Stoneman, while he, with Fitz's brigade, five regiments of about 1,600 men, and six cannon, would continue to pursue and harass the Federal infantry.[13]

Each of the Yankees was carrying eight days rations, whereas the Rebels had not had time even for breakfast, let alone to pack a lunch, so the prisoners were quickly relieved of their burden. It was mostly hardtack and bacon but it invigorated Scheibert and the Confederates. He had not eaten since the evening before, which was not his habit, and he pitched in and ate until he was full. Troopers, perhaps enjoying the show the plump man was making, gave him more, which he stuck in his pockets, and when still more was offered he protested that the men who captured the food should eat it. They laughed and told him not to worry, as they would soon catch more Yankees and more supplies.

Stuart and his men reached Raccoon Ford on the Rapidan after dark. The banks were rocky and steep and made for a treacherous crossing. The weather was getting worse. It was drizzling and the temperature was dropping. A fine sleet was coating horses and riders. The roads were muddy and the artillery struggled to avoid getting its guns mired.

About 1:30 a.m., they came in sight of the Federal army and Stuart allowed his men to go into camp. Scheibert wrote that they tied their horses to fences in a pouring rain, pulled off the saddles to use as pillows, wrapped themselves in blankets, and lay down in the mud for a precious two or three hours of rest. It was still dark on the 30th when a courier shook Scheibert awake and said the time had come. Cavalrymen were moving about, saddling horses, everyone still soaked. There was no feed for the horses but what grazing they could find and a few grains of corn. The soldiers had only the captured crackers and bacon not eaten the day before.

They were now in an area called the Wilderness, near a small church of that name, and around which another huge battle would be fought in a year. There were only two main roads through the dense brush and trees: the Orange Turnpike and the Orange Plank Road, which merged for a distance of about two miles before separating again at Chancellorsville, the large, stately home of the Chancellor family, located on seventy acres of cleared land. The three corps of infantry were between Stuart and Lee's army near Fredericksburg, and Stuart was determined to not only track their every movements and report them to Lee, but to make their march as unpleasant as possible.

This he accomplished by sending dismounted troopers forward to attack, snipe, and keep the Federals busy, and particularly by having the Horse Artillery shell the enemy whenever and wherever possible. Most of April 30 was spent in that manner, and the heavy woods on either side of the roads prevented the Federals from being able to turn and launch an infantry attack. Late in the evening, Stuart ordered his men onto a side road in the direction of Spotsylvania Court House and then went into bivouac about eight miles in that direction at Todd's Tavern.

Von Borcke and Scheibert each participated in what occurred after dark on April 30th, and each described the events in detail in their respective memoirs. Yet, as is often said about witnesses to the same car wreck, it is difficult to believe they were both at the same place at the same time. Essentially, Stuart decided to take Von Borcke, Benjamin White, Frank Terrell, a few other staff, and some couriers, and ride to Robert E. Lee's headquarters, which lay about twelve miles away as the crow flew, but a lot further along the winding roads and bridle paths through the wilderness. Scheibert either volunteered to go or was summoned to do so by Stuart.

There was a new moon, which provided little light, and even that was often covered by clouds. Von Borcke urged the General to take at least a squadron of troopers for protection, but Jeb was certain the roads were clear and declined. After their first encounter with enemy cavalry, however, which involved the General and staff getting chased and nearly caught by some thirty Federal horsemen, Stuart sent White back to bring up a regiment of Fitz Lee's brigade before proceeding further. Lee was ordered to follow with the rest of the brigade, which he did and thus turned the night from a simple journey to the commander's headquarters into a series of skirmishes, charges, retreats, and debacles.

Von Borcke's and Scheibert's accounts contain many similar incidents, but it is hard to match them up. Von Borcke wrote that the original purpose of the ride, which lasted all night, was to go to Lee's headquarters. Von described no less than four separate encounters with the enemy, whereas Scheibert described only two. In both accounts the riders got separated, confused, lost their way, rode "hither and thither," and couldn't distinguish friend from foe in the forest, but Von Borcke's account included wild, helter skelter races through the trees with the enemy in pursuit and on all sides, while Scheibert wrote of being pursued only once. Both wrote of being chased into a rail fence, which Von Borcke found too high to leap over, so that it was only with "rider pressing on rider, and horse plunging against horse" that "the fence at last yielded to the accumulated weight of the impetuous horsemen, and broke down with a loud crash, leaving the way open to the disorderly flight." Scheibert wrote they were saved by "a hard jump" over a rail fence, the top two feet of which had already been taken down in the rush, and that enemy cavalry would not venture in the dark against a fence still more than three and a half feet high.

Without passing judgment on which account is the more credible, it seems unlikely that a portly, ungainly rider like Scheibert could clear three and a half feet riding a rawboned old black mare. Perhaps, in the section he approached, the fence had been knocked down to only a foot and a half, which was still a "hard jump" for Scheibert.

Thomas L. Rosser, one of Jeb Stuart's hardest fighting lieutenants in 1862–63.

W.H.F. ("Rooney") Lee, son of Robert E. Lee and younger brother of Custis.

Fitzhugh Lee (above) was a nephew of Robert E. Lee and a cousin of Rooney's. Earning the respect of friend and foe alike, it was never possible to attribute his rise in the ranks to nepotism.

Beverly H. Robertson commanded one of Stuart's cavalry brigades during the summer of 1862.

William E. ("Grumble") Jones was never a favorite of Stuart's, but he helped save the day at Brandy Station.

John Singleton Mosby rode with Stuart on the Peninsula before embarking on his independent career as "The Grey Ghost" of the Confederacy.

John Pelham, or as Robert E. Lee termed him, "The Gallant Pelham," became a legend in his own short time as the commander of Stuart's Horse Artillery. Long after the war he was still being commemorated, as in the 1939 painting at left by Jared French.

They both recorded Von's horse being shot from under him, and Von gave a blow-by-blow account of an enemy charging him, firing one shot into his hat and a second into the head of his bay horse, which fell and pinned Von Borcke beneath it. After getting out and up and finding his assailant gone, Von removed his saddle and bridle and a courier rode up leading a riderless Yankee horse he'd caught in the woods. Trouble was, "it was an odd-looking, stumpy-legged little pony," and when mounted on it, Von's legs dangled nearly to the ground and his large saddle covered the pony's neck, leaving only its ears only sticking out." Stuart was in an ill humor when Von found him, but the ludicrous sight cheered him up. Von traded the pony for another captured animal the first chance he had.

There were many other scenes and episodes that night—Stuart running from the enemy for the first time in anyone's recollection, Stuart drawing his saber, shouting "Charge" and personally leading an attack only to have his regiment break and flee in the face of withering enemy fire, Confederates attempting to identify each other in the dark by saying in a low voice "Rebel?" and hearing in return, "All right. Rebel," and particularly the 1st and 3rd Virginia regiments, under the mutual delusion that the enemy was in their front, charging headlong into each other "in a splendid attack before they discovered their error, which was fortunately attended with no worse consequences than a few sabre-cuts."

All in all, it was a night from hell, and it led Von Borcke to understate, "All this was a lesson how dangerous night-attacks always are, and taught me that, whenever possible, they should be avoided." Stuart and his men took about eighty prisoners, two of which were personally captured by the General, and an equal number of horses. They finally arrived at Lee's headquarters camp at dawn on May 1.

Lee's camp was not asleep. Infantry was forming into battle lines. Stuart delivered his report on the status of the enemy—digging in near and around Chancellorsville. There'd been fighting in the area and dead bodies, mostly Federals, were scattered about. Scheibert saw General Lee near the infantry, which was about to advance in line of battle. Once Stuart gave his report and received orders for the day, he established temporary headquarters under some trees next to the road where, as Von wrote, they got "a large amount of sleep in a very short time."

Stuart, Von, and the rest of the staff were in the saddle and heading back to Fitz Lee's brigade camp only an hour or two after they arrived. They left Scheibert at Lee's camp, probably because he'd requested being close to the action, but perhaps just because Jeb wanted him to get some rest. As a result Scheibert got a little more sleep, and once awake he set about trying to find something to feed Old Black. The enemy was shelling sporadically, and fragments of shrapnel were falling about. He went from dead body to dead body, searching haversacks for hardtack, then carrying the biscuits back to feed to the horse by hand.

There were also some boxes of hardtack dropped by the Yankees, two of which would serve later that day as seats for Generals Lee and Jackson, but Scheibert was more interested in their contents. Coming upon a pile of crackers that had spilled, he was reaching down to collect some when a chunk of an enemy shell landed in the middle of the bread, turning it into crumbs and scattering it in all direction, so that Scheibert's hand was reaching for empty air. Scheibert claimed he didn't mind the bombardment, which would continue for eight days.[14]

Leaving Jubal Early's division and Barksdale's brigade in Fredericksburg, Lee was concentrating his army and moving on Hooker's main force. Anderson's and McLaws' divisions engaged in serious fighting that compelled the Federals to pull back and dig in around Chancellorsville. Stuart and his cavalry were guarding the army's flanks, with the 4th Virginia and part of the 3rd, under Colonels Wickham and Owens, on the right, and the remainder of Fitz Lee's brigade on the left.[15]

About 4 p.m. on May 1st, Stuart and his staff arrived at Catherine's Furnace, the site of a former ironworks. Enemy infantry were drawn up half a mile or less ahead, and Stuart ordered the 1st Virginia to attack in order to test the strength of the enemy's position. Heavy fire and rough ground ended the assault, and the troopers returned as a brigade of Georgia infantry of Jackson's Corps arrived to press the attack. The Federals fell back, but came under the protection of several batteries of artillery that began firing shells into the Rebels.

Jackson galloped up and collected Stuart. Together they rode forward to examine the Federal position and look for a point to place artillery to direct enfilading fire on the enemy's batteries. Finding a small bridle path leading from the main road to the right, the two generals and their staffs turned onto it, followed by six guns of the Horse Artillery. They found a position that offered the angle of fire they wanted, but the woods were so thick there was only room to place a single cannon in position, and the road so narrow behind that it was completely blocked by the limbers, caissons and artillery pieces of the rest of the battery.

Nevertheless, the one cannon was positioned and a shot was fired. Almost immediately, two "masked batteries" of Federals opened up from close range, firing shell and canister. Men and horses went down. Horses in harness began plunging and kicking, and everyone started looking for a way out. Jackson ordered the single gun to limber up and retire, but there was no room for the other cannon to turn around and go back. The gunners had to back and fill, turning their teams and vehicles around in short spurts like a modern driver does in a tight parallel parking space, inching around slowly, while enemy shrapnel and canister balls shredded leaves, tree trunks, branches, and flesh all around.

Jackson, Stuart, their staffs and most of the Horse Artillery troopers were finally able to get out of the precarious position without getting killed . . . with one exception.

Channing Price, Jeb's marvelous adjutant, was hit behind one knee by a piece of shrapnel. The wound seemed minor, just as Albert Sydney Johnston's similar wound had appeared at Shiloh, and just as Johnston did then, Price insisted on staying in the saddle and remaining in the field. It was a fatal mistake. The shell fragment had severed an artery, and Price's boot was soon filling with blood. Nobody realized it until Channing fainted and fell from his saddle. Stuart asked for a surgeon but none were present. Other members of the staff began rummaging about for a tourniquet, but nobody had one.

It was such a waste. A belt, haversack sling, saber sling, or any number of items could have been used to staunch the flow of blood, but it did not happen. Price was carried a mile back to the Furnace Road and the home of Charles Welford. Tom Price was summoned. Blood typing and blood transfusions in the field were not yet practiced. Stuart, Von, and others returned to the house after dark to see how Channing was doing. Von said, "It was a cruel spectacle to see the gallant young fellow stretched on his deathbed surrounded by his sorrowing friends, just able to recognise them and answer the pressure of their hands as a last farewell." Tom leaned over him near the end, watching helplessly. About midnight Channing Price passed away.[16]

In the meantime, at Lee's headquarters, Scheibert saw General Lee again. He was standing by a tree in a gray coat with no insignia, waiting for someone who proved to be Stonewall Jackson. Scheibert described him as thin, somewhat stooped, with a weather-beaten countenance that looked more like that of a thinker than a warrior. He and Lee shook hands and sat down on the cracker boxes to engage in serious conversation. Artillery fire had not abated, and Scheibert recalled that it was nearly silent as the two men conferred, except that shrapnel whirred through leaves and branches.[17]

At some point, Jedediah Hotchkiss, Jackson's topographical engineer, visited with Stuart at the Welford house. He asked Jeb and Mr. Welford about the existence of one or more little-known roads, then returned to Lee's headquarters and told Lee and Jackson what he'd learned.[18]

The two commanders were seated near the tree where they'd greeted each other. Lee removed his hat, and Jackson's face contorted several times. Then he removed his cap, put his hands together and looked up. One of the members of Lee's staff, watching with the others, whispered, "Look! Stonewall is praying as if in battle. That portends a bloody day." Then the two generals rose, shook hands in obvious agreement over what they had discussed, and parted for the last time.[19]

Once Jackson left, it was as if a spell had broken. The staff officers and others knew that whatever the two men had decided might dictate the outcome of the war. Couriers, cooks, and chroniclers went back to their respective tasks. Pieces of oil cloth were spread on the ground or tent halves were propped into lean-tos as the camp bedded down. Prayer books were taken out of haversacks and pockets. Everyone knew the next day would bring battle, but there was nothing to do but make peace, say prayers, and get some rest. Scheibert watched, marveling that men who had known nothing but pleasure and luxury before the war seemed comfortable in the open air and the hardship. One of Lee's staff officers told him that during the great events about to come that "many a mother's son will embrace the grass," because when Lee and Jackson get together, "history becomes pregnant and bears blood for us and hell for the Yankees!"[20]

At the Welford home, Stuart and his staff were devastated at Channing's death. Jeb told them to get some sleep, but Von, at least, was too grieved to do so. He wandered about in the woods, listening to the sounds of the armies. It is not known how Jeb Stuart spent the rest of the night. He had not slept in twenty-four hours, and was operating on pure adrenalin. His indomitable spirit must have been strained to the point of breaking under the weight of so many deaths of so many close members of his two families in such a short time. Yet immediately ahead of him lay the greatest forty-eight hours of his life.

Scheibert was up and active early on May 2. He arrived at the Welford house, where he'd been told he'd find Stuart, at 5 a.m. As soon as he arrived, Von told him to be quiet because everyone was in mourning over their favorite, Channing Price. A daughter of the Welford family, whom Scheibert described as beautiful, was arranging Price's body. Dr. Lacy, Jackson's chaplain, arrived and spoke words of last rites. Stuart was holding his head in his hands and sobbing. Then a courier stepped to the door and brought him back to reality. "General Jackson wishes to see General Stuart!"

Stuart, "as if awakened by a stroke of magic, quickly donned his hat with waving plumes and went with long strides toward Jackson," who was sitting atop Little Sorrell. Stonewall saw the distress on his young friend's face and asked, "What's the matter, Stuart? You look so disturbed." "Channing is dead," Jeb replied. "A shell fragment opened his artery, and he bled to death before help could come." "May God comfort you," said Jackson, "but come, I need your cavalry."[21] The time for what would become Stonewall's famous flank march had come. What Lee and Jackson had decided the night before was that while Lee would demonstrate against the main body of Hooker's army with barely 15,000 men, Jackson would take his entire corps of some 25,000 by hidden roads to reach the Federals' rear.

Stuart's job was to screen Jackson's march by putting mounted troopers between the Rebels and the Federal infantry on Jackson's right as he moved along a backwoods road. It was necessary to construct a bridge over a stream called Poplar Run in order to use the road, but that was accomplished and the march began about 7:30 a.m. Despite his best efforts, Stuart was unable to prevent the Yankees from learning about the movement. By 9 a.m. word reached Hooker's headquarters that part of Lee's army was on the move. Hooker directed his commanders to be alert and to advance skirmishers in case of attack. However, the goal of his maneuvers so far had been to dislodge Lee and force him to retreat. Accordingly, he believed the enemy's movement was proof of his own success, not an audacious flanking movement. In a clearing near Catherine's Furnace, the rear of Jackson's column was spotted by troops from Daniel Sickles' Federal Third Corps and they moved out to attack. A rearguard was able to hold them off, even as Sickles' own impression was that the Rebels were indeed in retreat. The rest of the Confederate column marched on silently and quickly. It was hot, the woods were stifling, and some fell out. One veteran of the march recalled, "I thought that he [Jackson] would kill us before we would get to the enemy."[22]

Von Borcke and Scheibert rode with Stuart near the head of the column. They could see the enemy from time to time and small bodies of Federal cavalry even placed themselves in the road ahead more than once. At other times the line of march took them so near the main enemy camps that the Rebels could hear the ring of axes chopping wood and even the sound of voices.

About 4 p.m. Munford's cavalry directed the head of the column from the woods to the Orange Turnpike. They had covered sixteen miles and were on the right flank of Hooker's army, occupied by Oliver O. Howard's Eleventh Corps. Howard's men thought they were far from the enemy. They'd done nothing but sit in camp all day and were now preparing to form up for evening dress parade, after which they would have their evening meal. Some were in groups, playing cards, or talking. Many were asleep and others lounged around campfires. Scheibert recalled hearing a drum begin beating the call for dress parade just before the attack began.

Howard's unit was commonly called "the German Corps" because it contained so many central European immigrants. They were what Rebels thought of when they claimed the Yankees employed foreign-born mercenaries. The Corps was formed in September 1862 by combining the divisions of Schenk, von Steinwehr, and Schurz, which had served under Franz Sigel in the Valley. They were the "I vites mit Sigel," men, and had known only hard luck. After getting whipped by Jackson in the Shenandoah, the newly formed Corps saw no action at Sharpsburg or Fredericksburg, and was intentionally assigned to the part of the field at Chancellorsville expected to be the most inactive.[23] Now they were about to receive the brunt of the most hard-hitting surprise attack of the war.

The Rebels formed three long battle lines. Once men were in position they lay down while the other units maneuvered into their respective places. Stuart placed a pair of guns under Beckham where they could pour fire into the Federal camp. The woods were so thick that no one could see more than a few dozen yards ahead, but the cavalry was still in position in front of the infantry, still ready to chase any probing Federals back to their camps if they came close to seeing what was assembling in the woods.

Von Borcke was sitting on his horse gazing toward the enemy's camp, and was so lost in thought he did not notice approaching Federals. A patrol of six or eight came out of the woods. Von heard them and turned. They saw him and froze.

Von turned his horse, dug in his spurs, and fled. The Yankees fired at him, but even this close encounter did not serve to alert Howard's men of their impending doom. Von rode back to where Stuart, Jackson, and their staffs were sitting at the base of a huge oak tree, waiting while the infantry moved into position. At about 5 p.m. Sandie Pendleton, Jackson's adjutant, rode in and reported the lines were formed.[24] Stuart sent word for Munford to move his cavalry out of the way, and at about 5:30, Jackson gave the command to his lead division commander, Robert Rodes. The Confederates moved forward.

They came out of the woods "yelling like devils let loose." The Eleventh Corps had built no breastworks to speak of, and its men were caught unawares. They fled in a panic with the Rebels on their heels and shells from Beckham's guns falling among them. Hooker's entire right flank collapsed in a matter of moments.[25]

Scheibert watched it all, seeing confusion spread and grow, with enemy infantrymen trying to save themselves by running or hiding in the woods. Horses ran or wandered about, some simply grazing. All manner of equipment, weapons, uniforms, packs, and cartridge boxes were thrown away or dropped. Artillery teams were abandoned and left standing in harness. An entire battery stood on a hill, ready to fire but deserted by all of its gunners. In the camps were decks of cards, open writing cases, pens and inkstands, and half-prepared meals. Scattered throughout were the dead and wounded.

Von Borcke saw a similar scene and noticed oxen lying about that were "half-slaughtered." Darkness temporarily brought the battle to an end. Scheibert rode around the battlefield, looking at the scenes of carnage, noticing, on the crest of a hill, a young Federal soldier with the features of a young woman who was clearly, to him at least, a German. Among the spoils he found a bag of oats for Old Black, and when he poured its contents on the ground in front of her, she was so famished that she dropped to her knees in order to gobble the grain as quickly as possible. Scheibert watched, happy to finally be able to reward the old mare, which he'd been riding for five days with extremely scant provisions. He marveled at how, in peacetime, he would never have thought that the act of feeding a horse could bring such joy.

Jackson himself was not ready to call it a day. He wanted to continue pressing the enemy, believing that continuing the offensive might cause the entire Federal army to disintegrate. He ordered Stuart to ride ahead toward Ely's Ford, where he believed Hooker would direct his retreat, not to either reconnoiter or attack, but to get in position to barricade the road and impede Hooker's flight while Jackson's infantry closed in on their rear.

Accompanied by Von and other staff members, Stuart led Fitz Lee's brigade and the 16th North Carolina Infantry Regiment to the ford. Leaving the infantry and the rest of the cavalry there, under Fitz, he took the 1st Virginia forward to locate the enemy. Trotting down a bridle path with Stuart and Von Borcke in the lead, they reached a slight rise in the path and saw, less than quarter of a mile ahead, campfires of a large body of the enemy. Stuart halted the regiment and he and Von rode closer until they could hear the enemy talking and get an idea of their numbers. This was not what they had hoped for, having expected to find the tail of a fleeing body of disorganized men.

Just the same, Stuart decided to give them a "slight surprise," and sent back for the 16th North Carolina Infantry to advance and get in position to attack. It did not take long for them to catch up and form line of battle, but before the attack could be ordered, two of A.P. Hill's staff officers rode up "in great haste and excitement." They spoke to Stuart in low tones, out of hearing of anyone else, and what they said visibly startled the general. He rode to Von Borcke and in a whisper said, "Take command of that regiment, and act on your own responsibility." Then he took the rest of his staff and the regiment of cavalry and rode away at top speed.

Artillery fire had commenced in the distance while Stuart and his men were riding toward Ely's Ford, and now it increased in volume. Von Borcke thought it meant that Jackson had reopened the battle, but the lack of information and Stuart's sudden, unexplained departure made him anxious. He was not familiar with the country, was nearly six miles away from the main body of Lee's army, and in supposed command of a body of infantry he didn't know and who didn't know him. Nevertheless, he told the North Carolinians to advance and open fire when they were within fifty yards of the enemy. It had the desired effect.

The Federals panicked. Men could be seen dashing past campfires and horses breaking loose and running. Shouts, bugles, drums, and scattered return fire filled the night with the sounds of chaos. Von learned later they had fired on nearly a full division of enemy cavalry commanded by Gen. William W. Averill, who was relieved of command the following day. They fled, probably believing that Jackson's corps or another large body of infantry had accomplished another bold ambush. Many of Averill's men did not stop running until they reached and crossed the Rapidan River, two miles away. Others became lost in the woods and straggled away from the battle.

Von Borcke had the North Carolinians keep firing for half an hour, and when other Federal units began moving in their direction, he ordered the regiment to retire, relinquished command to the 16th's colonel, and rode away in the direction Stuart had gone, anxious to learn what was happening.[26]

The news brought to Stuart by Hill's staff officers was that Stonewall Jackson had been seriously wounded. While the 16th North Carolina Infantry was about to pour volleys into Federal cavalry in the dark, the 18th North Carolina had poured a volley into what they believed were Federal cavalry in the dark. It had been Jackson, with some of his staff and couriers, however, being led through the woods by Private David Kyle, one of Stuart's men. A native of the area, Jeb had loaned Kyle to Stonewall earlier in the day as a guide.[27]

As soon as Jackson was wounded, command devolved on A.P. Hill, a friend of Stuart but not of Jackson. Hill came to his commander's side and had him removed from the field, but at that point Federal artillery fire opened up and a piece of shrapnel hit Hill in the leg. He sent for Jeb Stuart to take command of Jackson's Corps.

The next man in line of command was Robert Rodes, who had just recently been promoted to lead a division. Like Hill. Rodes was a capable officer who had done good work that day, but his promotion to Major General would not be official for five more days, making him lower in seniority than Stuart. One of Jackson's staff officers recalled later that he, Rodes, "distrusted his ability to take command" due to "modesty." Rodes wrote later that he did not consider Stuart entitled to assume command of the corps, but believed it was the wish of Jackson and Hill, so he did not hesitate in yielding it to him. Hill's chief of staff, Major William Palmer, did not like Stuart and did not want him in command, but after the war he admitted it was the right decision, as "Stuart was well known in our corps," and by then everyone knew what he accomplished.[28]

Stuart, answering the summons, found Sandy Pendleton, Jackson's chief of staff, on the Orange Plank Road. Pendleton was no great fan of Jeb's either. He, like Palmer and Kyd Douglass, thought Jeb was vain and pretentious, possibly overrated. Yet even Kyd Douglas wrote later that Jeb's reputation in the Second Corps was "second only to Jackson," and that he was "the best man" for the job. The fact that Jackson himself adored Stuart could not have been far from his mind.

Stuart sent Pendleton to find out about Jackson's condition and learn if he had any instructions. Jackson's chief of artillery, Colonel Stapleton Crutchfield, was also wounded, and Jeb summoned Lt. Colonel Edward Porter Alexander to command in Crutchfield's place. He then directed Alexander to reconnoiter and locate firing positions for his batteries, after which he rode out to learn where the different units of the Second Corps were located.

Pendleton found Jackson in a corps hospital near the Wilderness Tavern. His surgeon, Hunter McGuire, had just amputated Stonewall's left arm, Jackson was sleeping, and McGuire would not let Pendleton wake him. Pendleton pleaded, McGuire refused, but then Jackson woke anyway. Sandie described the situation at the front and asked if Stonewall had instructions, but the general was too addled to provide meaningful advice. "I can't tell," he said. "Say to General Stuart he must do what he thinks best."[29]

It took Von an hour, riding through dark woods filled with dead and dying men, to find Stuart. Jeb was sitting under a plum tree next to a lantern, writing dispatches. He paused long enough to give Von details of the bad news about the man they both loved, told him the attack would be renewed at dawn, and reported that another member of the staff, Lt. Hullihen, was wounded.

Stuart had sent Hullihen to carry a message to Jackson earlier in the day, and after delivering it, the lieutenant turned back to find Stuart. It was dark by then and he came on a battery of Confederate artillery that had unlimbered and set up in the road to open on the enemy. He asked its commander, "a big, surly fellow," who must have been another of Stuart's non-admirers, if he'd seen the general or his staff. "No," was the officer's curt response, and Hullihen rode on, knowing the road might not be safe.

Soon a picket stepped out and said, "Halt, who is there?" Hullihen replied, "An officer of Stuart's staff." The picket told him to advance and Hullihen did, admitting later that he was "fatigued and not on the alert." He had blundered into an enemy picket post, not more than fifteen yards away. He tried to wheel and flee, but the pickets opened fire. Hullihen recalled later that it sounded like the whole Yankee army was shooting at him, and one of the bullets hit him in the right shoulder.

He was nearly knocked from his saddle, but managed to stay aboard. His horse broke into a gallop, and Hullihen crouched over its neck and escaped. He came to the battery of artillery, which had not bothered to mention what lay down the road, but which now thought he was the enemy and was "in pandemonium." He rode on, found Stuart and his staff, and had his wound dressed. Von Borcke sat up with him, having abandoned hope of getting any sleep that night, and the next day Hullihen began a journey with hundreds of other wounded Rebels toward Richmond. He would not return to active duty until late that autumn.[30]

It is unlikely Stuart got any sleep that night either, so that he was coming up on three days with no more rest than probable brief naps.

May 3, the climactic day of Chancellorsville, like the last day of the siege of the Alamo and the Little Big Horn, was a Sunday. Despite Jackson's flank march, surprise attack, and the humiliation of the Eleventh Corps, Hooker remained in an extremely strong position and, having been joined by John Reynolds' First Corps that evening, he still outnumbered the Confederates two to one. Rather than abandoning the field and retreating across the Rapidan, as Jackson had hoped, Hooker put his men to work building breastworks and digging in around Chancellorsville. They were an army on an offensive campaign given the marvelous advantage of fighting a defensive battle against a woefully understrength opponent. There is more to winning battles than numbers, however, and no matter how superior the Army of the Potomac was in some respects, it lacked an advantage in will to win, spirit, and confidence.

The Federal position was U-shaped, both flanks on the river, its center held by the Second, Third, and Twelfth Corps, its right by the First and Fifth Corps, and its far left by the beleaguered Eleventh Corps, which had been sent there to regroup. Lee's smaller army was in three disconnected segments, Early back at Fredericksburg, Stuart on the left near Chancellorsville, and Lee personally commanding the center-right. Just before dawn Stuart received orders from Lee to attack, but he had already been making preparations to do so. Jeb placed his three divisions astride the Plank Road, Henry Heth (who had taken over for A.P. Hill) in the lead, Raleigh Colston about 400 yards behind, and Rodes this time in the rear. At the dawn of day they attacked.

May 3 saw one of the bloodiest days of the war. Heth's and Colston's assaults were beaten back with severe losses, while Federal counterattacks were likewise repulsed. The woods became a living hell as fortified Federal batteries ringing the field around Chancellorsville shredded the Confederate assaults, while on their side of the woods, Rebel artillery could find scarce openings through which to fire. It seemed that the Confederates could only painfully butt their heads against the prepared Union positions.

But then Joe Hooker's crippling caution once again came to the Rebels' rescue. Sickles' Third Corps had been positioned at the southernmost tip of the "U," where it had almost been able to intercept Jackson's flank march, and where it still stood as a barrier between Lee's and Stuart's wings of the army. Hooker, however, thought the Third Corps was vulnerable in its exposed position and ordered it to pull back closer to his main line. This uncovered a superb artillery position—an elevated plateau called Hazel Grove—which the Federals themselves had used to great effect the night before. Stuart and the brilliant young artillerist Porter Alexander were quick to perceive the new opportunity.

As Alexander wrote, "Gen. Stuart, who was at the spot at the moment, sent me word to immediately crown the hill with 30 guns. They were close at hand, & all ready, & it was done very quickly. . . . The position turned out to to be one of great value. It gave us fire over a larger part of the Chancellorsville plain, & we could even see the Chancellorsville house from it, about 2,000 yards away."[31] The Confederates finally had an open field of fire, and began to hammer at the Federal line. Alexander said, "They had built about 25 pits for guns, in one long row, on the edge of the sort of plateau looking over the stream which ran across the Plank Road. Against their fire & the strength of their breastworks, we might have never gotten them out but for our beginning to crumble their line on its left."[32] Stuart and Alexander then rode over to the Plank Road itself to place artillery to fire straight down the lane. Hit obliquely from the massed battery, and now by more guns directly in front, the Union position began to wither under the fire.

"Stuart was in fine spirits," wrote Alexander, "& was singing 'Old Joe Hooker, would you come out the Wilderness'." As the Federal line came apart, Jeb raced back to bring up more guns while Alexander rode to Hazel Grove to push forward the 30 cannon there. "By the time we could get over," he said "the enemy had abaonded his 25 gunpits, & we deployed on the plateau, & opened on the fugitives, infantry, artillery, wagons—everything—swarming about the Chancellorsville house, & down the broad road leading thence to the river."[33]

One of the earlier Confederate shells did unique damage to the Army of the Potomac. Hooker was at the Chancellor house about 9:15 a.m. when a cannon-shot hit a column he was leaning against and caused it to fall on him with enough strength to knock him unconscious for nearly an hour. He almost certainly suffered a concussion, but when he came to he refused to turn over command to the next ranking officer, Major General Darius

Couch. He continued giving orders, which some generals considered timid if not completely addled. To complicate matters, the two generals Hooker trusted most, John Sedgwick and Daniel Butterfield, were back at Fredericksburg facing Early, were out of communication due to faulty telegraph lines, and Hooker didn't have confidence in anyone at headquarters. As a practical matter, nobody exercised overall command of the Federal army for the rest of the day.

At about 10:00, the Second Corps men saw troops advancing from the right, and they turned out to be from McLaws' division. Stuart's wing and Lee's had now linked up, presenting one solid line, and a concentrated push was made along the entire front. Victory was in Confederate hands.

Scheibert awakened that morning from what he called a deathlike sleep and found Stuart's command in motion, advancing to the right. He saddled Old Black and headed toward the right flank, knowing that General Lee was in that direction but riding without companions. After an hour he came to a cabin belonging to a black man and decided to try to purchase some grain for the mare, but just as he put his hand in his pocket to see how much change he had, five soldiers emerged from the house—"Unionists."

Scheibert was wearing his Captain's coat, but he had only a dull saber as a weapon. He was about to be killed or captured, and probably would have made an easy target if he'd tried to escape. In a move he later credited to Pomeranian instinct, he pulled the saber from its scabbard, rode toward the Yankees and shouted as loudly and sternly as he could, "Surrender! You are surrounded by cavalry!" The Yankees stared at him and he shouted again in what he admitted was poor English "Down with your weapons, or you are dead men!" The five soldiers hesitated, then did as he said.

If Pomeranian instinct was what saved Scheibert, it kept working, because once he had the five unarmed men in front of his horse and moving away from the cabin, he had the presence of mind to shout "March," and "There are more of them in the house. We have counted all of them, and they will all be killed!" As the little knot of men began moving, a sixth Federal soldier came running out of the house and joined his comrades.

They were members of the 6th Ohio Infantry, and not only did they allow themselves to be taken prisoner by a single fat man who spoke bad English armed only with a sword, but they allowed him to march them through the woods for half an hour before coming upon other Confederate troops who took them into custody. Scheibert learned later that some of the six men were near the end of their enlistment, which might explain why they offered so little resistance. Still, when Scheibert turned them over to an amused regiment of Rebels and recounted how he'd captured them, the "duped enemy pulled long faces."[34]

The story of Scheibert's triumph ran like electricity through the ranks and the high command. General Lee and Stuart both had a hardy laugh over it. Von heard about it when he arrived at headquarters that evening and included the tale in his memoirs with only slight embellishment.[35]

The real story, the real triumph of the day, belonged to Jeb Stuart.

As usual, he led from the front rather than directed from the rear. He galloped back and forth along the lines of his divisions, shouting, commanding, and singing. At the beginning of the day he was mounted, appropriately, on Chancellor, but the horse was killed before mid-morning. Remounted on a blood bay, he twice led the 28th North Carolina in a charge, as though he was a regimental rather than a corps commander. Seeing another of his regiments about to break under withering fire, he rode the bay into their center, snatched their battle flag, and rallied the men in his ringing baritone, then led them toward the enemy. In the last major assault by Rodes' division, he rode ahead and leaped the bay over the Federal fortifications, then brought the excited horse to a halt between two abandoned enemy cannon, where it pawed the ground and flared its nostrils as the gray infantry caught up and swarmed past.[36]

His battle cry was "Remember Jackson!" His song was *Jine the Cavalry* with the new verse about "Old Joe Hooker." In some corners of history the tune handed down and attributed to Jeb on that day was *Old Dan Tucker*. The new lyrics fit, and the tunes are similar, but Jeb stuck with what he loved most.

Von Borcke marveled that Stuart and his staff were not killed. He watched them gallop back and forth while men died all around. While Von was giving directions to a courier a cannonball tore off the man's leg, mortally wounding him. Von's horse was hit twice, once in the back by a bullet and then in the chest by a piece of shrapnel, causing it to die the next morning. "Stuart all activity, and wherever the danger was greatest there was he to be found, urging the men forward, and animating them by the force of his example. The shower of missiles that hissed through the air passed round him unheeded; and in the midst of the hottest fire I heard him, to an old melody, hum the words, 'Old Joe Hooker get out of the Wilderness.'" Jeb rode, and sang, commanded half the army, and occupied the apex of his glory.

Stuart acquired a new member of his staff that day. He'd been sending so many messages to the components of his command that he ran out of couriers and staff officers. By accident he ran into Captain Andrew Reid Venable, Jr., commissary for the 1st Virginia Artillery. Venable and Stuart were friends, having met in late November 1862 near Fredericksburg and having shared dinners at Gay Mont. Venable's commander was Colonel John Thompson Brown, another friend of Jeb's. Brown had also dined with them at Gay Mont, and had good-naturedly complained about Venable's tendency to arrange his affairs during battles so that he wound up in or near the fighting. This was not the role of a commissary officer, but it impressed both Brown and Stuart.

The Venable family name was well known in the South, and during the war no fewer than four Venables served as staff officers. Charles Scott Venable served on General Lee's staff from April 1862 to Appomattox, and Paul C. Venable served on Wade Hampton's staff from January 1863 to January 1864. Then there was Andrew Reid Venable, also known as "Black Andrew," who served on Stuart's staff, and there may have even been another Andrew Venable, close in age (though there is also some possibility that in certain historical records birth dates were mistaken).[37] Students of the war sometimes get the impression there were only one or two very busy, very versatile Venables who flitted from staff to staff.

Andrew Jr. was trying to find Colonel Brown when Stuart found him. "Venable," Jeb shouted, "I've sent off my last man. You must take this order to the left. There is no one else. I will take all responsibility." "Certainly, sir," Venable responded. He took the message where Stuart directed, then returned. During a slight lull, Venable confided to Stuart that he was not happy as an artillery commissary officer. There was not enough action and it was like being in a "bomb-proof." Stuart slapped him on the back and said, "I'll ask for your services today, to be assigned to my staff." Venable soon became his assistant adjutant and inspector general.[38]

Scheibert stayed at Lee's headquarters after he delivered his six prisoners. The general was standing near a battery of artillery observing the battle through field glasses, and Scheibert was honored when he was invited to stand next to Lee. He naturally complimented the commanding general, telling him how impressed he was with the bravery of the Confederates. Lee responded in kind, telling the honorary captain, "Give me also Prussian discipline and Prussian forms, and you would see quite different results!" Marse Robert then waxed philosophical, telling Scheibert he hated the war and that one of his uppermost goals was to keep his own men "morally disciplined and to guard against barbarism."

He told Scheibert that the men of his army were the elite of Southerners from sixteen to forty-five years of age, who after the war would need
to pursue peaceful occupations and practice quiet civic virtues, whereas
war was a savage business to which they had become accustomed. It was
his job to help them learn self-control in order that they might succeed
when the fighting ended.

Lee was watching the battle through field glasses and talking when a
spent minie ball fell at the feet of the two men. Lee picked it out of the dirt
and handed it to Scheibert, saying, "Captain, this was meant for one of us.
Keep the little piece of lead as a souvenir of this day." The bullet became
Scheibert's most prized possession of the American war.[39]

After some eight hours, Lee called a halt to the Confederates' advance,
after he and Stuart had connected at the Chancellor house. The enemy was
on the run, but they still greatly outnumbered the Rebels, who were now
exhausted and disorganized. The lead division was pulled back, entrenchments were thrown up across the Plank Road in case of counterattack, and
the inevitable business of collecting wounded and burying dead began.

Bodies and abandoned equipment were everywhere. Von Borcke was
famished, and set about looking for something to eat, finally settling on the
contents of the haversack of a disfigured enemy soldier. He made a hearty
meal of what the man was carrying, but recalled that he would have considered such a thing impossible only months before.

Von's servant, Henry, came up with Kitt and began loading the mule
with spoils. Soon the animal was so burdened that only its legs were visible.
Von saw Henry staring wistfully at a dead Federal wearing a nice pair of
boots. Knowing his servant needed them, Von told him to take them before
somebody else did, but Henry declined, predicting that if he did the dead
Yankee's ghost would come in the night to get them back. Von wrote in his
memoirs that it was only the fact that the enemy was already dead that prevented Henry from taking the prize, and had the man only been wounded,
Henry "would have little hesitation in cutting a living man's throat for the
sake of the same alluring prize."

Von Borcke was sent about 11 a.m. to carry a message to a lead Confederate division, and at the front he spied a rare prize lying between the
lines—a large box of candles. Candles had become so hard to obtain that
after dark he crawled into the equivalent of no man's land and pulled the
box to safety. After removing a large number for himself, he took the rest
to Lee's headquarters and presented them to the army's commander. In his

calm, all-knowing way, Lee responded, "Major, I am much obliged to you; but I know where you got these candles, and you acted wrongly in exposing your life for a simple act of courtesy." Even General Lee had heard about the location of those candles!

In the evening, Stuart and his staff went into camp in an orchard about 150 yards from a barn that had become a Federal field hospital. Scheibert claimed that Confederates considered it a disgrace to groan or cry aloud with all but the most painful types of wounds, and that by listening to the groaning one could tell from afar whether a particular field hospital was filled with Confederates or Yankees. As examples he recorded seeing an officer walk by with his hat covering one hand, but splattered with blood, so that Scheibert asked if he was severely wounded. "No, only the hand is gone, Captain," the officer replied. Another officer was shot in the abdomen and was carried from the field on a litter born by four men on their shoulders. Soldiers from his regiment called out to him and the officer raised up on the stretcher, smiled, and waved to his men in a friendly manner. Scheibert, mounted on Old Black was able to see the officer's face, and that as soon as he lay back down it became deathly pale and distorted.[40]

Between the groans of the approximately 300 wounded Federals inside and around the barn, frequent incoming rounds of artillery fire, and false alarms that the enemy was attacking, nobody got much sleep that night, just as they'd gotten very little since April 29. At one point a battery of enemy artillery focused its fire on the area, hitting a cherry tree beneath which Von Borcke was lying, covering him with leaves and branches. More tragically, the shells also hit the barn several times, killing and giving new wounds to men who had already been mangled in the battle. [41]

At sunrise on May 4, Stuart wrote an order to Colonel William Payne, commanding the 4th Virginia, telling him that Fitz Lee was coming to his relief, asking if he knew where Stoneman and his cavalry were, and enclosing a telegram he asked Payne to send for him.[42] The Battle of Chancellorsville continued, but the principal scene of action was at Fredericksburg. Hooker had left Sedgwick's Corps there to threaten the Confederate rear, consisting of only one division and one brigade. Sedgwick drove the Confederates from Marye's Heights, which Burnside had been unable to do, and Lee sent two more divisions, McLaws' and Anderson's, to the aid of Early and Barksdale.

Lee, Stuart, and A.P. Hill, whose wound from the night of the 2nd was not serious, established their headquarters on Fairview Hill, the principal artillery position of the Federals the day before. Now the area was the target of that same artillery and when shells began falling, the officers and their staffs rode away until the firing subsided. The location offered a good view of the Federal positions or it would have been abandoned. By the end of the day the area looked as though it had been recently plowed, and an apple tree located next to Lee's tent had received three direct hits and several scrapes and scars from shrapnel.[43]

About noon the firing ceased. The weather was warm again, and unburied bodies were becoming odorous. As was the custom on other battlefields, the army in possession of the field tended to its own dead first, so that most of the offenders left above ground were Federals.

Hooker remained in a defensive position all day, which made Lee confident that he could spare the two divisions sent to deal with Sedgwick. He was so confident, in fact, that Lee accompanied Anderson's division in the direction of Marye's Heights, which Jubal Early had already reoccupied that morning. Anderson's and McLaws' troops swelled the Confederate strength to about 21,000, which outnumbered Sedgwick, and although neither of the two Confederate generals performed admirably or quickly, an assault launched at 6 p.m. pushed the Federals back to the river, which they crossed in retreat before dawn on May 5.

Still on the alert, Stuart sent a message to Lee the night of the 4th that the enemy was strengthening his position, still "fortifying and chopping." Early on the 5th he sent another message, proposing an assault on the Federal position, but Lee wrote back at 8:15 a.m. to say, "I do not know the circumstances which induce your wish to attack the enemy. With your present strength as reported in field returns, it might be beyond us. If the Enemy is recrossing the Rappk or attempting to do so, or if other circumstances warrant the attack, you can withdraw Heth. If you have to storm entrenchments, unless the Enemy can be driven from them by cannon, I cannot recommend an attack except under very favorable circumstances."[44]

It was a classic Robert E. Lee communication . . . do not know the circumstances . . . might be beyond us . . . if other circumstances warrant the attack . . . unless . . . I cannot recommend . . . ." Jeb understood. He did not attack.

Hooker called a council of corps commanders on the 5th to obtain their opinion on whether to fight or withdraw. A majority voted to renew the offensive, but that wasn't what Hooker wanted to hear, and that night he ordered the army to withdraw at the United States Ford. It was raining again and the river rose and threatened the pontoon bridges, but once Hooker was personally across the river, he gave explicit orders not to continue the battle. Both Darius Couch, who took command when Hooker left, and General Lee, who wanted to mount another attack on the dispirited enemy, were disappointed. The battle was over, with the Federals once more abandoning an "on to Richmond" attempt.

With Hooker no longer a threat, the Confederate infantry returned to its camps in and around Fredericksburg. A.P. Hill resumed command of the Second Corps on May 6, and Stuart returned to his cavalry, making his headquarters at Orange Court House.

Jackson appeared to be recovering, but on the 8th his condition deteriorated and on the 10th he died, causing greater grief for Southerners than any other loss of the war thus far. Of course it also gave immediate rise to another concern—who would replace him?

Stuart was an obvious choice. Had anyone been asked to name the four leading commanders in the Army of Northern Virginia on May 1, 1863, they would have named Lee, Jackson, Longstreet, and Stuart, probably in that order. With a vacancy in one of those positions, an obvious expectation was that a fourth name, perhaps A.P. Hill would be added, not that one of the three remaining luminaries would be squeezed to the side to make room for two others.

Stuart, as admitted even by men who did not particularly care for him, was the best-known and most popular choice of the men of the Second Corps. They loved Jackson and knew that Jackson loved Stuart. The comrade of their commander deserved to be their commander.

The votes were split among ranking officers and their staffs, with some shuddering at the thought of Stuart's promotion and others grieving it did not occur. Edward Porter Alexander, who served remarkably at both Chancellorsville and Gettysburg, may have summed it up best. Writing after the war, he opined that Stuart's not replacing Jackson was "an injustice to Stuart" and "a loss to the army he was not from the moment continued in command of Jackson's corps. He had *won* the right to it. I believe he had all of Jackson's genius and dash and originality, without that eccentricity of character which sometimes led to disappointment. . . . That Sunday morning's action [on May 3] ought to rank with whatever else of special brilliancy can be found in the annals of the Army of Northern Virginia."[45]

There is no doubt that Jeb wished for the appointment. On May 9, responding to criticism and rumors circulating in some corners, or perhaps just fishing for reassurance, he wrote General Lee, and although the letter is lost, Lee's response makes it clear that Jeb concluded by asking if his performance at Chancellorsville had been unsatisfactory. Lee replied on May 11 with, "As regards the closing remarks of your note, I am at a loss to understand the reference or to know what has given rise to them. In the management of the difficult operations at Chancellorsville, which you so promptly undertook and credibly performed, I saw no errors to correct, nor has there been a fitting opportunity to commend your conduct. I prefer your acts to speak for themselves, nor does your character or reputation require bolstering by out-of-place expression of my opinions." He then added, "I regret to inform you that the great and good Jackson is no more. He died yesterday at 3:15 p.m. of pneumonia, calm, serene, and happy. May his spirit pervade our whole army; our country will then be secure."

The words Lee wrote provoke many thoughts. As a man who rarely gave compliments (so that his referring to one officer as "gallant" caused the man to be so labeled for all time), his "I didn't see anything to correct" message was actually high praise. At the same time, the message sounds as though Lee was mentally shaking his head about how tender some people's feelings were, how much time they wasted on vanity, and how inappropriate it was for Jeb to worry about his own reputation while Lee's and the nation's concerns were all about the loss of Jackson. One wonders whether Stuart was relieved or embarrassed when he read the letter. Considering that he kept it, the former seems more likely.

There is nothing in the historical record to suggest that Lee gave serious thought to replacing Jackson with Stuart. Later that month, after visiting with and corresponding with President Davis, Lee reorganized the Army into three corps, creating a new one for A.P. Hill and turning the Second Corps over to Richard S. Ewell, who had been Jackson's chief lieutenant during his Valley Campaign and other battles up until Second Manassas.

Shortly after Jackson's death, Col. Tom Rosser visited Stuart and told him that on his deathbed, Jackson had stated that he desired that Stuart succeed him in command of the Corps. Humbly, Stuart said, "I would rather know that Jackson said that than have the appointment."[46] Perhaps so, but he longed for both. After the battle he prepared an order of congratulations to the men of he commanded at Chancellorsville. It hinted he would continue to command them, and he was still carrying the original of it in his pocket on the day he died.[47]

While such matters were developing, there was fatigue to overcome, meals to eat, and a war to be fought. Stuart got some much-needed sleep on May 5. On the 6th, he, Von and other staff officers dined with a "Mrs. F," who owned a plantation near Fredericksburg and with whom Von Borcke had established friendship. Earlier that day, Scheibert rode back to Chancellorsville, at Lee's request, to make a sketch of the battlefield. On his return he stopped at the house where Channing Price died on May 1 and learned that on the 2nd, Federal soldiers had visited and "had acted like mad men, and had naturally turned everything upside down."[48]

On the morning of May 7, Jeb sent Von to Lee's headquarters to report what he had learned about the Federal cavalry under Stoneman, then set off after them with Rooney Lee's brigade. Stoneman had been galloping about with over 7,000 troopers in what was intended as a devastating raid deep into Confederate territory, but which only did minor damage to railroads and burned a few supply wagons. Rooney Lee had only about 1,000 men in the saddle, but he'd kept Stoneman busy, distracted, and minimally destructive. On the night of the 7th, Stoneman recrossed the Rappahannock and brought the raid to a close. Stuart and Rooney Lee returned to camp.[49]

Scheibert was still with Stuart's military family, and he took time to record the routine for meals, saying there were normally two—breakfast at 7 a.m. when in camp and 4 a.m. on the march, followed by dinner at 6 p.m. or the end of a day's march. The menu was limited—cornbread, sometimes wheat bread or hardtack, coffee made from parched corn or wheat, sometimes sassafras tea, sometimes only water, plus molasses, and whatever meat might be available, usually bacon. Butter and eggs were rare.[50]

On May 8, Stuart worked on a report of cavalry operations in the Chancellorsville campaign, expressing the opinion that with more men he could have prevented Stoneman's raid altogether.[51] Had he been off chasing Stoneman, of course, he might not have been available to take command of Jackson's Corps on May 2.

On either the 7th or the 8th, hearing there was a horse for sale at a plantation in Louisa County, Von obtained permission to ride there and investigate. He still had the horse he'd captured from the enemy the night of April 30, but needed another. With one courier he set off. The horse turned out to be "a tall thoroughbred bay, of beautiful form and action," and the thousand dollar price tag did not seem excessive, so Von purchased the animal, spent the night at the plantation, and headed back toward Orange the next day on board his new steed.

The return route took them through Verdiersville and, remembering the lady who lived in the house who was instrumental in his escape from the onrush of Federal cavalry, Von stopped to pay his respects. She was in the yard when he rode up, but instead of delivering the welcome Von expected, she took one look at him, screamed, and fled into the house.

Utterly confused, Von Borcke dismounted and followed. Begging for an explanation, the lady handed him a copy of a Richmond newspaper and pointed to an article that began, "Among those who fell at the battle of Chancellorsville we regret to report the death of Major von Borcke." She had believed the story. In fact a great deal of Virginia accepted it without question, but in her case she'd been visited by an obvious ghost, and Von had a little difficulty convincing her he really was alive and in her parlor.

Upon returning to cavalry headquarters, he found that the tale of his demise was resulting in letters of condolence to Stuart, who was greatly amused. The joke got better when Governor Letcher sent a dispatch to General Lee asking that Von Borcke's body be forwarded to Richmond where, like Pelham's, it could be laid in state at the capitol before burial. In reply, General Lee wrote the Governor, "Can't spare it; it's in pursuit of Stoneman."[52]

On May 10, Scheibert attended a religious service delivered by Dr. Lacy that Jackson, still alive, had directed him to conduct. Lee was in attendance, and Lacy began his saying "God turns all things to the good of those who believe in Him. General Jackson, whom I left yesterday, gave me this text. He also cheerfully suffers his disability and considers himself fortunate in the loss of his arm, which he says has exalted his spirit more than any previous occurrence. In his case God has also turned the severe wound to the best. But, our gallant leader, children, hovers in greatest danger of being taken from us by death. Let us pray for him, that the Dear Lord God may sustain him for us."

Hundreds of ragged Rebels who made up the congregation knelt and prayed that Jackson would be spared. After the service, Scheibert accompanied Lee and they discussed the sermon. As if to explain why Lacy's prayers would not save Stonewall, he said, "But the doctor forgot the conclusion of the prayer: 'Thy will be done always. The spirit of the noble Jackson will be with us, his example must sustain us. Indeed, he will still lead us, even though his body may be called away!"[53]

Later that day, Scheibert said farewell to his friends in Lee's army and departed for Richmond, planning to tend to business there and depart in a few days for the western theatre of the war, particularly Vicksburg. He would not be gone long.

On May 11, Stuart wrote to Thomas Price, Channing's father, to express his deep grief over the young man's death. He said that as an adjutant general "he had no superior," said that General Lee knew and appreciated his worth, called him a "universal favorite," wrote that "no one about me could have been less spared," and said he missed him "hourly now." As with Pelham, he directed his staff to wear mourning for thirty days.

There was a lot of mourning during those days, and a photo of Stuart taken in Richmond about this time shows him standing erect, hat in his right hand with crown toward the camera, left hand on his saber, gray pants tucked into boots only knee, rather than thigh, high, and wearing a black mourning band on his left arm. Whether he donned it for Pelham, Price, or Stonewall Jackson is not known, but it served them all.

Scheibert arrived in Richmond on May 11. He met with President Davis and members of his cabinet and made arrangements to leave for Vicksburg on May 15, but then came down with dysentery and a fever so intense he was unable to leave his bed. He was still sick on his birthday, May 16, when Von Borcke showed up unannounced at his hotel room with an invitation to return to Stuart's headquarters. A great expedition was in the works, possibly toward the north, and Jeb thought the Prussian captain might like to go along.

Scheibert declined, explaining to Von his plans to go west as soon as he was feeling better, but Von said it was too late, that Vicksburg was surrounded and it was difficult for even the boldest scouts to get in. He showed Scheibert reports that convinced him that trying to get into the Mississippi city would be a waste of time, so he agreed to return to Stuart's camp.

Stuart received a gift the same day in the arrival of the newly promoted Henry McClellan, now a major and Jeb's assistant adjutant general. He had been tapped for the position before Channing Price was killed, but now he faced the daunting challenge of trying to fill Price's shoes. He came close to doing so.

On May 20, Stuart moved his headquarters back to Culpeper Court House, pitching his tents near their former camp in a grove of hickory and tulip-poplar trees surrounded by clover fields, christened "Camp Channing Price." In reply to Stuart's report on Chancellorsville and his assertion that the cavalry division was undermanned, General Lee had arranged to send him reinforcements, although some of them were not to Stuart's liking.

The 4th and 5th North Carolina regiments were summoned from that state, where they were serving under Beverly Robertson. Neither Lee nor Stuart intended that Robertson come with them, but he did. A small brigade commanded by Brig. Gen. Albert Jenkins was transferred from western Virginia to the Shenandoah and ordered to relieve Grumble Jones' brigade so it could join Stuart. Jeb appreciated the new troops, but he was now saddled with the two subordinates he most disliked. He asked that Jones be given command of the Stonewall Brigade, whose commander, Elisha Paxton, had been killed on May 2. Lee said he was willing to transfer him if Jones desired it, but if not, he knew of no reason to force him to go, adding in reference to Stuart's well-known dislike of "Grumble," "Do not let your judgment be warped."[54]

In addition to the new troops, the grass was green and the horses, so terribly depleted and miserable during the winter, where fattening up. Von Borcke wrote that men in camp were in high spirits and that hundreds, particularly in Hampton's brigade, were returning from their homes with fresh horses. The Horse Artillery received replacement guns—rifled Blakleys —to replace worn-out smoothbores, and Stuart sent a letter to General Cooper on the 21st to request that Beckham be promoted to Lt. Colonel.[55]

Stuart also wrote to General Chilton in Richmond, on the 21st, attempting to kill two birds with one letter. The stated purpose of the correspondence was to propose establishment of a "Reserve Camp for recuperation and mounting." The recent experience of losing so many horses over the winter followed by an equal number of troopers who had to journey home to get another mount convinced Stuart it made good sense to have a station where fresh horses could be shipped in from afar and to which sick or injured animals could be sent to recover. He thought it ought to be located in either Albemarle or Fluvanna Counties as soon as possible in light of operations on the horizon, and that it should be under the orders of General Lee. That was the responsible, military purpose of the letter. His second, more ingenuous, purpose was in regard to who should command the camp. It needed to be "an experienced and capable Cavalry Officer of rank," and he had just the man in mind—Brigadier General Beverly H. Robertson.

He despised Robertson and wanted to get rid of him in any manner possible, but on this occasion he praised the man. Robertson was "eminently fitted . . . a good disciplinarian, and excellent Instructor and Organizer of Cavalry . . . [who] . . . could in no way render as efficient service as in the capacity proposed."[56] We might suspect that General Lee shook his head knowingly when he read Jeb's letter. Robertson remained where he was.

Scheibert returned to Stuart's camp, in response to Von Borcke's invitation, on May 21st, feeling shaky from his recent illness. Blackford also returned from his illness and long furlough. On that day, too, the *New York Times* published Tom Price's diary. It's not known how long it took for the newspaper to work its way south into Stuart's hands, but it probably was not long. All who read it would have wanted to make certain Jeb learned of it as soon as possible.

The diary entries covered the period February 10, 1863, when Tom Price put on his uniform and left home to join Stuart, to April 19, 1863, when he described the "narrowest escape" of almost being blown up by the artillery shell that did not explode when it landed in the middle of Stuart and his staff on April 14. From the perspective of Nnorthern readers, the charm of the diary was its first person, intimate views of Stuart, Pelham, Von Borcke, and Robert E. Lee. Jeb's joke about "stalled beef" was included, as was his remarkable prediction, a month before the battle, that Chancellorsville would be the site of the next great engagement.

From Jeb's perspective the diary had no charm. To the contrary, it embarrassed and hurt him. Stuart loved the Price family. Nannie was his darling and Channing was one of his military favorites. He went out of his way to get Tom Price on his staff, making room, as an assistant engineer, for a man whose specialty was ancient languages. He'd invited him to his table, been concerned about the books he read, and carried gifts to him from Dundee. What Tom wrote in his diary in return, while not hateful, revealed no gratitude plus an attitude of dismissiveness for Stuart and the position on his staff. "Our fare is very bad. . . . Oh! to be back at my favorite studies! Oh for Berlin, or Paris, or Athens. I long so to hear literary conversation, and have my thoughts once more directed to agreeable topics." "The General tickled his staff and threw them down in the mud." "General Stuart was with us and prattled on all the evening in his garrulous way— described how he commenced the war. . . . " A few later entries put Jeb in a positive light, but they were thoroughly overshadowed by the earlier, dismissive ones.

Stuart's detractors must have loved it—a member of his own staff dismissing him as a silly, garrulous, prattling fool. Jeb was cut deeply. To have Channing's brother disrespect him so thoroughly, right on the heels of losing Channing, was doubly injurious.

Tom's days as a member of Stuart's military family were over. He was relieved of his duties and transferred to the engineer department in Richmond, gone by the end of the month. Blackford wrote a letter of recommendation to Colonel Gilmore, the department's commander, saying Price's dismissal was due to causes "in no way connected with his professional duties but of a character wholly personal between Gen. Stuart and himself," and that Price "discharged his duties satisfactorily and would after a little while . . . make a most valuable officer."[57]

On May 22, Stuart held a review of the brigades of Fitz and Rooney Lee, about 4,000 men, at Brandy Station.[58] Flora and Jimmie visited in time to see the review, but she left soon after and Stuart wrote her on May 26. He reported the arrival of goods he'd ordered from Nassau, a wedding he did not plan to attend, and that a newspaper reporter had requested being assigned to his camp for the upcoming campaign. He'd declined, uncharacteristically, and the reporter left "with a flea in his ear," so that Jeb warned her to watch out for articles in which he was abused. There'd been discussion of donating money to erect a monument to Jackson, but he believed it was the legislature's job to pay for it while individuals donated money to charities.[59]

The next day, May 27, Stuart wrote a report to General Lee with alternatives for how to reorganize the cavalry "division," but which sounded like the creation of a corps. It would result in either three or four divisions, with division commanders Hampton, Fitz Lee, and Rooney Lee, if the former, and a fourth commander to be selected later if the latter. He acknowledged Lee's "natural disinclination to promote those so near to you"—a son and a nephew—but he begged to be allowed to be the judge based on his "long and intimate official relations."

Mid-May through the first week of June 1863 was a period of lull and recuperation as both sides licked their wounds from the recent battle. It was anticipated that the Confederates would follow up their victory by launching a major offensive, while Hooker was now thinking only in terms of defense. It was generally quiet along the front, but three events occurred during the last of May and the beginning of June 1863 that are as humorous as any that occurred in the war, all recorded by Blackford and all involving Captain Scheibert.

It is not possible to pinpoint the exact day that any of the three events occurred, but all happened between May 28 and June 9. Blackford did not specify a date, but inserted them in his memoirs immediately following

Jackson's death, on May 10, and military events that occurred after May 18. Scheibert's book and the state of his health indicates he could not have participated in any of the three slapstick adventures before the 28th, and one sentence he wrote establishes that the first, and most comical, probably occurred on May 31.

May 31 was a Sunday, a leisurely day in camp with womenfolk visiting and General Stuart and his staff stretched out on blankets in the sun. Mrs.W.H.F. "Rooney" Lee was visiting her husband and boarding at a house in town. Her name was Charlotte Wickham Lee, she liked to paint, and on this particular afternoon Scheibert made an appointment to "touch up an oil sketch of a small-size female head which Mrs. Lee had just finished." He was dressed in a short jacket and white trousers that made him appear, according to Blackford, as if "his fat person . . . had been melted and poured in, so tight was the fit." He also wore a hat and gloves, and carried a walking stick.

Scheibert was a bit of a renaissance man—a soldier, an engineer, an author, an artist and a historian. He made maps and sketches of scenes he witnessed during the war and he welcomed an opportunity to assist a young lady with her oil painting. After they worked on the portrait, it was laid on a chair in the parlor to dry and they talked. One of Scheibert's odd ways "was that when he became interested in conversation he would start up on his feet, in the eagerness of his gesticulation, walk about the room and then pop down on any chair that happened to be nearest to him." That is what happened. Scheibert paced about, talking and gesturing, then sat down abruptly in the nearest chair, which happened to be the one in which the wet painting was lying. Neither Scheibert nor Mrs. Lee noticed.

When it was time for Scheibert to leave, Mrs. Lee thanked him and said she would keep the picture as a souvenir of their acquaintance. She then turned to get the picture but it was gone. "Bless my soul!" said Scheibert. "I laid it down on one of the chairs, but I don't see it now." They looked from chair to chair but it was nowhere to be seen.

Oh," said Scheibert, "the wind must have blown it under the piano!" He fell to his hands and knees and began crawling toward the piano. Mrs. Lee shrieked.

"Here it is!" she announced, and screaming with laughter as she peeled the portrait from his rear end, leaving the lovely face, "somewhat blurred" but transferred "most conspicuously" to the white canvas of Scheibert's wide posterior.

Scheibert backed out from under the piano, twisted to see where Mrs. Lee was pointing, and without speaking or stopping to get his hat, cane, or gloves from the hall, bolted out the door and began running across the fields toward the headquarters camp, "waving his arms wildly and roaring like a bull with laughter." Blackford and the others sat up, wondering what was going on. The large man charged into the midst, threw himself down on the grass and, still convulsing with laughter, rolled over and over. Every time he turned, the bright but blurry picture of a lovely face on the seat of his trousers flashed at the headquarters group. It took him awhile to regain enough composure and breath to explain what had happened, and as Blackford wrote in gentle understatement, "You may rest assured we enjoyed the joke."

A day or two later, Scheibert struck again. This time it was not his artistic but his musical talent that set the stage. It was not the same house or piano, but it was a similar scene. Scheibert arrived with a few staff officers, including Blackford. Some young ladies were upstairs and, probably intending to announce their arrival with as much pomp and circumstance as possible, the honorary captain sat down at the piano and began to play one of his favorite pieces of German classical music.

His playing was excellent, and he became enthralled with his own performance. As the dramatic piece moved toward a musical crescendo, he pounded harder on the keys and rose up on his feet with his rear end hovering above the piano stool. He played with feeling and flair, reached the dramatic zenith of his selection, pounded out the climax, and crashed back down. The piano stool collapsed in a cloud of broken mahogany. He went sprawling backwards, just as the ladies began descending the stairs.

The foot of the stairs was in an adjoining room, so Scheibert had a few seconds to scramble to his feet, "in an agony of terror and embarrassment," before the ladies appeared. In standing, he kicked part of the broken stool, then hastily snatched up a stool leg, perhaps thinking with Pomeranian instinct that he could conceal all that had just happened. When the ladies walked in he quickly put the stool leg behind his back "and stood transfixed with eyes and mouth wide open, a perfectly ludicrous picture of embarrassment." Blackford and the other officers were so convulsed with laughter they couldn't talk, let alone introduce their friend to the women, who stood staring as Scheibert turned redder and redder.

The last of the three Scheibert incidents that Blackford recorded might have occurred as early as the Chancellorsville campaign or as late as Brandy

Station, with early June seeming most likely. This time it was Scheibert's horsemanship that got everyone's attention. As mentioned previously and confirmed by Blackford, "Captain Scheibert was not much of a horseman and his awkwardness in this accomplishment was a never-ending source of amusement." The staff made numerous jokes about it, usually to his face, and he took it all with good humor. Considering his memoirs contain numerous references to his riding of Old Black on long rides, night rides, rides along the front, and at least one "hard jump," he may have wanted to pad his record as a horseman as much as possible out of concern that one of those staff officers would carry some of the jokes forward to his own memoirs.

So it was that Blackford not only revealed Scheibert's equestrian short-comings, but a lack of skill in packing as well, saying, "He had a way of attaching all his belongings to his saddle in separate packages by strings and straps, and not being skilled in the art, these packages, when his horse galloped, would flop wildly, and becoming loosened would often fall to the ground."

On this occasion Stuart utilized Scheibert as a genuine member of his staff, or at least a courier. Jeb, in advance, came upon a force of the enemy and a skirmish broke out. The area was not heavily wooded, but it contained scrubby trees and several different roads. Scheibert wanted take part in the action, so Stuart directed him to ride back and summon a Confederate regiment to come forward quickly. Scheibert received the order and dashed away, down the wrong road and in the direction of the enemy.

Jeb was horror-struck and immediately sent a courier to bring Scheibert back. Soon the man was close enough to see the honorary captain galloping ahead, his packages and bundles dancing and bouncing around him. The courier shouted for him to stop, but Scheibert, seeing he was being pursued and assuming it must be the enemy, spurred his horse to go faster. The bundles and packages began to come loose and to litter the road.

The courier knew Scheibert was headed straight for disaster, and let his horse go full out. The enemy was in sight when the courier overtook and managed to rein Scheibert in.

Crestfallen at having not only bungled his chance to perform genuine service for Stuart, but at having littered the road with his property, he came trudging back, stopping every few yards to retrieve another item, while Stuart and his staff observed with glee.[60]

CHAPTER TWELVE

FLEETWOOD AND YEAR'S END
JUNE 1–JUNE 23, 1863

He was movement, excitement, baritone song,
a pinpoint in time, which dazzled, long gone,
boots to the thigh, sword at the waist,
a sparkling blue eye, a life lived in haste.
Plume on his hat brim, spur made of gold;
those who die youthful, never grow old.
He who died youthful, but lived every hour
God granted glory, to the cavalier flower.
—First verse of *J.E.B.*, as sung by Bill Coleman[1]

Jeb Stuart started the month of June with a letter to Major Walter H. Taylor, Assistant Adjutant General on Robert E. Lee's staff. The stated purpose of the letter was to reply to Taylor's inquiry regarding Colonel Matthew C. Butler, commander of the 2nd South Carolina Cavalry, who was being considered for promotion. Stuart was generous in his praise, calling Butler zealous, thoroughgoing, dashing, and fully deserving promotion to the command of a South Carolina brigade. He'd spoken to Wade Hampton about Butler the day before, and he agreed with Stuart's estimate. In comparing him to other colonels in Hampton's brigade, however, he stated that Col. Lawrence Baker of the 1st North Carolina was the most deserving of advancement, and expressed hope that both could be promoted.[2]

The success of the grand review on May 22 made Stuart decide to hold another on June 5. He began preparing on June 1 and the planning and

arrangements occupied his and his staff's attention through the 4th. This
one would be grander than that on the 22nd, with more troopers partici-
pating and more dignitaries to impress. Scheduling it for the 5th was ideal,
because Lee's army began moving out of its camps around Fredericksburg
on June 3, marching up the Rappahannock toward Culpeper Court House
where Stuart was already camped. Knowing trains loaded with officers,
dignitaries and visitors would roll into town, Jeb issued invitations throughout the surrounding area, as far away as Charlottesville, to attend a ball on
the night of the 4th, followed by the grand review in the morning.[3]

The hotels in Culpeper soon filled, and households willing to open their
doors to guests were solicited. When those accommodations ran out, tents
were set up for additional guests. General Randolph would return, and Von
Borcke arranged to have the locomotive that carried him from Gordonsville
decorated with the Confederate battle flag. More trains carried more guests,
and Stuart had wagons and ambulances waiting at the depot to pick them
up and deliver them to their respective lodgings.

The ball at the courthouse, in Von Borcke's words, "went off pleasantly
enough, although it was not, in the language of the reporter, 'a gay and
dazzling scene, illuminated by floods of light streaming from numerous
chandeliers.'" That was due to the fact that candles were still hard to come
by. Von Borcke had a few left from the box he'd risked his life to retrieve at
Chancellorsville, but the revelers had to depend mostly on the moon for
light that night.[4]

Stuart and his staff donned new or best uniforms. Horses were in the
best condition they'd been for months. The site for the review was at
"Auburn," a farm near Brandy Station belonging to an avowed Unionist
named John Minor Botts.[5] In particular it was held in a large open area at
the foot of a hill that "was admirably adapted to the purpose . . . of afford-
ing a reviewing stand from which the twelve thousand men present could
be seen to great advantage."

A designated line of approach from the courthouse to the reviewing
stand passed homes with second story porches and first story verandahs.
Ladies in attendance had prepared for the event by bringing baskets of
flowers and petals, and when Stuart and his staff approached they threw
the blooms into his path. Three bands of musicians were present to provide
stirring background music. Jeb Stuart was again at the zenith of his glory,
the apex of his element.

As Blackford pointed out, the accumulation of so many cavalrymen was equal in magnitude to the gathering of three times as many infantry. At 10 a.m., as Stuart and his staff took position on the hill overlooking the cavalry division, there were "nearly a hundred horsemen, all officers, dashing through the field" to make certain all units were in position and prepared. "Then the lines broke into column of squadrons and marched by at a walk, making the entire circuit; then they came by at a trot, taking the gallop a hundred yards before reaching the reviewing stand; and then the 'charge' at full speed past the reviewing stand, yelling just as they do in a real charge, and brandishing their sabres over their heads. The effect was thrilling, even to us, while the ladies clasped their hands and sank into the arms, sometimes, of their escorts in a swoon, if the escorts were handy, but if not they did not." While the charge was underway, Beckham's Horse Artillery rapidly fired blank rounds.[6]

The grand scene was not flawless. Grumble Jones, who would have preferred to be anywhere else as much as Stuart would have preferred the same, elected to be difficult. As Frank Robertson wrote fifty-plus years later, Jones' brigade "was scattered around generally as if unknowing of the Grand Review." Stuart directed Robertson to ride to Jones and ask him why his command was not ready. Robertson knew to look for a "claybank horse" that belonged to Jones, and found him lying on the ground acting as if he was completely unaware of what was going on. Robertson delivered Stuart's message and Jones "blazed all sorts of language" at him. Robertson turned to ride back to Stuart and report what had transpired, but heard behind him Jones's bugler blowing *boots and saddles,* meaning that Jones was putting his men into motion to join the review.[7]

Another ball was held that night in Stuart's camp, and for this one "enormous wood-fires" provided illumination. Those fires, plus Sweeney and his band, were a foundation for both dancing and strolling in the dark. As Von Borcke recalled, "The ruddy glare . . . upon the animated groups of our assembly gave to the whole scene a wild and romantic effect." [8]

On June 6, the expectation among Stuart's staff was that life would return to what passed for normal, but that expectation lasted less than a day. Robert E. Lee arrived at Culpeper and expressed willingness, or desire, to participate in yet another grand review.

The grand review on the 8th differed from that of the 5th. There was no ball, no invited guests, no ladies to strew flower petals in Stuart's path. It was, as Blackford said, "a business affair, with only soldiers on hand to observe." There was no mock artillery bombardment, and particularly different was the presence of several thousand infantrymen from Hood's Division.

The Army's infantry was moving steadily toward Culpeper and was strung out from that place back to Fredericksburg on the 8th. Two divisions of Longstreet's First Corps and three divisions of Ewell's Second Corps had arrived and gone into camp, while Hill's Third Corps was still manning the works at Fredericksburg and other divisions were in between. Hood's division, of Longstreet's Corps, was camped closest to Brandy Station. It consisted of four brigades, including the regiments of Texans who comprised most of Hood's former brigade. Predictably, their purpose in attending the grand review was not merely to watch the show.

The agenda for the review was the same as before. First the division marched by, then trotted, and then charged with sabers drawn and the Rebel Yell echoing off the hills. As they thundered by, hats and caps flew off by the dozens, perhaps hundreds. It had happened at the previous reviews also, but in those the spectators were either fellow cavalrymen or dignified guests. This time the charging cavalrymen had hardly passed by before a swarm of Hood's men dashed out and retrieved—stole—every piece of headgear on the field.[9]

The five brigades that participated in the review were camped long distances apart in order for their horses to have plenty of grazing area. Hampton was southeast, between Brandy Station and Stevensburg. Robertson's two North Carolina regiments were at Bott's farm, where the review was staged. Rooney Lee's five regiments were at Welford's Ford on the Hazel River, about three miles from the Rappahannock. Fitz Lee's brigade, commanded temporarily by Colonel Munford because Lee was suffering from rheumatism, was across the Hazel River, near Oak Shade Church, seven to eight miles from Fleetwood. Only Jones' brigade was on the Rappahannock, strung out from Beverly Ford and back from the river for two miles to St. James Church. Company A of the 6th Virginia, of Jones' Brigade, was picketing Beverly Ford, and a picket from one of Beverly Robertson's regiments was at Kelly's Ford.[10] Stuart headquartered at Fleetwood, but all but two of his tents were struck and loaded on wagons in anticipation of moving camp on June 9.

The Union cavalry movement that became the Battle of Brandy Station began officially on June 7. The Federals knew that Stuart, whom they believed commanded from twelve to fifteen thousand troopers, was near Culpeper. They believed his presence there was for the purpose of launching a huge cavalry raid into Maryland that an intelligence report to Hooker characterized as "the most important expedition ever attempted in this country." However, they were uncertain of the location of the rest of Lee's army. They knew he'd begun moving out of his lines at Fredericksburg, but Stuart had been successful in keeping them from learning of their destination. Accordingly, Hooker ordered General Pleasanton to take the entire Federal cavalry corps, 8,000 men, plus two brigades of infantry, 3,000 men, and four batteries of artillery to "disperse and destroy the rebel force assembled in the vicinity of Culpeper." A secondary goal was to learn all they could about the location of Lee's infantry.[11]

The huge force of Union cavalry moved toward the fords on the Rappahannock and arrived on the 8th at Beverly's and Kelly's Ford, which were eight miles apart. The Federal horsemen were no longer the ineffectual force they had been a year previously. One of the things Hooker accomplished during his command of the Army of the Potomac was to reorganize the cavalry into its own corps and give them what one officer described as "a new life." The corps was commanded by Alfred Pleasonton, and for the first time in the war it went into action as a separate, well-organized body instead of a scattering of regiments and brigades attached to different infantry units.

They attacked before dawn on June 9 at Beverly's Ford.

The moment Stuart became aware of their presence afterward became an issue of great debate. As already described, Von Borcke claimed the enemy's presence was known on the 8th, but if so it suggests that Stuart was careless in leaving only one brigade near the river. Scheibert wrote that a courier arrived at Stuart's headquarters at 3:30 a.m. Other accounts say the first word Stuart had of the enemy's presence was the sound of gunfire from the direction of Jones' brigade. No matter how one dissects it, Jeb Stuart was taken by surprise.

Von Borcke wrote, "I was awakened about day-break by the sound of several cannon-shots. In an instant I was on my legs, and stepping out of my tent I distinctly heard a brisk firing of small-arms in the direction of the river. An orderly shortly afterwards rode up, reporting that the enemy, under cover of the fog had suddenly fallen upon our pickets, had crossed the river in strong force at several points . . ." Scheibert, in the same tent, remembered it differently, writing that a courier rushed in about 3:30 a.m. shouting about Yankees and that it was necessary to forcefully pull Von Borcke out of bed. Blackford wrote that the camp was awakened by the sound of gunfire and that a courier from Jones arrived "presently."[12] Frank Robertson recalled that as soon as firing was heard from the direction of the river that Captain Will Farley threw his hat into the air and shouted, "Hurrah, we are going to have a fight!" It would be Farley's last.

There was a blanket of fog over the countryside, and Stuart was eight miles from the Rappahannock with his division scattered in three directions, miles apart. Jones was heavily engaged and all alone. Scheibert painted a picture of instant, efficient response, with couriers flying in all directions, all brigades present within an hour, and Stuart firmly in charge. Von Borcke was not as generous, reporting that he and Stuart could not agree on the best course of action, with Jeb ready to attack the enemy with his entire division while Von argued to place the artillery and most of the cavalry on Fleetwood Heights and draw the enemy into an attack. Blackford wrote that Jones stopped the enemy's attempted crossing, that the enemy fell back to await the rest of the cavalry to arrive, and that "everything remaining quiet, Stuart accompanied by his staff rode down to the scene of action about the middle of the day."

That three accounts of what happened at Stuart's headquarters in the early hours of June 9, all written by men who were there, are so wide-ranging they might be an example of what witnesses to the same car wreck see, and may also be symptomatic of what three admirers of Stuart hoped the world would conclude. The Battle of Brandy Station is remembered today as the greatest cavalry battle ever to occur on American soil. It is remembered as a Confederate victory—another Jeb Stuart victory—in a long line of similar successes. It is remembered as the battle in which the Union cavalry proved its mettle, essentially for the first time, and as foreshadowing what would follow at Gettysburg and in 1864.

The Battle of Brandy Station was all those things, but it was something entirely different as well. Jeb Stuart was far from perfect. He'd made plenty of errors on various battlefields, but he was the type of military leader, like Custer and a few others, about whom most people could not be ambivalent. Those who knew him, or believed they did, usually either adored or despised him, and those who despised him wanted to see him "get his comupin's." Brandy Station became their greatest opportunity to date for that to happen. That, in turn, made Stuart desperate to redeem his reputation, only to accomplish the exact opposite by being absent when he was most needed, prior to Gettysburg.

The chain of events of the battle was that the 8th New York Cavalry, commanded by Colonel Benjamin "Grimes" Davis, of Brig. General John Buford's brigade, crossed at Beverly's Ford before dawn at a time reported by witnesses ranging from 3 a.m. to 5 a.m.[13] Company A of the 6th Virginia, commanded by Captain Bruce Gibson, opened fire and fell back. Jones was summoned and soon the rest of the 6th Virginia plus the 7th Virginia were on the way to the ford.

Chew's Battery of the Horse Artillery was parked in a vulnerable position and was ordered to withdraw toward St. James Church and go into battery. Jones then summoned the 11th Virginia, under Colonel L.L. Lomax, the 12th Virginia, under Colonel Asher Harmon, and the 35th Virginia Battalion, under Lt. Colonel "Lige" White, to protect the guns. Major Beckham placed a single gun from Hart's South Carolina Battery in the middle of the road along which the Federals were advancing and fired canister, delaying them long enough for the Confederates to better organize. There followed a series of attacks and withdrawals by the Rebels, accompanied by Beckham's artillery firing from high ground near St. James Church, that brought the Federal offensive to a halt. The opposing troopers went at each other saber to saber in "real cavalry style," as a trooper of the 12th Virginia recalled.

In the meantime, Stuart's other brigades were responding and riding either toward Fleetwood or Beverly's Ford. Rooney Lee's and Munford's brigades came to Jones' aid and drove the Federals back toward Beverly's Ford. Stuart made Fleetwood his command post and remained there, dispatching and receiving reports, until riding to Beverly's Ford about 11 a.m.

However, the Federals did not limit their assault to a single ford. The plan had been to attack in two columns at both Beverly's and Kelly's Fords. The attack at Beverly's Ford came first, but the column at Kelly's Ford, under the command of Brig. Gen. David Gregg, was soon across, encountering only a token resistance from Robertson's pickets. Stuart dispatched the rest of Robertson's two regiments toward Kelly's Ford, but Gregg, with two brigades, was intent on flanking Stuart at Fleetwood.

For some reason, Robertson did little to stop them. He saw them and realized what they were doing—heading for Stuart's flank and command post. He even sent a courier with a report that he'd seen them, although it isn't clear where the courier went. Instead of either attacking or trying to get in front of Gregg, however, Robertson chose to let him alone and, instead, to send out skirmishers to oppose Federal infantry that were coming down the road behind Gregg. He would later report, "Had I pursued the flanking party, the road I was ordered to defend would have been left utterly exposed. I acted according to orders and the dictates of judgment." In other words, had he pursued the horses, the inside of the barn would have been utterly exposed by the open door through which the horses had just escaped.

Stuart had left Major McClellan in charge at Fleetwood, but there were very few troops there. Suspecting an attack from Kelly's Ford, he sent Lt. Robert Goldsborough, the new member of the staff, with an order to Colonel Wickham of the 4th Virginia to move toward the ford in support of Robertson. Goldsborough never made it. He rode headlong into Gregg's advancing Federals and was captured. He spent the next twenty months, until March 1865, in various prison camps, then was released in time to participate in the retreat from Petersburg and the Battle of Sayler's Creek, at which he was killed on April 6, 1865.

Grumble Jones learned of Gregg's flanking movement and sent a courier to Stuart to warn him, but Jeb sent a message back that Jones should "tend to the Yankees in his front and I'll watch the flanks." Jones read the message and said, "So he thinks they ain't coming, does he? Well let him alone. He'll damned soon see for himself."

Major McClellan, at the command post, also received and scoffed at a report that Federals were coming from the direction of Kelly's Ford. He knew Robertson was between Fleetwood and the ford and that he would have at least reported, if not stopped, any Federal advance from that direction. Nevertheless he sent a courier to reconnoiter. Within moments the man came galloping back to say the enemy would be at Fleetwood in five minutes. The blue horsemen hove into view about 1 p.m.

Stuart had now been taken by surprise a second time, and in neither case had he been at the scene of critical action when it occurred. The only Confederates occupying Fleetwood Hill were McClellan, a handful of couriers, and one six-pounder howitzer from Chew's battery, under the command of Lt. John W. Carter, which had exhausted its ammunition in the morning's fight and retired. It was sitting idle at the foot of the hill. The only shells Carter had for his gun were a handful of solid shot and a few projectiles believed to be defective.

McClellan sent couriers to find Stuart, and Carter brought his gun to the crest of the hill and began firing his precious rounds at the approaching Federals. The first courier who found Stuart was met with incredulity. Jeb heard him out and turned to Captain James Hart, who commanded one of Beckham's batteries, and told him to "ride back there and see what all that foolishness is about." Almost at the same instant, a second of McClellan's couriers, Private Frank Dean, arrived with the same message and, hearing the sound of Carter's single gun banging away, Stuart decided the reports were true. He sent Frank Robertson to find Wade Hampton and direct his brigade toward Fleetwood, sent other couriers pounding in other directions, and then rode hard for his command post.

The nearest Confederate cavalry—Harmon's 12th Virginia and Lige White's Comanches—were a mile and a half from Fleetwood. Both were summoned immediately and they rode to the sound of Carter's gun. Incredibly, when Carter began shelling the Federals, they stopped for a few moments to determine what they were facing, and then resumed their advance at a cautious pace. Also incredibly, the 12th Virginia did not realize the seriousness of the situation and was approaching from the other direction at a trot. McClellan saw them coming, rode to meet them and ordered them to charge at a gallop. The lead elements of the 12th Virginia arrived at Fleetwood just as Carter was withdrawing his cannon after firing his last shell. The enemy, a brigade commanded by Colonel Percy Windham, was only fifty yards away.

Harmon and a handful of troopers pounded pell-mell into the leading units of Windham's brigade, the 1st New Jersey Cavalry, which was also charging. White's 35th Battalion was close behind the 12th Virginia, and they threw themselves into the fight, but the combination of a rush to the scene and violent collision of the opposing forces splintered the Rebels. White's battalion was split into two parts and mixed with Harmon's 12th, after which both units were driven back in total disorder. Harmon engaged an officer of the 1st New Jersey in a saber duel and was severely wounded. The Federals brought up three artillery pieces of the 6th New York Battery to the foot of the hill and prepared to open fire.

White reformed the half of his battalion that had stayed with him, galloped around the west side of the hill and charged the three guns. Federal cavalry supporting the artillery was driven back but the gunners remained and fought hand to hand. Many of the battery's horses were killed and the thirty-six gunners employed every weapon available, including rammers, sponges and worm screws. Within minutes thirty of the thirty-six were dead or wounded.

White held the guns for mere minutes. The Federals counterattacked and drove him back. Other Confederate units were arriving, Hampton

bringing four regiments in column of squadrons at a gallop. Jones was
bringing the 11th Virginia. A series of charges and counter-charges, as
glorious and sweeping, as chaotic and confusing as any ever made, swirled
around Fleetwood Hill. The 1st New Jersey made six full regimental
charges and numerous smaller ones. On other parts of the field microcos-
mic battles within the larger battle raged. A division of Federal horsemen
commanded by Brig. Gen. Alfred Duffie was attacked by 500 Rebels of the
2nd South Carolina and the 4th Virginia, resulting in the capture of half
of the 4th. One of the attacks by the 1st New Jersey was on two batteries
of the Horse Artillery, McGregor's and Hart's, while they were unsupported
by cavalry. Rebel artillerymen, like those of the 6th New York, fought
enemy cavalry with pistols, sponge staffs, and handspikes.

The day's fighting was also filled with a myriad of individual adventures and tragedies. Von Borcke was in the center of things, alternately rallying disorganized units to meet the enemy and being chased at full speed
by them. At one point, while galloping to deliver an order of Stuart's, Von's
horse fell with him and nearly broke one of his legs.

Blackford was sent on various missions to deliver orders and reports,
writing that as he galloped about he emptied his revolver twice at close range
but was never able to learn what effect his shots had as he couldn't stop to
find out. He added that pistol practice at a gallop was a favorite amusement
of the staff, that it was surprising how accurate one can shoot that way and
that he "seldom failed to hit a hat at that distance and in that manner."

In one of the dozens of back and forth charges and retreats, a regiment
of Federals was in flight when its bugler rode his horse over what he
believed to be only a large wooden plank on the ground. It was the covering
of a subterranean icehouse. The wood gave way beneath the weight and
sent man and mount straight down. The horse was killed instantly, but the
bugler survived and was pulled from the hole by a rope, to the amusement
of bystanders.

Captain Benjamin White was shot in the neck and, supported in the
saddle by Von Borcke, was chased and nearly captured. Frank Robertson,
like all members of the staff, was sent with orders and messages, sometimes
alone, sometimes with Chiswell Dabney, and sometimes with Von Borcke,
nearly getting shot or captured several times. He was handicapped by
having a horse, Bostonia, who refused to turn once she began running. This
worked to his advantage once, when a Federal sergeant gave chase and
could neither catch nor hit him with pistol shots; but it was a serious prob-

lem when he attempted to deliver a message. Only by grasping the left rein in his hand and hauling hard in that direction while simultaneously stretching his left foot as far back as possible and spurring furiously was he able to bring the mare around in a huge wheeling maneuver. In doing so he often sent other men and officers scattering to avoid being trampled,

Wade Hampton's brother, Lt. Col. Frank Hampton, was mortally wounded, and Colonel Butler of the 2nd South Carolina, as mentioned previously, lost a foot. It was the manner in which Butler was wounded, however, that was particularly tragic for Stuart. Captain Will Farley and Butler were sitting side by side on their horses, facing opposite directions, when an enemy artillery shell passed through both of the men and their mounts. Butler lost a foot but Farley's leg was torn off above the knee.

Several men came to the aid of the fallen officers, and both Farley and Butler directed them to tend to the other first. Farley was placed in an old, flat horse trough lying nearby. He was in great pain but was smiling and composed. As they were about to carry him away, he called to an officer named John T. Rhett. Pointing to the leg that had been torn off, Farley asked that it be brought to him. When Rhett did so, Farley hugged it to his chest and said, "It is an old friend, gentlemen, and I do not wish to part with it." As is the case with so many events associated with the war that seem small, unimportant, or odd today, the credit for who actually picked up and delivered the leg was claimed by at least two persons—Rhett and Capt. James Louis Clark, another of Stuart's aide-de-camps. Clark made several other post-war claims that push the limits of credibility, so Rhett probably has the better credentials for the incident. In any event, Farley then clasped hands with Rhett and a Capt. Chesnutt, and said, "Goodbye gentlemen, and forever. I know my condition and we will not meet again. I thank you for your kindness. It is a pleasure to me that I have fallen into the hands of good Carolinians at my last moment."

He was carried from the field to an ambulance. A Captain Blocker, a friend of Farley's, stayed with him and, at his request rode to a Dr. Jones and asked if Farley could be brought to his house. Jones told him certainly, and Farley was carried in from the ambulance to be laid on a mattress in the parlor. As he was lowered to it, Farley said, "Hold on Blocker, let your arm stay under my head." Blocker did so and Farley closed his eyes for several seconds, then opened them, looked around the room and demanded, in a clear, distinct voice, "To your post, men! To your post!" Those were his last words. He lived only a few moments longer.

Like most of Stuart's staff, Farley had obtained a new uniform for the grand reviews, and he left his coat with a girl in Culpeper with the directions, "If anything happens to me, wrap me in this and send me to my mother." When John Esten Cooke saw Farley's body in Culpeper that night, he was wearing the new coat.

Eventually, a little past 2 p.m., the Federals began to withdraw. They did so in large part because Confederate infantry, Robert Rodes' division, was seen moving toward the battlefield. General Lee was riding at the head of the division.

Pleasonton did not accomplish the mission of dispersing or destroying the Rebels around Culpeper, but he obtained reliable information that a significant part of Lee's infantry was there in addition to the cavalry. He also showed the Southerners that his cavalry were a force to be reckoned with, and that Jeb Stuart was not the military genius he'd been made out to be. Casualties for the day were 866 for the Federals and 523 for the Confederates.[14]

Returning together to Fleetwood after the enemy withdrew, Robertson and Blackford came upon a handsome sorrel horse standing on three legs, the fourth having been torn off at the knee. Intending to put the animal out of its misery, Robertson approached to within eight feet of the animal, aimed his pistol at its forehead and fired. Instead of falling, the sorrel bolted forward and knocked Robertson's horse to the ground, injuring Robertson's leg and covering him with blood from the death wound he'd inflicted on the animal. At camp everyone thought he was severely wounded when they saw the blood and his limp.

Except for desultory exchanges of cannon fire, the battle was over. Stuart wanted to have his headquarters tent and those of his staff pitched in the same spot they had been that morning, principally as a matter of pride. He wanted it to be remembered that he held the field and was not driven from any part of it. There were so many dead men and horses lying about, however, there was no room to pitch tents. Bluebottle flies were swarming around the bodies and puddles of congealed blood, so Stuart reluctantly ordered his camp moved about a mile away, further from the river, to an oak grove on a farm belonging to a man named Bradford. Following a recent pattern, the new headquarters was named "Camp Farley." After Camps Pelham and Price, it must have occurred to some of Jeb's remaining staff that having a camp named in one's honor was not a particularly appealing prospect.

Criticism of Stuart's performance began almost immediately after the battle. On the 10th a lady in Culpeper—definitely not one of those who had spread flower petals in Stuart's path—felt so disgusted that she wrote a letter of complaint to the man at the top. It follows, with its original spelling:

> Culpeper Co.
>
> President Davis
>
> I have assumed a privilege which in no doubt will seem strange to you but I have deliberately premeditated over the matter & the true love I have for the Confederacy have dared to address our, President, allow a Lady who deeply wishes our Confederacy success to say if General Stuart is allowed to remain our Commanding General of Calvay we are lost people, I have been eye witness to the manuevering of General Stuart since he is been in Culpeper & do know the whole of our unsuccess is his fault, General S loves the admiration of his class of Lady friends, too much to be a Commanding General he loves to have his repeated reviews immediately under the Yankees eye too much for the benefit & pleasure of his Lady friends for the interest of the Confederacy & Citizens who deeply suffer for his pleasure, I have also been eye witness to General Hampton during his winter campaign in Culpeper & plainly say he is the General he knows his place as a Gentleman & Officer does not devote his Military life seeking the admiration of Ladys as General S does but for General H yesterdy in the fight we know would have been surrounded by hords of those miserable creatures Yankees, Oh, what a life to endure then to see our Commanding General in fault, disgrace. President allow a true Southern Lady to say General S conduct since in Culpeper has been perfectly ridiculous having repeated reviews for the benefit of his lady friends he riding up & down the line thronged with those ladys, he decorated with flowers apparently a monkey show on hand & he the monkey in fact General S is nothing more or less than one of those fixed up fops devoting his whole time in his Lady friends company, President, I shall send a copy of this to our Chief Commander General Lee as I feel confident you or him are not posted with General S conduct hopeing a change may take place & more success may attend our army is my sincere pray to God.
>
> Respectfully, A Southern Lady

PS:
President Davis allow a true friend to the Confederacy to make a few more remarks upon the great destroyer of the Confederacy "Ardent Spirits" if something is not done to stop the distillers in Culpeper Madison Green & Rappahanoc God only knows the consequence it is not only destroyeing the army but starving the citizens you can scarsely go to a farm house beyond Culpeper Ct House but they have a distill making Ardent Spirits bringing to Culpeper Ct Hou & you can scarsely find a house in the Town but they are selling it out to the Army Ladys actuly keeping jug under their beds selling out to the soldiers this thing must be stoped ever to have success in our army Officers & privates more than half their time drunk & when the enemy comes they are unprepared. I am a citizen of Culpeper Co have made it my business to watch the manuevering of our army & do plainly see the fault rest in our Officers for want of discipliam in their selfs & army.

Stuart would not see the letter for another couple of weeks, and when he did it is unlikely he found any humor in it. It is probable, in fact, that it added another log to a raging internal fire kindled by criticism from newspapers and the army. That criticism was scathing, and speaks for itself:

There is little doubt, from all accounts, that our cavalry, resting secure in believing there was no danger with so much infantry surrounding them, allows the enemy to surprise them everywhere.... The whole affair was, to say the least, very discreditable to somebody.—*The Savannah Republican*

If General Stuart is to be the eyes and ears of the army, we advise him to see more and be seen less. . . . Gen. Stuart has suffered no little in public estimation by the later enterprises of the enemy. —*Richmond Enquirer*

Vigilance, vigilance, more vigilance is the lesson taught us by the Brandy surprise, and which must not be forgotten by the victory which was wrested from defeat. Let all learn it, from the Major General down to the picket.—*Richmond Sentinel*

The more the circumstances of the late affair at Brandy Station are considered, the less pleasant do they appear. If this was an isolated case, it might be excused under the convenient head of accident or chance. But the puffed up cavalry of the Army of Northern Virginia has been twice, if not three times, surprised since the battles of December, and such repeated accidents can be regarded as nothing but the necessary consequences of bad management. If the war was a tournament, invented and supported for the pleasure of a few vain and weak-headed officers, these disasters might be dismissed with compassion. But the country pays dearly for the blunders which encourage the enemy to overrun and devastate the land, with a cavalry which is daily learning to despise the mounted troops of the Confederacy. The surprise on this occasion was the most complete that has occurred. The Confederate cavalry was carelessly strewn over the country . . . .—*Richmond Examiner*

The *Charleston Mercury* called the battle an "ugly surprise." The *Richmond Dispatch* claimed the Federals were shelling Stuart's headquarters before he figured out they were crossing the Rappahannock and that Stuart and his staff were "rollicking, frolicking, and running after girls." Various officers, from Longstreet to McLaws, as well as individual enlisted men, wrote home that Stuart was surprised, that only desperate fighting saved the day, that Stuart was "whipped," that he was "caught napping," that he was paying more attention to the ladies than to his business as a soldier, and that "Stuart had best stop his reviews and look to his laurels." The chief of the Bureau of War, Robert H.G. Kean, wrote in his diary that "Stuart is so conceited he got careless." One of Longstreet's staff, Charles Blackford, wrote that "Stuart was certainly surprised," "the fight . . . can hardly be called a victory," and "Stuart is blamed very much."[15]

The morning of June 10th, Stuart and his staff rode over the battlefield. Hundreds of turkey buzzards were already at work on the dead bodies. In the area that had been occupied by Stuart's headquarters, Von counted thirty dead horses. Blackford noted that most of the dead men in that same area bore saber wounds—"cuts or thrusts"—whereas bullet wounds were more common on other parts of the battlefield.

Pleasonton sent a message to Stuart on the 10th requesting permission to bury the Federal dead and tend to the wounded still within Stuart's lines. Jeb replied that he had already attended to both tasks. For the next few days, through the 15th, Stuart and his men not only buried dead, but burned horse carcasses, prepared for the upcoming campaign—an invasion of Maryland and Pennsylvania—and kept a wary eye out for another attack. On the 13th there was a false alarm that put most of the cavalry division in the saddle, but no Federals appeared.

Jeb wrote a disjointed letter to Flora on the 12th to tell her of the recent battle, proclaiming that it would be called "Battle of Fleetwood Heights." He reported mournfully the death of Farley, the capture of Goldsbourough, the death of Lt. Colonel Hampton and of Colonel Sol Williams, commander of the 2nd North Carolina Cavalry. Williams was one of the ten officers in the hotel room the night of March 16, about whom Harry Gilmor had written that seven were marked for tragedy. He also praised Rooney Lee, who was wounded, as well as Colonel Pierce Young of Cobb's Legion.

Many of Jeb's letters were written in a rather stream-of-consciousness manner, with sudden changes of subject in mid-paragraph. This may have been because he was frequently interrupted as he was writing, and then simply started a new subject when he returned, but it may also have been a reflection of a restless mind, a short attention span, or that something was eating at him. In this particular letter, Jeb changed subjects suddenly three times, and each time to return to the same subject—the "lies" in the newspapers about the recent battle.

The *Richmond Examiner* of June 12 was the most upsetting to him. It may have been the only one he'd seen so far as it is the only one he identified by name, but his first comment on the subject, was "The papers are in great error, as usual, about the whole transaction." He stated emphatically that he had not been surprised, and that "The enemy's movement was known and he was defeated." Then, after writing more about the battle, of Lee's review of the cavalry on the 8th, and commenting that Rosser's regiment was absent, he suddenly switched subjects and declared, "The Richmond Examiner of the 12th lies from the beginning to end. I lost no paper—no nothing—except the casualties of battle. I understand the spirit and object of the detraction and can, I believe, trace the source. I will, of course, take no notice of such base falsehood."

His refusal to take notice lasted for five more sentences in the letter before he returned to the subject. "I lost nothing whatever," he wrote, "The Examiner to the contrary notwithstanding. I believe it all originates in the Salt question. You must be careful now what you say."

The "salt question" was whether Stuart's brother's salt works, located at appropriately named Saltville, Virginia, should be turned over to the government. Like nearly everything in the Confederacy, salt was in short supply. It was particularly vital for preserving meat for the army, and the Stuart family had been caught up in a political debate. Many believed the saltworks were too valuable to be in private hands, and that they should be nationalized, either voluntarily or otherwise. Considering that the saltworks were the principal source of income for the Stuart family, they did not see it that way. Jeb was convinced he performed perfectly well on June 9 and was above criticism. Because there was criticism—a lot of it—it must have its roots in evil political forces.

On June 13, Stuart wrote his report on the battle to General Lee. It was two and half times as long as his report on Chancellorsville, and did not contain as much flowery prose as many of his reports. Lee's response, on June 16, was, "The dispositions made by you to meet the strong attack of the enemy appear to have been judicious and well planned. The troops were well and skillfully managed, and, with few exceptions, conducted themselves with marked gallantry."

While the cavalry remained in camp, Lee's infantry continued moving northward, although it had not yet commenced an invasion. Ewell's Corps was headed for Winchester, and one of the pickets who had been on duty at Beverly's Ford the morning of June 9, Private Luther Hopkins, saw something moving with Ewell's men he'd not seen before. A long line of wagons, each pulled by six horses, were carrying something large covered tightly with white canvas. Everyone's curiosity was aroused, and eventually someone was able to get a peek beneath the covering—pontoons. The Army of Northern Virginia was planning to do some serious river-crossing somewhere. Rumors were that it might be Ohio. Longstreet had let it be known that that is where the army ought to be going, via Tennessee and Kentucky.[16]

Stuart wrote a letter to his brother, William Alexander, about this time, although the exact date is uncertain. In it he wrote, "I am standing on the Rappahannock, looking beyond, and feel not unlike a tiger pausing before its spring. . . . that spring will not be delayed much longer . . . I ask now, my dear brother, and best friend, that you will pray for me in the coming struggle."[17]

Stuart knew the Confederate army was about to invade the North in a campaign he hoped and believed would bring the war to an end with a victory for the South. Yet one suspects his particular need for more action was not tied directly to that campaign, nor was it driven by a tiger's need to spring and kill in order to survive. Jeb's need was the survival of his reputation, his pride, and his personal glory. He had tasted it, then feasted and drank deeply of public acclaim the previous year, but it had taken a toll. The deaths of little Flora, Burke, Pelham, Price, Jackson, Farley, and others carried more grief than most men know in a lifetime, and he had gathered it all in less than eight months. That much sorrow, even for a man as emotionally solid as Stuart, required a great deal of stamina to endure.

Stuart's faith in God was certainly the foundation of such stamina, but he needed more. He needed to be as beloved in the eyes of his nation as he was following the first ride around McClellan. He needed more flower petal strewing-adoration, more worshipful gazes, more ecstasy-inspiring words of love. He'd become addicted to it. Instead, in just five weeks, he'd been passed over for promotion, refused permission to reorganize his command, and most recently, been defamed and libeled in at least a dozen newspapers. He was suffering from serious withdrawal. He was in need of either complete rehabilitation or a massive fix of emotional opiate. He needed to spring back into the limelight, and was determined to do so.

At 8:30 a.m. on Tuesday, June 16, 1863, bugles blew to call three brigades of Stuart's cavalry division to mount and fall into formation. Leaving Hampton and Jones behind to wait for A.P. Hill's corps, now moving up from Fredericksburg, they rode to the Rappahannock, crossed, and stopped for lunch at Orleans, where Stuart and his staff visited a "Mrs. M." before continuing toward Rector's Crossroads. Fitz Lee's brigade, commanded by Munford, was in the lead. Rooney Lee's brigade came next, commanded by Colonel John Chambliss due to Rooney having been severely wounded at Fleetwood. Robertson brought up the rear.

Stuart's orders were to secure the gaps in the Blue Ridge Mountains and screen the movement of Longstreet's corps, which was marching north by way of the Blue Ridge. Ewell, who led, had arrived at Winchester on June 13 and fought a battle with the Federals, driving them out of the town and taking nearly 4,000 prisoners. His men—the spearhead of Lee's invasion—were now approaching the Potomac, while Hill, the tail, was a hundred miles behind.[18]

By evening, the three cavalry brigades had covered nearly forty miles, and were about to go into bivouac when Stuart and his staff, at the head of the column, saw a handsomely dressed man riding toward them across a field. He jumped a fence gracefully and approached. Blackford could scarcely believe his eyes. It was John Mosby, but not the same Mosby Blackford remembered. Stuart and other staff members had seen him within the last year, but Blackford had not. The Mosby he had known, first as a fellow private in the same company, then as a regimental adjutant and finally as a scout, had been unkempt, with little concern for his appearance, and scorn for military protocol. The John Mosby that rode up that June evening was every bit as dashing in appearance as Stuart.

He had, in that year, become famous, particularly after the capture of Gen. Stoughton, and he was a welcome guest in camp that evening at Rector's Crossroads. He also brought information. The Federal cavalry was no longer near Culpeper. It was moving rapidly on a line parallel to Stuart's and was already in adjacent Loudon County, although principally only in small detachments.

Stuart's cavalry started again at dawn and rode to Upperville, where each of the three brigades were sent in different directions to cover mountain passes and stay ahead and to the right of Longstreet's corps. Munford was sent with his brigade east to occupy a gap in the Bull Run Mountains at Aldie. Chambliss, with Rooney Lee's brigade, was sent west toward Thoroughfare Gap. Stuart and his staff, with Beverley Robertson's brigade a few miles back, also rode east, toward Middleburg, which they reached about noon. Munford was six miles further ahead on the same road, gathering corn at a farm and within sight of Aldie.

Stuart and his staff stopped to rest. They had friends in Middleburg and the entire town was happy to see them. Saddles were pulled off and plans were to stay a couple of hours. Some of the friends had heard the news of Von Borcke's death, "but not its contradiction," and the big man "underwent another ovation at [his] quasi-resurrection." He felt obliged to drop in at the home of everyone he knew, and did so while the rest of the staff gathered in the yard of a burned house to eat what Frank Robertson called their "scanty mid-day ration."

Two couriers galloped in from different directions. A regiment of Federal cavalry had been seen moving toward town from the south at a trot, while Munford, to the east, had been attacked near Aldie.

Von Borcke was busy giving "bodily assurance of [his] presence in the world of the living, and relating adventures to a circle of pretty young ladies, [when] the streets suddenly resounded with the cry of 'The Yankees are coming!'" Stuart had been surprised yet again.

The regiment coming from the south was the 1st New Jersey Cavalry,

commanded by Colonel Alfred Duffie. The Federals attacking Munford
were four regiments commanded by Brig. Gen. Judson Kilpatrick. Pleasonton, the overall cavalry commander, had been ordered by Hooker to
obtain reliable information on where Lee's army was and what it was doing.
Gregg's division was in the lead for that purpose, and Kilpatrick's brigade
was at the head of the division. Duffie was dispatched by Gregg to bypass
Aldie on the south, ride to Middleburg, and wait there for the rest of
Gregg's division to catch up, spending the night if necessary.

Stuart and his staff hurriedly saddled up and rode hard toward Beverly
Robertson's brigade, approaching from the west, but after covering only
about half a mile, Jeb reined in and shouted for Frank Robertson. Robertson's horse, Miranda, was considered to be one of the fastest of any of his
staff. Stuart had just realized that the enemy regiment coming from the
south was going to cut Munford off from the rest of Stuart's division, and
he told Robertson to ride back through Middleburg, find Munford, and tell
him the enemy was behind him, to "press a guide," and join Stuart that
night by "roundabout roads" at Rector's Crossroads.

"Pressing a guide," had specific meaning. As Frank Robertson explained
after the war, it meant to find any man who is a native of an unknown area,
whether awake or asleep, and impress him into service as a guide by placing
a cavalryman with a drawn saber on either side of him, and having those
three men lead the column. The two cavalrymen's orders were to kill the
pressed guide "should he show any signs of treachery or guide us wrong."

"Look out for yourself," were Jeb's last words to Robertson, and "good-
bye Robertson," was "cheered" to him by his comrades as he rode away.
He was galloping toward a full regiment of the enemy and admitted that
the farewell "meant more than usual." The citizens of Middleburg were
all behind closed doors, except one young lady sitting on a porch, when
Robertson cantered through town—until he came to an intersection with
a road going north and south. Forty yards to his left that road was "full of
Yankees." As soon as they saw him they began shouting, cussing and shooting. Robertson spurred Miranda and gave the mare her head.

The Federals chased him for three miles, but only one, on a blaze-faced
sorrel, was as fast as Miranda. The sorrel got close but could not gain on
Miranda, and although the rider occasionally fired a shot at Robertson,
none hit him. Robertson rode full out until he came to a long hill. Halfway
up, knowing being above his pursuer gave him an advantage, he stopped,
wheeled, aimed and fired. The Federal became "loose in his saddle," but

Robertson did not "have time to go back and inquire after his health." He rode on until he found Munford.[19]

Munford was briskly engaged, and was driving the enemy back. The battle at Aldie had been a hot one, with numerous charges and counterattacks. Munford wrote later, "I do not hesitate to say that I have never seen as many Yankees killed in the same space of ground in any fight I have seen."[20] Another Confederate wrote, "I had never known the enemy's cavalry to fight so stubbornly or act so recklessly."[21] Nevertheless, Munford obediently disengaged and fell back. He'd lost 119 men, but had inflicted 305 on the Federals, 138 being prisoners. As directed, he "pressed a guide" and rejoined Stuart after dark.[22]

After the Battle of Aldie on the 17th, the following days through the 21st would see fierce clashes at be Middleburg and Upperville, although all the fights were close, sometimes overlapping, and sometimes given each other's names. Aldie also involved an incident unique in the history of Stuart's cavalry. At the beginning of the engagement, when Kilpatrick advanced and opened fire on Munford's pickets, Colonel Rosser's 5th Virginia led a saber charge through the town, driving Kilpatrick back. Rosser then placed a squadron of troopers—fifty men of Company I, under the command of Captain Reuben Boston—on a hill as dismounted sharpshooters, the men's horses being held in a ditch on the far side of the hill. A squadron of the 2nd New York Cavalry charged, dislodged the Confederates, and scattered their horses. Boston and his men fell back to another hill on a farm belonging to a family named Adams, but they were attacked by both the 2nd New York and the 6th Ohio on three sides. Boston was overwhelmed and forced to surrender, the first and last time any unit under Stuart did so.[23]

Stuart, meanwhile, met Robertson's brigade and returned to Middleburg, arriving outside town as the sun was going down. The Federals had barricaded the road, and after skirmishing for a while, Confederates led by Captain Woolridge of the 4th Virginia rushed the barricade and took it, followed by Robertson's brigade. Von Borcke, embarrassed by being chased out of the town earlier, made a point of being next to General Robertson when the Rebel horsemen galloped back. He was more gratified when they found the enemy directly outside the house he had fled, and was able to drive into and scatter them while the same young ladies watched from their windows.

Once Middleburg was again free of Yankees, Stuart established his headquarters two miles out town, at the Rector plantation, on a hill and at a crossroads. Then he and Von Borcke resumed their socializing in town, even though many of the young ladies were by then busy tending the wounded from the day's fighting. It was late when they returned to camp.[24]

Fighting resumed the morning of June 18. Chambliss discovered that most of Duffie's 1st Rhode Island, after being driven out of Middleburg, were surrounded by Rebel units so that they spent the night hiding in the woods. He took 140 prisoners and drove away the rest of the regiment. Pleasonton sent Gregg's division toward Middleburg to support Duffie, but there was little left to support and he fell back toward Aldie. Munford fought him near there, capturing another sixty men, including a colonel.

The day became exceptionally hot, with temperatures above a hundred, and Stuart spent the day in Middleburg. One of Mosby's men brought in enemy dispatches captured from one of Hooker's staff, which were immediately forwarded to General Lee. Von Borcke was given the responsibility of overseeing the transfer of the several hundred Federal prisoners to Upperville, from which they were sent to Winchester. It rained late in the day, cooling things off, but also came the sound of artillery. The Federals were advancing again on Middleburg.[25]

Stuart's goal, and orders, were not to beat the enemy but to keep the Federals from learning the location of Lee' army. Accordingly, he fell back that night toward Rector's Crossroads and Upperville, and was near that town at dawn on the 19th when the enemy opened fire with rifles and artillery.

Robertson's and Chambliss's brigades contested the enemy's advance, and Stuart established a command post on a hill about a half mile from the front that afforded a good view of the countryside. Major Beckham contested the enemy advance, and Stuart sent Von Borcke to direct the placement of a battery where it could deliver a crossfire with other batteries when the Federals approached. After doing so, Von Borcke rode to the edge of the Confederate left and did not like what he saw. The enemy was more numerous than he or Stuart had suspected, and were about to overrun the Confederates. He reported this to Stuart but Jeb was not alarmed. He believed he could hold his position, and was busy sending directions to Chambliss regarding the Federals advancing from Aldie. He sent Von Borcke back to have another look.

Once again Von came back to report that the enemy was about to overpower their left, and again Stuart argued. "You're mistaken for once, Von;

I shall be in Middleburg in less than an hour." Stuart was so confident, in fact, that he directed Von Borcke to write out a pass for a major in Longstreet's commissary[26] who wished to visit friends in Middleburg. Von Borcke did as he was told, and was telling the major that he was afraid he would not be able to make use of the pass, when firing on the left became significantly louder and Confederates began running from that direction, pursued by a large body of the enemy.

"Ride as quickly as you can, and rally those men," Stuart directed Von Borcke. "I will follow you immediately with all the troops I can gather." Von had the satisfaction of being proven correct, and just as he reached where the Confederate line had broken, the 9th Virginia charged up from its position in reserve, and the battery Von Borcke had helped place earlier opened fire. The Federals were driven back and the Confederate line was reformed. Stuart came riding up and was cheered by his men who, as Von recalled, "always felt relieved by his appearance in the moment of extreme danger."

Stuart directed that the regiments on the left withdraw by squadrons, which they did under the cover of artillery fire, until only Stuart and his staff were left. Von believed the enemy knew Stuart was there and that he was being specifically targeted. If so, then his admiration of Stuart worked to his disadvantage. He was dressed almost exactly like the general and both were mounted on good-looking chargers, with Von being a larger target than Jeb.

Bullets in abundance flew uncomfortably close. A minie ball hit Von Borcke's trousers and snipped off part of the gold lace stripe. Stuart was on Von's left and he told him, "General, those Yankees are giving it rather hotly to me on your account." Then another bullet took Von Borcke out of the war.

It hit him in the neck. He said it felt like someone had struck him with a fist. "Fiery sparks glittered before my eyes and a tremendous weight seemed to be dragging me from my horse." Blackford and Frank Robertson were there, and both heard the bullet hit. Blackford described the sound as that made when a barrel is struck a violent blow with a stick. He knew one of their party had been shot, and looked around at Stuart, but Jeb was "as firm as a rock in his saddle." Then he saw Von drop his bridle, become limp, and begin sliding sideways to his right. His mount, feeling the reins loosen, thought it meant he should move and bounded forward. Von clutched at the horse's mane but kept falling. As he fell, one spur caught on his blanket, which was rolled and tied behind the saddle. Blackford was on his left and spurred Magic alongside Von's horse, caught hold of his foot with both hands, pulled it clear of the blanket and threw it over the saddle. At the same time, Robertson jumped from his horse and caught Von, or at least broke his fall, so that he landed easily on the ground on his back.

Blackford dismounted and he and Robertson knelt beside the wounded man. The wound appeared to be mortal, and Blackford was afraid the best he could do for his friend was get his body off the field before it fell into the enemy's hands. Von had once told him that he had a horror of winding up in a nameless grave, and had asked Blackford that "if the occasion should ever arise, to mark the place so that his friends could find it." That became Blackford's goal.

The enemy's skirmishers were closing in. They had seen Von go down and believed they had a great prize within their grasp. Stuart had also seen Von's wound and feared the worst, but he had a battle to fight and a division to command. He left it to Robertson, Blackford, and some couriers to tend to this latest tragedy.

Bullets were hissing and splatting all around. Von's horse was rearing and plunging. Blackford did not know what to do, but then remembered something Von Borcke had told him that applied to this very situation. It was, in fact, something taught in Prussian cavalry schools. He directed one of the couriers to grab Von Borcke's horse's ear and twist it. Nobody likes having an ear twisted, but when it happens to horses it distracts their attention from whatever else is going on, so that the animal has no other thought than the status of its ear. Von's charger stopped lunging and stood calmly while Blackford and a courier endeavored to lift the huge man onto its back.

As they picked him up from the ground he was first completely limp, but once upright he came around, realized what had happened, and stiffened his legs enough to stand, then to get a foot in a stirrup and then, "with a mighty effort," be hoisted into the saddle. Von recalled it only slightly differently, saying he regained his senses while still on his back and saw men trying to raise him. He could not move his left arm and blood was pouring from his wound on the side of his neck and from his mouth. He could not speak, but claimed he motioned his companions to leave him and save themselves. If he really did so, and if he was understood, his request was ignored. Von Borcke also claimed the enemy was so close and the fire so heavy that two of the soldiers trying to assist him were killed. This, plus the sight of the enemy coming from nearby woods gave him the energy to mount his horse and, supported by Blackford and Robertson, ride slowly and painfully for almost a mile, until they found an ambulance.

As they were loading him into the ambulance, Robertson got a clear look at the wound, but didn't think it looked bad. "It's only a graze wound," he told Von Borcke, who managed to utter, "Oh I hurt to death," in response. When he did so, Robertson saw blood on his lips and realized that the bullet must have hit a lung.

The enemy was advancing and shells were bursting nearby. The ambulance driver, more concerned about his own safety than his passenger's, whom he figured was about dead, drove fast. The road was rocky, the ambulance was without springs, which caused Von so much pain that he crawled forward and shoved his pistol against the driver's head until he slowed down.

Dr. Talcott Eliason, Stuart's surgeon, overtook the ambulance and signaled for it to stop. He climbed inside and examined Von Borcke's wound. The ball had entered the lower part of his neck, cut through a portion of his windpipe, taken a downward course and, as Robertson had surmised, lodged in his right lung. Von Borcke watched the doctor's face and did not like what he saw. Eliason liked Von Borcke, but he had to be honest. "My dear fellow," he said, "your wound is mortal, and I can't expect you to live till the morning." He asked Von Borcke if there was any last wish he could fulfill, but what Von wanted was for Eliason to be wrong. He made up his mind to make it so.

Eliason lived in Upperville. Von had been his guest the previous October 30, when he established a bond with the doctor's blind ten-year-old daughter. Now Eliason directed that the wounded major be taken there to die.

A bed was prepared in the parlor and Mrs. Eliason and other women of the house tended to him while the little girl held his hand and cried. He was given opium, and soon his comrades began arriving. Von was unable to move. His face and neck were swollen and discolored, but he could hear what was being said. The question and answer were the same for each visitor— "Is he still alive?" and "Yes, but he will not live over the night."

Stuart came, bent down, kissed his forehead, and let two tears drop onto Von Borcke's cheek. "Poor fellow," he said, "your fate is a sad one, and it was for me that you received this mortal wound." Von wanted to grasp Stuart's hand and say what he felt for the general but he could not move or speak. Such words would be exchanged between the two less than a year later, but then it would be Stuart who was wounded and dying.

He slept that night, and did not die.[27]

On the battlefield, after Von Borcke's wounding, Stuart continued to fall back slowly, daring the Federals to attack in force. They did not do so, and the day ended with estimated casualties of ninety-nine on the Federal side and about forty on the Confederate.[28]

Stuart was reinforced the evening of the 19th by the arrival of Jones' brigade and in the morning by the arrival of Hampton, who had just fought a small battle near Warrenton. Mosby and his Rangers were doing what they did best, and had captured dispatches that alerted Hampton to the enemy's location. Stuart placed Hampton on the Upperville Pike and moved Chambliss to a position in front of Union. With his five brigades he was trying to cover three roads leading to three different mountain passes, beyond which was the Shenandoah and Lee's long, laboring columns of northward-bound infantry. There were artillery exchanges and skirmishing most of the day, which Von could hear from Dr. Eliason's. A courier kept him informed of events, which for the most part consisted of Stuart falling back toward Upperville. If the town fell into enemy hands, so would the big Prussian, and an ambulance was standing by to carry him to safety before that occurred.[29]

At about 8 a.m. on June 21, three Federal brigades commanded by John Buford advanced from Middleburg toward Union, attempting to turn Stuart's left flank. Gregg's division, plus a brigade of infantry under Strong Vincent, over 1,500 men, advanced toward Hampton and Robertson in front of Upperville. Gregg's movement was intended as a feint, and Buford was supposed to accomplish the real goal of turning and driving away the Rebel cavalry. When Buford ran into the brigades of Chambliss and Jones, however, he could go no further and Gregg's movement became the significant Federal offensive.

Stuart continued the strategy of the previous few days—stop the enemy but do not be drawn into a serious battle; fall back and take up another defensive position and let them come on again. He was thus delaying the enemy, denying him significant intelligence, and giving Lee's three corps time to move further toward or into enemy territory. At the same time, however, Jeb's troopers were discovering that the Federal cavalry was more of a force to be reckoned with than ever. As Blackford described, "The improvement in the cavalry of the enemy became painfully apparent. . . . It was mainly in their use of dismounted men, and in their horse artillery, however, for they could not stand before us yet in a charge on horseback." However, "They were much better provided with long-range carbines than our cavalry, which gave them an advantage dismounted. Their cavalry too had been largely recruited from the infantry and had seen service and been drilled as such, which of course was greatly to their advantage serving on foot, while our cavalry had served from the beginning in their branch of the service, and had been drilled mainly mounted."[30]

Shortly after noon on the 20th the sound of firing became louder and nearer to Dr. Eliason's home. Wounded men and stragglers began passing by in the street, and Von was helped into his uniform, so as to be ready to move if word came to do so. As Von waited, he was thrilled to see an unexpected visitor arrive—Captain Scheibert!

Since departing Stuart's headquarters immediately after Brandy Station, Scheibert had traveled with General Lee to Winchester. He met and spent time with Longstreet and fellow Europeans, Frank Lawley and Colonel Arthur Fremantle of Britain's Coldstream Guards. When he heard on the morning of the 20th that Von Borcke was wounded and might lie in the path of advancing Federals, he did not hesitate to go to his assistance.

He'd returned Old Black to Von Borcke, and was riding a borrowed white horse, which he saddled and rode toward Upperville. It was a long ride, through Berryville and Millwood, across the Shenandoah, through Paris and then to Upperville. He found Von weak and barely able to whisper. Blackford added, in describing the wound, that "The bullet passed through the collar of his jacket an inch or two from the spine and entered his throat, and for months he coughed up pieces of his clothing which had been carried in."[31]

Von wrote that Scheibert brought General Longstreet's personal ambulance with him, but Scheibert said that Stuart had an ambulance waiting. Either way, the time had come to get Von Borcke out of harm's way. The courier Von had been waiting for—Captain James Clark, claimant of being Farley's leg-retriever—arrived with word from Stuart that he was holding off the enemy at the last defensive position available before Upperville was overrun, and to get loaded and head for Paris immediately. Dr. Eliason advised against attempting to move him. He'd declared the wound mortal two days earlier and still believed that was the case. Scheibert and Von Borcke decided that they must disobey the doctor because they believed Von would be taken to Washington as a trophy and treated roughly. An alternative was to hide him in the woods, but the final decision was to split the baby, load him in the ambulance and head for Paris, but to hide him in the home of a friendly citizen if the opportunity presented itself.

Shells were bursting overhead as Scheibert, Captain Clark, Von's servant, Henry, and Dr. Eliason assisted Von Borcke into the ambulance. Then everyone climbed in or onto a horse and headed out of town in a scene reminiscent of Rhett and Scarlet fleeing Atlanta as the city burned. Scheibert wrote that Von Borcke winced at every little jolt.

The fighting came closer until the ambulance was between the two opposing forces. Enemy cavalry were in sight and riderless Federal horses came alongside the vehicle. Each time one came near enough, Scheibert, Henry, or another member of the party snagged its reins and lead it along, figuring they might need them as the equivalent of lifeboats. Soon they had four such horses in addition to Von Borcke's charger and the faithful, but obstinate mule, Kitt.

Von recalled that a decision was made to carry him to the home of a "Mr. B.," who lived about two miles out of town on a small road the enemy might not notice, whereas Scheibert said they found a hospitable house whose owner was unknown but who told them to leave Von Borcke and escape. Scheibert claimed Von first demanded then pleaded to be taken along, but they believed it would kill him, so they mounted their horses and ambulance and hurried away.

Typically, Von Borcke recalled it differently, saying that bullets were whizzing about while Henry led horses and Kitt, while Scheibert, riding behind, whacked the mule's rear with the flat of his saber as it kicked, plunged and generally making an ass of itself. According to his version, Mr. B. was waiting for them at the gate and was "very willing to receive me into his house," but that he urged the ambulance and escort to leave quickly. Von did not mention demanding or begging to be allowed to go with them—only that he saw them plunging into the woods as two black servants helped him into the house and to a bed on the ground floor.

He fell asleep, but was awakened half an hour later by a servant who said Yankees were outside. Von resolved to die fighting, and gathered his saber and a revolver onto the bed and waited, Jim Bowie-like, to shoot down the first enemy trooper who came through the door.

None came. Some Federals entered the house, but Mr. B. told them the Rebels had ridden into the woods, and he then lavished refreshments on them. After half an hour they rode away. The Federals told their host they were looking for a large Rebel, possibly Stuart, who'd been severely wounded and was possibly dead and buried in the vicinity. A Northern newspaper printed a similar story, saying, "The big Prussian rebel, who was Stuart's right arm, had been killed at last, and his body buried at Upperville."

Scheibert and the rest of the group that rode away into the woods became separated. Scheibert and Henry remained together, leading the extra horses and the mule, but when they rode into a green meadow, Henry could not bear to not let the horses and Kitt get a bite to eat. To Scheibert's amazement, he unbridled and let them start grazing.

Scheibert lost it. He thought he heard shouts of the enemy behind them, but his English was too poor to make Henry understand their situation. He shouted at the servant, then drew his saber and, as he'd done earlier with Kitt, struck Henry with the flat side until he retrieved the horses, mounted Kitt and made good their escape. Scheibert wrote that he could no longer consider Henry reliable after that incident, merely good but also dumb.[32] In all the various first-person accounts of the year of glory written by those present, this is one of only two recorded instances of Stuart's companions being physically abusive to a black man acting as a servant. The other was Von Borcke.

Scheibert, Henry, and the others arrived in Paris and found Stuart waiting anxiously for them and news of his friend. He was very upset and said, "I must dig him out again. He may still be lying there unobserved!" The other members of his staff agreed. They were ready to "dig out" the one they routinely called "our gallant von Borcke."[33]

It turned out to be the faithful Henry, with some direction from Scheibert, who dug him out. Scheibert sent Henry from Paris with all but one of Von's horses, plus Kitt and Scheibert's white horse, which was worn out.[34] He was the first rescuer Von Borcke saw the morning of June 21. According to Von, Henry was so anxious about Von's fate that he staked Kitt and the horses on the Shenandoah, crossed and worked his way on foot past Federal pickets to find Von Borcke. He stayed at his bedside all day, watching every breath the Prussian drew.

Late in the evening Dr. Eliason arrived, reported the Federal cavalry were retreating, and examined Von Borcke's wound. To his surprise it looked as though Von might recover, and he told him if he could last nine days from the day he was shot, he might get well.

On June 22, others arrived to see how he was doing, including Stuart, Wade Hampton, and Beverly Robertson. General Longstreet sent three surgeons, along with an apology for not coming himself, and declared he would have advanced an entire division to save him had it been necessary. The army was still moving north and soon it was gone, leaving Von Borcke with the memories of the greatest year in his life.

On June 23, with the enemy's cavalry no longer pressing him, and the bulk of Lee's infantry approaching or across the Potomac, Stuart turned his attention to his own route north.

Perhaps the sting of the criticism of his performance at Fleetwood Heights had faded by then. He wrote Flora that day, beginning with "Scarcely a moment to write. God has spared my life and blessed us with success thus far. The entire Cavalry and a large force of infantry making a forced reconnaissance day before yesterday." He'd already notified her of Von Borcke's wounding by telegram, and reported that the "noble fellow" was better. His next letter to her would be dated July 10, 1863, after much had happened.

Sometime about then he received the letter from the "Southern Lady" dated June 10, in which she declared Stuart a disgrace and predicted that if he was allowed to remain in command of the Confederate cavalry the citizens of the Confederacy were a "lost people." The letter had gone to President Davis, been passed around to everyone's amusement, and was given to Custis to send to Stuart. He did so with a wry smile and a prodding jibe—"Respectfully referred to Genl. J.E.B. Stuart with the Compliments of the President's Staff & the suggestion that he cease his attentions to the ladies or make them more general."

Jokes at his expense were something Jeb could not abide. Whether it was John Esten Cooke playfully telling Flora he'd shaved his beard or a trusted staff officer saying he prattled in a garrulous way, a barb against Stuart cut him deeply. One from an anonymous lady in a town where he thought all the ladies loved him, written to the President, no less, must have driven him as close to a ragged edge as he was capable of being. He could not allow such sentiments to go unanswered.

So it was, on the morning of June 24, 1863, that Jeb Stuart began what Blackford described as "an expedition which for audacious boldness equaled if it did not exceed any of our dashing leader's exploits."[35] That is not how history would remember it. Historians, Civil War students, novelists, poets, and lyricists would analyze, debate, defend, castigate, and try to explain Stuart's actions between June 24 and July 2, 1863. He almost certainly intended to salvage all of his lost glory during those few days, to rekindle the fires of adoration that had been ignited a year before when he made the first ride around McClellan. Perhaps he dwelled on the words of the newspapers from mid-June, and perhaps he fumed over the scathing letter from the unknown lady in Culpeper. Perhaps neither even crossed his mind. We can never know.

What we do know is that Jeb Stuart's year of greatest glory ended on June 24, 1863, and that what afterward began has forever linked his name less with glory than with a significant reason the South lost the war. He would win more victories and would occupy a position in the hearts of Southerners nearly equal to that of Stonewall Jackson and Robert E. Lee, but his reputation would forever bear a dark, lusterless stain.

With glory came tragedy that long year—little Flora, Burke, Pelham, Price, Jackson, Farley, and Von Borcke—the people and personalities who made the year so much of what it was for Jeb Stuart were gone from his life after June 23. He would see Von Borcke again, but not in a way either could have wished.

On June 24, 1863, however, Jeb Stuart did not dwell on what he had lost. He carried a burden of grief wherever he went, but it was overshadowed by his dauntless optimism, his great spirit, and his absolute faith in God. He still had battles to fight, songs to sing, and a war to win. It was only a year of glory in a lifetime of glory in the mind of James Ewell Brown Stuart that Wednesday, when the bugles blew, the gray troopers swung into their saddles, and Stuart turned them north toward what would become the road to Gettysburg.

EPILOGUE
And So the South Lost the War

I rid with ole Jeb Stuart and his band of Southern Horse
and there never were no Yankees what could meet us force to force.
No, they never could defeat us, but we never could evade
their dirty foreign politics and their cowardly blockade.

Now there ain't many left of us as rode out at the start,
and them that are are weary, weak of body, sad of heart,
but we fought a fight to tell about and I am here to say,
I'd climb my horse and follow Marse to hell come any day.
—Old Reconstructed

Von Borcke, Blackford, Chiswell Dabney, John Esten Cooke, Hagen, Mosby, Hullihen, Henry McClellan, Wade Hampton, Fitz Lee, Rooney Lee, Beverly Robertson, Frank Robertson, Tom Rosser, and Scheibert survived the war. They led interesting lives, and wrote of their experiences.

Jeb Stuart did not. He was mortally wounded at the Battle of Yellow Tavern on May 11, 1864, and died the next day, a Thursday. Riding in the ambulance from the battlefield, he shouted to his men, who were shocked and disorganized by his wounding, "Go back, I would rather die than be whipped." A little later he turned to Lieutenant. Hullihen, who had joined him in the ambulance and asked, "How do I look in the face, Honeybun?"

He was taken to the home of his brother-in-law, Dr. Brewer, in Richmond. President Davis came to see him, as did Von Borcke. Flora was

329

summoned and hurried to his side. She was too late. His last thoughts were of her. His last words were, "God's will be done."

In the 150 years since Stuart gained his glory there have been countless debates and a number of books about the "what if's." What might have been done differently, what particular actions, failures to act, mistakes, lost opportunities, failures to follow orders, or simply demographics that caused the South to lose the Civil War. What could have been done differently, perhaps something minor, perhaps major, that would have caused a different outcome and a completely different history of the United, and the Confederate, States? In all likelihood the Southerners never had a chance to win, and the miracle is not that they didn't, but that they came so close. There are die-hard Rebels who wish the South had won and who might still secede if allowed, but for most Southerners the feeling is sentimental pride, something like:

> It's the dream of Pickett charging and never being stopped;
>   it's the thought of Stonewall Jackson, never being shot.
> Though we'd never change America; she is as she should be,
>   we can't help but try once more to win that one last victory.[1]

Yet to that list of "what if's" must be added: What if Jeb Stuart had been placed in command of the Second Corps of the Army of Northern Virginia, or perhaps its newly formed Third Corps, after Stonewall Jackson's death?

To be clear, the young cavalryman, when unexpectedly given command of the entire left wing of Lee's army at Chancellorsville, executed his task with an acute grasp of battle rarely seen in the war. Porter Alexander said that he had seen many attacks "planned" for crack of dawn, but hardly any that had done so. But at 4:00 a.m. on May 3 at Chancellorsville, the entire Rebel left surged forward. This was due to the preparations made by Stuart and his closest lieutenants at hand—Rodes Ramseur, Paxton, Alexander—during the night, and thus not an ounce of impetus from Stonewall's original attack was wasted. When the Federal front finally caved in completely, the cheers that went up when Jeb Stuart met Robert E. Lee at the Chancellor house, were burned in the memory of every Confederate who witnessed it.

The best argument for Stuart not gaining permanent command of an infantry corps was the reckless way he commanded—always in the thick of the fight, personally leading attacks, or rallying troops, never giving consideration for his personal safety when his inspiring presence could attain greater goals. This style of battlefield leadership would not have lasted Jeb long as commander of an infantry corps.

There is also the factor that he had become renowned as the best cavalryman in the Confederacy, so there is little evidence that Lee even considered him for permanent command of the Second Corps, or Third. There were many ambitious generals in the Army of Northern Virginia, who had led troops in confrontational infantry combat since the onset, so the idea of a glamorous cavalry leader supplanting them could hardly have been well accepted. On the one hand Lee simply wished to retain his supreme cavalry leader; on the other, it is remarkable that when fate gave Stuart the opportunity to lead infantry—after both Stonewall and A.P. Hill had been wounded—he did a superb job with his emergency command, in fact providing Lee his most stellar victory.

In the campaign that followed, just weeks later, Dick Ewell, who had been Jackson's most trusted lieutenant through the Vally Campaign and up until his wounding at Groveton, commanded the Second Corps. A.P. Hill commanded the Third. The imagination boggles at the notion that Stuart might have continued to command either of those units, which were first on the scene at Gettysburg, and if so what further dynamism he might have displayed. With Stuart's acumen and on-the-spot leadership in battle, one can doubt that any opportunity would have been missed, and at the same time that any strategic surprises might have been encountered.

As it stands, after Chanellorsville, Jeb Stuart returned to his role as cavalry leader, and thence went largely missing from the great campaign in Pennsylvania. He did enormous service on the third day of that fight, and also during the Army of Northern Virginia's subsequent retreat; however the "year of glory" fairly ended during the first days of July 1863, whereupon afterward the grim mathematics of the war would gradually drive Dixie down. There was only a brief period when gallantry, or truly exceptional battlefield leadership, might have turned the relentless arithmetic around.

If the South ever had a chance to win, it was because of the historical anomaly of the confluence of a few "invincibles" on its side—Lee, Longstreet, Hood, the Hills, Stonewall, Ewell, Gordon and all the rest. In the western theater there was also Cleburne, Forrest, Cheatham, Stewart and Morgan. But among these giants in American military history, none surpassed the record of bravery, achievement, and devotion to duty of Jeb during his—and the Confederacy's—greatest year. When America fully engaged in World War II it employed two main battle tanks, one which was called the Sherman, after the Union general who raged across Georgia. The other, a lighter tank, was called the Stuart.

Jeb's style of combat leadership all but guaranteed he wouldn't survive the war, and he was mortally wounded on May 12, 1864, while trying to stave off a Union thrust under Sheridan against Richmond. Lee said afterward, "I cannot think of him without weeping." Indeed, the loss of the South's most gallant cavalier marked an entire turn of the war from maneuver and initiative to morbid attrition. Robert E Lee, despite his losses, would continue to hold out as long as he could. But he must have often reflected on that singular year, 1862–63, when anything seemed possible for his cause, when he had Jeb Stuart alongside him. It was a rare period—perhaps lost in warfare forever—when personalities determined the course of events, and temporary disappointments always gave way to further hopes.

At the very end, General Lee went to see General Grant and his large staff at Appomattox with only a single aide alongside. One wonders if he could have done so if Stonewall Jackson had still been alive, or particularly Jeb Stuart. His humiliation by then complete, he must have reflected on the year, so recent, when anything seemed possible. The gallantry already earned paid dividends at the surrender, however, when Grant, supported by Lincoln, provided generous terms to simply end the war.

Jeb Stuart was a fascinating man surrounded by fascinating men. If he were alive today, he might be a beloved popular figure, or perhaps one equally reviled.[3] He might be another successful general, a popular singer, politician, minister, or comedian. The latter would require some serious upgrading in humor quality, but if he could make Stonewall Jackson laugh in 1862, who might resist him today? Or perhaps his remarkable combination of personality traits worked only in the unique and unlikely time that was the American Civil War.

So we gaze at the old photos, read the old letters, gaze upon the artifacts, and visit the scenes of his glory. He and his time grow ever more distant. Those who care about him grow fewer. Stories about him grow less in popularity, which is a shame. Jeb Stuart was, as John Mosby said, "so unique that he seemed able to defy all natural laws." Mosby knew him and was a legend himself, the source of books, stories, even a television series. The memory of Jeb Stuart, once the heartthrob of a nation, fades ever further, becomes less and less relevant, becomes a topic of trivial pursuit.

But for those who were there, for those who rode with him, saw him, read of him in the contemporary newspapers, for those who wrote the memoirs, sat at the feet of the old men and heard tell of him, or simply read or wrote books about him, his memory and the year of his glory, will live forever.

NOTES

PROLOGUE

1. J. Thomason, *JEB Stuart*, p.1 (New York: Charles Scribner's Sons, 1930), cited hereafter as "Thomason."
2. Fitzhugh Lee, "Speech at Army of Northern Virginia Banquet, October 28, 1875," 1 *Southern Historical Papers*, 80 (1876).
3. J. Wert, *Cavalryman of the Lost Cause*, pp. 137, 163, 198, 199 (New York: Simon & Schuster Paperbacks, 2008), cited hereafter as "Wert."
4. Thomason at 5.
5. Wert at 101.
6. Thomason at 15.

CHAPTER ONE

1. Heros von Borcke, *Memoirs of the Confederate War for Independence*, 33 (Philadelphia: J.P. Lippincott & Co., 1867), cited hereafter as "Von Borcke."
2. Adele H. Mitchell, ed., *The Letters of General J.E.B Stuart*, 227 (Stuart-Mosby Historical Society, 1990), hereafter cited as "Letters."
3. J. Maxwell, *The Perfect Lion: The Life and Death of Confederate Artillerist John Pelham*, 70 (University of Alabama Press, 2011). Cited hereafter as "Maxwell."
4. E. Thomas, *Bold Dragoon: The Life of J.E.B. Stuart*, 110 (New York: Harper & Row, Publisher, 1986), cited hereafter as "Thomas."
5. W.W. Blackford, *War Years With JEB Stuart*, 69–70 (Louisiana State University Press, 1993), cited hereafter as "Blackford."
6. Letter dated January 9, 1864 from J.E.B. Stuart to Samuel Cooper; Letter dated April 1, 1864 from J. E.B. Stuart to Braxton Bragg.
7. Mark Boatner, *The Civil War Encyclopedia*, 880–81 (New York: David McKay Co., 1949), cited hereafter as "Boatner."
8. George Cary Eggleston in *A Rebel's Recollections*, quoted in *They Followed the Plume*, by R. Trout, at 162–63.

9. Wert, at 200.

10. *Ibid.* at 102.

11. Blackford at 91.

12. Thomas at 91.

13.*Ibid.* at 122.

14. *Find a Grave*,http://www.findagrave.com/php/famous.php?page=gSearch& page=gSearch&globalSearchCriteria=redmond+burke.

15. R. Trout, *The Followed the Plume: The Story of J.E.B. Stuart and His Staff,* 75 (Mechanicsburg, PA: 1993), cited hereafter as "Trout, *Plume.*"

16. *Ibid.*

17. *Ibid.* at 76.

18. The saber was taken by Farley at the battle of Williamsburg from a captain of the 47th New York and carried by Farley until his death, then passed down through the next generation of the Farley family until, in November 1923 it was returned to a descendant of its owner by Farley's granddaughter. Trout, *Plume* at 108–110.

19. Thomas at 87.

20. Thomason at 119.

21. J. E. Cooke, *Wearing of the Gray: Being Personal Portraits, Scenes and Adventures of the War*, 7–8 (Indiana University Press, 1959), cited hereafter as "Cooke."

22. J. Ramage, *Gray Ghost: The Life of Col. John Singleton Mosby*, 37 (University of Kentucky Press, 1991, Paperback edition, 2010), cited hereafter as "Ramage;" Wert at 207.

23. Blackford at 16.

24. *Ibid.* at 32.

25. *Ibid.* at 79.

26. *Ibid.* at 89.

27. H. K. Douglas, *I Rode with Stonewall: The War Experiences of the Youngest Member of Jackson's Staff,* 193 (University of North Carolina Press, 1968), cited hereafter a "Douglass."

28. *Ibid.* at 194.

29. Wert at 199.

CHAPTER TWO

1. Letter to Flora dated May 28, 1862; Emory at 106. Stuart was close to a family named Fontaine that included John B., Edmond, Elizabeth. Lucie, Mollie and Maria Louisa, and while it is probable that this is the same family the letter from Stuart simply said "My Hd Qrs are at a charming place in the outskirts of Richmond. Mr. Fontaines."

2. Owned by a Mr. Mellon, Thomas at 90.

3. Lee was Superintendent at West Point when Stuart was there. Lee's son, Custis, was one of Stuart's best friends and Lee's daughter, Alice were close to Stuart since West Point. Jeb once wrote that Mrs. Lee "was like a mother to me," and, of course, Jeb had served as Lee's volunteer aide at Harpers Ferry when John

Brown was captured. Lee's son, Rooney, served under Stuart as commander of the 9th Virginia Cavalry and Lee's nephew, Fitzhugh, was commanding the First Virginia Cavalry. Thomas at 108.

4. The army was given this new name on March 14, 1862, having previously been considered the "Army of the Potomac" during its days under P.G.T. Beauregard and Joseph E. Johnson. Naming the army after a portion of a state was consistent with the war-long tradition of Southerners naming their battles and armies after geographic sites, states or areas, while Federals named theirs after rivers and bodies of water.

5. Wert at 92.

6. Von Borcke at 23.

7. *Ibid.* at 25.

8. *Ibid.*

9. J.S. Mosby, quoted by Ramage at 358, n. 28.

10. Wert at 93, Thomas at 111.

11. The entirety of Lee's order to Stuart, read as follows:

Headquarters Dabb's Farm, 11th June, 1862
General J.E.B. Stuart, Commanding Cavalry

General,—You are desired to make a scout movement to the rear of the enemy now posted on the Chickahominy, with a view of gaining intelligence of his operations, communications, etc., and of driving in his foraging parties and securing such grain, cattle, etc. for ourselves as you can make arrangements to have driven in. Another object is to destroy his wagon trains, said to be daily passing from the Piping-Tree Road to his camp on the Chickahominy. The utmost vigilance on your part will be necessary to prevent any surprise to yourself, and the greatest caution must be practiced in keeping well in your front and flanks reliable scouts to give you information. You will return as soon as the object of your expedition is accomplished; and you must bear constantly in mind, while endeavoring to execute the general purpose of your mission, not to hazard unnecessarily your command, or to attempt what your judgment may not approve; but be content to accomplish all the good you can, without feeling it necessary to obtain all that might be desired.

I recommend that you take only such men and horses as can stand the expedition, and that you use every means in your power to save and cherish those you do take. You must leave sufficient cavalry here for the service of this army, and remember that one of the chief objects of your expedition is to gain intelligence for the guidance of future movements.

Information received last evening, the points of which I sent you, leads me to infer that there is a stronger force on the enemy's right than was previously reported. A large body of infantry, as well as cavalry, was reported near the Central Railroad.

Should you find, upon investigation, that the enemy is moving to his right, or is so strongly posted as to make your expedition inopportune, you will, after gaining all the information you can, resume your former position.

I am, with greatest respect, your obedient servant, R.E. Lee, General

12. It is a minor mystery why John Pelham was not selected to command the section of artillery that accompanied the expedition. He had proven his talent and Stuart had already become attached to him. The most likely explanation is that Pelham was ill, possibly with measles, which was common in the army that season. Other suggestions are that Pelham was either on furlough or a recruiting mission, or that he was considered too valuable to be put at risk, but none of those theories seem likely considering the importance of the situation and the likelihood that Stuart would have selected Pelham if he was available. One writer insisted that Pelham did, in fact, accompany the expedition, a claim a more recent writer characterized as being interesting but incorrect. Yet topping off the minor puzzler are the recollections of William Todd Robins, who served as Rooney Lee's regimental adjutant and who rode on the expedition. He mentioned that Pelham was a fellow rider. J. Maxwell, *The Perfect Lion: The Life and Death of Artillerist John Pelham,* 86, fn 22 to Ch. 8 (University of Alabama Press, 2011); R. Krick, *Staff Officers in Gray: A Biographical Register of the Staff Officers in the Army of Northern Virginia,* 256 (University of North Carolina Press, 2003).

13. Wert at 94; Thomas at 113.

14. It is noteworthy, and characteristic of Von Borcke, that he wrote that Stuart's force was comprised of "about 2500 cavalry" whereas all other sources state there were only 1200. Von Borcke at 26.

15. Thomason at 142.

16. The regiment's companies were originally named the Stafford Rangers, the Caroline Light Dragoons, Lee's Light Horse, the Lancaster Cavalry, the Mercer Cavalry, the Essex Light Dragoons, the Lunenburg Light Dragoons, Lee's Rangers, the Potomac Cavalry, and the Richmond County Cavalry.

17. Like the Virginia regiments they had started as individual, local cavalry companies—the Natchez Cavalry, the Chickasaw Rangers, the Southern Guards, the Sumter Mounted Guards, the Canebrake Legion, the Dixie Cavaliers, Screven's Company, the Morehead Rangers, McKenzie's Company, and Robert's Company.

18. H. McClellan, *I Rode with Jeb Stuart: The Life and Campaigns of General J.E.B. Stuart,* 54 (Bloomington: De Capo Press, 1994), cited hereafter as "McClellan."

19. Wert at 95. Other accounts are that he visited Wickham briefly and left while yet another is that he stayed and breakfasted with the family. Thomas at 114–115.

20. Wert at 95.

21. Boatner at 634.

22. Ramage, *supra,* at 47; Boatner, *supra,* at 174; P. St. G. Cooke, *Cavalry Tactic or Regulations for the Instruction, Formations, and Movements of The Cavalry of the Army and Volunteers of the United States* Philadelphia: J. P. Lippincott, 1862).

23. Von Borcke at 27.

24. Robert J. Trout, *With Pen &Saber: The Letters and Diaries of J.E.B.Stuart's Staff Officers,* 72 (Mechanicsburg, Pa.: Stackpole Books 1995), cited hereafter as "Trout, *Pen.*"

25. Thomason at 144.
26. Wert at 96.
27. *Ibid.*
28. Ramage at 48; Thomas at 118.
29. Wert at 98.
30. Thomason at 145.
31. McClellan at 59, fn 1.
32. Thomason at 145.
33. *Ibid.* at 146.
34. Ramage at 48.
35. Brass wedding rings sold by sutlers are a very common relic hunter find in Civil War camps, but there is no clear explanation for the purpose. Were they simply not considered to be wedding rings back then, did a lot of soldiers buy them as wedding rings, were they popular because married men were often subjected to less hazardous assignments than single men, or is there some other explanation?
36. Wert at 98.
37. Ramage at 48 & 49.
38. *Ibid.* at 48.
39. Von Borcke at 28.
40. *Ibid.* at 28–29.
41. Thomason at 146.
42. Ramage at 49.
43. Thomas at 121.
44. Von Borcke at 30.
45. Wert at 99.
46. Thomason at 148.
47. Cooke at 177.
48. Wert at 99.
49. Von Borcke at 31.
50. McClellan at 64.
51. Cooke at 177.
52. Wert at 99.
53. McClellan at 64.
54. Von Borcke at 31.
55. Wert at 99.
56. McClellan at 64.
57. Von Borcke at 31.
58. Wert at 99.
59. Cooke at 179.
60. McClellan at 65.
61. Cooke at 180.
62. *Ibid.* at 179.
63. *Ibid* at 180; Wert at 100; McClellan at 66.
64. McClellan at 66.

CHAPTER THREE

1. Wert at 100–101.
2. Thomas at 125.
3. *Ibid.*
4. Thomason at 153.
5. After the Seven Days Battles, Cooke would serve on court martial duty, then be sent west to take charge of the Baton Rouge District, where he remained until May, 1864, when he was places in command of the army's recruiting service. Boatner at 174.
6. Appendix reproduced in McClellan at 69–70.
7. Thomas at 126.
8. Wert at 102.
9. McClellan at 70–71.
10. Ramage at 33.
11. Contrary to what James Ramage concluded in *Gray Ghost* at pp. 40–41, Lord Cobham was not a religious dissenter who was hanged and burned, but a noted governmental leader whom Pope admired and in whom he saw the future of England. Lord Cobham died of natural causes, and Fitz Lee's comment to Mosby was not meant to imply that Mosby would also be hanged, but simply that he was not what he pretended to be, and Fitz could see through him. Anyone seeking to find more meaning or another interpretation of Lee's esoteric comment may visitt http://www.inspiringshortstories.finecrypt.net/index.php?b=EPISTLE_I_TO_SIR_RICHARD_TEMPLE_LORD_VISCOUNT_COBHAM for the full poem.
12. Ramage at 45.
13. *Ibid.* at 50.
14. Wert at 117.
15. Trout, *Plume,* at 65.
16. Boatner at 739.
17. Thomason at 171–72.
18. Wert at 48.
19. J. P. Smith, *With Stonewall Jackson in the Army of Northern Virginia,* 73 (Gaithersburg, Md., Zullo & Van Sickle, 1982, reprint of earlier edition).
20. Blackford at 71.
21. *Ibid.* at 72.
22. Von Borcke at 38.
23. *Ibid.* at 39.
24. Maxwell at 93.
25. Battles and Leaders, Vol. II, page 341.
26. Ibid., page 364.
27. *Ibid.*
28. Blackford at 74.
29. John C. Hotten, *A Dictionary of Modern Slang, Cant, and Vulgar Words,* 1859; The Phrase Finder, http://www.phrases.org.uk/meanings/302700.html.

30. Blackford at 76.
31. *Ibid.* at 76–77.
32. Von Borcke at 42–43.
33. Thomas at 134.
34. McClellan at 77.
35. Blackford at 74–75.
36. *Ibid.*
37. Von Borcke at 41, 43.
38. Von Borcke at 44.
39. *Ibid.*
40. *Ibid.* at 45.
41. Maxwell at 94.
42. Trout, *Pen* at 77.
43. Blackford at 75.
44. McClellan at 78.
45. Blackford at 75.
46. *Ibid.*
47. *Ibid.* at 77.
48. *Ibid.* at 76.
49. Thomason at 200.
50. *Ibid.* at 77.
51. Von Borcke and Stuart concluded that this was unlikely. Von Borcke at 48.
52. McClellan said Long Bridge; Von Borcke said Bottoms Bridge.
53. Blackford at 77; McClellan at 79; Thomason at 201; Maxwell at 98.
54. Thomas at 136.
55. R. Krick, *Civil War Weather in Virginia*, 63 (University of Alabama Press, 2007).
56. McClellan at 82.
57. Maxwell at 100.
58. Wert at 111.
59. Maxwell at 100.
60. Wert at 112.
61. *Ibid.* at 101.
62. Maxwell at 102.
63. W. Taylor, *Four Years With General Lee* at 41, quoted in McClellan at 83–84.
64. Wert at 112.
65. *Ibid.*
66. Blackford at 80–81.
67. Thomason at 206.

CHAPTER FOUR
1. Trout, *Pen* at 82.
2. Von Borcke at 56.
3. *Ibid.* at 54–55. Von identified the Colonel of the 9th Virginia as Fitzhugh Lee, but he apparently confused the two cousins, as Rooney commanded the 9th Virginia.

4. Trout, *Pen* at 82.

5. Blackford at 85–87.

6. Thomason at 3, 317, 385, 416, 467, & 479; Letter from J. Stuart to William Stuart dated August 15, 1862, from *J.E.B. Stuart Papers,* online at http://6whitehorses.com/cw/jebs/jebs.htm, cited hereafter as "Papers."

7. Blackford at 296.

8. *Ibid.* at 165.

9. Von Borcke at 56–57.

10. Thomason at 70.

11. *Ibid.* at 71.

12. Von Borcke at 57.

13. Blackford at 87.

14. Von Borcke at 58.

15. Trout, *Plume* at 52–55.

16. Blackford at 87.

17. Von Borcke at 59.

18. Trout, *Pen* at 84.

19. Blackford at 88.

20. Von Borcke at 59–60.

21. Letters at 258.

22. Von Borcke at 62–63; Blackford at 88.

23. Trout, *Plume* at 115–16.

24. *Ibid* at 116.

25. *Ibid.* at 251–53.

26. Trout, *Plume* at 218.

27. Blackford at 204–205.

28. Wert at 115.

29. Maxwell at 107 and notes 9–10 to Ch. 10.

30. Maxwell at 107.

31. Letters at 259–260.

32. Maxwell at 107–108.

33. Trout, *Plume* at 254; Von Borcke at 64.

34. Blackford at 93.

35. Von Borcke at 64.

36. Krick, *supra,* at 62–63.

37. Trout, *Pen* at 85.

38. *Ibid.* at 86.

39. Wert at 141.

40. McClellan at 86 and 91; Wert at 115.

41. Thomason at 214.

42. Ezra J. Warner, *Generals in Gray,* 122–23 (Louisiana State University Press, 1959).

43. *Ibid.* at 259.

44. Boatner at 101–02.

45. Thomason at 215.

46. Maxwell at 110.
47. Blackford at 95.
48. Ibid.
49. Blackford at 95; Von Borcke at 67.
50. Trout, *Plume* at 111.
51. Blackford at 95–96.
52. Wert at 120.
53. Blackford at 98, n. 1.
54. Wert at 122–23.
55. Letter of Aug. 15, 1862, Papers.
56. Wert at 124.
57. Von Borcke at 72.
58. Blackford at 97; Wert at 124.
59. Von Borcke at 73.
60. Ramage at 54–55; Von Borcke at 74.
61. Wert at 124.
62. Letters at 260–61.
63. Von Borcke at 75–77; Maxwell at 113.
64. Frank S. Walker, Jr., *Remembering: A History of Orange County, Virginia*, 171–72 (Orange County Historical Society, 2004).
65. Blackford at 97–98; Thomason at 225;
66. Letters at 261.
67. J.E.B. Stuart's Official Report dated Feb. 5, 1863, Virginia Historical Society.
68. Thomason at 228; Wert at 126.
69. Frank S. Walker, Jr., *supra* at 171; Boatner at 102; Wert at 125; Maxwell at 114.
70. Wert at 126.
71. Maxwell at 114.
72. Wert at 126.
73. Von Borcke at 79–81.
74. Blackford at 99.
75. *Ibid.* at 80.
76. Von Borcke at 78.
77. Wert at 126–27.
78. Thomason at 231–32; Wert at 127.
79. *Ibid.* at 232.
80. Blackford at 100.
81. *Ibid.* at 233.
82. *Ibid.* at 101.
83. *Ibid.* at 107; Thomason at 233; McClellan at 94.
84. Von Borcke at 89 and 93. Considering that Von Borcke supplied the dollar amounts for the treasure in the strongboxes, we may surmise that the real value was in the order of $2000 in gold and $50,000 in greenbacks. He was probably more accurate about the cigars, at least to the extent of there being at least one box of them.

85. Blackford at 106.
86. *Ibid* at 108.
87. *Ibid.*
88. Von Borcke at 91.
89. Letter to Flora dated Sept. 4, 1862, Letters at 263.
90. Blackford at 107; Wert at 129.
91. Thomason at 236–37.
92. Wert at 129.
93. Thomason at 239; Wert at 131–32.
94. Thomason, *Ibid.*
95. Douglas at 135.
96. *Ibid.* at 162.
97. Wert at 132.
98. Maxwell at 122–23.
99. Wert at 8–9, 133.
100. Boatner at 103.
101. Thomason at 244.
102. James Longstreet, *From Manassas to Appomattox* (New York, Da Capo Press [reprint ed.], 1992), at 184.
103. John Bell Hood, *Advance & Retreat* (Lincoln, Neb.: University of Nebraska Press [reprint ed.], 1996), at 37.
104. Cooke at 144.
105. *Ibid* at 145.
106. Trout, *Plumes* at 256.

CHAPTER FIVE
1. Thomason at 292.
2. Wert at 78–79.
3. Thomas at 90, 160.
4. Von Borcke at 125–26.
5. *Ibid.* at 126.
6. McClellan at 109.
7. Papers, September 12, 1862.
8. Wert at 140.
9. *Ibid.* at 141.
10. Blackford at 140.
11. Wert at 141, 143.
12. Von Borcke at 134; Burke at 195; Thomas at 164; Thomason at 261.
13. Wert at 141.
14. Maxwell at 143.
15. Von Borcke at 136.
16. *Ibid.*
17. Blackford at 141.
18. *Ibid.*

19. Von Borcke at 137.

20. Maxwell at 143.

21. Author's visits to both houses, February 27, 2012.

22. Wert at 143.

23. *Ibid.* at 144.

24. Thomas at 167.

25. Von Borcke at 141.

26. Wert at 144.

27. Von Borcke at 145.

28. Maxwell at 145–47

29. Wert at 145–46.

30. Davis at 264.

31. Wert at 150.

32. Blackford at 146.

33. McClellan at 124.

34. Wert at 151.

35. Burke Davis, *JEB Stuart: The Last Cavalier,* 203 (New York: Rinehart & Co. 1957) cited hereafter at "Davis."

36. Von Borcke at 159–60.

37. McClellan at 127; Blackford at 147; Wert at 151–52.

38. Von Borcke at 161.

39. Blackford at 148; Davis at 204.

40. Wert at 153.

41. *Ibid.* at 154–55.

42. *Ibid.* at 156–57.

43. Maxwell at 160, quoting Jennings Cropper Wise.

44. McClellan at 132.

45. Blackford at 151.

46. Von Borcke at 166.

47. Wert at 159.

48. Blackford at 152.

49. Von Borcke at 168.

50. Blackford at 153.

51. Von Borcke at 169–70.

52. *Ibid.* at 170.

53. *Ibid.* at 172.

54. *Ibid.* at 176–78.

55. *Ibid.* at 163.

56. Blackford at 151.

57. Letter dated September 33, 1862 from Jeb Stuart to Flora Stuart.

58. Von Borcke at 179; Maxwell at 175–76.

59. *Ibid.* at 180.

60. *Ibid.* at 181

61. Maxwell at 176.

62. *Ibid.* at 176–77
63. *Ibid.* at 178.

CHAPTER SIX

1. Thomason at 291.
2. In 1881 this was replaced with the long, columned porch that exists today. Joan Brzustowicz. *The Bower.*
3. Maxwell at 178. Unfortunately, Stuart's Oak died more approximately 80 years ago.—Author's interview with Louise McDonald, descendant of the Dandridge family and occupant of The Bower, February 26, 2012.
4. Maxwell at 179.
5. Joan Brzustowicz. *The Bower, supra.*
6. Davis at 211.
7. Douglass at 192.
8. National Register of Historic Places Inventory—Nomination Form, dated December 1, 1981. http://www.wvculture.org/shpo/nr/pdf/jefferson/82004321.pdf.
9. Blackford at 155.
10. *Ibid.*
11. *Ibid* at 188; http://law2.umkc.edu/faculty/projects/ftrials/lincolnconspiracy/lincolnaccount.html.
12. Joan Brzustowicz. *The Bower, supra.*
13. Von Borcke at 193.
14. *Ibid.*
15. Blackford at 86.
16. Von Borcke at 196–200.
17. *Ibid.* at 161.
18. *Ibid.* at 189–90.
19. *Ibid.* at 190.
20. Blackford at 158–59; Maxwell at 184.
21. Von Borcke at 205.
22. Blackford at 158–59.
23. Von Borcke at 207.
24. Marrow Stuart Smith, *Life After J.E.B. Stuart,* 21–23 (Lanham, MD: University Press of America, 2012).
25. *Ibid.* at 21.
26. Maxwell at 185.
27. Thomason at 297.
28. John Allen Miller, *Emmitsburg During the 1862 Chambersburg Raid,* http://www.emmitsburg.Net/archive list/articles/history/civil war one.htm .
29. Maxwell at 186.
30. Von Borcke at 207.
31. Trout, *Pen* at 105.
32. McClellan at 137.
33. The meaning is "fault-finding," "objecting unnecessarily, quibbling, carping, or

capriciously criticizing," which suggests that those who gave the word the most thought might have also been the most "caviler," and therefore "caviler cavaliers."

34. Wert at 168; Burke at 116; Maxwell at 187.

35. McClellan at 138.

36. *Ibid.* at 139.

37. Peggy Vogtsberger, *The Chambersburg Raid*, The John Pelham Hist. Association, http://www.gallantpelham.org/articles/showart.cfm?id art=21.

38. McClellan at 139.

39. Blackford at 165.

40. *Ibid.*

41. *Ibid.* at 166–67.

42. Davis at 220; McClellan at 141.

43. Blackford at 165.

44. Davis at 219.

45. Maxwell at 195.

46. *Behind the Marker, supra;* McClellan a 143; *Blackford* at 168.

47. McClellan at 140.

48. Blackford at 167–68.

49. *Behind the Marker, supra.*

50. Thomason at 306.

51. McClellan at 142.

52. *Ibid.* at 142–46.

53. Trout, *Pen* at 107.

54. Davis at 210.

55. Maxwell at 196.

56. *Ibid.*

57. McClellan at 141; Blackford at 168.

58. Thomas at 175; Davis at 221; Thomason at 305–06; Maxwell at 197; Peggy Vogtsberger, supra.

59. *Behind the Marker, supra;* Wert at 172.

60. Blackford at 168.

61. Maxwell at 197; McClellan at 147.

62. Trout, *Pen* at 107, 111.

63. McClellan at 146.

64. Maxwell at 197.

65. *Ibid.*; McClellan at 148–49.

66. Blackford at 169.

67. McClellan at 148. Both Blackford and McClellan recorded this incident, which happened only to Blackford. It is interesting that McClellan, whose book was published in 1885 before Blackford began working on his, includes considerably more direct quotes of Stuart's words than does Blackford's account.

68. Blackford at 170.

69. John Allen Miller, *supra.*

70. John B. Paxton, John C. Martin, Sanford Shroeder, Shields Hunter, Abraham

Stockslager, Andrew Hartman, Nelson Boyd, Lewis Pittinger, Andrew Lowe, Andrew Warren, David Baer, John Hartman, and Alexander Benchoff. John Allen Miller, *supra.*
71. *Ibid.*
72. *Ibid.*
73. Blackford at 171.
74. *Ibid.*
75. Davis at 227–28.
76. Blackford at 173.
77. *Ibid.* at 174.
78. Peggy Vogtsberger, *supra.*
79. Blackford at 179.
80. *Ibid.*; Davis at 229–30.
81. Wert at 174; Blackford at 178–79.
82. Davis at 225.
83. *Ibid.* at 231; Peggy Vogtsberger, *supra.*
84. Wert at 174.
85. Blackford at 176–78.
86. Wert at 176.
87. Trout, *Pen* at 108.
88. *Ibid.* at 180.
89. McClellan at 160–61;
90. John Allen Miller, supra.
91. Davis at 235; McClellan at 161.
92. John Allen Miller, *supra.*
93. *Report on the organization and campaigns of the Army of the Potomac,* Operations After Antietam, p. 419.
94. Peggy Vogtsberger, *supra.*
95. Davis at 235.
96. McClellan at 161.
97. Greg Goebel, *In The Public Domain,* 35.1 "The Fall of McClellan/Burnside Takes Command," http://www.vectorsite.net/twcw_35.html.
98. Thomas at 180.

CHAPTER SEVEN

1. Freed was detached to Stuart's staff from his company and was first mentioned by Stuart in a report to General Longstreet on September 11, 1861, although Trout states that the exact dates of his service as the General's bugler are unknown. *The Letters of General J.E.B. Stuart* at 215; Trout, *Plume,* at 308.
2. Von Borcke at 210.
3. Trout, *Pen* at 109.
4. *Belle Boyd, Cleopatra of the Secession,* http://www.civilwarhome.com/belleboyd.htm.
5. This officer was identified by Trout as "Major Morse" in *They Followed the Plume: J.E.B. Stuart and His Staff* at 115, but no staff officer named Morse is included in

Krick's *Staff Officers in Gray: A Biographical Register of the Staff Officers of the Army of Northern Virginia.* Fitzhugh's cellmate was almost certainly Alfred Moss, who served as a Voluntary Aide de Camp for General Ewell in 1862. He was taken prisoner in the summer of 1862 and sent to the Old Capitol Prison, but was less fortunate than either Fitzhugh or Boyd, as he contracted jaundice while incarcerated, and died in Richmond on October 5, 1862. Krick at 227, 375.

6. Trout, *Plume* at 115.
7. Trout, *Pen* at 109.
8. *Ibid.* at 110.
9. Von Borcke at 216.
10. *Ibid.*
11. *The Letters of General J.E.B. Stuart,* p. 283.
12. *General R. E. Lee's War-Horses, Traveller and Lucy Long,* Southern Historical Society Papers, Vol. XVIII. Richmond, Va., January–December. 1890; *General R. E. Lee's War-Horses,* Southern Historical Society Papers, Vol. XIX. Richmond, Va. 1891.
13. *Ibid.*; Wert at 177.
14. Blackford wrote that the enemy went into camp a mile from The Bower, but he may have exaggerated, as Jeb's letter to Flora said that they were "about 8 miles near Charlestown and The Bower," while Von Borcke wrote that after further advance the next day they were a mile and a half from The Bower.
15. Maxwell at 212.
16. Although technically Porter was still in command of the V Corps of the Army of the Potomac, he were relieved of duty and was facing charges for his actions at the end of the Second Manassas Campaign for which he would ultimately be court-martialed and dismissed from service, almost certainly unfairly. It is unlikely that Stuart would have known that Porter was not physically in command as of October 16, 1862, Boatner at 104, 372, 417, 661–62, 818.
17. Letter dated October 16, 1862 from J.E.B. Stuart to Flora Stuart.
18. Blackford at 182.
19. Blackford at 181–82; Von Borcke at 218.
20. *The Letters of General J.E.B. Stuart,* pp. 270–77.
21. Douglass at 196.
22. Maxwell at 179.
23. *Ibid.* at 293–94.
24. Maxwell at 180–82, and fn 21 to Ch. 15.
25. *The Bower,* John Pelham Historical Association, http://www.gallantpelham.org/articles/showart.cfm?id_art=10, Maxwell at 358, fn 18; *Find A Grave,* http://www.findagrave.com/cgi-in/fg.cgi?page=gr&GRid=65527517.
26. *Ibid.* 225.
27. Wert at 179.
28. Von Borcke at 227.
29. *Ibid.* at 228.
30. McClellan at 169.
31. Von Borcke at 231.

32. McClellan at 179; Blackford at 170.
33. Von Borcke at 233–34.
34. Wert at 179.
35. Von Borcke at 236–37.
36. Wert at 181.
37. Von Borcke wrote his memoirs shortly after the war ended, relying on his journal, but was careful not to identify anyone by name if he believed that doing so might subject that person to punishment or suspicion. Of course he rarely failed to record what they served at mealtime, and it is probably safe to say that the descendants of those who hosted Stuart would much rather have verification of their ancestors' association with him than knowledge of what was on the menu. Von Borcke at 240.
38. *Ibid.* at 244.
39. Wert at 181–82.
40. McClellan at 178.
41. Blackford at 183–84.
42. Von Borcke at 247.
43. *Ibid.* at 252.
44. *Ibid.* at 253–60.
45. Wert at 182.
46. Thomason at 33–34; Wert at 182; Von Borcke at 261.
47. *The Letters of General J.E.B. Stuart,* p. 279.
48. Von Borcke at 262–66.
49. Cooke at 14.
50. Wert at 184.
51. Thomason at 334–35; Von Borcke at 268–69.
52. Maxwell at 235; Thomason at 335.
53. Wert at 183.
54. Von Borcke at 271–72.
55. *Friends Forever: James Dearing & the Wash. Arty.,* http://www.washingtonartillery.com/Dearing%20page.htm
56. *The Letters of General J.E.B. Stuart,* pp. 280–81.
57. Trout, *Pen* at 114.
58. *The Fredericksburg Campaign,* http://www.civilwarhome.com/fredricksburgcampaign.htm.
59 Wert at 188.

CHAPTER EIGHT
1. Trout, *Pen* at 114.
2. Trout, *Plume* at 78.
3. He records their arrival as being on November 26, whereas a recent biography of Pelham sets the date as December 7. Maxwell at 241.
4. Von Borcke at 282–84.
5. McClellan at 187–88.

6. Maxwell at 236–37.

7. Wert at 186.

8. Trout, *Pen* at 115–16.

9. *Ibid.* at 117.

10. McClellan at 188.

11. *The Letters of General J.E.B. Stuart*, p. 281–82.

12. Wert at 186–87; Maxwell at 237.

13. Wert at 183.

14. Trout, *Pen* at 118.

15. *Ibid.*

16. Maxwell at 238–39.

17. Wert at 188.

18. *Ibid.* at 286. Von Borcke records the snowball fight as beginning on December 3 and carrying over to the 4th, but other sources put the date of the fight as the 5th. Considering that Von Borcke recorded that Pelham had driven off gunboats prior to the snowball fight, the 5th seems the most likely.

19. The poem was as follows:

When genius wealth & fashion bow in homage at thy feet
and youth and beauty smile in all thy happy glances greet.
When I shall pitch beneath the sky my bivouac on the lea—
I ask not then (for 't would been in vain) that thou wouldst think of me.

When music's soft enrapturing swell delights thy list'ning ear,
when Zephyrs whisper "all is well" & thou lovst are near—
when skies are bright & thou are all that thou couldst wish to be,
I dare not ask for 't would be in vain that thou couldst think of me.

But when misfortune frown's upon that lovely dimpled face
and o'er the past my mem'ry's dove can find no resting place;
when friends are false save one whose heart beats constantly for thee,
'tis then I ask thou would turn confidingly to me.

The other recipients of this poem were "The One I Love," in 1854, Robert E. Lee's daughter, Agnes, in 1863, and a mystery woman identified only as "George" on January 28, 1864.—*Jeb Stuart Papers*, http://6whitehorses.com/cw/jebs/jebs_1862.htm.

20. *The Letters of General J.E.B. Stuart*, p. 282–83.

21. Maxwell at 241.

22. Von Borcke at 287.

23. Blackford at 187.

24. *Ibid.* at 187.

25. Maxwell at 241.

26. *Ibid.* at 188; Von Borcke at 290–91.

27. Von Borcke at 298.

28. *Ibid.* at 298–304.

29. Maxwell at 245.

30. *Ibid.* at 246; Von Borcke at 305–306.

31. Wert at 190–91; Maxwell at 249–57.

32. Blackford at 193; Von Borcke at 315.

33. Trout, *Plume* at 263–64.

34. Letters at 283.

35. Blackford at 194–95.

36. Trout, *Pen* at 123.

37. Von Borcke at 325–27.

38. Trout, *Pen* at 123

39. *Ibid* at 124.

40. *Ibid.* at 123.

41. *Ibid.* at 128.

42. Letters at 284; Boatner at 226; Summary of Magruder's service record, http:// kristenlp5virtualnotebook.wikispaces.com/Civil+War; *Civil War] William T. Magruder, late US Dragoons,* http://gs19.inmotionhosting.com/~milita8/cmh/member/member.cgi/noframes/read/5680. Note that footnote 67 on p. 421 of *The Letters of General J.E.B. Stuart* is in error identifying Magruder as Major Gen. John B. Magruder.

43. Maxwell at 272.

44. Tony & March Parvord, *The Complete Equine Veterinary Manual,* 116–17, 168 (United Kingdom: David & Charles, 1997).

45. Von Borcke at 335–36.

46. Cavendish, Spencer Compton, Marquis of Hartington and eighth Duke of Devonshire 1833–1908, http://thepeerage.com/e688.htm.

47. Blackford at 199.

48. *Ibid.*

49. Trout, *Pen* at 128.

50. *Ibid.*

51. Von Borcke at 342; Maxwell at 273; Wert at 193.

52. Douglass at 209.

53. Trout, *Pen* at 135.

54. McClellan at 197–201; Thomason at 351; Wert at 196.

55. Trout, *Pen* at 138.

56. Ramage at 58–59; Wert at 197.

57. Trout, *Pen* at 135–41; Wert at 193–98; Maxwell at 273–281.

58. *Ibid.*

CHAPTER NINE

1. Von Borcke at 347.

2. Trout, *Pen,* at 142.

3. Blackford at 199.

4. *Ibid.* at 140, 142.

5. Von Borcke at 348.

6. *Ibid* at 349.

7. Trout, *Plume,* at 225–26.

8. Letters at 285–90; Robert Trout, ed., *In the Saddle with Stuart: The Story of Frank Smith Robertson of Jeb Stuart's Staff,* 21 (Gettysburg: Thomas Publications, 1998); *11th Virginia Cavalry Regiment,* http://www.civilwar.n2genealogy.com/units/csa-va/va_cav_11_reg.html.

9. Trout, *Pen,* at 143.

10. Trout, *Plume,* at 173–74.

11. Von Borcke at 350; *Colbun's United Service Magazine and Naval and Military Journal,* 1862, Part II, p. 469.

12. http://www.gettysburgframe.com/mkramn.html.

13. Trout, *Pen,* at 147–48. Cached Cached–S

14. *Dundee,* http://www.gallantpelham.org/articles/showart.cfm?id_art=11.

15. Von Borcke at 350–52.

16. *Burnside's Mud March* http://www.civilwarhome.com/mudmarch.htm; *Battles And Campaigns—1863* "Mud March "Burnside's Quagmire, January 20–22, 1863, http://civilwar.bluegrass.net/battles-campaigns/1863/630120-22.html; http://en.wikipedia.org/wiki/Mud_March_(American_Civil_War), citing: Boatner, pp. 409 & 573; Furgurson, Ernest B. *Chancellorsville 1863; The Souls of the Brave,* 16 (NY, NY: Vintage Books, 1992), and Stine, James H., *History of the Army of the Potomac,* 297, (Phila., PA: J. B. Rodgers Printing 1892).

17. Trout, *Pen,* at 145.

18. *Ibid.* at 147.

19. *Ibid.* at 149.

20. *Ibid.,* at 150–51, 153; *Webster's New World Dictionary.* Cached

21. Trout, *Pen,* at 156.

22. Von Borcke at 352–53. One of these autographs by General Jackson, accompanied by one secured from General Hood on the same paper by Captain Bushby, recently came up for auction at Christies and sold for $4,180.00. It was described in the online auction as "Jackson, Thomas J., General, C.S.A. autograph closing and signature (T.J. Jackson) clipped from a letter, n.d., one page, a narrow strip of blue lined paper . . . rare in any form . . . written for j. wm. bushby at his camp before Fredericksburg Jany. 1863. Bushby, an Englishman, apparently visited the Confederate army encampments near Fredericksburg in January 1863." http://www.christies.com/LotFinder/LotDetailsPrintable.aspx?intObjectID=2364833.

23. Trout, *Pen,* at 152–53; *Ann Herbert, Countess of Pembroke, en.wikipedia.org/wiki/Anne_Herbert,_Countess_of_Pembroke.* Cached—Similar.

24. Trout, *Pen,* at 154.

25. *Ibid.* at 160; Wert at 199. This trip to the home of former Congressman Taylor, which occurred during the first week of February, may have been the trip that Stuart was on in connection with the visit to Senator Hunter and "the Essex girls."

26. Von Borcke at 353.

27. Trout, *Pen,* at 155–56. Cached—S

28. Except when he was drinking, which Stuart never did.

29. Letters at 290–92.
30. Trout, *Pen*, at 156–57.
31. *J.E.B. Stuart Papers*, 1863.
32. *Pen*, at 157.
33. Cooke at 14.
34. Trout, *Pen*, at 158.
35. *Ibid.*
36. *Ibid.* at 294.
37. Trout, *Pen*, at 158,
38. Maxwell at 289, 384 n. 14.
39. Trout, *Pen*, at 158.
40. Von Borcke at 354–55.
41. Von Borcke at 356; Maxwell at 291–93.
42. Trout, *Pen*, at 165.
43. Trout, *Pen*, at 161–63.
44. Letters at 294–96.
45. Papers at 1863, letter of February 26, 1863 to Flora.
46. *Ibid.*
47. Trout, *Pen*, at 162–64; Blackford at 200; Von Borcke at 356.
48. Wert at 207; Trout, *Pen*, at 172.
49. Papers, 1863.
50. Trout, *Pen*, at 164.
51. Von Borcke at 357.

CHAPTER TEN

1. Robert J. Krick, *Civil War Weather in Virginia*, 91 (U. of Alabama Press, 2007).
2. Trout, *Pen* at 167.
3. Krick, *supra.*
4. The title of Jomini's book is sometimes translated as *The Art of War* or *The Theory and Practice of War.*
5. Letters at 298.
6. Papers at 1863.
7. Robert Trout, ed., *In the Saddle with Stuart: The Story of Frank Smith Robertson of Jeb Stuart's Staff*, 21–22 (Gettysburg: Thomas Publications, 1998), cited hereafter as "Trout, *Saddle*"; Blackford at 200.
8. Blackford at 201; Maxwell at 295. Maxwell places the receipt of the candy at or around March 12, but it was almost certainly the same candy mentioned in Stuart's letter to Flora on March 4, whereas Pelham's scheming to visit Nannie Price came to fruition a week or so later.
9. Trout, *Pen* at 167.
10. Papers at 1863.
11. Trout, *Pen*, 114, 145. 152, 154, 156–57, 159–62; Papers at 1863; Blackford at 202–03.
12. Maxwell at 375, n. 25.

13. Maxwell at 294–95.
14. Ramage at 67–70.
15. Wert at 206–07.
16. Trout, *Pen* at 172.
17. *Ibid.* at 174–75.
18. *Ibid.* at 177.
19. Maxwell at 296. The ladies were staying at the home of a Mr. Bull, which is still standing in Orange and is known as "Rebel Hall." It is possible that "Miss Brill" was actually a daughter of the Bull family and that the name has been misinterpreted from cursive writing. Author's visit to Rebel Hall, February 28, 2012.
20. The exact day of his departure is unclear. Channing Price wrote in a letter to his parents dated March 9 that if he wasn't so busy "I might perhaps steal a short visit to you to-day, as the General goes through Richmond on the way to Culpeper C.H. as a witness in the case of Lt. Col. Pate. . . ." John Esten Cooke wrote on March 10 that "the Gen. went to Culpepper via Richmond." A modern biographer of Stuart determined that he left on either the 11th or the 12th. Von Borcke wrote that Stuart left on the 15th. Stuart wrote to Flora from Culpepper on the 13th saying he was sorry to have not seen her in Richmond "the other day," so his leaving on the 11th or 12th seems probable. The record of the court martial shows that "Major" J.E.B. Stuart testified on the 12th, 13th, and part of the 16th. The date of his departure is important mostly for the purpose of figuring out when the events at Camp No Camp related to John Pelham just described occurred, and which make the dates just attributed to those events unwieldy. Whatever date he left, he was still there and the court martial was continued for two weeks on the 16th, to be re-convened in Richmond. Trout, *Pen* at 173; Wert at 206, which incorrectly says that Stuart took Von Borcke and Pelham with him; Von Borcke at 357; e-mail to the author from Lisa Wehrmann, Virginia State Library, January 19, 2012.
21. Wert at 206.
22. Papers at 1863.
23. *Ibid.*
24. *Ibid.*
25. Maxwell at 293–94.
26. *Ibid.* at 298.
27. *Ibid.* at 299.
28. *Ibid.*
29. *Ibid.* at 300–09.
30. Blackford at 201.
31. Von Borcke at 350–60.
32. Trout, *Pen* at 182.
33. Maxwell at 316.
34. *Ibid.* at 384, n. 10.
35. *Ibid.*; Letters at 300–301; Maxwell at 317.
36. Maxwell at 317–22.

37. Von Borcke at 361.
38. Trout, *Pen* at 184–85.
39. *J.E.B. Stuart Papers,* 1863.
40. Trout, *Pen* at 185–86.
41. *Ibid.* at 187.
42. *Ibid.* at 186.
43. *The Letters of General J.E.B. Stuart* at 302–04.
44. Trout, *Plume,* at 57–60.
45. Trout, *Pen* at 187.
46. Byron Farwell, *Stonewall: A Biography of General Thomas J. Jackson,* 488 (New York: W.W.Norton & Co. 1992).
47. Channing Price, who mentioned the offer in a letter home dated March 30, 1863, identified Goldsborough's company as being an escort for Jubal A. Early, but other accounts identify it as serving Ewell.
48. *The Letters of General J.E.B. Stuart* at 304–05.
49. Trout, *Pen* at 192–93.
50. *Ibid.* at 190.
51. In fact, the two letters from Jeb to Flora dated April 3, 1863 simply do not match up. Either there is a date error for one, probably that written from Dundee, or Jeb simply didn't tell the same tales to his wife. In the one from Dundee he is "here on that everlasting Ctmartial" but he expected to return the next day, apparently the 4th, to Fredericksburg. In the one written from Fredericksburg he had already returned and attended morning church services, and because he headed the letter "Good Friday," as well as April 3, it makes the date of that letter unimpeachable. The Pate Court Martial met on April 2 and 3, but Stuart did not testify. In the letter from Dundee, which is located between Richmond and Fredericksburg and not handy to either city, he said he had not seen Maria in Richmond, but in the letter from Fredericksburg he said "I saw a good deal of Maria in Richmond and that sweet little girl—Bonnie." The Brewers definitely had a daughter named Bonnie, although at least one source lists her birth year as 1864. To complicate matters slightly more, Channing Price wrote his mother on April 5 that "This morning I was much pleased to see the General back. . . ."
52. Wert at 210.
53. Trout, *Plume,* at 230.
54. Trout, *Pen* at 192; Krick, *Civil War Weather in Virginia,* at 92.
55. Trout, ed., *In the Saddle with Stuart,* 124 n. 1.
56. Papers, April 6, 1863.
57. Trout, *Plume* at 146.
58. Wert at 132.
59. Trout, *Plume* at 201–02.
60. Trout, *Pen* at 195–97.
61. Von Borcke at 365–66.
62. *Ibid.* at 367; Trout, *Pen* at 196.

CHAPTER ELEVEN

1. Justus Scheibert, *Seven Months in the Rebel States During the American War, 1863*, translated from German by Joseph C. Hayes, edited by William S. Hoole (Confederate Publishing Co., Inc. 1958), cited hereafter at "Scheibert."
2. Phillip Van Doren Stern *Robert E. Lee*, 167–68 (New York: McGraw Hill, 1963).
3. Papers at April 19, 1863.
4. Letters at 313–14.
5. Trout, *Plume* at 200–201.
6. Scheibert at 42.
7. Letters at 315.
8. Trout, *Plume* at 264, 266.
9. Wert at 214.
10. Von Borcke at 369–70.
11. Scheibert at 45.
12. *Ibid.* at 55; Von Borcke at 370–71.
13. Wert at 216.
14. Scheibert at 60.
15. McClellan at 231.
16. Von Borcke at 382; Trout, *Plume* at 222.
17. Scheibert at 60–61.
18. Wert at 221.
19. Scheibert at 60–61.
20. *Ibid.* at 62.
21. *Ibid.* at 63.
22. Wert at 222.
23. Boatner at 193.
24. Von Borcke at 384–85.
25. Wert at 223.
26. Von Borcke at 386–87.
27. Wert at 224.
28. *Ibid* at 224–25.
29. *Ibid.* at 225.
30. Trout, *Plume* at 181; Von Borcke at 389.
31. Edward Porter Alexander, *Fighting for the Confederacy* (Chapel Hill: University of North Carolina Press, 1989), at 209.
32. Ibid.
33. Alexander at 210.
34. Scheibert at 69–70.
35. Von Borcke at 398.
36. Thomason at 385–86.
37. Robert E.L. Krick, *Staff Officers in Gray: A Biographical Register of the Staff Officers in the Army of Northern Virginia*, 292–93 (Chapel Hill: University of North Carolina Press, 2003).
38. Davis at 296.

39. Scheibert at 75–76.

40. *Ibid.* at 76–77.

41. Von Borcke at 395–99.

42. Letters at 316–17.

43. Scheibert at 77.

44. Wert at 231.

45. *Ibid.* at 231–32.

46. Trout, *Pen* at 202.

47. Davis at 418.

48. Scheibert at 81–82.

49. Wert at 232.

50. Scheibert at 78–79.

51. Wert at 232.

52. Von Borcke at 406–07.

53. Scheibert at 80–81.

54. Wert at 236.

55. Von Borcke at 410; Robert J. Trout, *Galloping Thunder: The Stuart Horse Artillery Battalion,* 211–12 (Mechanicsville, Pa.: Stackpole Books, 2002).

56. Letters at 319–20.

57. Trout, *Plume* at 225–31; Blackford at 205–06.

58. McClellan at 261.

59. Papers at May 26, 1863.

60. Blackford at 206–09.

CHAPTER TWELVE

1. From the C.D. *Chantilly Remembrance* (Woodbern Or.: Cold Comfort Productions, 1998) lyrics by Monte Akers.

2. Papers at June 1, 1863.

3. *Ibid.*

4. Von Borcke at 411.

5. Wert at 238.

6. Blackford at 212.

7. Robertson at 58.

8. Blackford at 212; Von Borcke at 412–13.

9. Blackford at 212–13; Von Borcke at 413.

10. Wert at 239–40; Gary Gallagher, *Brandy Station: The Civil War's Bloodiest Arena of Mounted Combat,* BLUE & GRAY MAGAZINE, October, 1990.

11. *Ibid.* at 240.

12. Scheibert at 87; Von Borcke at 414; Blackford at 213.

13. Compare Downey's book, supra, and Gallegher's periodical article, supra.

14. Downey, supra; Gallegher, supra; Blackford at 213–217; Von Borcke at 414–21; McClellan at 264–292; Robertson at 55–59; Trout, *Plume* at 147–49; Wert at 241–49; Davis at 305–10; Clark B. Hall, *The Battle of Brandy Station,* pp. 32–45 CIVIL WAR TIMES ILLUSTRATED, June, 1990; Sherman L. Fleek, *Swirling Cavalry*

Fight, pp. 43–49, AMERICA'S CIVIL WAR, September, 1989.

15. Wert at 250–51.
16. Davis at 313–14; *The War was a Grievous Error: General James Longstreet Speaks His Mind*, p. 36, CIVIL WAR TIMES, April 2010.
17. Thomason at 412. This letter, quoted in Thomason's 1930 book without a foot-note, is also in Wert, at 253, but the authority for it in the latter is Thomason. It is not contained in either the Letters or the Papers.
18. Wert at 253–54.
19. Robertson at 66–67.
20. Davis at 316.
21. Wert at 254.
22. Robertson at 67.
23. Thomason at 414; *Aldie, Middleburg, and Upperville*, http://johnsmilitaryhistory.com/aldie.html.
24. Von Borcke at 427–28.
25. *Ibid.* at 428; Wert at 255.
26. Von Borcke identified the officer as "Longstreet's commissary, Major N," but Long-street's commissary at that time was Major Thomas Walton. In fact, Longstreet did not have any staff officer whose name began with an N during the entire war. Von Borcke may have been mistaken about Walton's name, or Major N. may have been a commissary for someone other than Longstreet.
27. Von Borcke at 430–33; Blackford at 218–20; Robertson at 68–69.
28. McKay at 548.
29. McClellan at 307; Von Borcke at 429–30.
30. Blackford at 221.
31. Scheibert at 105; Blackford at 220.
32. Scheibert at 108.
33. *Ibid.* at 106.
34. Blackford at 221.
35. *Ibid.*

EPILOGUE
1. *The Southern Birthright*, music and vocals by Bobby Horton, lyrics by Monte Akers, HOMESPUN SONGS OF THE CSA, Vol. 6 (CD: Birmingham, AL: Bobby Horton, 2001).
2. Attributed to Jackson by Longstreet, *The War was a Grievous Error: General James Longstreet Speaks His Mind*, p. 36, CIVIL WAR TIMES, April 2010.

INDEX